JEWISH IDENTITIES IN POLAND AND AMERICA

Jewish Identities in Poland and America

The Impact of the Shoah on Religion and Ethnicity

SEBASTIAN REJAK

VALLENTINE MITCHELL
LONDON • PORTLAND, OR

First published in 2011 by Vallentine Mitchell

Middlesex House,	920 NE 58th Avenue, Suite 300
29/45 High Street, Edgware,	Portland, Oregon,
Middlesex HA8 7UU, UK	97213-3786 USA

www.vmbooks.com

British Library Cataloguing in Publication Data

ISBN 978 0 85303 872 6 (cloth)

Library of Congress Cataloging in Publication Data

The publication of this book has been made possible thanks to a generous grant of The Auschwitz Foundation (Belgium) and The Kosciuszko Foundation – An American Center for Polish Culture, Promoting Educational and Cultural Exchanges and Relations Between the United States and Poland since 1925.

Printed in Great Britain by the MPG Books Group, Bodmin and King's Lynn

Moim synom Kubie i Maćkowi
To my sons Jacob and Matthias

The very day the edict [banning pregnancy] *was issued, a pregnant Jewish woman passed by the ghetto hospital. A German noticed her swollen belly and shot her for violating the German order against reproduction. His bullet penetrated her heart and she fell dead on the spot. A passer-by immediately carried her into the hospital, thinking there might be a chance to save her or the baby ... A Jewish obstetrician was rushed over. He said that if surgery was performed immediately, the baby could be saved ... The baby, miraculously, was alive. However ... the cruel murderers ... soon entered the hospital to record the name of the murdered woman in their book of the dead. When they found the baby alive, their savage fury was unleashed. One of the Germans grabbed the infant and cracked its skull against the wall of the hospital room.*

(Ephraim Oshry, *Responsa from the Holocaust*)

Contents

Acknowledgements

This book owes a lot to individuals and institutions whose names I wish to mention in order to express my gratitude. First and foremost I would like to thank Prof. Daniel Grinberg of Białystok University and the Graduate School for Social Research, Warsaw. Not only was he the person who constantly supported the idea of writing this book, but he was also an attentive, critical reader, as well as a friend who always cared about my intellectual progress. I do hope his efforts have not been wasted.

I should also like to thank Prof. Henryk Domański, Director of the Institute of Philosophy and Sociology at the Polish Academy of Sciences, Warsaw, and the late Prof. Stefan Amsterdamski, the Founder of the Graduate School For Social Research, Warsaw. They both encouraged me to pursue my research project, of which this book is a fruit.

My deep thanks go also to those who were helpful in establishing personal contacts with my potential interviewees: Helena Datner, PhD, of the Jewish Historical Institute, Warsaw; the late Zofia Zaks of the 'Children of the Holocaust' Association, Warsaw; members of the Jewish Socio-Cultural Society in Poland; Robert Cherry, PhD, of the Brooklyn College, CUNY; and John Ranz – a Polish Jew from Będzin and an American Jew from Brooklyn, but above all a great person full of optimism and inspiration.

I also want to thank those whose scholarship and thought-provoking – sometimes provocative – ideas have had a tremendous impact on my research: Richard L. Rubenstein, Professor Emeritus of Bridgeport University, whose *After Auschwitz* has been one of the most important books I've ever read and gave me an impulse to critically analyse theology in light of the Holocaust; Peter Novick, Professor Emeritus of the University of Chicago, author of *The Holocaust in American Life*, who not only changed my way of seeing identities shaped by history and memory but also epitomizes a true scholar whose ultimate goal is to establish facts, rather than to please the public; and Prof. Alan Rosenberg, lecturer in the Philosophy Department at Queens College, CUNY, whose scholarship has given me a new and stronger desire to see the Shoah as a watershed event for western civilization. Although they differ in their views and methodologies, they all have been to me examples of honest and courageous scholars immune to the changing fads of academia. Meeting them was for me no less important and inspiring an event than reading their books.

Doing my research and publishing this book would have been goals difficult to realize if not for generous support from several institutions: first and foremost, the New York-based Kościuszko Foundation whose grant made my research in the USA possible; the Graduate School for Social Research and the Foundation for Polish Science, both based in Warsaw; the New York-based New School University (and Prof. Elżbieta Matynia in particular), as well as the Fondation Auschwitz in Brussels.

And, of course, my gratitude and appreciation to Heather Marchant, Vallentine Mitchell Publishers, who made my idea of a book into a reality. I am also indebted to Sigrid Pohl-Perry and Phillip Perry, PhD, who were the first native speakers of English to read the whole manuscript and who offered invaluable remarks, and to Joanna Lawson, for copy-editing the manuscript.

Last but not least, I wish to express my deepest thanks to my parents, Maria Danuta and Janusz Rejak, who have always encouraged me in my academic work.

Sebastian Rejak
Warsaw 2010

Introduction

For several decades the Nazi Holocaust has been drawing the attention of innumerable brilliant scholars, among whom historians constitute the largest group. Thousands of historical works on the Shoah have been issued so far, and tens or hundreds of new books and articles are being published every year. Thus, is there anything novel left to be said on this topic? One answer seems possible and satisfactory: as long as new research is being done in this field of study, there is potentially a chance for new observations to be made and new conclusions to be drawn.

The present book is a study based mostly on two types of sources. One is the written material published as books or articles in American Jewish periodicals (where relevant, Polish-language literature was also used). The other is empirical research conducted in Warsaw and in New York City in the years 2000–02.

Before I present a detailed description of the research instruments and techniques used and the scope of the study, I would like to answer one critical question, namely: Why did I undertake to delve into a subject which is focused on a disaster, and one that has triggered numerous controversies? My general interest in Jewish topics started some fifteen years ago. I was initially fascinated by what may be called Jewish folklore: I used to read Hassidic tales, study Jewish religion and rituals as well rabbinic exegeses of biblical texts, and commentaries on Jewish holidays and symbols. In short, I was interested in learning more about Judaism. Then I also began to study the Hebrew language. As a native of Lublin, once a city with a strong Jewish presence, I studied Jewish history. Being immersed in the world of Jewish traditions, ideas, concepts and interpretations, I wondered why so many people are so interested in the Holocaust. Why, of all Jewish history, have they chosen this particular period of six war years? In 1998 I learned about Richard L. Rubenstein and his ideas. After having read his most important work, *After Auschwitz*,[1] I decided that I would write my doctoral dissertation in the field of Holocaust studies. Rubenstein's book was a shock for me. It raised questions I had virtually never asked and, more importantly, it gave answers that to some might have seemed blasphemous, yet they were intellectually and morally honest, if controversial. Thus I understood those who have been pulled into the abyss of the Shoah. Paradoxically, this impenetrable abyss has incited me to search for meanings in the darkness of life.

Reading Rubenstein, and then also Eliezer Berkovits, Irving Greenberg and Emil L. Fackenheim, led me to pose vital questions. I wondered how classical Judaic doctrines – or any other theological doctrines, for that matter – could be reconciled with the unimaginable suffering and the mass death of the Holocaust. This was a clash between theology and philosophy on one hand and history on the other. The outcome of this is a historiosophical problem upon which I have reflected ever since that time; it is a double question. Firstly, *Can we believe what we believe in, regardless of history?* Secondly, *Does history – our factual historical experiences – impact our views?* The former is a more theoretical issue; it deals with concepts – their credibility, sensibleness and coherence. The latter is practical, so to speak, for it inquires whether, in our proper *Sitz im Leben*, we do change our beliefs in response to dramatic historical changes. I shall seek answers to these two problems in the first and second parts of this book respectively.

If I were to briefly explain the meaning of the title of this book I would say: It is a book about how the Holocaust is understood by Polish and American Jews; it is a study of social concepts and attitudes. The very terms 'Holocaust' and 'Shoah' necessitate some more in-depth elucidation. The word 'holocaust' comes from the Greek language; its original form is *holokauston* and the plural is *holokausta*. The Greek word was coined by joining an adjective and a noun: *holos* (all, whole) and *kauston* (a burnt offering, or anything 'that is burnt'). Thus, *holokausta* were offerings wholly burnt, consumed by fire. In the *Septuagint* the terms *holokauston, holokausta* were used to render the Hebrew *olah* (see 1 Samuel 7:9) and its plural form *olot* (see Deuteronomy 27:6). In fact, the Greek term *holokauston* first appeared in the fifth century BCE and signified not only a whole-burnt sacrifice but also such phenomena as an enormous destruction consuming material objects and human beings, especially if the devastation was done by fire. Later on, in secular literature the word *holokauston* meant a complete destruction, the slaughter of a group of people. In the nineteenth century this use of the word became even more pervasive.

The Hebrew term *shoah* means 'catastrophe' or 'destruction' (see

Psalm 35:8 and Psalm 63:10). The word *shoah* was first used in the context of mass murder of Jews in a booklet titled *Shoat Yehudei Polin* (The Destruction of the Jews of Poland), published by the United Aid Committee for the Jews of Poland (Komitet Pomocy Żydom Polskim) in Jerusalem in 1940. In November 1942, the Jewish Agency declared that what was happening to the Jews of Europe was a *shoah*. At a conference of Jewish poets and writers held in the Jewish Agency offices in Jerusalem on 12–13 July 1942, 'Saul Tchernichovsky, an outstanding Hebrew romantic poet, entitled his moving address "The Command of the Horrible Sho'ah that Is Coming Over Us"'.[2] Probably the first person to use this term in scholarly historical literature in the context of the events that were going on in Europe was Ben-Zion Dinur (Dinaburg), who stated in 1943 that the murder of Jews was a *shoah* which symbolized the plight of the Jews among the nations of the world.[3] Also, about the same time, in July 1943, Fishl Shneerson, addressing the participants of the writers' conference held at Kibbutz Hulda, noted that the term *shoah* was at times employed in psychology – in the context of feelings of guilt, repression of facts, paralysis, or in instances of extreme grief.[4] Until the spring of 1942, however, the term was used only scarcely. A much more widely, even spontaneously, employed word was the Yiddish word *churbn* or *churban*[5] (catastrophe, ruin, demolition) also taken from the Hebrew language. *Churban* was the word which East European Jews used to describe the demolition of both Jerusalem Temples. Then it also came to signify any mass destruction of the Jewish people, be it during the Crusades, the Spanish Inquisition or at the time of the Bohdan Chmielnicki massacres.[6]

The meaning of the word *shoah* was studied and elucidated by many a Jewish scholar. Rashi, for instance, in order to explain the term, resorts to the word *churban* and claims it is a catastrophe that brings destruction. Yet hardly anyone has alluded to the fact that when the term *shoah* is used in the Torah, it is almost always seen as an act of God and it implies God's retribution, as is clearly demonstrated in Isaiah 6:11; 10:3; Zephaniah 1:15; Job 30:14; Proverbs 1:27; 3:25; Psalm 35:8 and Psalm 73:18.[7] Thus, the biblical meaning of this term has a specific theological connotation: an event that is named *shoah* is categorized as divine punishment. The view of the Shoah as punishment is of crucial importance to the ideas I present in this book, and I will elaborate on it more broadly in the first chapter.

I will now reflect on the use of the word 'holocaust' in pre-war and early post-war texts. My main source for this passage was an online article by Jon Petrie,[8] who has shown that before the Second World War the term was used in non-Jewish contexts, and that when it was mentioned after the war it meant a nuclear destruction. I will give below several citations from the 1938 issues of the *Palestine Post*:

> For the first time since last September Japanese aeroplanes again raided Canton ... Although the damage exceeds September's holocaust, the death toll was somewhat less.
>
> (29 May 1938, p.1, col.1)

> Yesterday was also an anniversary of destruction. It was the day on which Great Britain entered the World War 24 years ago. Since that holocaust swept over the world, it has had no real peace.
>
> (5 August 1938, p.6, col.2)

> ... the holocaust of 1914–18 ...
>
> (11 September 1938, p.8, col.3)

> thanks to the general dread of yet another European holocaust ... [Hitler] has brought them peace with territorial aggrandisement.
>
> (11 October 1938, p.6, col.2)

> the planning system of the Bolshevist regime has broken down ... The holocaust of directors and engineers shot as 'wreckers' to stimulate others has brought only spasms.
>
> (27 October 1938, p.3, col.2)[9]

Similarly, in the early 1960s the general American public understood the word 'holocaust' as pertaining to a nuclear destruction, for a nuclear war seemed almost inevitable at that time. *The Reporter* of 17 August 1961 titled a review of two books on nuclear war and nuclear strategy, 'A Cold Look at the Holocaust'. And the cover of the 4 November 1961 *Nation* displays in upper case: SHELTERS WHEN THE HOLOCAUST COMES'.[10] Petrie claims that it is precisely because of that association with the total destruction that an atomic bomb could cause that the word 'holocaust' started to circulate among American Jews in the 1960s. This seems to be a legitimate statement only to a certain degree. For, as Petrie has demonstrated in another passage, there had been other uses of the term which appeared in times and circumstances having little to do with fear of atomic destruction.[11]

However, we ought to note that early on in the war the term *holocaust* was already being used to describe the plight of European Jews, as Robert Shapiro has shown. The Jewish Telegraphic Agency's bulletin dated 24 December 1942 reported from Moscow that in a place called Zajcewo, the Nazis had burned forty Jews alive. 'In other towns of the Orłowski district Jews are also being massacred, some were hanged, some shot dead, and others were burned. In one town the Jews were thrown into a huge cauldron under which fire was lit. In this holocaust perished women as well as children.'[12] Shapiro also noted that on 15 December 1942, the *News Chronicle* reported that 'Holocaust' was the fate of the Jews under Hitler and that it is incomparable to any other tragedy.[13] As he discovered, probably the first use ever of the word *holocaust* meaning Nazi persecution of the Jews appeared in A.A. Brill's introduction to Sigmund Freud's works published in 1938: 'we have been shaken by the horrible news that Hitler's holocaust surrounded Vienna, and that professor Freud with his family are captives of this greatest plague of our civilization'.[14]

As early as 1938, shortly after the *Kristallnacht*,[15] in a telegram dated 16 November, the chief rabbis of Palestine suggested to their British counterpart: 'Propose you ... proclaim Jewish day of mourning ... for holocaust synagogues Germany ... '[16] Also, in the London *Times Literary Supplement* of 26 August 1939, the editors prophetically warned that a 'holocaust' loomed over the Jews in Hitler's Germany.[17] As far as official documents are concerned, the word 'holocaust' was used for the first time in the preamble to the Israeli Declaration of Independence (1948 – 'Nazi *shoah*' was translated in the English version as 'Nazi *holocaust*'), as well as in the English translation of the Knesset law (1951) on *Holocaust Remembrance Day* (Hebrew: *Yom HaShoah uMered HaGetaot*).[18]

Another term that is quite often used to describe the planned annihilation of the Jews by the Nazis is the word 'genocide'. This notion was coined by Raphael Lemkin, a Polish Jew and renowned lawyer, in his *Axis Rule in Occupied Europe: Laws of Occupation – Analysis of Government – Proposals for Redress*.[19] Lemkin, who fortunately managed to flee the German invasion, intended to show the world the actual situation of occupied countries, and especially of the plight of Jews living in them, as a humanitarian catastrophe. He did it by proposing a specific legal terminology on which a new category in international law would be based:

> By 'genocide' we mean the destruction of a nation or of an ethnic group. This new word, coined by the author to denote an old practice in its modern development, is made from the ancient Greek word *genos* (race, tribe) and the Latin *cide* (killing) ... Generally speaking, genocide does not necessarily mean the

immediate destruction of a nation, except when accomplished by mass killings of all members of a nation. It is intended rather to signify a coordinated plan of different actions aiming at the destruction of essential foundations of the life of national groups, with the aim of annihilating the groups themselves ... Genocide is directed against the national group as an entity, and the actions involved are directed against individuals, not in their individual capacity, but as members of the national group.[20]

What is meant in the present study by 'understanding of the Holocaust' is a specific perception of the catastrophe by Polish and American Jews. In this book – and in the research done – I have focused on two aspects of that perception: (re)interpreting one's *ethnic* and *religious* identity in the light of the Holocaust. Thus the term 'understanding' is coterminous in this case with 'self-consciousness'. I intend to approach the problem from the point of view of sociology of religion – but religion viewed very broadly as a life system, which seems a legitimate way to investigate this issue, for Judaism is not only a religion *sensu stricto* but also a religion *sensu lato* – it is an ethnic religion and a multi-level tradition which can be practised in a secular way. This, by the way, is one of the observations of this work: that Judaism is to many Jews a secular religion, one that includes plenty of non-theological elements: rituals, literature, myths, ethical teachings, art, cuisine, political tradition, specific behaviour patterns and social stratification.

At an early stage of my research I already knew I was interested in studying both social concepts and social attitudes. Why do I distinguish between concepts and attitudes? I simply treat the former as theoretical constructs, and the latter as personal psychological and spiritual responses to a particular event. Thus, in the first part of the book, I will analyse the theological and historiosophical conceptions of leading American Jewish thinkers: Richard L. Rubenstein, Eliezer Berkovits, Emil L. Fackenheim and Irving Greenberg. These four authors, I contend, have had a significant impact on contemporary American Jewry. Their responses to the Shoah illustrate the intermingling of two elements: the facts as they appear to our senses, on the one hand, and our theoretical constructs – theologies and philosophies – on the other. Each of the authors is quite different from the others, yet, on one plane, they exert the same social task: they act as representatives of society in trying to reconcile reality with our ideas of reality. They test hitherto existing conceptions against the realm of factuality. As a result, what their scholarship offers are new concepts meant to be in accord with the facts. I shall explore in the first chapter whether they do put forward novel solutions to existential problems. For one thing, these priest-philosophers are taken from the people, are children of the masses, are shaped by their families and educational systems; their families and their pedagogues, in turn, are obviously a result of the past generations. For another, these thinkers – and all thinkers – have the might to shape the coming generations, to influence them, to offer them new ways of thinking, or even to shock them with their conclusions. They possess a quasi-Nietzschean power to create new people by means of their teachings.

In analysing the concepts of these scholars I sometimes juxtapose them with other Jewish authors and pay close attention to the Holocaust debate which was held in Jewish American periodicals in the last twenty years of the previous century. Also, to give the philosophico-theological reflections a proper context, I begin the first chapter with a historical section summarizing the high and low points of the discussion on the Holocaust which swept over the American public (Jewish and non-Jewish alike) from the early post-war years until the end of the century. Then, also for reasons of clarity and respecting the demands of chronological order, I present an overview of the first reactions to the catastrophe voiced by outstanding Jewish religious authorities – Orthodox rabbis and commentators, not always American residents – who gave their *responsa* to the *Churban Europa* during and after the war. Only after these things are clarified do I proceed to a detailed analysis of the works of contemporary American Jewish thinkers. In the third chapter, I have tried to present an overview of the Polish discussion on the Shoah and Jewish identities; it has to be born in mind, however, that such a debate took place only to a limited extent and that it could hardly be likened to the American scholarly debate.

As for exploring attitudes, this task proved feasible thanks to conversations with individuals whom I interviewed in person. In the interviews I asked the respondents the same questions I asked when analysing the texts of the scholars mentioned above. The problem I focused on in both parts of the book was: How, facing the Shoah, can the Jew believe in the God of Israel? What is the Jewish response to this Jewish catastrophe? Thus, as I have tried to demonstrate, in conducting the research in all its stages, and then analysing the data, attempting to find out what a Jewish understanding of the Shoah is, and how this perception – and memory – of the Holocaust was transformed by individuals and how it functions as a group memory and group identity – in all this, it was of uttermost interest and importance to me to explore the Jewish aspect of the phenomenon studied. I wanted to know about 'the Jewish way' of coping with the Shoah, and whether there is any one and only Jewish way.

PRIOR RESEARCH IN THE AREA

To write a decent summary of all that has been said so far in Holocaust studies, even excluding the field of Holocaust history, would take a separate book. That is why I will limit myself here to an enumeration of major works and a brief description of the themes they deal with. Also, I will refer only to publications in specific areas that are crucial to the subject matter of this study: namely, the history of Holocaust debate, and the sociology of post-war Jewish societies.

So far the best and the most comprehensive publication about the history of Holocaust debate on the American continent is *The Holocaust in American Life* by Peter Novick. The book spans the period of time from the war years, through the 1960s, to the late 1990s. Novick explores how information about the Nazi destruction of the European Jews was accepted by American authorities and American Jewry, as well as how Palestinian Jews reacted to it. One of the most important parts of his book is dedicated to the situation of the 1960s and 1970s – when the Eichmann trial and the Israeli–Arab wars, as Novick claims, had an enormous impact on Holocaust discussion in the United States. In the last two chapters, Novick dwells on the recently discussed issues: the memorialization of the Shoah, on creating innumerable museums and university Holocaust study centres, the rivalry for victimhood, and the delicate – if loaded with controversies – topic of the uniqueness of the Holocaust.

Interesting information regarding the role of the Holocaust in the American Jewish community can also be found in Eli Lederhendler's *New York Jews and the Decline of Urban Ethnicity, 1950–1970*.[21] Lederhendler analyses the social changes that New York Jews had undergone in the first two decades after the war. He shows how Jews, as an urban population, were moving on the social ladder; how they accepted the East European immigrants; how they changed their identificational strategies, and – which is extremely interesting from our point of view – in what ways the Holocaust influenced those changes.

Another important publication is a set of articles collected and edited by Hilene Flanzbaum under the title *The Americanization of the Holocaust*.[22] Flanzbaum has noted that American discussion on the

Holocaust is becoming more and more Americanized, and at the same time entering the mainstream American culture as one of its most important elements. Three chapters by other authors in the volume also merit a mention. Jeffrey Shandler ('Aliens in the Wasteland: American Encounters with the Holocaust in 1960s Science Fiction Television') shows how the Holocaust became a popular topic of television programmes, how it came to be used as a touchstone of social problems, and, last but not least, how the very word *holocaust* became a household word. Henry Greenspan ('Imagining Survivors: Testimony and the Rise of Holocaust Consciousness') argues that the survivors and their written and oral accounts have shaped America's collective memory. James E. Young ('America's Holocaust: Memory and the Politics of Identity') presents an unusually insightful and well-researched chapter on commemorations of the Shoah in America: on public ceremonies and Holocaust museums. Finally, Young reflects on the problem of American culture as a culture of competing disasters.

In his revealing book, *Preserving Memory: The Struggle to Create America's Holocaust Museum*,[23] Edward Linenthal tells the story of the United States Holocaust Memorial Museum – how the project to build it was made, what political issues stood behind the idea, and what were the obstacles to completing the construction of the museum. Linenthal's book is a historic-sociological analysis of the process of politicization of Holocaust memory.

One last publication I would like to mention here is Alan Mintz's *Popular Culture and the Shaping of Holocaust Memory in America*.[24] Analysing selected film productions, Mintz tries to find out how the Shoah has moved from 'silence to salience', as one of his chapters is titled. One of the values of this book is its contribution to the methodology of Holocaust studies. Mintz argues that there are generally two paradigms of the Holocaust which are employed by the historians as well as the philosophers. One is the exceptionalist model, according to which the Shoah is an all-shattering event that excludes all analogies and comparisons; the other is the constructivist model which points to the social context of interpretation as the crucial element determining the meaning of the Shoah: in other words, the latter model implies that there is no meaning or sense in the Holocaust as such; all we see in it is the outcome of our subjective perception.

In the field of the sociology of Jewish life, I will mention a few works that are more comprehensive in scope, and also those which explore the issue of Jewish identity vis-à-vis religion and the Shoah. Charles E.

Silberman, in his work, *A Certain People: American Jews and Their Lives Today*,[25] presents an overview of the problems of contemporary American Jewry. He deals with issues of identity, religious choices, intermarriage and the danger of dwindling numbers looming over the Jewish population in America. He also analyses the impact of Israel and the Holocaust on American Jewish life, especially after the 1967 war, and also touches the issue of Jewish memory. Silberman argues that although for the older generations both Israel and the European catastrophe that preceded its establishment occupy an exceptional place in their self-definition, for the younger Jews Israel is a taken-for-granted political fact, while the Shoah appears as distant as the destruction of the temples thousands of years ago. The question of Jewish identity seen against the background of Jewish social structure (based on a quantitative research) is also thoroughly elaborated by Arnold Dashefsky and Howard M. Shapiro in *Ethnic Identification Among American Jews: Socialization and Social Structure*.[26]

In his oft-cited work, *Observing America's Jews*,[27] Marshall Sklare describes several sociological perspectives of writing about American Jewry: a dying people and an anachronistic community whose existence is sustained by the hostility of Gentiles; a corrupted class of people who acquired a new, higher social status; and finally, Jews seen from the survivalist perspective – as a people torn apart between the will to continue its existence and the temptation to assimilate. His general observations regarding American Jewry indicate that this social group has not experienced what Sklare calls the paradigmatic process of integration with the majority society (self-segregation – acculturation – assimilation). While there are still some Jewish groups which are on the stage of self-segregation, most of the American Jewish community have arrived at the stage of acculturation. Sklare maintains, however, that they seem not to tend to proceed to assimilation in large numbers. The reason for this, he claims, is twofold. Firstly, that anti-Semitism in America is not so strong as to trigger the desire to assimilate (and therefore avoid discrimination). Secondly, that Jews in general, Sklare contends, are prone to think of themselves as an elite group; thus to assimilate completely to American (meaning: Gentile) society would imply leaving the elite. Sklare is also very interested in the intellectual character of American Jewry and dedicates a whole section to Jewish sociologists, claiming that they constitute a specific group: secularized and quite alienated from the Jewish community at large, which partly explains why few of them made any contribution to the study of American Jews.

With regard to sociological studies on the topic of religious denominations and religious beliefs of American Jewry, it is expedient to mention Samuel C. Heilman's *Jewish Unity and Diversity: A Survey of American Rabbis and Rabbinical Students*[28] and *Portrait of American Jews: The Last Half of the 20th Century*,[29] as well as Jack Wertheimer's *A People Divided: Judaism in Contemporary America*.[30] All these books focus on Jewish religious identity and how it is affected by the social changes of American culture at large. In *Jewish Unity and Diversity*, Heilman, using statistics, shows how Orthodox Jews differ from non-Orthodox, and in what ways the youngest generation (rabbinical students) differs from the older ones. It is telling that while in his sample all Orthodox students were men, in all non-Orthodox denominations he surveyed, the rate of women was about 50 per cent. What is also interesting is that while 98 per cent of the Orthodox rabbis (and 100 per cent of students) believe in God, the numbers for the Conservative and Reform are, respectively, 94 per cent (92 per cent), and 93 per cent (89 per cent). In the second of Heilman's works mentioned above he investigates the issue of Jewish fluctuating denominational loyalties and the impact of the existence of the state of Israel on their identity as Jews. Jack Wertheimer concentrates on the question of Jewish culture war – a result of, inter alia, the general fragmentation of American culture in the 1960s. In parallel with that Jewish fragmentation, Wertheimer maintains, American Jews started to be preoccupied with survivalism: the bare survival of American Jews as an ethnic group came to be seen as the number one problem of that community. Also, Wertheimer has observed a shift from interest and immersion in East European Jewish culture to Israeli culture, from Ashkenaz to Israel.[31] He also noted an attempt initiated by the Reconstructionist milieus to launch a new Copernican revolution which 'would substitute the Jewish people for God as the center of Jewish universe'.[32]

Topics connected to the role of politics in Jewish communal life and in determining the role of American Jewry in American society were elaborated upon by Seymour Martin Lipset and Earl Raab in *Jews and the New American Scene*,[33] and also by Jacob Neusner. Lipset and Raab analyse American Jewry as generally one community that undergoes numerous social changes, that tries to determine its cultural specificity, that fears both assimilation and anti-Semitism, and finds the Shoah and Israel as important identity-building factors. This, certainly, is a topic most thoroughly dwelt on by Jacob Neusner. In his book, *The Religious World of Contemporary Judaism: Observations and Convictions*,[34]

Neusner argues that there are in fact two Judaisms. One is the traditional Judaism of the Dual Torah (written and oral), the other is the Judaism of 'Holocaust and Redemption'. He contends that if the Holocaust was a difficult question, Israel is the answer to that question. To that particular subject Neusner dedicated his book, *Stranger at Home: 'The Holocaust', Zionism, and American Judaism.*[35]

In an important volume, *Jewish Identity*,[36] edited by David Theo Goldberg and Michael Krausz, the latter editor, in a chapter entitled 'On Being Jewish', argues that there is no essence of the Jewish people, and therefore it is difficult to determine what Jewish identity might be. Krausz opposes what he calls the essentialist approach and asserts that apart from the view of the Halacha there is a multiplicity of Jewish identities. Basically, he divides these identities into two types: he distinguishes between Jewishness-by-descent – that is, by birth – and Jewishness-by-assent – that is, by self-identification. Krausz also claims that the Holocaust, as an integral part of Jewish history, constitutes part of American Jewish identity: identification with Holocaust narrative 'can hardly not be constitutive of being Jewish'.[37] In the same volume, in the chapter 'Jewish Identity and the Challenge of Auschwitz', Lionel Rubinoff analyses the influence of the Shoah on Jewish faith. In his opinion, the very existence of places like Auschwitz is a terrible test of the Jewish belief in God. It can be perceived as a shocking alarm, the significance of which is that Jews have been abandoned by the God who had allegedly chosen them, or even that they made a mistake believing in him. Rubinoff argues that the question of the Holocaust is undetachable from the issue of Jewish identity. And though seeking answers to the catastrophe is unavoidable, these answers can be only as absurd as the event itself. The radical uniqueness of the Shoah, he contends, lies in its incomprehensibility, in its refusal to be interpreted and searched for any meaning, and finally it is unique because it transcends human language.

The single most important publication based on empirical research on the impact of the Holocaust upon Jews is Reeve Robert Brenner's *The Faith and Doubt of Holocaust Survivors.*[38] Surveying a group of over 700 survivors living in Israel, Brenner was interested to learn whether and how the faith of his respondents had changed during or after the Holocaust. He assumed that the Shoah had the potential to impact the faith of Jewish people; thus his purpose was to see if this event brought the respondents to unbelief or if it incited them to believe in God. Brenner argues that 16 per cent of those who had been believers before the war lost faith because of the Holocaust; after the war, out of the 38 per cent who claimed they were believers, 2 per cent came to believe in a non-personal God. What is striking is that a full '*47 percent* [of the survivors] *averred that the Holocaust had no influence on their beliefs about God. That is, nearly half of the entire survivor population were unaffected.*' (Italics in the original.)[39] Brenner also argues that of the 16 per cent who lost faith in God due to the Shoah, one half ceased to believe in God since they saw the Holocaust as clear evidence that there is no providence or providential force. Yet what might seem surprising is that 5 per cent of the sample gained faith in God because of the Holocaust, which did not happen to any of the Jews I have interviewed in Warsaw and New York. William B. Helmreich's *Against All Odds: Holocaust Survivors and the Successful Lives They Made in America*[40] is also an interesting book – based on 170 interviews – but for the most part it concerns the topics of the well-being of the survivors who came to America after the end of the war. The author explores the life histories of his respondents: how they fared upon arrival to the United States, how they were accepted by native-born American Jews, and finally how their professional and family life developed after several decades in America. Though very insightful and inspiring as a well-researched work, it has little relevance for the topic of this book.

The same might be said about Nechama Tec's *When Light Pierced the Darkness: Christian Rescue of Jews in Nazi-Occupied Poland.*[41] Tec interviewed Jewish survivors and Poles who had extended their help to Jews during the war. If the question of religious beliefs was present in her study, it pertained mostly to the religious motivation of the rescuers in deciding to help the Jews. Tec did not ask her respondents whether, according to them, the Holocaust could be squared with the existence of a good God. Yet an interesting outcome of her research is that, in fact, most of the rescuers hid Jews because that was, they said, what their religion demanded from them, even if before the war some of them had been declared anti-Semites. For those with a weaker religiosity it was just the call of duty, Tec argues.

As for English-language publications dealing with the history and social issues of post-war Polish Jews, two books should be mentioned: *A Social Analysis of Postwar Polish Jewry* by Irena Hurwic-Nowakowska,[42] and *Neutralizing Memory: The Jew in Contemporary Poland* by Iwona Irwin-Zarecka.[43] Hurwic-Nowakowska's book is based on an extensive survey she conducted between 1947 and 1950. With regard to methodology, she assumed an extended definition of the Jew, including not only Jews but also people who regarded themselves as Poles but admitted to having Jewish roots. She accepted this definition on the grounds that such people often registered with Jewish Committees after the war. Hurwic-Nowakowska is concerned with issues of Jewish identity. She has noted that the basis for Jewish identification among post-war Polish Jewry was predominantly Jewish religion and/or the Yiddish language. When asked about their homeland, some of her respondents mentioned Poland, whereas others mentioned Palestine. This was not surprising, for, as she shows, after the Kilece pogrom and other smaller incidents, after having experienced Polish anti-Semitism personally, many Jews did not believe in a peaceful Polish–Jewish coexistence. It is also interesting that in her questionnaire, Hurwic-Nowakowska included questions concerning religious beliefs. Though religion played an important role for her informants, either in terms of faith or in terms of ethnic bonds, a significant proportion of the sample rejected Jewish messianism and the idea of chosen-ness. More than 50 per cent of the sample were non-believers, while only 7 per cent were both believing and practising. In general, Hurwic-Nowakowska discovered, for these Jews tradition and cultural values were more important than belief in God.

In *Neutralizing Memory: The Jew in Contemporary Poland*, Iwona Irwin-Zarecka focuses on the question of Jewish identity and of continuing the existence of a Jewish community. She argues that of those Jews who survived the Shoah, most were committed to Polish culture, and after the war they hoped to be able to live in the 'democratic' Polish society; thus, she contends, many favoured complete assimilation. Those who did not advocate outright assimilation were in favour of silent Jewishness, 'keen on rendering the whole issue [of Jewishness] irrelevant, both in public and in private. At home, steeped in secular tradition, there was no room for Jewish ritual; oftentimes, there was even no room for any talk about the past. [They] were migrating symbolically into the world of Polish priorities'.[44] To some, the awareness of being Jewish was not something that was underscored by the memory of the Holocaust. If anything, memory of the war made them 'less special', as tragic war experiences were part of the Polish society at large. To others, memory was becoming more and more focused on suffering, even to the exclusion of everything else.

Two other important publications are Joanna Wiszniewicz's 'The First Postwar Generation of Polish Jews: The Legacy of the Holocaust Handed down by Parents With Regard to Jewish Identity',[45] and

Marcin Starnawski's 'Historically Conscious Cosmopolitans: Jewish Identity and the '68 Generation of Polish Jews in Exile'.[46] Both these authors argue that Holocaust memory proved to be one of the crucial elements of the identity of contemporary Polish Jews. These two articles will be commented on in more detail in Chapter 4, section 2.

Barbara Engelking, in her *Holocaust and Memory: The Experience of the Holocaust and Its Consequences: An Investigation Based on Personal Narratives*,[47] explores the psychological consequences of the Shoah for those who survived. In her interviews she attempts to provoke her respondents to talk about their war experiences, and about their present fears, their feelings of regret or remorse. In short, she is interested in analysing the phenomenon known as PTSD (post-traumatic stress disorder). Since the book is generally a psychological work, the author does not ask her interviewees about their faith and their views on religion. On rare occasions the respondents themselves say how the Shoah impacted their relationships with God. Yet we find a piece of information which, from the standpoint of the present book, is interesting. Engelking admits that a considerable majority of her interviewees were non-religious people.

One of the most important publications on the post-war history of Polish Jews that has appeared over the last decade is *Poland and the Jews: Reflections of a Polish Polish Jew*[48] by Stanisław Krajewski. In his book, Krajewski, a mathematician by profession and an active member of the Warsaw Jewish Community, covers a broad spectrum of topics: from historical and sociological essays on the significance of Auschwitz for Jewish and Polish identities, through communism and Solidarity to contemporary Polish–Jewish relations and Jewish–Catholic dialogue. It is essential reading for anyone wanting to have even a perfunctory knowledge about Polish Jews and their role in Polish society.

I found a lot of inspiration in Joanna Wiszniewicz's *opus vitae*: *Życie przecięte: Opowieści pokolenia Marca* [Life Cut Through: Stories of the March Generation].[49] Wiszniewicz, who prematurely passed away in 2009, has managed to gather an immense amount of material (twenty-seven interviews) that will certainly trigger further research into the sociology of post-war Polish Jewry. Without her book my research would have been incomplete.

Another book I would like to mention is one published originally in Polish and titled *The Holocaust and Identity*,[50] by Małgorzata Melchior. A sociologist, Melchior concentrates on the question of identificational transformations of the Polish Jews who survived on the 'Aryan' side equipped with forged documents. In her book, Melchior analyses three periods in the lives of her informants: before the war, during the Nazi occupation, and after the war. She tries to find out how the identities (both individual and social) of these persons were changed when they had to act as Polish Christians; how they behaved when they were 'suspected' of being Jewish or even attacked by Polish blackmailers; and, finally, how they reacted to the new reality after the war when they could either keep their Polish identity or come back to their original Jewish identity. Melchior underscores the fact that for different people the same situation could have had different emotional and practical consequences. She argues, for example, that living under an assumed identity might have been relatively easy for those who had already identified with Polishness to a large extent, while for those who had had little to do with Polish culture and Polish everyday life, assuming a new external identity might have been like wearing a mask or acting a difficult role. Thus Melchior concludes that the war experiences of those Jews depended greatly on their pre-war biographies. This, in turn, weighed heavily on the identity choices they had to make after the liberation. The author contends that these choices were often excruciating moral and psychological dilemmas. As was the case with Engelking, Melchior was not significantly interested in exploring the question of the religious beliefs of her informants.

METHODOLOGY AND SOURCES

My basic methodological assumptions are in a way puritan: I do not make use of tens of conceptions that endlessly reinterpret one another and split hairs over issues of secondary importance. My aim is to follow a rational procedure in conceptualization, operationalization, and analysis. From the very beginning, and throughout my whole research, I have found inspiration in Max Weber's methodology. I certainly do not consider myself an 'orthodox Weberian', which means I do not take all of his social concepts to be irreproachable, nor do I think that all his concepts are applicable to my research. What I do value greatly in Weber is his sober and innovative methodology. I am especially indebted to Weber for his conception of the 'ideal type'. It proved to be an ideal solution, an ideal tool with which to plan and achieve the aims of my research project.

It may be helpful to briefly explain what I mean by the ideal type. In these reflections I rely on the best currently available study on Weberian methodology, authored by Sven Eliaeson.[51] Weber's scientific career was that of a lawyer, economist and historian. With time, he also made himself known as a sociologist. This passage from history and economics to sociology marked an important change in his scholarship. Although he never really stopped being a historian, Weber made an invaluable contribution to social sciences' methodology through his polemics with both the historicists and the psychologists. He was anti-historicist and at the same time his research was history-focused. Eliaeson aptly describes Weber's move from historicism to the study of society where historical facts were only the point of departure, which, inter alia, led the German thinker to the formulation of the ideal type:

> The ideal type exemplifies Weber's liberation from the historicist milieu in which he was raised. This 'break' with historicism was gradual, as indicated by the original character of his conceptual tool as a vehicle for history; in retrospect we use it as a tool for social science. It is not a dramatic parting; on the contrary it takes the form of building a bridge between historicism and the more modern ideals of science. Or perhaps it is even a release of something that is already inherent among historians. In helping the historicists to save themselves Weber, as the American saying goes, 'put the hay where the horse could get it' – or so it seems.[52]

The ideal type has to do with evaluating the logic of thinking or of a process or action, yet it has nothing to do with value judgment. In other words, the ideal type, properly understood, is a conception of an ideal concept or model and not a theory of ethical evaluation.[53] So, the ideal type is a theoretical structure, a provisional map of an unknown area, so to speak, which is sketched with rough strokes and which is continually being corrected and modified as the unknown land is being explored: 'this mental construct cannot be found empirically anywhere in reality. It is a *Utopia*. Historical research faces the task of determining, in each individual case, the extent to which this ideal-construct approximates to or diverges from reality.'[54] Thus, Weber's ideal type is an excellent exemplification of his 'end-rational' approach to science. *Zweckrationalität*, purpose-oriented rationality or instrumentality, is one of Weber's most basic rules or organizing principles, which make genuine research possible. To create an ideal type when making a research project is therefore a rational step that leads to the next stages of a scholarly investigation. It is an instrument or a tool of primary importance in pursuing a methodologically coherent research. The ideal type, however, is not a hypothesis – it is nothing more than a practical (and purpose-oriented) tool which is meant to help formulate hypotheses or hypothetical assumptions in the course of study.[55]

There is one more theoretical problem concerned with Weberian methodology which I would like to elucidate at this point. It pertains to the category of 'interpretative understanding' (*Verstehen*). What Weber called interpretative sociology is not exactly the same as what is usually understood by this term today. We cannot forget that Weber thought in terms of empirical evidence. His opposition to psychology was in large part due to his inability to accept empathetic understanding as reliable scientific explanation. But he was an advocate of interpretative understanding in general. This seems to be somewhat confusing. Yet, as Eliaeson shows, there is a way to comprehend this apparent inconsistency. He claims that there are two kinds of interpretative understanding: one is Weber's, the other is non-Weberian. Weber's way of interpretative understanding is purely rational (he finds the scheme of 'cause and effect' indispensable); the other is empathetic or hermeneutic. Now the difference is clear: for Weber, the only genuine explication of a phenomenon is to answer the question 'What is the actual cause of a given phenomenon?', while to understand an event hermeneutically is to point to the meaning or significance thereof.

I shall therefore make it clear at the very outset of this book that I do not intend to engage in seeking empirical cause-and-effect explication of the phenomena I want to explore. This decision has to do with the nature of my research. It is a study of human attitudes, thinking, opinions and worldviews; also of concerns, fears, uncertainties and ambiguous feelings. As a *qualitative* and not a *quantitative* research it is subject to empathetic and hermeneutic interpretation, rather than to strict causal explication.[56] Also, I do not intend to seek 'hard' sociological laws which allegedly govern human behaviour, for I do not believe that there are such laws. Nor do I agree with the Hegelian perspection of history which is but a progressive self-realization of the absolute *Geist*. That does not mean, however, that I reject the need for a rational explanation. Given that any logical analysis is an act of rational thinking, my attempts at an empathetic interpretation of the Holocaust and its impact upon Polish and American Jews will be a rational content analysis of the research materials. After all, 'for Weber *Verstehen* [understanding] is an act of *rational* interpretation'. (Italics in the original.)[57] Thus, my method consists of trying to reach an empathetic and rational understanding of the phenomena that are being explored. I therefore dissent to some extent from Norman Denzin's stance, which is that in studies in meaning and interpretation there are no methods to be followed. While he contends that in qualitative research (especially in biographical analysis) meaning takes precedence over method, my conviction is that hermeneutics, or seeking for meanings, is our simplest method.[58]

CONCEPTUALIZATION

In the first stage of the research conceptualization, I made a general outline of the subject I intended to investigate and formulated a tentative title for the book which was: *The Impact of the Holocaust upon the Jews of Poland and America.* Then I had to establish what I really wanted to examine, which were the questions that should be asked, and what my suppositions were. To this end I constructed my ideal type. It was my deep conviction that such an immense humanitarian catastrophe as the Holocaust must have had a significant impact on the beliefs of the group which had been targeted for mass destruction. I thought that the ubiquity of suffering and death caused by the Nazi extermination policy had to affect the beliefs of the Jewish people. Therefore my ideal type took the form of a hypothetical assumption, a premise I was to confront with reality: *The Holocaust, as the destruction of the Jewish people, on an unheard-of-scale, has had a tremendous impact on all contemporary Jews. First and foremost, it must have shaken their belief in the God of the Bible, leading many of them to atheism. It seems very probable that the survivors – those who experienced the horrors of the Shoah with their own bodies and minds – because of the torment they went through, will be in a large percentage nonbelievers. Also, the Shoah must have affected what it means to be a Jew today.*

The next stage of conceptualization was to determine the object of my interest and to set limits in time and space. I decided to base the research on two kinds of data: books and articles by American Jewish thinkers, as well as publications by Polish Jews, and also in-depth interviews with Polish and American Jews. Analysing the textual data, I focused on books on the Holocaust issued in the United States, regardless of the time of their publication. With regard to the periodicals, however, I had to impose some time limits. I thought it would be reasonable to concentrate on four or five Jewish periodicals published between 1980 and 2000. I consider the last twenty years of the past century to be the period of time when Holocaust debate was at its peak in America. I will dwell at length on this issue in the first chapter. As regards literature on Polish Jews and the Holocaust, the question has been truly troubling, since reliable material providing information on that issue is really scant, consisting of a dozen books analysing historical aspects of post-war Jewry plus a few sociologically-oriented publications. To that should be added a few dozen articles published in various periodicals, specifically in *Midrasz* and *Puls.*

With regard to the interviews, it seemed both sensible and feasible to conduct them in Warsaw and in an American metropolis with a significant Jewish population. Warsaw was a natural choice, for this is where the largest Jewish community in Poland dwells and where a number of Jewish organizations are active. In fact, these organizations proved to be a good source of information. Considering the United States, it appeared that New York City would be the most appropriate place in which to interview American Jews. New York is the American city which has the largest Jewish population; it is the seat of numerous Jewish organizations which also could serve as sources of information and of contacts with potential respondents.

OPERATIONALIZATION

The concept of research had then to be 'put into motion'. In order to conduct interviews it was necessary to construct a specific research tool. Since it was intended to be a qualitative study, I decided to prepare a structured in-depth interview scenario. Originally the scenario was written in Polish and included nineteen questions of which seventeen were open-ended. A special form was also devised to collect the background data of each informant. This form comprised thirteen questions plus two additional sections where answers to questions two and fifteen of the main scenario were to be noted. During each interview I had the written scenario with me as a guide and in order to make sure I had asked all the questions. Of course, each interview had its own atmosphere and tempo, and there were moments when the interviewee was especially interested in the topic of the conversation, as well as moments when s/he seemed even bored with the interview or surprised to hear a particular question. That is why the scenario was only loosely structured: that is, the order of questions varied from conversation to conversation. Often I had to change the subject of discussion when I had the impression that the respondent felt uneasy or annoyed, and later on, using other words or auxiliary questions, I used to come back to the topic I was interested in. Also, it was not infrequent that an interviewee would answer unasked questions by dwelling on a particular theme for a relatively long time and touching many points. In such cases I did not have to ask the question formally for the interview to be valid. The purpose was to obtain important data; therefore, if the interviewee started to speak about such important issues, my task as the interviewer was just to control the conversation and, when necessary, to ask additional questions in order to get more explicit or detailed answers, or to clarify some ambiguous expressions.

I chose to interview Warsaw and New York Jews as representing, from a historical perspective, two communities important for world Jewry. The former are not only descendants of the largest and most influential Jewish community in pre-war Poland, but also constitute a large proportion of the now very small group of Polish Jewry. The latter are nowadays the largest Jewish community the world over – American Jews make up 43 per cent of the whole Jewish population and almost 69 per cent of total diaspora Jewry.[59] And New York's Jewish community, counting 1.97 million, is the second-largest Jewish urban population after Tel Aviv's 2.56 million, and constitutes more than one-third of all American Jews (5.7 million). What is more, New York's Jewish population is three times larger than that of Haifa, and much more than three times as large as that of Jerusalem.[60]

In contemporary Poland, Jews constitute a statistically insignificant minority – according to some sources the figure is close to a thousand times less than just before the outbreak of the Second World War.[61] The *American Jewish Yearbook* estimates Poland's Jewish population in 2001 at about 3,500.[62] In 1997, Helena Datner and Małgorzata Melchior estimated Polish Jewry to number from 6,000 to 15,000.[63] In a lecture on *Contemporary Polish Jews*, given by Datner on 6 May 2004 at Warsaw University, she argued that the number is now estimated at between 3,000 to 5,000 of affiliated Jews. In a private conversation she told me that the number of those officially affiliated with a Jewish organization and the number of all who consider themselves Jewish, at least in some way, is significant. There are, as Datner put it, many 'closet Jews' or 'forest Jews', who hide their identity not only from the general public but sometimes also from their closest family: children, grandchildren, spouses.[64] Altogether, the number of Polish Jews probably ranges between 15,000 and 30,000 – including those formally unaffiliated and unwilling to reveal their identity. Between 10 and 30 per cent of Poland's Jews live in the capital.[65] Active Jewish communities also exist in Cracow, Łódź, Wrocław, Gdańsk, Katowice and Poznań.[66] In the United States, the cities which host significant numbers of Jews, apart from New York, are: Los Angeles (621,000), south-east Florida (514,000), Philadelphia (276,000), Chicago (262,000), Boston (227,000), San Francisco (210,000), Washington, DC (165,000), Baltimore (95,000) and Detroit (95,000).[67]

In the summer and fall of 2000 I carried out a series of forty-nine in-depth interviews in Warsaw[68] with people regarding themselves as Jewish. The research sample was obtained in the simplest and at the same time the only possible way. I got the names and addresses of the Jewish inhabitants of Warsaw from two sources:

1. The Jewish Community of Warsaw (Gmina Wyznaniowa Żydowska w Warszawie).
2. Warsaw department of the Social-Cultural Society of Polish Jews (Towarzystwo Społeczno-Kulturalne Żydów Polskich).

Altogether I received 104 full addresses of Warsaw Jews. I mailed about eighty special letters (using the Polish Academy of Sciences letterhead) in which I introduced myself and briefly summarized my research project, explaining that I was conducting interviews with Warsaw Jews and asking the person addressed whether s/he would be willing to meet with me for a tape-recorded conversation. In the letter I also ensured my potential informants that all interviews would be kept confidential and that their names would not be revealed to any third party. About half of these people said that they would meet with me when I called them some two to three weeks after the letters had been posted. During the research it turned out, however, that 'snowball sampling' could also be used – some of the interviewees gave me the telephone numbers of their Jewish friends and advised me to contact them. So finally it was a kind of mixed-sampling method that I adapted to my study.

Most of the interviews were conducted either in my apartment or in that of my respondents. A few I carried out in the building of the Jewish Community of Warsaw, 6 Twarda St, and two meetings took place in restaurants since the respondents insisted on that.

Conducting my research in New York was made possible thanks to a research grant I was given by the Kosciuszko Foundation. I was formally invited by the New School University (formerly New School for Social Research), and the Foundation provided me with financial support.

In New York City my technique for contacting Jewish people was in a large measure different, as I had no access to any comprehensive list of Jewish inhabitants of New York. The first person I interviewed was a university professor. I received his address and phone number from the Kosciuszko Foundation's Holocaust Committee, who asked me to read a research proposal that the person mentioned above had submitted to them (it was a study in Polish–Jewish relations). I contacted that person and agreed to discuss his project, and asked whether he would be willing to participate in my research, to which he said yes. After the interview the professor not only gave me some methodological and linguistic hints, but also offered his help in contacting people whom I could interview. It was from him that I got the first phone numbers of Jews living in New York. So, the snowball method was a major way to get in contact with potential new respondents. Another way was participating in conferences and lectures organized by the Center for Jewish History (a superinstitution located at 15 West 16th Street, housing YIVO Institute for Jewish Research, Yeshiva University Museum and the Sephardic House), Arbeter Ring (Workmen's Circle), the Generation After (a group gathering survivors and their children), the Jewish Theological Seminary of America (school for theological studies of the Conservative branch of Judaism) and Hebrew Union College – Jewish Institute of Religion (Reform Judaism). After these lectures were over I would approach one or two people and tell them about my research. Every time I asked someone to agree to an interview, I had with me a short letter (typed on a New School University letterhead) explaining the nature and objective of my research and assuring the reader that all information would be kept confidential. Also, I sought New York-based Jewish organizations on the Internet. That is how I found the City Congregation (local community of Secular Humanistic Judaism) and an organization called Jews for Racial and Economic Justice. In many cases, when I met people who agreed to be interviewed, the snowball method subsequently proved practical and efficient.

Altogether I interviewed fifty-two Jews in New York. As in Warsaw, all interviews were tape-recorded. In one case the interviewee asked for a formal letter in which I stated that the person would not be identified in any way in my dissertation or any published material, and of course I provided the letter. Among the informants there were people from all five boroughs of New York: Manhattan, the Bronx, Queens, Brooklyn and Staten Island. At the time of the interview one person lived in New Jersey, just across the Hudson River, in a town included in the Greater New York metropolis. About half of the interviews were conducted either at my place or at my respondents' places. Around fifteen were carried out in my informants' workplaces, some in the building of a Jewish organization, and three conversations were recorded in a restaurant.

Upon completing the fieldwork, all interviews were computer-transcribed and saved as text files. Subsequently, these files were exported into a qualitative data analysis software.[69] Then all Polish interviews were saved in one file and the American interviews in another one. The next stage consisted of coding the transcribed interviews. I created only a few categories, which were a kind of keyword with which I marked those segments of the interviews which contained information pertaining to a given topic. The categories I found useful were the following: Jewish/Identity, Holocaust/Shoah/Identity, Assimilation, Holocaust/Shoah/God, Torah/Bible. Every fragment that pertained to one of the above-mentioned categories was properly coded. However, I did not only use the coding system, but often also used Boolean search. Yet I did not limit my analysis to those computer-generated reports (although they were extremely helpful for keeping away the danger of 'data overload'); many times during the stage of analysis I would read and reread selected interviews or selected segments of interviews in search of specific information or just to get some background data. Assuming that the very person of the researcher is the best 'tool of analysis,' I thought that a direct 'contact' with the interviews was unavoidable and useful for obtaining a more nuanced picture of what my respondents' views and attitudes were.[70]

Before I started interviewing the respondents, and during each and every interview, I had to answer the question of 'Who is a Jew?' Knowing that there is the Halachic law saying that a Jew is either born of a Jewish mother or converted – which law, however, is contested or neglected by many non-Orthodox Jewish circles – I decided to accept a subjective definition of being Jewish: anyone who considers him/herself Jewish is a Jew. Certainly, this definition can be questioned on the grounds that it does not do justice to Jewish matrilineal tradition. Yet this study is not meant to conform to any particular Jewish legal principles – Orthodox or otherwise – but to take an unbiased position toward all social phenomena to be analysed. My methodological assumption concurs with what Sergio DellaPergola labelled the '*enlarged Jewish population*': this operative concept of his includes both core Jews and people of Jewish parentage whose religion is other than Judaism. Who are core Jews, according to DellaPergola?

The *core Jewish population* includes all those who, when asked, identify themselves as Jews ... This is intentionally comprehensive and pragmatic approach. Such definition of a person as a Jew, reflecting *subjective* feelings, broadly overlaps but does not necessarily coincide with Halakhah (Jewish law) or other normatively binding definitions. It does *not* depend on any measure of that person's Jewish commitment or behavior – in terms of religiosity, beliefs, knowledge, communal affiliation or otherwise. [Italics in the original.][71]

As we can see, in his concept of the *extended Jewish population* DellaPergola includes all respondents claiming they are Jews, either of Jewish or other religion, or not believers at all. It is worthwhile mentioning that whenever I contacted potential respondents, either by mail or by telephone, I made it perfectly clear that I was interested in interviewing Warsaw (or New York) Jews – I never used the category 'Poles of Jewish origin' or 'people of Jewish ancestry', just to avoid misunderstandings. Thus anyone to whom I addressed my letter, or my oral introduction to the research I was doing, was aware that my target group was Warsaw (or New York) Jews. Therefore, all those who agreed to the interview I considered to be Jewish. Moreover, the question with which I began all interviews was: 'What in your life makes you a Jew? What are the ways in which you identify yourself as a Jew?' If I had heard anyone answer that there must have been some kind of misunderstanding, or that the person thought I would be interviewing people who survived the war, also of Polish ethnic identity, I would have ended the interview without asking any other questions. Yet no one ever said s/he had no Jewish identity at all.[72]

As with most studies of a qualitative nature, the samples of Warsaw and New York Jews are not highly representative of the Jewish populations of Poland and America respectively. Although I sought to include in the groups interviewed a similar number of women and men, to have survivors and non-survivors, members of various Jewish communities and organizations, and people with different educational backgrounds, it would be naive and invalid to claim that I eventually obtained statistically representative samples. Nevertheless, it can be said that both groups analysed are in some ways phenomenologically representative.

I have dedicated quite a few paragraphs to describing how both samples were obtained and how I made sure of the identity of each particular respondent. But the identity of the researcher is not to be neglected, either. It is not an unusual case nowadays for a Pole to study

Jewish history, culture or religion, or Jewish social issues in general. Yet it was not unimportant for many of my interviewees whether I was a Jew or a Pole, and what my religion was. Most of my informants took it for granted that I was a Polish Catholic – this at least could be inferred from many conversations, for often the interviewees would say: 'you as a Catholic', or 'in your Christian religion', or else 'as a Pole you surely know that ... '. When I was asked to reveal my ethnic and/or religious identity I usually answered that I would willingly do so after the interview was over. In some cases, nonetheless, urged by the respondent, I said that I am not Jewish. Did this information actually affect the responses of my informants? The first answer is *Yes*. One might expect at least some of them to be less critical of the Poles (this is a common psychological reaction in the situation of interview: the person interviewed tries not to say things that would supposedly be uncomfortable or vexatious to the researcher). Certainly, even if this were the case, it would have had hardly any impact on the final outcome of this work, as its main topic has little to do with Polish–Jewish relations. Yet I can honestly say that it was only in rare cases that I would feel that the interviewee was unwilling to use harsh words with regard to Polish people because of the researcher's alleged ethnic identity. What is more, I could even observe that often the informants were more eager to express critical views on Poland or Poles if they knew that the interviewer was Polish.[73] What might have encouraged them to be forthright and sincerely speak about their feelings was that I assured them that I was not there to judge anyone's opinions but to listen to them, and that I would not find offence in whatever they said, because from my point of view – as a researcher – the perfect situation would be if what they told me was what they thought. Altogether, my guess is that if my being a Pole did affect the content of the answers my respondents gave to me, the impact was rather that they were more candid in expressing their criticisms and negative feelings.

The other sources of material on which I based my study were books and articles by American Jewish authors. This material is analysed in the first half of my dissertation. It includes books by Richard L. Rubenstein, Eliezer Berkovits, Emil L. Fackenheim and Irving Greenberg, as well as articles that deal, in one way or another, with the Holocaust in the American context. The articles I analysed come, in the majority, from the following five American Jewish periodicals: *Commentary, Judaism, Midstream, The Reconstructionist* and *Tikkun*. The monthly *Commentary* is published in New York by the largest Jewish organization in the United

States – the American Jewish Committee. It is said to be one of the most prestigious American periodicals and at the same time a tribune of the neoconservative movement; it publishes articles dealing with political, social and also religious questions. Published in California, *Judaism: A Quarterly Journal of Jewish Life and Thought* is sponsored by the American Jewish Congress and 'is dedicated' – the editors reveal – 'to the creative discussion and exposition of the religious, moral and philosophical concepts of Judaism and their relevance to the problems of modern society'. *Midstream* is a Zionist periodical; the editorial board gives preference to articles on social and religious aspects of Jewish life. *The Reconstructionist*, published in Pennsylvania, is the only one among the analysed journals that is edited by a religious institution – the Reconstructionist Rabbinical College. It is one of the oldest Jewish-American periodicals (founded in 1935). 'By focusing on a single theme in each issue, and bringing to bear multiple perspectives on it, *The Reconstructionist* is a forum for significant dialogue and fresh approaches within the contemporary Jewish community', claim the editors. *Tikkun* (Hebrew: to transform, heal, and repair) has been published bi-monthly since 1986 in San Francisco. According to its founders and the editorial board, it is meant to be '*the liberal alternative* to the voices of Jewish conservatism and spiritual deadness in the Jewish world and as the *spiritual alternative* to the voices of materialism and selfishness in Western society'. (Italics in the original.) Out of over 120 articles gathered in the course of study, eighty-two have been cited in this book.

As mentioned above, Chapter 3 is dedicated to a social history of post-war Polish Jewry; it is based, for the most part, on books and articles by Irena Hurwic-Nowakowska, Iwona Irwin-Zarecka, Stanisław Krajewski, Joanna Wiszniewicz, Helena Datner, Paweł Śpiewak, Bożena Szaynok, Małgorzata Melchior, Konstanty Gebert, Grzegorz Berendt and August Grabski, Natalia Aleksiun and Alina Cała, among others.

OBJECTIVE OF THE STUDY

My objective in writing this book was to try to show how the Holocaust has impacted contemporary Jews. To this end I chose to analyse texts of American Jewish writers who have shaped Holocaust debate from its very inception. I also assumed that conducting interviews with Polish and American Jews would provide interesting research material which could be confronted with the theoretical works of Jewish authors.

Describing the goal of the study in detail I should like to underscore once again two points already mentioned. One was that I planned to so conduct the field research as to obtain answers to my initial question of whether the Shoah impels Jewish people to reject traditional biblical historiosophy – one that draws the picture of a caring God who intervenes in human lives and can be experienced from within Jewish history. The second thing I wanted to test was the assumption that the European destruction, or rather the awareness thereof, now plays a significant role in the general structure of Jewish identity.

It can also be said that this study was motivated by a common curiosity encountered by most sociologists and anthropologists: Do people change in response to cataclysmic events or do they only modify their belief systems to the reality they have to face? This work is also an attempt to find answers to this question.

Last but not least, this dissertation is meant to be a contribution to the sociology of contemporary Jewish societies. Although historical research in the field of Jewish studies is well established in Poland (in spite of the catastrophe, or maybe because of it), studies in the sociology of contemporary Polish Jewry are a forlorn territory where only a few scholars enter. Certainly, the comparative approach I applied in this research is a novelty in the field of Jewish social studies in Poland. As far as is known to me, there has been no significant publication in Poland which focuses on both Polish and American Jewry. On one side, Polish Jews, a tiny minority in today's Poland, though once the largest and the most vibrant community in all of Europe; on the other side, American Jewry, presently the largest, most powerful and at the same time the most innerly differentiated Jewish community in the world. Are these two groups totally unlike one another? Do they have any features in common? Does the Holocaust play a similar role in both communities? Do their members see Jewish identity in the same way and do they have the same identification strategies? I will attempt to answer these questions through comparative analysis.

What still remains to be done? In all honesty I must admit that the two major objects of my interest – the issues of identity and religious beliefs – are such vast subjects that I have found it infeasible to embrace in this study all thinkable questions, and to analyse the phenomena of identity-constructing and the attitude toward religious ideas in all respects. My focus was on the impact of the Shoah on these two spheres of life. What remains to be further explored in the contemporary history of Polish Jewry are issues of their cultural and religious revival as well as the role they played in Polish society in the politically turbulent years between the Martial Law period (1981–82) and the regaining of full independence by Poland in 1989.

Also, I have purposefully not included literary works in my study. There is of course an immense literature of the Holocaust – memoirs, personal diaries, fiction, poetry – in Polish as well as in English. This is, in my opinion, the kind of material that deserves still to be analysed and commented upon by Polish scholars, especially experts in literary studies. Analysis of Holocaust literature – and Holocaust-related episodes in other works – certainly would shed new light on the issues of identity and the question of God versus the destruction of European Jewry.

NOTES

1. R.L. Rubenstein, *After Auschwitz: History, Theology, and Contemporary Judaism*, 2nd edn (Baltimore, MD, and London: Johns Hopkins University Press, 1992). The first edition was titled *After Auschwitz: Radical Theology and Contemporary Judaism* (Indianapolis, IN: Bobbs-Merrill, 1966). All citations from this book, unless otherwise stated, are taken from the second edition.
2. Uriel Tal, 'On the Study of the Holocaust and Genocide', *Yad Vashem Studies*, 13 (1979), p.48.
3. See Israel Gutman (ed.), *Encyclopedia of the Holocaust* (Tel Aviv, New York and London: Sifriat Poalim Publishing House, 1990), s.v. 'Holocaust'.
4. See Tal, 'On the Study of the Holocaust and Genocide', p.49.
5. In Hassidic circles the expression *Churban Europa* is often used in reference to the Holocaust, yet this term was earlier used to refer to any great massacre that claimed the lives of European Jews.
6. For more on this particular term see Chapter 2, section 1.
7. There are, indeed, thinkers who criticize the use of the term 'holocaust' because, allegedly, it has misleading religious connotations, bringing to mind sacrifices offered to God, which might suggest that the millions of Jewish victims were in some way a sacrifice to God. Michael Berenbaum, for example, argues that 'the word [holocaust] itself softens and falsifies the event by giving it a religious significance'. Michael Berenbaum (ed.), *The World Must Know: The History of the Holocaust as Told in the United States Holocaust Memorial Museum* (Boston, MA: Little, Brown, 1993), p.1. The point is, however, that no matter whether we use the term 'holocaust' or 'shoah', we do utilize, if only unconsciously, biblical categories. And in biblical standards, in traditional Judaic interpretations, whatever happens is done by the will of God. Thus, whichever of the two words we employ, they both have religious connotations.
8. Jon Petrie, 'Jon Petrie investigates the etymology of the word 'Holocaust' (accessed 7 December 2003). http://www.fpp.co.uk/Auschwitz/docs/HolocaustUsage.html.
9. All five fragments are quoted in the online article 'Jon Petrie investigates'.
10. Ibid.
11. In this context it may seem surprising that in both Raul Hilberg's widely-known *The Destruction of the European Jews* (1961) and Elie Wiesel's *Night* (1960), the word 'holocaust' did not appear.
12. R.M. Shapiro, 'Holocaust: Usankcjonowanie terminu historycznego [Holocaust: Sanction of a Historical Term], *Biuletyn Żydowskiego Instytutu Historycznego*, 169–71 (January–September 1994), p.3.
13. See ibid., p.4.
14. Sigmund Freud, *The Basic Writings of Sigmund Freud*, edited by A.A. Brill (New York, 1938), p.32, quoted in Shapiro, 'Holocaust: Usankcjonowanie terminu historycznego', p.4.
15. Now called, in Germany, *Reichspogromnacht*.
16. Hartley Library, University of Southampton Special Research Collections, information brochure [1998], p.12, MS 175/142/1, ms. copyright J. Schonfield, quoted in the online article 'Jon Petrie investigates'.
17. Editorial, *Times Literary Supplement*, 26 August 1939, p.503.

18. P. Novick, *The Holocaust and Collective Memory: The American Experience* (London: Bloomsbury, 2000), p.133. The American edition was published a year earlier under the title *The Holocaust in American Life*. There are many German terms which were used by the Nazis during the war as key words denoting the mass murder of Jews. We should keep in mind that the Nazi government introduced a special terminology in order to pass information (between particular German offices and departments) about their politics of annihilation without calling it by its proper name. These special language procedures were called *Spracheregelung*. By far the best known such euphemism is *Endlösung (der Judanfrage)*, which means the Final Solution (of the Jewish question). In current-day literature this word is often used interchangeably with 'the Holocaust.' For the NSDAP this was the *Kernfrage* – the crucial element of their politics. The Nazis planned to make Germany and all of Europe *judenrein* (free of Jews). The action that was to lead to this end was called *Arisirung* (Arianization). Hitler himself and his cohorts often used the following terms in relation to the policy or particular actions taken against the Jewish population: *Umsiedlung* or *Aussiedlung* (resettlement – deportation to the ghettos and camps located in the East), *Entfernung* or *Ausweisung* (removal), *Austreibung* (expulsion, banishment) *Ausschaltung* (exclusion), *Vernichtung* (annihilation, extermination), *Ausrottung* (eradication, extirpation), *Einzelaktionen/Sonderaktionen* (special actions), *Sonderbehandlung* (special treatment – extermination), *Sonderzüge* (special trains – transports to death camps), *Spezialeinrichtungen* (special devices – crematoria), *Wasch- und Disinfektionsraum* (gas chamber). In current Holocaust literature, besides the words Holocaust and Shoah, the following terms are used: Nazi genocide, Jewish genocide, European catastrophe, Jewish catastrophe, destruction of European Jews, extermination of European Jews.
19. Raphael Lemkin, *Axis Rule in Occupied Europe: Laws of Occupation – Analysis of Government – Proposals for Redress* (Washington, DC: Carnegie Endowment for International Peace, 1944).
20. Lemkin, *Axis Rule in Occupied Europe*, p.79.
21. Eli Lederhendler, *New York Jews and the Decline of Urban Ethnicity, 1950–1970* (Syracuse, NY: Syracuse University Press, 2001).
22. Hilene Flanzbaum, *The Americanization of the Holocaust* (Baltimore, MD: Johns Hopkins University Press, 1999).
23. Edward T. Linenthal, *Preserving Memory: The Struggle to Create America's Holocaust Museum* (New York: Columbia University Press, 2001).
24. Alan Mintz, *Popular Culture and the Shaping of Holocaust Memory in America* (Seattle, WA: University of Washington Press, 2001).
25. Charles E. Silberman, *A Certain People: American Jews and Their Lives Today* (New York: Summit Books, 1985).
26. Arnold Dashefsky and Howard M. Shapiro, *Ethnic Identification Among American Jews: Socialization and Social Structure* (Lexington, MA: Lexington Books, 1974).
27. Marshall Sklare, *Observing America's Jews* (Hanover and London, MA: Brandeis University Press/University Press of New England, 1993).
28. Samuel C. Heilman, *Jewish Unity and Diversity: A Survey of American Rabbis and Rabbinical Students* (New York: American Jewish Committee, 1991).
29. Samuel C. Heilman, *Portrait of American Jews: The Last Half of the 20th Century* (Seattle, WA, and London: University of Washington Press, 1995).
30. Jack Wertheimer, *A People Divided: Judaism in Contemporary America* (New York: Basic Books, 1993).
31. By way of example he notes that while the traditional Sabbath greeting of American Jews had been the Ashkenazic *gut shabbos*, after the Israeli–Arab wars it was replaced by the Hebrew *shabbat shalom*. See Wertheimer, *A People Divided*, p.31.
32. Ibid., p.35.
33. Seymour Martin Lipset and Earl Raab, *Jews and the New American Scene* (Cambridge, MA: Harvard University Press, 1995).
34. Jacob Neusner, *The Religious World of Contemporary Judaism: Observations and Convictions* (Atlanta, GA: Scholars Press, 1989).
35. Jacob Neusner, *Stranger at Home: 'The Holocaust', Zionism, and American Judaism* (Chicago, IL, and London: University of Chicago Press, 1985).
36. David Theo Goldberg and Michael Krausz (eds), *Jewish Identity* (Philadephia, PA: Temple University Press, 1993).
37. Michael Krausz, 'On Being Jewish', in Goldberg and Krausz, *Jewish Identity*, p.272.

38. Reeve Robert Brenner, *The Faith and Doubt of Holocaust Survivors* (New York: Free Press, 1980).
39. Brenner, *Faith and Doubt of Holocaust Survivors*, p.95.
40. William B. Helmreich, *Against All Odds: Holocaust Survivors and the Successful Lives They Made in America* (New York: Simon & Schuster, 1992).
41. Nechama Tec, *When Light Pierced the Darkness: Christian Rescue of Jews in Nazi-Occupied Poland* (New York and Oxford: Oxford University Press, 1986).
42. Irena Hurwic-Nowakowska, *A Social Analysis of Postwar Polish Jewry* (Jerusalem: Zalman Shazar Center for Jewish History, 1986). For the Polish edition see: *Żydzi polscy (1947–1950): analiza więzi społecznej ludności żydowskiej* (Warsaw: IFiS PAN, 1996).
43. Iwona Irwin-Zarecka, *Neutralizing Memory: The Jew in Contemporary Poland* by (New Brunswick, NJ: Transaction Publishers, 1989).
44. Ibid., p.55.
45. Joanna Wiszniewicz, 'Pierwsze powojenne pokolenie polskich Żydów: Rodzicielski przekaz pamięci Holocaustu a tożsamość żydowska' [The First Post-War Generation of Polish Jews: The Legacy of the Holocaust Handed down by Parents With Regard to Jewish Identity], *Biuletyn Żydowskiego Instytutu Historycznego*, 191 (September 1999).
46. Marcin Starnawski, 'Historically Conscious Cosmopolitans: Jewish Identity and the '68 Generation of Polish Jews in Exile', *East European Jewish Affairs*, 32 (Winter 2002).
47. Barbara Engelking, *Holocaust and Memory: The Experience of the Holocaust and Its Consequences: An Investigation Based on Personal Narratives* (London: Leicester University Press, 2001).
48. Stanisław Krajewski, *Poland and the Jews: Reflections of a Polish Polish Jew* (Kraków: Austeria, 2005).
49. Joanna Wiszniewicz, *Życie przecięte: Opowieści pokolenia Marca* [Life Cut Through: Stories of the March Generation] (Wołowiec: Wydawnictwo Czarne, 2008).
50. Małgorzata Melchior, *Zagłada i Tożsamość: Polscy Żydzi ocaleni 'na aryjskich papierach': Analiza doświadczenia biograficznego* (Warsaw: IFiS PAN, 2004).
51. Sven Eliaeson, *Max Weber's Methodologies: Interpretation and Critique* (Cambridge, UK: Polity, 2002).
52. Ibid., p.54.
53. What is important 'is the intrinsically simple demand that the investigator and teacher should keep unconditionally separate the establishment of empirical facts' and 'his evaluation of these facts as satisfactory or unsatisfactory'. Max Weber, *On the Methodology of the Social Sciences*, translated and edited by E.A. Shils and H.A. Finch (Glencoe, IL: Free Press, 1949), p.11.
54. Max Weber, *Gesammelte Aufsätze zur Wissenschaftslehre* (Tübingen: Mohr-Siebeck, 1922), p.191, quoted in Eliaeson, *Max Weber's Methodologies*, p.47.
55. See Eliaeson, *Max Weber's Methodologies*, p.47.
56. According to Eliaeson, interpretative understanding can be either rational (the Weberian type) or hermeneutic. This disjunctive alternative seems in one respect false, for it assumes that hermeneutic interpretation is irrational, or a-rational at best. It would probably be more correct to depict the two modes of understanding as cause-and-effect reasoning (Weber) and hermeneutic reasoning.
57. Eliaeson, *Max Weber's Methodologies*, p.42.
58. See N.K. Denzin, 'Reinterpretacja metody biograficznej w socjologii: znaczenie a metoda w analizie biograficznej', in *Metoda biograficzna w socjologii*, ed. J. Włodarek and M. Ziółkowski (Warsaw and Poznań: PWN, 1990), pp.55f.
59. See Sergio DellaPergola, *World Jewish Population 2001*, 4 March 2002 (3 September 2002), Table 8, accessed 4 March 2002, <http://sites.huji.ac.il/jcj/dmg_worldjpop_01.htm>. (From: *American Jewish Yearbook, Vol. 101* [New York: The American Jewish Committee, 2001]). The same figure was also given by the second-largest-circulation Polish weekly news magazine, *Polityka*, in its report dated 16 June 2001, p.3.
60. See DellaPergola, *World Jewish Population 2001*, Table 10.
61. Relying on the *Concise Statistical Yearbook* (Warsaw: GUS, 1939), Jerzy Tomaszewski estimates that the number of Jews in Poland in 1931 was slightly over 3.1 million, while in 1939 it was close to 3.5 million, or 9.7 per cent of the whole population of Poland. See Jerzy Tomaszewski, 'Niepodległa Rzeczpospolita', in Jerzy Tomaszewski (ed.), *Najnowsze dzieje Żydów w Polsce w zarysie (do roku 1950)* (Warsaw: PWN, 1993), p.159.
62. See DellaPergola, *World Jewish Population 2001*, Table 4.

63. H. Datner and M. Melchior, 'Żydzi we współczesnej Polsce—nieobecność i powroty', in Z. Kurcz (ed.), *Mniejszości narodowe w Polsce* (Wrocław: Wydawnictwo Uniwersytetu Wrocławskiego, 1997), p.63. In 1998, Laurence Weinbaum wrote: 'It would not be unreasonable to accept a figure of 10–15,000 as a rough reflection of the number of active, affiliated and "border-line" Jews in Poland.' *Polish Jews: A Postscript to the 'Final Chapter'?* (Jerusalem: Institute of the World Jewish Congress, 1998), p.9.

64. The expression 'closet Jews' or 'forest Jews' alludes to the German occupation when many Jews, in order to survive, had to hide in the flats of their Polish friends on the so-called 'Aryan side' (a closet would be a natural, though not the safest, place to hide during visits of suspected individuals or even German soldiers). Many others went to the forests and there, not infrequently in groups, they strove for survival, endangered not only by German police and military troops, but sometimes also by Polish underground units, Jewish ghetto police (*Ordnungsdienst*) and some hostile local people. Thus, the 'closet' or 'forest' mentality can be ascribed to Jews who are still hiding their Jewish identity. Of course, it is not only war memories that can entail such behaviour, it is also the continuing existence of anti-Semitism in Poland that makes some Jewish people not want to reveal their identity. I once faced this kind of situation when I was contacting Jews affiliated to Jewish institutions in Warsaw. When I called Mrs X, her mother answered the phone. After I had explained who I was and what my research was about, the woman said that I should not try to contact her daughter, because her husband did not know that she was Jewish and they were both unwilling to tell him.

65. In a conversation with some officials of the Jewish Congregation of Warsaw, I was told that they estimate there are at least 3,000 Jews in Warsaw.

66. As Tomaszewski indicates, in pre-war Warsaw, Jews constituted around 30 per cent of the city's population. Twenty-five per cent of Polish Jewry lived in five biggest cities: Warsaw, Lodz, Cracow, Lvov and Vilna. In many smaller cities and towns, in central and eastern Poland, they constituted 30 to 70 per cent of the number of inhabitants. On the other hand, in 1931 only 1 per cent of Polish Jews were farmers. See Tomaszewski, 'Niepodległa Rzeczpospolita', pp.160–2; Jerzy Tomaszewski, *Rzeczpospolita wielu narodów* [The Commonwealth of Many Nations] (Warsaw: Czytelnik, 1985), pp.152–4.

67. The urban character of Jewish societies all over the world is clearly demonstrated in DellaPergola's paper. In 2001, according to Table 10, over 70 per cent of the world's Jewish population lived in twenty metropolises in seven countries in Asia, Europe, and North and South America. A more detailed overview of American Jewry from the socio-demographic perspective will be given in Chapter 1.

68. The research was carried out in so-called Greater Warsaw, which includes the centre of the city as well as the suburban region.

69. I used CTANKS (Code-A-Text Transcription and Note Keeping System, version 1.0.3 [September 2000]) – a special software for textual data analysis.

70. As some argue, this interpretivist or phenomenological approach does not lead to the discovery of new sociological laws, but to a better understanding of meanings and acts. See M.B. Miles and A.M. Huberman, *Analiza danych jakościowych* [Qualitative Data Analysis] (Białystok: Transhumana, 2000), p.8.

71. DellaPergola, *World Jewish Population 2001* [section 'Definitions' in the online article cited].

72. There was, however, one problematic case when a woman, a child survivor, thought she had no right to be Jewish because she had been raised as a Catholic. I analyse this interview in Chapter 3, in the section presenting the profile of the sample of Polish Jews.

73. One illustration would be in order here. One of my New York interviewees [AM 25m], with whom I met at my place in Manhattan, made a remark regarding the pictures pinned to the walls. These were Xerox copies of the front pages of satirical Yiddish-language periodicals published in pre-war Poland. In his opinion they were typical anti-Semitic drawings. When I explained to him these were all pictures from the Jewish press, his answer was that this did not change the fact that they were viciously anti-Semitic. In any case, his conviction was that Poland was generally an anti-Semitic country.

PART 1

In the Wake of Catastrophe:
Cultural, Political and Religious Responses
of American and Polish Jews

CHAPTER ONE

Implications for Identity Strategies

1. JEWISH IDENTITIES IN AMERICA AFTER THE HOLOCAUST: THE ROLE OF MYTH AND INSTITUTION

AMERICAN SOCIETY, THE JEWS AND THE QUESTION OF RELIGION

In the present chapter I shall try to elucidate one of my two major theses, namely that the Holocaust has impacted the identity of American Jews considerably, especially in the last two decades of the twentieth century. To this end, I will seek an answer to the following question: If the Holocaust did affect the strategies of identity-building of American Jews, how did the process of change develop in practice?

At the outset of this chapter, it is expedient to present a brief sketch of the social situation of American Jewry from the 1930s until the Vietnam War. Between the First and the Second World Wars, Jews – just like the American society at large – tended to hold optimistic views of the world and its future. This outlook can clearly be seen in Mordecai M. Kaplan's vision of Judaism as expressed in his most famous work, *Judaism as a Civilisation*.[1] Kaplan's concept of Judaism is more sociological than theological in character: religion is seen as only one among many elements of Jewish identity. That perspective, however, was no different from the general world view of pre-war American Jewry (excluding the Orthodox milieus, of course). In the 1930s, the second generation of Jewish immigrants from Eastern Europe came to play a decisive role within the American Jewish community. At the socio-economic level, they were entering America's middle class while gradually shifting from activities such as peddling and working in factories to becoming white-collar employees, entrepreneurs and professionals.[2] Culturally, Yiddishism was still predominant, especially in New York, though many of those who had previously inhabited the traditionally Jewish Lower East Side moved to the so-called second-settlement areas – Upper Manhattan and beyond. In spite of a steady growth in the number of congregations and synagogue buildings,[3] most American Jews tended to hold secular world views. It was not atypical of the Jewish worker at that time to read an anti-religious Yiddish newspaper. Others, neither antagonistic toward religion nor especially involved in it, would visit a synagogue once in a while, and even recite by heart some Hebrew prayers. Jewish education, with the exclusion of religious schools, was totally secular. Jewish afternoon schools offered hardly any religious training. And the Yiddish school system – comprising Zionist, socialist (Workmen's Circle), communist and Sholem Aleichem schools – was overtly non-religious, if not atheistic.[4]

The overall status of religious practice was such that, according to a 1935 survey, 'seventy-two per cent of the young Jewish men and seventy-eight per cent of the young Jewish women had attended no religious service at all during the past year'.[5] That was in no way surprising, as most of those men and women were atheist or agnostic, with only a small proportion sharing traditional Jewish religious beliefs. This, too, was in accord with the ideas of Mordecai Kaplan, who proposed a kind of Judaism where there was no supernatural deity, but a cosmic force of evolution. In 1918 Kaplan was instrumental in founding the New York City Jewish Center, which became attractive to many Jews because it organized not only synagogue life, but had a school and offered a gamut of extra-religious activities and hobbies. This, of course, was based on his concept of Judaism as Jewish life in all its forms, religion being just one of them. As Nathan Glazer has observed, 'the assumption that Jewish life could be maintained without Judaism, or alongside it, was given substance not only by the fact that it was being so maintained but also by the rise of a special institutional form, the Jewish Center. The Jewish Center ... became very popular in the twenties and [its] popularity has continued to this day.'[6]

What happened in the late 1940s and 1950s was a complex, multi-level change in Jewish identities (it is more reasonable to use the word in plural than to speak of a 'Jewish identity'). From the mid-1840s to the 1940s, the Jewish population of New York grew from several hundred to about 2.25 million.[7] As they grew in number and shifted upwards on the social ladder, many of them decided to move out of the most densely populated areas.[8] Thus, the second generation of East European Jews was moving from second-settlement areas to the suburbs, while several thousand new immigrants came from Europe. It should be remembered that the second-generation Jews from areas of second settlement were chiefly secular:

The Jewish migration out of the areas of second settlement was a migration of just those elements in the past most immune to Jewish religion, the second and third generation of the East European group. The areas of second settlement ... were the strongholds of Jewish irreligion and of Jewishness. It was in these almost totally Jewish areas, paradoxically, that Jews could live lives almost completely unaffected by Jewish religion and that the proportion of synagogue members was always lowest.[9]

But what does Glazer mean by 'Jewishness'? The term enjoyed a real vogue in the pre-war period; in contradistinction to Judaism, Jewishness was meant to underscore the ethnic and cultural elements of identity instead of focusing on religion as was the case with Judaism. Certainly, Jewishness was not tantamount to *Yiddishkeit*, or the Yiddish culture of East European Jews,[10] nor was it coterminous with secular Zionism. Rather, it was a combination of all those elements that could be found in Jewish life, of which religion constituted just one aspect.

Thus, when secular Jews from metropolitan areas were making their homes in suburbia, they had to acculturate to the new societal surroundings, just as their grandparents had done in the Lower East Side and other such places across the United States two generations earlier. Another fact that should not be overlooked is that Jews are traditionally very family-oriented.[11] As such, the newcomers to suburbia wanted their children to feel at ease with their Christian, mostly Protestant, friends. They thought, for example, that it would be 'embarrassing to have children playing outside while the Christian children go to Sunday school and church'.[12]

Keeping and reshaping those third-settlement Jewish identities was a challenge not only due to the new societal circumstances. No less importantly, American anti-Semitism was becoming more visible and vexing. *The Protocols of the Elders of Zion* was published in America in 1920 under the title *The Protocols and World Revolution*, and the publication was widely distributed in the country. The famous business-man Henry Ford, in his newspaper the *Dearborn Independent*, also spread virulent anti-Semitism. In 1920 Ford published *The International Jew*, an anti-Semitic pamphlet.[13] Anti-Semitism was experienced by Jews in America between the two wars, not only by those in white-collar jobs and the professions but also on campuses.[14]

At the same time, the very pillars of secular Jewish culture were collapsing. Since the early 1930s, socialism in America – including Jewish Socialism – was gradually declining. Jewish Socialist milieus that had been advocates of Jewishness or 'secular Judaism' were also in retreat; after all, it became clear, especially after the war, that they had lost the battle for non-religious Jewish identity.[15]

Beginning in the mid-1940s, Jewish intellectuals – or at least some of them – were turning or returning to religion. In Glazer's opinion, this had something to do with 'the European catastrophe'.[16] Well-known Yiddish writers, the one-time propagators of secular culture, deeply impacted by the events in Europe, found a way back to religious Judaism. Glazer remarks, however, that the significance of the fact that a couple of intellectuals underwent a visible and significant change of their world views should not be overestimated. In any case, 'nothing quite like this had happened in Jewish life since the Enlightenment'.[17] Glazer has described that period of massive comeback to religion as 'the Jewish revival'.[18] In short, the new interest in religion was a social phenomenon that came to be seen in two (not always separate) groups: intellectuals and 'common' people. The former were disappointed with the radically socialist doctrine; the latter wanted to adjust to the suburban neighbourhood.[19] In both cases the new religious involvement was in accord with the general tendencies of American society at large. It was also a continuation of the pattern of social behaviour of the Jewish masses coming to America: peaceful accommodation, which at that time did not mean assimilation, as was the case in the interwar period, but acculturation. They were so successful at it that they could be called 'the first cosmopolites and citizens of the world'.[20]

But what, exactly, was the nature of this revival? Was it indeed a religious revival, as it may seem at first glance? I will argue that what a large portion of American Jewry underwent in the 1940s and 1950s was the reinvention of *secular religion*. The term may appear to be an oxymoron, but in fact it only attempts to grasp more accurately the social situation of the group under consideration. Yet the notion of secular religion requires further explication, and a redefinition of the very term 'religion'. This, as Jacob Neusner has pointed out, is especially relevant with regard to American Jews.[21] Though concurring, for the most part, with Peter Berger's diagnosis of desecularization in contemporary Western culture,[22] I also argue that his opinion can be deemed true only if we accept a specific meaning of the word 'secular'.

It is my conviction that religion should be considered in a more holistic manner than is usually the case. Etymologically, religion (Latin *re-ligare*) is something that reunites, re-links and renews bonds.[23] It is often assumed that the reuniting takes place between a human being and its deity (this concept presumes that an original unity between humans – or nature in general – and the divine once existed and will be restored). Historically this is evident, but from the sociological stand-point such an opinion underestimates the group aspect of religion. Religions have always been systems of beliefs and/or practices acknowledged by a group of people. It is hardly possible to imagine a one-person religion; one could arguably claim that even a few people or a single family can have a religion of their own, but not an isolated individual. It is usually maintained that, on principle, religion finds its expression in two elements: a doctrine of unification of humans and a supra-human being, as well as a kind of bond between members of a given religious community. It is, however, a common experience that people gather together on innumerable non-trivial occasions and cele-brate their unity or oneness *without* at the same time referring to a deity. Suffice it to recall ancient and contemporary folk and state cults: the cult of Caesar, army, power, wisdom, fecundity, democracy, equality, work, fun, law, constitution, reason, and so on. These cults have nothing – or close to nothing – to do with faith in a Higher Being. Of course, there are also non-theistic religions in which such a being is absent, the best example being Confucianism, but this is yet another premise on which to base the concept of an all-secular religion, in which bonds between members of a given group are an essential purpose – indeed the only real purpose – of the group's existence.

Thus, what happened to American Jews in the 1940s and 1950s was just an invention of a secular religion. Surely enough, the phenomenon did not appear suddenly and unexpectedly; in fact, the community was quite well prepared for it. If we take the whole Yiddish culture,[24] with its numerous schools, and political and charity organizations, and if we take the 'enlightened' version of Judaism which was its Reform branch, as well as Mordecai Kaplan's Reconstructionist movement, then the post-war return to religion structured as a secular institution hardly seems surprising. The Jewish centres referred to above were instru-mental in the process of secularization of Judaism *qua religion*. Those centres, with their schools and lay organizations for the adults, were a perfect place for the second- and third-generation Jews and their children. Nathan Glazer, though looking with a critical eye at 'privately collected statistics', gives figures showing a significant increase in the number of Jewish congregations during the 1940s and 1950s. In 1937, 250 Conservative synagogues (with 75,000 member families) and 290 Reform synagogues (with 50,000 families) are reported to have been active in the United States. In 1956, there were 500 Conservative congregations gathering 200,000 families, and 520 Reform congregations with 255,000 member families. The overall number of synagogues in America, however, rose only by some 5 per cent in the years 1937 to 1952 (from 3,700 to 3,900). That was due to the closure of a large number of Orthodox synagogues in poorer urban areas. Also, a significant number of young Orthodox Jews left their parents' religion and joined either the Conservative or Reform movements.[25] One has to bear in mind the fact that the sheer growing numbers of synagogues cannot be interpreted as an indication of the revival of traditional religion. It is important to know that many of the newly-opened synagogues were only part of larger community centres that attracted many people for cultural reasons. A significant growth of 73 per cent can also be observed in the overall number of children enrolled in Jewish schools between 1946 and 1956.

Describing the synagogue boom of the 1940s and 1950s, Glazer has pointed out:

> the religious services often seem the least vital of the many 'services' supplied by the new synagogues. The children almost certainly go to the school, the teenagers very likely go to the dances, the women probably join the sisterhood, the men possibly join the brotherhood, and last ... are the religious services, poorly attended by a core of old-timers and the merest scattering of young people ... During the past fifteen years, people have often asked whether the synagogue was meeting the religious needs of Jews. But the Jews themselves do not demonstrate any strong religious drive. They throng the Jewish centers and the center-synagogues but do not participate in any large numbers in the services of the synagogue ... Even the rabbinate is not very different in this respect from the people.[26]

We can argue, therefore, that the characteristic trait of the secular (not civil) religion of American Jews from the 1940s onwards has been its community-centredness. Many of those participating in Jewish communal life, even in the synagogue, may not share the belief in the existence of God, but they feel the need to live as Jews. They have that need to share one system of meaning with other Jews – which assumes some form of *communitas* or *kehillah* (Hebrew for 'community').[27] The community itself becomes the religion in secular terms; but it is not *any* community, it is a Jewish community.[28] Why, then, is the Judaism described above a secular but not a civil religion? According to Jonathan Woocher, who draws heavily on Emile Durkheim and Robert Bellah, civil religion is 'a system of shared beliefs and public rituals, defining and symbolizing the nation or polity as a moral community ... [It] operates in a sphere of its own, that of the nation's identity and destiny, and seeks to invest that sphere with religious meaning.'[29] Woocher claims, however, that a civil religion is focused mostly on the political element and, in contradistinction to traditional religion, it is unable to provide its members with a transcendent perspective.[30] Even if this is so with regard to American civil religion in general (Woocher reflects on both American and Jewish civil religion), this category fails if applied to the religion of American Jews as transformed in the 1940s and 1950s. Firstly, the Jewish Community Center (JCC) – our paradigm of an institution of secular religion – is not an entity focused on politics; its members hold different political views and the JCC does not aspire to unite them into one political group. The issue of shared beliefs is methodologically a troublesome one, too. While it cannot be denied that the new religious Jewish community is based on *some* shared beliefs, it should be acknowledged that faith in the existence of a transcendent, personal God (God of Israel) is not a belief all members share. There is a significant proportion of people who are agnostics or atheists but find it meaningful to participate in the religious life of their community. Thus, for them, religion must play a different role; it fulfils their social needs, having at the same time little to do with the realm of theology. On the other hand, the communal and cultural experiences these communities offer do transcend the mere group level of being. In contradistinction to Woocher's concept of civil religion, secular Jewish religion does produce a 'trans-human perspective'.[31] The notion itself is insightful and fits very well the concept of secular religion: participation in a religious community in a non-traditionally religious way begets a feeling of belongingness and of meaningful bonds. That, however, could not be further from the shallowness and one-dimensional character of mere politics-centred groups.

The non-traditional (non-theistic) involvement of many American Jews in religious communities should be seen as a 'natural' phenomenon,[32] one that does not contradict the age-old heritage of Judaism, because Judaism contains both the ethnic and the religious (traditionally understood as theological) elements. It is self-evident, as Lipset and Raab have noted, that 'the central core of Jewish identity has been religion, even though an ethnic culture is built into that religion. The religious core provides a special base for Jewish survival.'[33] Therefore, to contend, as Woocher does, that Judaism has been for centuries also a civil religion is to overemphasize its political aspect (*Geselschaft*) at the cost of the ethical and cultural layer (*Gemeinschaft*). This 'new' Judaism, understood as a civilization, a way of life, and the feeling of Jewish-*ness* had a specific 'negative' side to it. The negativity meant rejection of becoming a non-Jew – it was identifying oneself by way of a negative statement: 'I am not a non-Jew.' And in order to practically express one's non-Gentile identity, Jewish content proved indispensable.[34] We can assume that this strategic negativity might have led to a flourishing of Jewish institutions which offered to many a secular–religious membership.

1945–60: WAS THE HOLOCAUST DOWNPLAYED?

We have seen that American Jews in the 1940s and 1950s tended to become ever more involved in their secular religion. Many of them were registered members of Jewish congregations, regardless of whether or not they professed faith in God. What is more, 'any strong religious feeling', Glazer contends 'is looked upon with suspicion in the Jewish community and often considered a harbinger of conversion to Christianity'.[35] In Jewish intellectual milieus, the stress on belief in God was even weaker, though the group became resolutely more Jewish in terms of conscious identification. And the impact of these intellectuals was far from invisible in those days.[36]

Jews were widely accepted as members of the 'melting pot triad' – Protestant, Catholic, Jew – although anti-Semitism was still disturbing, even in academia. What, therefore, was the reason for an unusual interest in the Holocaust in the 1960s? And why did American Jews not pay more attention to the event in the preceding decades? During wartime, as Peter Novick argues, American Jewry was to some extent impacted by the Nazi atrocities, but the fact that they were also Americans did not allow for that impact to be too deep.[37] News regarding the persecution of the Jews in Europe would not appear on the front pages of leading American newspapers. Also, it ought to be underscored that some of the major Jewish organizations in America – out of fear of fanning anti-Semitism – refrained from taking official action to press the Roosevelt administration to stop the annihilation of European Jews.[38]

Novick claims that, contrary to what usually happens after a momentous event has occurred, the Holocaust was 'hardly talked about for the first twenty years or so after World War II; then, from the 1970s on, [it was] becoming ever more central in the American public discourse – particularly, of course, among Jews, but also in the culture at large'.[39] In his opinion, discussing the Nazi genocide was, in a sense, embarrassing in the late 1940s and 1950s. The whole Freudian concept seems to him to have little relevance, since 'the available evidence doesn't suggest that, overall, American Jews (let alone American gentiles) were traumatized by the Holocaust, in any worthwhile sense of the term'.[40]

Refuting psychological explanations, Novick proposes to analyse the political climate in America in the late 1940s and 1950s, to discover why the Shoah was rarely discussed at that time. He suggests that the major causes of that situation had to do with the new political alignments. After the Second World War, Germany was no longer Nazi Germany but the Federal Republic of Germany, an ally of the West; the Soviet Union, on the other hand, once an ally, now became public enemy number one of the United States. Mentioning Nazi crimes was out of place in those circumstances. As the Cold War gained momentum, speaking of the Shoah became even less desirable. The Cold War, too, influenced American policy regarding displaced persons in Europe. As time passed, Jews kept in the displaced persons or DP camps in Western Europe were given ever less attention; those fleeing communist regimes were now more 'interesting'. Also, there were fears of letting anti-Semitically disposed Eastern Europeans and ex-Nazis into the United States. This, Novick argues, could be seen in the debate over the 1948 and 1950 legislative acts dealing with the DPs. So, gradually, the issue of the Holocaust became more marginalized. The problem lay also in the fact that the Holocaust was relatively often invoked by the communists.[41] Thus, neither Jewish Americans nor other American citizens thought it wise or appropriate to speak about the catastrophe in public. The question became even more complicated in the McCarthy era when, in 1950, Julius and Ethel Rosenberg were arrested and charged with spying for the Soviet government between 1943 and 1950.[42]

Nathan Glazer spoke in a similar vein when he gave a description of the situation of American Jewry at the very time of his writing *American Judaism*. Trying to account for the significant religious changes that he witnessed within the Jewish community, he asserted that these changes had not been brought about either by the Shoah or by Zionism. 'The two greatest events in modern Jewish history, the murder of six million Jews by Hitler and the creation of a Jewish state in Palestine, have had remarkably slight effects on the inner life of American Jewry.'[43] Yet he claims there is one event that probably constitutes a real threat in the midst of American Jewry, and its consequences are more far-reaching, even more shocking than other twentieth-century historical events. 'Judaism, which was the religion of all the Jewish people, has become Orthodoxy', which is only one among many Jewish denominations. This event, Glazer contends, 'creates a more serious break in the continuity of Jewish history than the murder of six million Jews. Jewish history has known, and Judaism has been prepared for, massacre; Jewish history has not known, nor is Judaism prepared for, the abandonment of the law.'[44]

Not all Jewish scholars, however, agree with the opinion that the growth in Holocaust interest took place only some time in the 1960s. Eli Lederhendler,[45] for example, in his thought-provoking study on New York Jews, has presented an opposite view:

> Contrary to popular notions, I do believe that the Holocaust as an event had a significant impact on Jewish culture and concerns as early as the fifties and certainly by the beginning of the sixties. And, once again contrary to general assumptions, I do not share the idea that changes in the tenor of Holocaust consciousness at the end of the sixties are explained by the Six-Day War or the greater willingness of survivors to speak publicly (i.e., in English) about their experiences. Rather than focus on such internal Jewish factors, I believe that the paradigmatic change in this regard – from viewing the Holocaust as a potentially threatening precedent for human society at large, to viewing the Holocaust as proof of Jewish victimization and, therefore, as the moral basis for Jewish relationships with others – is related above all to the politicization of victimhood itself in late-sixties American society.[46]

Lederhendler claims that the *Churban Europa* elevated New York as a literary Yiddish centre, as did the 1952 murder of prominent Yiddish-language writers in Stalin's Soviet Union. The well-known Jewish artists who arrived in New York either shortly before or after the war included: Sholem Ash, Yankev Glatshteyn, Chaim Grade, Kadia Molodovsky, Shmuel Niger-Charney, Joseph Opatoshu, Isaac Bashevis Singer, Isiah Trunk and Aaron Zeitlin, among others. Few of these writers, however, talked about the catastrophe (with the exception of Grade, who wrote about the Shoah obsessively). Even though many of

Singer's books were translated into English in the 1950s, America could not have learned much about the Holocaust from them.[47]

Lederhendler mentions, too, several scholarly books, specifically Theodore Adorno's *The Authoritarian Personality* (1950), Hannah Arendt's *The Origins of Totalitarianism* (1951) and Bruno Bettelheim's *The Informed Heart: Autonomy in a Mass Age* (1960). In addition to these, he reminds us that during the early post-war years, many plays were staged and films produced in which the main topics were related to Jewish culture and/or history. Among the most important of these, he counts *Fiddler on the Roof* (dramatized version of Sholem Aleichem's *Tevye the Milkman*, 1964), Rolf Hochhuth's play, *The Deputy* (1964), Arthur Miller's plays, *After the Fall* (1964) and *Incident at Vichy* (1964), as well as such films as *Exodus* (1960), *Judgement at Nuremberg* (1961) and *The Shop on Main Street* (Czech production, 1965). Also, Lederhendler mentions the most famous Holocaust testimony, Anne Frank's *Diary* (1952), though he does it in just one sentence.

These various pieces of literature and art are supposed to confirm his claim that by the 1950s, America was not evading issues linked to the Shoah and, therefore, was affected by the event. But a mere enumeration of works more or less related to the extermination of European Jews seems to be a poor confirmation of his statement – especially because he puts works on general Jewish topics (especially those originally written in Yiddish about Yiddish culture) with those that do mention, if marginally, the European catastrophe. In spite of that, Lederhendler asserts that 'reading the literature of the fifties and sixties on modern mass society and on racial and ethnic prejudice as presented by Jewish observers, one comes away with the clear impression that it was pervaded by an awareness of the Holocaust'.[48]

The problem is that the impression is not clear at all, especially if we confront the alleged awareness of the Shoah in the 1950s with its salience in the 1980s. What is more, it is possible that arguments to back Lederhendler's opinion *could* exist; strangely enough, however, he himself does not invoke them. The scant attention he pays to Anne Frank's *Diary* is indeed surprising. During the two decades following its first impression in 1952, the book sold some five million copies. It provoked a heated discussion among Jewish and non-Jewish scholars on the issue of its particularity/universality. The play and the film (1959) based on the diary proved also controversial, although (or maybe because) the film was seen by millions of Americans. In 1996, in a survey carried out at the University of Michigan, *The Diary of Anne Frank* 'was still named as the predominant source of Holocaust education', as Hilene Flanzbaum has remarked.[49] Flanzbaum, too, asserts she has met many people who did not concur with the view that the Holocaust was hardly ever discussed in the 1950s. Relying on her interlocutors' reminiscences, she argues that Anne Frank's *Diary* 'has long been the most important landmark in the Americanization of the Holocaust'.[50]

Peter Novick shows himself to be more critical in assessing many of the alleged Holocaust-related works published or produced in the 1950s. He has analysed Frank's diary at length, as well as the debate about its various stage versions, and concluded that the diary was an exception: no other literary work had attracted such attention from the American public at large.[51] He conceded that the play based on the diary was a real success on Broadway, but the film (1959) did not become a hit at the box office, and neither did *Judgement at Nuremberg*.[52] The latter, Novick argues, though usually considered a Holocaust film, deals with the event only occasionally. Also, the 1955 film by Alain Resnais, *Night and Fog* (*Nuit et brouillard*), allegedly a film about the Shoah, was not, in fact, about the Jews, but about Nazi actions against the French Resistance. The word 'Jew' did not even appear in it.[53] Lederhendler's thesis is also arguable in light of the lack of historical Holocaust literature in the 1950s. Lederhendler simply ignores the issue, and rightly so, for there was not a single publication in this area of study in the United States at that time – that is, before Raul Hilberg's magisterial work, *The Destruction of the European Jews* (1961). The only English-language books on the history of the Shoah were translations from German and French: Gerald Reitlinger's *The Final Solution* (1953) and Leon Poliakov's *Harvest of Hate* (1954); both books, however, received 'only scant attention' on the American continent.[54]

There is yet another topic that Lederhendler has seemingly treated superficially: Elie Wiesel's first novel, *Night*. Today, translated into over thirty languages and read by millions of people,[55] it is one of the most famous pieces of Holocaust literature, second only to *The Diary of Anne Frank*. It is a widely accepted opinion that *Night* 'became a watershed event in Holocaust consciousness, enabling the writing of subsequent Holocaust narratives, and also creating a wider audience for other testimonies already in existence'.[56] Wiesel wrote the original Yiddish script in 1955, at around the time he met the French writer François Mauriac. The text was then heavily edited (of the original 862 pages, only 245 were left) and finally published in 1956, in Buenos Aires, Argentina, under the title *Un di velt hot geshwign* (*And the World*

Remained Silent).[57] Subsequently, Wiesel translated the book into French and it came out as *La Nuit* in 1958, this time cut to 127 pages. The English edition followed in 1960, based on the French text. But at first it proved difficult to publish the novel: 'several years passed before [Wiesel] was able to find a publisher for the French or English versions of the work. Even after Wiesel found publishers for the French and English translations, the book sold few copies.'[58]

Why, then, was Anne Frank's *Diary* so popular, as early as the 1950s, while Wiesel's *Night* sold poorly in the first half of the 1960s? The answer lies in the completely different characters of the two books. *Night* is a clearly Jewish narrative, not (only) because the author is a Jew, but because the content is focused on Jewish topics: Jewish fate, Jewish religion, Jewish doubts and pain. *The Diary of Anne Frank*, on the other hand, has usually been thought of as a book on suffering and strength, on weakness and overcoming it – in universal terms. Indeed, this is what occasioned many criticisms of the diary. In the 1950s and early 1960s, most of its editions, as well as stage and film adaptations, were criticized as 'dejudaized' and optimistic versions of the original text. But, in fact, 'the *Diary* was not twisted into an optimistic and universalist document by [theatre directors and scriptwriters, such as] the Hacketts, Garson Kanin, George Stevens, or anyone else; it *was* such a document' (italics in the original).[59] That positive mood of the diary made it also easily acceptable and 'digestible' for the American public at large. Contrarily to Wiesel's *Night*, the *Diary* was, as it were, of the American spirit. Its focus on problems universal to humankind all over the world, on surviving and strength, courage and hope (very much like American popular culture in general), made the book attractive and 'commended it to Americans in the 1950s, including most of the organized Jewish community. Every generation frames the Holocaust, represents the Holocaust, in ways that suit its mood.'[60] Wiesel's novel was right at the opposite pole of literature: it spoke of despair, bewilderment, unsupportable pain, the decay of human bonds, agony and death. The melioristic trend of American culture could hardly incorporate these experiences into its realm.

Yet it is telling that the book found little interest among more than two million American Jews. What is more, special policies were adopted by some American Jewish organizations that discouraged its members (and American Jewry at large, it might be assumed) from dwelling on the Holocaust too much. Just before the end of the Second World War, John Slawson, one of the leaders of the American Jewish

Committee, at a meeting of the National Community Relations Advisory Council (NCRAC), presented a report on anti-Semitism in America, based on the findings of social scientists. The study showed that most of those who claimed that Jews possessed too much power in the United States subconsciously imagined Jews as weak and vulnerable to acts of violence. Thus, Slawson insisted that Jewish organizations

> should avoid representing the Jew as weak, victimized, and suffering ... There needs to be an elimination or at least a reduction of horror stories of victimized Jewry ... The Jew should be represented as *like* others, rather than unlike others. The image of Jewish weakness must be eliminated ... In an effort to arouse the conscience of the world, as the one possible means of alleviating the tragic plight of our brethren in Europe, we have had to publicize the mass atrocities committed by the Nazis. That was unavoidable ...
>
> [Now] it is necessary ... to encourage the adaptation of the Jewish mores to the mores prevailing in this country ... [What is implied] is neither segregation nor assimilation, but an adjustment to the American scene by means of a cultural integration.[61]

The above passage shows with exceptional clarity that it was undesirable, even before the war ended and much more so afterwards, for American Jews to invoke the Shoah in public. This, however, is not surprising, for they wanted to be part and parcel of American society and not to stress the differences which could undermine the efforts towards acculturation Jews had undertaken at least since the 1920s. Thus, if they refused to talk about the Holocaust, it is because the desire to be American and behave like Americans was stronger than the fact of being Jewish, at least in this particular context. One may argue, in fact, that in the America of the 1940s and 1950s, on the whole, most people did not talk about the destruction of European Jews because it was an event of little relevance to, and did not suit, the American spirit and the predominant tenor of public discourse.

Even if it sounds sensible to assume that American Jews discussed the Shoah only on rare occasions, in private or in public,[62] since they did not want to evoke the stereotypical Jew-victim image as an epitome of their identity, evidence to the contrary does exist. In his *Annotated Bibliography of Holocaust Writing in American-Jewish Magazines, 1945–1952*, David G. Myers has listed over 170 features, which is not a negligible number.[63] Moreover, Hilene Flanzbuam says that many of her informants did not concur with the view that in the 1950s hardly anyone talked about the Shoah.[64] Also, from the historical point of view, it might be interesting to see how and when the Shoah victims began to be memorialized in America. Lederhendler mentions three commemorative ceremonies that took place in New York City in 1960. In March of that year, about 750 former Auschwitz concentration and death camp inmates gathered at the Concourse Plaza Hotel in the Bronx, to commemorate their dead fellow-prisoners. The following month, during the *Yiddisher Kultur Kongress*, 3,500 people were present at a memorial ceremony of the 1943 Warsaw Ghetto uprising. Letters were then read from some well-known statesmen, including the presidential candidate, John F. Kennedy. Also that same month, at a meeting organized by the National Committee for Labor Israel, a survivor and fighter in the Warsaw Ghetto uprising, Zivia Lubetkin Zuckerman, spoke to some 4,000 people gathered to pay tribute to the 'memories of six million Jews exterminated during World War II'.[65]

But why does Lederhendler begin with the year 1960? He wanted to show how the Holocaust had already impacted American Jewish culture in the 1950s, but he has failed to do that, though there is evidence that could possibly support his thesis. As James Young has discovered, 'the first public Holocaust commemoration in America took place not after the war at all but at the very height of the killing, on December 2, 1942 – as a mass protest'. On that day, the Jewish Telegraphic Agency reported, some 5,000 Jewish workmen in New York City stopped working for ten minutes.[66] The largest public memorial service before the end of the war took place on 19 April 1944, to solemnize the first anniversary of the Warsaw Ghetto uprising. The commemoration, held at the stairs of the City Hall, gathered about 30,000 Jews, who listened to the address of the then mayor, Fiorello de la Guardia, and some prominent Jewish activists.[67] As for post-war memorial services, during a public ceremony in New York in October 1947, Mayor William O'Dwyer declared a special lot in Riverside Park would be chosen to place a monument commemorating Jewish victims of the Shoah. On that spot he put a plaque bearing the following inscription: 'This is the site for the American memorial to the Heroes of the Warsaw Ghetto Battle, April–May 1943, and to the six million Jews of Europe martyred in the cause of human liberty.'[68] The plaque can still be found in its original place, but no memorial has been erected so far.[69]

With regard to the debate on the alleged Holocaust-silence in the first fifteen years after the war, one last conclusion seems appropriate. The only difference between authors maintaining, on the one hand, that the destruction of European Jews received but scant attention in those years, and those claiming, on the other, that the Shoah was discussed and did have some impact on American Jewry, is that in essence the two positions are not as remote from one another as it may look at first glance. In any case, it was surely the survivors themselves who began to talk about the catastrophe *among themselves*, not with other Jews, and even less so with Gentiles. William Helmreich has convincingly remarked that most Holocaust-related activities were initiated and organized by the survivors:

> There is a perception that interest in commemorating the Holocaust really began to grow after the Eichmann trial. Perhaps; but it is equally clear that the survivors themselves were memorializing the Holocaust almost from the time they arrived in the United States. In an article that appeared in *Der Yiddishe Farmer* ... readers are reminded that the Holocaust martyrs had exhorted their fellow Jews: 'Don't forget us! Tell the world! Take revenge.' ... Interviews now being done suggest that it was through the *landsmannschaften* that the Holocaust experiences were shared and recalled. All of the major cities in the United States with substantial survivor populations had 'Newcomer' organizations, in addition to the *landsmannschaften*, and these served as bridges between the old culture and the new.[70]

1961–78: The Eichmann Trial, the Six-Day War and Yom Kippur War

Let us now move forward to the 1960s. In May 1960, Adolf Eichmann, the infamous Nazi criminal and the architect of the 'Final Solution', was captured in Buenos Aires. His trial began the following year at the Jerusalem Court of Justice. Also in 1961, Raul Hilberg's magisterial history of the Holocaust, *The Destruction of the European Jews*, was published in America. In 1963, Hannah Arendt's *Eichmann in Jerusalem*, a collection of reports she had written for *The New Yorker* during the trial, came out in the United States. All this marked a new era in Holocaust debate and a further step in the developing Holocaust consciousness.

While one may debate whether there really was silence in American (and Jewish American) society about the Shoah, there is no question that in the 1950s, no scholarly or theological debate was ignited.[71] It was only in the 1960s that American Jews started to reflect on the catastrophe, not only in a more systematic, serious way, but in a way that rendered it possible for the event to become one of the pillars of Jewishness.

Although many articles dealing with the Holocaust appeared between 1945 and 1959, few books by American authors, having the Holocaust as their main theme, were published before 1960. It should be stated once again with all clarity: I do not claim that within American Jewry, discussion on the Shoah was negligible or virtually non-existent in the late 1940s and the 1950s. Instead, I believe that, compared with the role the Holocaust played in the 1980s and 1990s, it was far from being salient. It was only of minor importance for American Jews and, characteristically, the event's influence on the group was limited, due to the politics of some of the Jewish institutions. I cannot totally concur with Novick, in whose opinion, 'compared with the omnipresence of the Holocaust in the 1980s and 1990s – nobody in these years seemed to have much to say on the subject, at least in public'.[72] It can be claimed, upon even perfunctory examination, that the intensity of Holocaust debate in the 1950s was utterly different from what it was in the 1980s; nevertheless, one can arguably contend that *many* people had *much* to say about the Shoah in the first twenty years after the war. What is of utmost importance, however, is that we have to ascribe one meaning to the words *many* and *much* when applied to the 1950s, and another meaning when they are applied to the 1980s. It is possible to maintain that Holocaust-related discussion was initiated as early as the latter half of the 1940s, and at the same time to claim that the discussion was very limited in scope – if judged by the standards of the 1980s and 1990s.

I would argue that the transformation – and intensification – of Shoah debate was a complex and long-lasting process. Thus, all simple (or simplified) explanations of the phenomenon must be deemed insufficient and misleading. The clue to the problem is the double identity of American Jews: they are both Jews and Americans, and as such are affected by what occurs on the American and the Jewish historical scenes. And the American aspect is not to be overlooked; as Jacob Neusner has observed, 'after four generations, to be Jewish is a mode of being an American, taken for granted by Jews among other Americans, and no longer problematical'.[73] What is more, 'American Jews ... manifest so many of the traits that sociologists and social critics attribute to the new American bourgeoisie (the familiar affluent society) that they may be said to epitomize it.'[74] Thus we have two levels of social consciousness that are affected by two different kinds of *Sitz im Leben*: one is the political situation of the state of Israel; the other is American culture at large. With regard to Israel, we can assume that what happened there in the 1960s and early 1970s had an exceptional consequence for the identity of American Jews. From this point of view, it can be argued that the increasing concentration on the Shoah was a two-phase process: the first phase occurred during the Eichmann trial, which was widely commented upon in the United States, especially by Hannah Arendt, who became famous for *The New Yorker* reports she was sending from Jerusalem; the next stage fell at the end of the 1960s and the beginning of the 1970s, which was directly connected with the Six Day War of 1967 and the Yom Kippur War of 1973.[75]

As far as the American context is concerned, two factors should be mentioned as having an impact on the transformation of Jewish identity strategies in the 1960s and 1970s: namely, the rise of *ethnic America*,[76] and – not unrelated to that – the ever more effective *politics of victimhood*. The growing hunger for ethnicity was a sort of counter-reaction to the melting-pot ideology that dominated America from the 1920s well into the 1950s. Published in the 1966 *Commentary* symposium, Arnold Wolf's view in this regard is symptomatic:

> God often causes [the Jews] to be or permits them to be caused to be what no man would ever like to be: victims ... He chose us willy-nilly to be enemies to Pharaoh, Haman, Torquemada, and Stalin. He chose us to be victims of Sargon II, Godfrey de Bouillon, and Hitler. The doctrine of the chosen people ... is not a Jewish idea, but only our interpretation of historic fact.[77]

It is a historic fact that for long centuries Jews were victims, especially on the European continent. But why did victim identity become so important for American Jews in the 1960s? Why in America? And why at that particular time? It has to be born in mind that what Jews anamnestically remember (as is the case with Pesach) is often suffering and being victimized: *We* were in Egypt and *we* were freed.[78] The presentness-by-memorialization of things past is typical of Judaism; this includes the memory of being wronged and persecuted. As Harold Bloom has aptly remarked, the Epicurean concept of memory, where only pleasurable things are to be remembered, 'is antithetical to Judaism': so much so that 'nothing could be more un-Jewish'.[79]

Yet we still have to answer the question: Why did this new focus on victimhood appear more than fifteen years after the war? One of the possible explanations for this phenomenon seems to be the emergence of ethnic and cultural minorities on the American public scene. With their stress on victim status, groups such as blacks, Latinos, native Americans, women and homosexuals started a more-or-less organized campaign, the aim of which was to gain political significance. Also, the Vietnam War (1965–73) veterans claimed to be victims of American militarism and hoped to benefit from their victimhood status. As Eli Lederhendler has it, this new victimhood culture was more responsible for the 'changes in the tenor of Holocaust consciousness at the end of the sixties' than the Six Day War was responsible for the need of the survivors to speak in public (and in English) about their experiences. He believes that if, since that time, the Shoah has been viewed 'as proof of Jewish victimization and, therefore, as the moral basis for Jewish relationships with others', it is above all due to 'the politicization of victimhood itself in late-sixties American society'.[80]

Americans were probably bored with the ideology of the melting pot and felt a need for *difference*. The status of victim could easily be used in order to define oneself, or even a whole group, as positively different. Moreover, being a victim meant acquiring a privileged social status, even if only in a symbolic way. It is clear that American Jews were not passive observers in the drama of change of societal priorities; they co-shaped the gradually emerging image of the noble American victim. The new cult of victimhood was not completely unlike the cult of hero, of self-made wo/man; it was just a novel (postmodern?) version of the old idea. Now, to be a real hero meant to be a hero born out of his/her victimization, someone who had been wronged but who had the courage and the nerve to take a stand against their perceived status as underdog. By the same token, being acknowledged as a victim equalled climbing on the ladder of social prestige.

Therefore a totally new public discourse appeared – one in which victims were both its authors and main characters; and, not least important, it was not a discourse of the elite. This phenomenon was also observable within American Jewry: 'a new Jewish public discourse ... assigned new prominence to the Holocaust – a metasymbol of vulnerability, uncertainty, and victimization'.[81] Lederhendler claims that this could happen in the 1960s only because Jews had introduced the Shoah into American public discourse a decade earlier. But while during the first fifteen years after the war the destruction of European Jews was regarded as a warning against total annihilation of the world and as an example of totalitarian rule, in the 1960s it became 'a specifically Jewish tragedy. From the Eichmann trial to Elie Wiesel's books, through a spate of new scholarly and popular writings of Hilberg and Arendt, the spotlight began to shift from the perpetrators to the victims.'[82]

As I have contended earlier in this chapter, it is risky to claim that

Jews introduced the Holocaust into the public sphere *in the 1950s*. What can be argued, however, is that in the 1960s the Shoah changed its status from a topic of discussion among Jews – which it had been previously – to an issue of general interest to all Americans.[83] Of course, I am not attempting to present the situation in black and white. The claim I am making here is that the shift was, in large part, from an intra-group question to an inter-group question. The group to which the subject 'belonged' transformed it in such a way that it became ever more widely known. Hence, all the other groups, ethnic and/or religious, of American society became aware of the Jewish Holocaust, and – which is extremely important in this context – felt compelled to find in their own histories sufferings that would be at least 'equal' to that of the Jews. Therefore, we can assert that the elevation of the Holocaust to the pedestal of all-American consciousness was due to a process of change that had a dual source: the desire of most minorities to present themselves as victimized – and thus deserving of special privileges – and an increasing salience of the event within American Jewry.

How, then, did American Jews come to view the Shoah as relevant to their contemporary situation? It cannot be denied that the Eichmann trial was instrumental in bringing the European catastrophe to their attention. In spite of the numerous articles in the American Jewish press (as indicated by Myers), the Holocaust did not constitute an important element of Jewish identity; in other words, being Jewish had nothing to do with the Shoah. What happened in Europe during the war was just a minor topic of discussion. It did not even trigger any serious theological debate among Jewish scholars – until Richard Rubenstein's controversial *After Auschwitz* came out in 1966.[84] What happened in the 1960s was that the Shoah became politically useable. As Eli Lederhendler has put it, American Jews 'found themselves in a now more crowded field of claimants for political and cultural recognition ... [and] recover[ed] the rage for victimhood'.[85] Although few of them had lived through the Holocaust, they felt like victims, even more so after the Six Day War and the Yom Kippur War. Having experienced an actual threat to the newly established state of Israel, American Jews thought another Holocaust was possible, and were compelled to retrieve the Nazi Holocaust from oblivion.

Characteristically, the Holocaust, seen through the prism of the Six Day War of 1967, motivated a one-time pulpit rabbi, Meir Kahane, to found (in 1968) what would later come to be one of the best-known, if controversial, American Jewish organizations – the Jewish Defense

League (JDL). Kahane's organization was obviously a response to the catastrophe of European Jews:

> 'Never Again!', the JDL's slogan, was a direct Holocaust reference and this phrase encoded a further set of inferences: 'Never again' would American Jews 'sit still' while their relatives were in peril ... (be it in Israel or in the Soviet Union). The JDL, however, deployed the terminology of 'Never Again!' not only to rally the troops, but also to overcome the shame of victimhood. 'Never again' would Jews be weak, be slaughtered with impunity ... In creating a Jewish pseudo-underground, Kahane was acting out a Holocaust fantasy in which the dignity of the murdered could be retroactively and symbolically saved. [He] needed to assert a further claim: that the Holocaust was not over and, indeed, that the 'next Holocaust' could be prevented *in real life*. [Italics in the original.][86]

The creation of the JDL, though just one among many Jewish organizations in America, testifies to the claim that the emergence of Holocaust discourse, and its elevation to salience, was directly linked with the Arab–Israeli wars of the 1960s and 1970s. It is curious, however, that the very establishment of the state of Israel was not decisive in the process of the Holocaust's becoming a prominent part of Jewish identity in America. It was not in 1948, but after 1967 and then again after 1973, that the Shoah gained unquestionable interest among America's Jews (and Gentiles, too).[87] The two wars in Israel meant two things to American Jewry: first, that another Holocaust is possible, for the enemies of Israel are many, and wish it wiped off the map; and second, that Israel can overcome the looming danger and survive.[88] That is why not only 1948 but also 1967 and 1973 can be assumed to be the years of the rebirth of Israel,[89] for it was after these two great victories of the Jewish state that American Jews could let the Holocaust break through to the surface of Jewish communal and institutional life, and draw the attention of their Gentile co-citizens to Nazi atrocities committed in Europe.[90] Hence, from the psychological point of view, the Six Day and the Yom Kippur Wars were crucial in triggering Holocaust debate in the United States. Put simply, it was easier to talk about the European catastrophe knowing that the Jewish people is no longer weak, that it will not falter in fighting its adversaries, that *Am Yisrael chai* – the Jewish people lives.[91]

This twofold experience of Jewish death and Jewish victory, as Jacob Neusner has noted, is one of the most curious phenomena in the history of American Jewry:

American Judaism ... shapes its conceptions of meaning out of the materials of events of Europe and the Near East. These events, far from America's shores and remote from American Jews' everyday experience, constitute the generative myth by which the generality of American Jews make sense of themselves and decide what to do with that part of themselves set aside for 'being Jewish' ... What is to be called 'the myth of Holocaust and redemption' shapes the day-to-day understanding of those who live within the myth ... So, a sizeable sector of the American people sees the world in and along the lines of vision of reality beginning in death, 'the Holocaust', and completed by resurrection or rebirth, 'Israel'.[92]

The years 1967 and 1973 were thus instrumental in the process of transforming the catastrophe into one of the major points in American Jewish life.[93] The relevance of the Holocaust could only then be confirmed: for what happened *then* was possible *now*. Yet, contrary to the Second World War, the Arab wars brought victory to the Jews of Israel. But was it only the Israelis who had won the new wars? Surely not – and that is exactly why American Jews understood these victories as their own. The Holocaust could therefore be turned into a myth (understood as 'truth told as story'[94]), which means that it proved useable – and useful – for the American Jewish community, for its functioning as a minority among other minorities. The Holocaust myth (together with its Zionist part) constituted a new and meaningful structure in the realm of Jewish life. It was a very specific and powerful frame of reference. But if this new myth of American Jewry meant a growth of prestige and an increase in social influence, it also created a stumbling block in their re-lations with other minorities. Jews were perceived as white Americans of European descent, and thus were excluded from the class of oppressed people of colour. This was especially true in Jewish–black relations; once their allies in fighting for equal rights for all American citizens, Jews were now regarded by some blacks as rivals who wanted to steal the 'wreath of victimhood'.[95] The new rising conflicts with other minorities were partly due to the perception that American Jews were becoming the most influential minority and the least oppressed, at one and the same time. Achieving what could be called a privileged social status (thanks to the Holocaust myth) stood also in contradiction to the specific *social contract* that Jews in America had voluntarily accepted, and actually lived, up until the 1950s. In its traditional formulation, 'the "social contract" calls for American Jews to be "prepared to render unto America that which belong(s) to America"', while at the same time it is expected that they should 'abstain from asking for special rights and privileges or that the public order accommodate itself to the sectarian demands of Jews as Jews'.[96]

The process whereby the Holocaust, as a 'salvific myth', has taken a strategic place 'accorded to it in normative American Judaism',[97] was critically assessed by many a Jewish scholar:

> [There is an] insidious ... tendency among Jewish lay and religious leaders to use the Holocaust as a means of arousing feelings of latent Jewish identity. They 'invoke' it and make it a code word for a series of Jewish experiences. Leaders cite the memory of the victims in what seems to have become a meaningless, reflexive action. They use it to capture the attention and to arouse the emotions of followers.[98]

We might understand these harsh words of Deborah Lipstadt as a kind of warning: that the now-symbolic act of recounting Holocaust narratives is becoming parallel to (or is even replacing) the Passover Haggadah with its central tale of the Exodus. Remembering the Holocaust has now become 'less and less an exercise in collective memory and more and more the basis of an identity built on victimization'.[99] Thus, a new solidarity arose, that has transformed American Jewry as a whole; the change consists in that, contrary to many other things hitherto common to most Jews, it is now the Holocaust that binds Jews together, as Novick maintains. 'Insofar as the Holocaust became the defining Jewish experience, all Jews had their "honorary" survivorship in common',[100] for they knew (and still know) that if not for their grandparents' decision to emigrate from Europe, they would have been among the victims of the Shoah.

The elevation of the role of victimhood in American Jewish identity is also sometimes viewed as an aspect of Americanization of the Holocaust.[101] Being immersed as it were, in the 'cultural climate that virtually celebtrate[s] victimhood',[102] they take on the current behavioural patterns of the society they are part of; they confirm their Americanness by 'shar[ing] in the trendy cult of victimhood'.[103]

It is curious, however, that Holocaust-related discourse, with its stress on victim identity, is a double-edged sword: it incites ambivalent feelings – not only of belongingness to the American culture, but also of being endangered by it. For to dwell on the victim aspect of the Shoah is to draw an image of the world in which others (that is, Gentiles) hate the Jews. The fear of anti-Semitism and, in fact, the conviction that it is gaining power, then becomes an ever-present feeling. Some even go so far as to call the Holocaust an idol, or god, and say that victims of the Shoah are objects of veneration. This is allegedly intrinsically linked with a reappearing distrust toward Gentiles, for, as David Klinghoffer contends, 'with constant invocations of a fabled nationwide anti-Semitism, scare-mongering groups like the Anti-Defamation League keep this god's altar-fire burning'.[104] This, however, is nothing really new for American Jews, as most of them are descendants of European Jews who had experienced oppression in their host countries before coming to the United States. So it seems legitimate to claim, as Peter Novick does, that the ' "culture of victimization" didn't *cause* Jews to embrace a victim identity based on the Holocaust; it *allowed* this sort of identity to become dominant'.[105]

The rediscovered anti-Semitism (or rather the reappearing fear of it) became parallel to Holocaust imagery; the two elements formed together a new frame of reference for American Jews.[106] In fact, however, what was happening in American society at large was an increasing openness toward the Jewish minority. Since the 1970s, sociologists have noticed a rising rate of mixed marriages within the American Jewish community. Most authors interpret this phenomenon as a result of quitting theistic Judaism, and – paradoxically – as a 'side-effect' of the openness and tolerance of American society. As Jack Wertheimer has opined, 'situated in an open society that welcomes Jews with unprecedented hospitality, American Jewry is losing a significant portion of its population to assimilation and intermarriage'.[107]

If we do accept Novick's claim that all America's Jews share 'honorary survivorship', then they will share some sort of survivor mentality as well. And survivor mentality, as Neusner wants to define it, is to 'see the world as essentially hostile and [to] distrust, rather than trust, the outsider. [To] exhibit the traits of citizens of a city under siege, feeling always threatened, always alone, always on the defensive.'[108] It is beyond question that in the 1920s and 1930s, anti-Semitism was a real problem for American Jewry,[109] but was Jew-hatred still rampant in America in the 1960s and the decades that followed?

> In 1946 an unpublicized poll commissioned by the American Jewish Committee asked a national sample of gentiles whether there are 'any nationality, religious or racial groups in this country that are a threat to America'. Eighteen percent named Jews. By 1954, after which the question was abandoned, this was down to one per cent ... The perception of the 'end of the golden age' for

Jews in America, and of mounting anti-Semitism, persisted throughout the 1970s and 1980s, and into the 1990s. [But] the reality in those years was that the 'golden age' for American Jews, rather than receding, became even more golden. The last pockets of anti-Jewish discrimination disappeared; surveys showed anti-Semitic attitudes continuing to decline; Jewish senators came to be regularly elected in states with virtually no Jewish voters; any hint of anti-Semitism from a figure in public life was immediately and roundly reprobated.[110]

It seems, therefore, that the rising awareness of the Holocaust has brought with it a pervasive and virtually unavoidable fear of an anti-Jewish mood in America. In an effort to continue and deepen their American identity (which in the 1960s and 1970s had something to do with being a survivor-victim), American Jews arrived at a troubling situation in which they were, as a minority, emotionally isolated from the rest of the society; and the Gentile society, on the other hand, came to be seen as at least potential anti-Semites. As late as 1989, in 'a poll by the American Jewish Committee, 85 per cent of American Jews called anti-Semitism a "serious problem" '.[111] And that was presumably due to the 'shadow cast by the Holocaust'.[112] With time, the mentality of inhabitants of a city under siege, of which Neusner has spoken, penetrated that branch of Judaism which is said to be the most open and Americanized among Jewish denominations, namely the Reform. Surprisingly enough, more than one out of three Reform rabbis agreed that 'ideally, one ought not to have any contact with non-Jews',[113] as a 1988 survey revealed.

EXCURSUS: JEWISH IDENTITY

Thus we have come to the (lately) problematic issue of Jewish identity. What does it mean to be Jewish in America after the Holocaust? Is Judaism a religion or an ethnic entity? Is Judaism something different from Jewishness? These questions are very much relevant to our analysis of post-Second World War American Jewry, for answering them will help us to find out whether the Shoah has had a factual – not only an imagined – impact on their identity. In biblical and Talmudic times, being a Jew was anything but a question of formulating definitions: it was historically and theologically determined.

Before Emancipation, the issue of being Jewish was hardly a problem; from the legal point of view it was clear: according to the Halakhah (Jewish law), anyone born of a Jewish mother or who converted to

Judaism was a Jew.[114] For practical reasons we may assume that the question of Jewish identity became a problem after 1789, which is directly connected with the *Declaration of Rights of Man and Citizen*. According to that document, every right should be granted to the Jew as a *citizen*, but s/he should have no right as a *Jew*. In other words, a French Jew could be a citizen on the street, and a Jew at home. As a citizen s/he was part of *la nation française*, the French nation.

Perhaps the most important thing (from the point of view of our analysis) that Neusner says about the modern crisis of Jewish identity is his assumption that being Jewish had been, in the past, understood in religious terms. Thus, if religious interpretation of Jewish identity is no longer convincing, does it mean it has become completely irrelevant to the life of the modern Jew? Is Judaism, then, still a religion, or is it an ethnicity, or something else? During the Jewish Emancipation, or *haskalah*, the view of Judaism as ethnicity was advocated, which meant that a Jew should be a German or a Frenchman of Mosaic persuasion. The issue of religion versus ethnicity then appeared in America with the German Jewish emigration of the nineteenth century (and with the Reform movement), as well as with the arrival of East European Jews (a significant portion of them leaning toward social justice, socialism and Yiddishism) from the 1880s till the 1920s. Although Judaism is generally thought of as a religion, this now seems to be a questionable claim. This has to do not only with the present-day situation of American Jewry, but with Jewish holy scriptures, too. In the whole Hebrew Bible, any word that could be translated as 'religion' simply does not exist. Also, in the Talmud, what could be understood as Judaism appears as 'Torah'.

Obviously, however, to contend that Judaism is not a religion would be undeniably false. We can, therefore, argue that Judaism is *not only* a religion; it is more than that.[115] The ethnic component incorporated into Judaism is equally important to it; moreover, the aspect of ethnicity is so undetachable from the religion that the word 'Jew' refers both to a member of the Jewish nation and to a person of Mosaic persuasion.[116] Even if some authors claim, as Lipset and Raab do, that religion constitutes the core of being Jewish, they always seem to point out that the religious character of Judaism serves ethnic ends: 'The central core of Jewish identity has been religion, even though an ethnic culture is built into that religion. That religious core provides a special *base for Jewish survival*' (italics added).[117] What, then, is the place of religion in Judaism? Is it decisive in identifying oneself as a Jew? If being Jewish 'means to believe in a particular doctrine, how is that doctrine defined? We look around and we find a dozen different doctrines, each called Judaism; we look inside ourselves and find we subscribe to none.'[118]

It is a widely shared opinion that there exists no single, authoritative Jewish creed or set of Jewish dogmas: that Judaism is not about believing but about living.[119] Though there are the 'Thirteen Principles' of Jewish faith, formulated by Moses Maimonides, they have been subjected to critique all through the ages and, with the exclusion of strictly Orthodox Jews, there are few people who would claim they believe in any 'truths' of Judaism. Glazer, describing the situation of Jewish immigrants who arrived in America in the nineteenth century, asserts that 'Jews in Eastern Europe, as in Germany, tended to ignore everything that might be considered theology.' They were taught to practise *mitzvot*, or the commandments, and ritual practices of Judaism; for most of them, that was all they had as Jewish education. Accordingly, it was relatively easy for them to lose faith, since, in fact, 'they had no faith to lose: that is, they had no doctrine, no collection of dogmas to which they could cling and with which they could resist argument. All they had, surrounding them like armour, was a complete set of practices.'[120] And even the practices, in certain milieus, were abandoned or denounced outright as reactionary or obscurant.

That is why, at some point, it became evident that Judaism is not to be considered an identity code for all Jews. A new notion had to be coined to refer to those who were Jewish, and thought of themselves as Jews, but had little or nothing to do with Judaism as a religion (understood in traditional terms). They described their identity as Jewishness.[121] The conflict between Judaism and Jewishness started in earnest in the early 1900s. Jewish culturalists (mostly Bundists and those associated with all sorts of Yiddishist organizations – in short, politically and culturally leftist) were advocates of *Jewishness*,[122] whereas those affiliated with any of the Jewish religious denominations defended *Judaism*. In the 1950s, however, and still more in the next decade, Jewishness (as defined above) was losing the battle with Judaism, as Glazer believes.

But was it really a triumph of Judaism in its hitherto dominant version – as the religion of believers in the God of Israel and performing his commandments? To answer this question we have to relate it to two concepts: firstly, the aforementioned theory of Peter Berger about the desecularization of the world, and secondly, Mordecai Kaplan's idea of Religious-Culturalism (Reconstructionism). With regard to the former, it must be said that while Berger is generally right in his observation that in most parts of the world, religion is gaining both in absolute numbers and in cultural and political influence, it ought to be noted, at the same time, that American Jewry is an exception to this theory. Berger is certainly well aware that there are exceptions to the theory he proposes; he points, for example, to the European continent, where modernization goes hand in hand with secularization. It is curious, however, that, *mutatis mutandis*, the same may be said about the community of American Jews. They, too, tend to be more and more secular in a specific meaning of the term: what I mean here by 'secular' or 'secularity' is not a lack of involvement in religion, but a lack of belief in a supernatural, biblical God.[123] Therefore, as far as belief in God is concerned, American Jews tend to be more European than American. What is characteristic is that they become members of religious congregations en masse, while many of them do not believe in God. And this, exactly, is the essence of *secular religion* of American Jews: while the feeling of belonging to a group is important and significant, the belief in God is unimportant and/or irrelevant to their lives. Hence, secular, God-*less* Judaism is an expression of identity for many American Jews; it is the way they live their Jewishness. In a desecularizing world, American Jews have invented secularized Judaism and thus become more secular and religious at the same time.

We should also consider the ideas of Judaism and God as propounded by Mordecai M. Kaplan, the founder of Reconstructionism. It seems advisable here to have a closer look at this denomination of Judaism, for, as Charles Liebman has properly remarked, 'Reconstructionism is the only religious party in Jewish life whose origins are entirely American and whose leading personalities view Judaism from the perspective of the exclusively American Jewish experience', though today it is 'numerically and institutionally insignificant'.[124] Kaplan's view is a deeply humanistic one, though not anti-theistic or anti-religious. He intended to establish a new philosophy of Judaism which would be acceptable to Jews of all denominations; therefore his ideas of Judaism, God and tradition tended to be generic and inclusive rather than exclusive. His religious–culturalist conception of Judaism, was, however, rejected by most branches of Judaism, for it looked either too traditional and backward or too modernist and progressive. Kaplan argued that religion is 'inescapable ... in any civilization that tends to deal with the whole man and not merely with part of him'.[125] He also thought that the idea of God, 'in whatever form it is expressed',[126] bears with it universal significance and is existentially necessary for humans to function as individuals and members of society. His idea of God was thus a functional one, and it was to be an alternative for those who could not accept the traditional biblical deity. God was supposed to be a universal force responsible for human progress, and for Jews – an idea conditioning their survival.[127]

Kaplan, however, was not too much interested in theological nuances and embellishments; his idea of Judaism as a civilization was rather philosophical and sociological in character – in short, an intellectual attempt to find positive and rationally tenable values in Jewish religion.[128] Furthermore, Kaplan argued that Judaism is an *evolving religious* civilization of the Jewish people.[129] Thus, he saw Jewish religion as a product of the Jewish people,[130] which theologically is false (it runs counter to the biblical narrative, but historically and sociologically is legitimate: Judaism has evolved as an outcome of the life of the Jews throughout the centuries.[131] Therefore, the problematic question posed by many, 'Is Judaism a religion or an ethnicity?',[132] is, in fact wrongly constructed, for in Judaism both elements are intrinsically and inexorably linked with one another. The nexus is all the more strong because for almost 2,000 years, Jewish religion has served as cement, binding them into one group forced to live in the Diaspora. Throughout the centuries, Judaism, with only a small portion of theology, provided an ethnic identity to the Jewish people, which can be clearly seen in how it functions in the United States:

> American Jews no doubt are more ethnic, or peoplehood-oriented, than religion oriented. But only Reconstructionism makes a virtue of this, and most American Jews are not quite willing to admit to this virtue publicly. The entire basis of Jewish accommodation to America, of the legitimacy of Jewish separateness, has been that Judaism is a religion, like Catholicism or Protestantism, and that Jews are not merely an ethnic group, like the Irish or the Italians ... Although Jews may know in their hearts that their identity stems from peoplehood and ethnicity, they are reluctant to display this truth in public. This is not a matter of deluding the American public. Above all, Jews delude themselves.[133]

Therefore, Jewish peoplehood or, more broadly, Jewish civilization, emphasized by Kaplan, turns out to be one of the essential elements of Jewish group identity, if not the decisive one. But what exactly is Judaism when understood as peoplehood or civilization? – for the notion cannot be an empty one. What elements does it comprise?

According to Kaplan, it is '*that nexus of a history, literature, language, social organization, folk sanctions, standards of conduct, social and spiritual ideals, esthetic values, which in their totality form a civilization*' (italics in the original).[134] Most of the components of the Jewish civilization enumerated by Kaplan are cultural values (broadly understood). Thus, at face value, it might be assumed that cultural identity is in practice tantamount to Jewish identity, at least for non-Orthodox and non-believing Jews.[135] According to the latest surveys, Jewish identity in America is ever more dependent on Jewish culture. In *A Study of Jewish Culture* in the Bay Area (San Francisco), Gary Tobin proposed 'a definition of Jewish culture elastic enough to encompass customs, daily rituals, and popular culture as well as intellectual life, historical preservation, the visual and performing arts'.[136] The study has revealed that some 90 per cent of Bay Area Jews participate in various forms of cultural Jewish life (film shows, concerts, lectures). It would seem legitimate, therefore, to assume the view that cultural Judaism is the most pervasive expression of Jewish identity and a form of secular religion.

But is Jewish identity in present-day America coterminous with Jewish culture? Would all Jews subscribe to secular cultural Judaism as the main or sole determinant of their identity? It seems highly unlikely. As Jacob Neusner argues, it is progressing secularization that caused a crisis of Jewish identity, and the gist of the crisis was, and still is, that 'there is no consensus shared by most Jews about what a Jew is, how Judaism should be defined, what "being Jewish" and "Judaism" are supposed to mean for individuals and the community'.[137] Therefore, Neusner concludes, we live in a time when there is no single Jewish identity, because various cultural settings can, and do, define the Jews' identity in a way that suits *them* best and is meaningful in *their* particular *Sitz im Leben*.[138] If, then, one single Jewish identity *does not exist*, it is because Jewishness is not a static but a dynamic reality; it is multiple and multifocal. People who claim to be Jewish may choose different elements of the 'Jewish world' and shape their identity in a way they feel is appropriate to their existential situation. This 'pick-and-choose'[139] identity seems to be, of late, a characteristic phenomenon of American ethnic culture. It emphasizes those modalities of one's culture that one sees as the most interesting, inspiring and socially useable. The 'pick-and-choose' identity is also a specific way of keeping one's tradition. Etymologically, tradition means something passed or transmitted from one generation to another (Latin *tradere*, to transmit); a set of values, rituals, literature, habits of behaviour, often a language (if not practised in everyday life, at least present in liturgical rituals or particular words, sayings, swear words). Thus, nowadays in America (but not only there), people's identities are based on selective traditions. Certainly this is not an 'invention' of modern times; all tradition is a selection-cum-reinterpretation of elements coming from yet older traditions and deemed worth preserving.[140]

The same applies to the multiple identities of America's Jews. I venture to suggest that there is not one Jewishness but many Jewishnesses.[141] Since generally one's identity is not a given, an unchangeable whole, but a plastic reality, it follows that Jewish identities are subjected to change or transformation, and are created by selecting particular components from a larger aggregation. I also claim that Jewish culture, though not a term determining all Jews' identities, is the most widely shared 'space' of being Jewish and expressing one's Jewishness – a sort of common denominator. Therefore, the notion of Jewish identity (and all other identity) must be seen not as a set of precisely described features which one would have to 'possess' in order to be regarded a Jew. *Rather, the identity of a person (be it viewed from the ethnic, cultural, or religious perspective) is a multi-layer, multi-focus and selective mental entity. It is a modality of what could be called an ideal identity (for example, an ideal Jewish identity); that is, we may assume the existence of a purely theoretical Jewish identity which is embodied in countless personal life histories (all of them different from each other and non-identical with the theoretical identity). And each personal identity is an amalgamate of (a number of) those traits that together form the ideal identity. It could also be said that a person's identity is not 'one' but is plural in character, for its multiple dimensions desingularize it.[142] Personal identity (rather 'an' identity than 'the' identity) is always shaped by two factors: the subjective and the objective. The former factor is the personality of an individual (with all his/her uniqueness and particular decisions), while the latter is his/her immediate social and natural environment.* Thus it is something totally different to be a Jew in sixteenth-century Morocco than in twentieth-century America; to be Jewish in thirteenth-century Marseilles is different than in a nineteenth-century Polish shtetl or twentieth-century Birobidzhan, East Siberia.

1978–2000: THE HOLOCAUST AS A MAJOR COMPONENT OF AMERICAN JEWISHNESS

A pessimistic, though legitimate, conclusion might be that there is no authoritatively defined Jewish identity; that is, each and every Jew defines for him/herself what it means to be Jewish. One of the possible implications of this statement is that most American Jews may be in disagreement with one another as to what Jewish identity is. Some may want to term it very restrictively; others may simply claim they do not know whether there is any Jewish identity; and still others say that they just don't care about it. Hence, Leonard Fein infers: 'We yearn for some sign, some mark that will indicate to us in a way we can comprehend what it is that's special about the Jews.'[143] He then continues to indicate a sign that has lately come to provide a content for the concept of Jewishness:

> Along comes the Holocaust, and makes us special. It's not the kind of special we'd have chosen, but there it is, ours by right, and awesomely substantial. If you have the Holocaust, what more do you need? Other answers may be more precise, but none is more comprehensive. And if the Holocaust becomes a definition, then you don't have to hunt for other answers, other ways of defining yourself ... So we engage in a veritable orgy of Holocaust museum construction – and learn that it is far easier to raise money for the construction of such museums than it is, say, to offer higher wages to the scandalously underpaid teachers in Jewish schools ... My point is that the explosion of Holocaust-related activities tells us something about how we have come to understand Jewish history.[144]

Before the Jewish catastrophe became 'the Holocaust', however, and before the Holocaust came to occupy the important role in American Jewish life that it does today, some important events had taken place. In the 1970s, courses on the Holocaust had already started to attract more and more students at American colleges and universities; plans were made to build Holocaust memorial centres. In the early 1970s, for instance, Raul Hilberg began teaching a course on the Shoah at the University of Vermont. He intended to lecture on the topic for two years, yet it proved so popular, with almost half of his students non-Jewish, that Hilberg decided to go on. He said that 'against the single occurrence [of the Holocaust], one would assess all other deeds. And so, memorialization began in earnest, that is to say it became organized.'[145] Indeed, it was in the 1970s that a considerable growth of Holocaust interest became observable. As Michael Berenbaum has noted, 'between the Six Day War [of 1967] and the Yom Kippur War [of 1973] the Holocaust' had already stopped being just one among many events in Jewish history and 'became a central part of Jewish consciousness'.[146] At that time, numerous higher education institutions introduced Holocaust courses into their curricula;[147] the first Center for Holocaust Studies was founded by the historian Yaffa Eliach in Brooklyn in 1976. By 1978, there were eight Holocaust museums/memorial centres already existing or being planned, while still other programmes for official memorialization were submitted to various financial support institutions.[148]

The year 1978 turned out to be really exceptional in its consequence for the future development of Holocaust consciousness in America. In that year, four important events took place: President Jimmy Carter created the President's Commission on the Holocaust (later called the United States Holocaust Memorial Council),[149] which was to create a project for a national memorial to 'the six million who were killed in the Holocaust';[150] also in that year, the First International Conference on the Teaching of the Holocaust was organized by the Anti-Defamation League in Philadelphia; in April of the same year, the mini-series *Holocaust* was aired by NBC Television – the nine-and-a-half-hour hour programme was watched by some 120 million Americans; also in 1978, the egregious Nazi march took place in Skokie, Illinois, after which the federal Office of Special Investigations was formed, whose purpose was to bring former Nazis living in the United States to trial and to deport them.[151]

All these events made a considerable difference for the general American public: after that time the Holocaust would cease to be a purely 'Jewish affair' and would become an all-American concern. As Berenbaum admitted, it was beneficial from the point of view of the American Jewish community as well. For if America started to learn more about the Shoah, the Jews, too, would not be left untouched, and their growing awareness of the Holocaust would, in some way or another, affect their identity.[152] That, in turn, was seen as a way of shocking the group, which was becoming dejudaized at an alarming pace. Thus what was deemed undesirable for American Jewry in the early 1940s and 1950s was now thought to be a way of awakening their Jewish identity. The *Holocaust* mini-series and the plan to build a national memorial were instrumental in making the Holocaust a salient event, in both Jewish and American collective memory. The televised version of Shoah history was shown only a year after America had seen *Roots* – a television series recounting the story of American slavery. Jacob Neusner concluded, in an article published in 1979, that the role

Holocaust played for American Jews was to some extent similar to what *Roots* meant to American blacks.[153] Though the 1978 series aired by NBC was criticized by many intellectuals,[154] it doubtlessly impacted the views of a large part of American society and was an example of how the entertainment industry could appropriate the Holocaust and make it part of American popular culture.

Among those who backed the plan to construct a memorial to the Shoah was Elie Wiesel, who, for the first seven years, presided over the Commission on the Holocaust. When it was decided in 1979 that the memorial would take the form of a museum, there arose the question of 'Where?' Finally the decision was made that the museum would be constructed in Washington, DC, on a lot at 14th Street SW, in the immediate vicinity of the Mall, some 1,500 yards from the Washington Monument. Yet the idea to build a national memorial to the Holocaust did not meet with support and warm acceptance among all Jewish intellectuals and leaders. In 1979, one year after the President's Commission had been established, Jacob Neusner had already noted that 'not a few Jews find the Holocaust Commission puzzling'.[155] Some were afraid of petrifying the victim-image of the Jew on the one hand, and of fanning anti-Semitism on the other; others suspected that the museum would distort Jewish history by centring on the Shoah. A few citations must do justice to the many voices of those who criticized the concept as a whole or in part.

Arnold J. Wolf wrote about what he felt might be the consequences of constructing a Holocaust museum:

> Young Jews could be frightened and/or inspired by the Holocaust and would more likely decide to be better Jews. On the other hand, many other Americans were sick and tired of the continual message that Jewish suffering was somehow more terrible than others'. How could a Black or Native American feel about a huge museum dedicated to the murder of European Jews and nothing to mark his own story of genocide here on American soil – especially since the government sponsored Museum was going up on American sacred space, the Mall in Washington, DC.[156]

Philip Lopate alluded not only to the Washington Museum but to the very idea of creating Holocaust museums in American cities:

> I just don't get why both New York and Washington, DC, should have to have Holocaust memorial museums. Or why every major city in the United States seems to be commemorating this

European tragedy in some way or another ... I view museums primarily as places for the exhibitions and contemplation of interesting objects. Institutions like Yad Vashem ... and the Museum of the Diaspora in Israel – which have few artifacts, consisting mainly of slide shows, blown-up photographs, and accompanying wall texts [just the way United States Holocaust Memorial Museum was to be designed] – are, in my view, essentially propaganda factories, designed to manipulate the visitor through a precise emotionalexperience. They are like the Tunnel of Horrors or as a Disneyland park devoted to Jewish suffering.[157]

Writing for the *Commentary*, Edward Norden affirmed:

There were some wise heads who thought the entire congression-ally-approved idea [of building a United States Holocaust Memorial Museum on federal land] a poor one. For example, Henry Kissinger: 'Building a memorial on national ground is likely to reignite anti-Semitism... [by raising] too high a profile.' Between the lines of Kissinger's objection stared the hurt faces of the Irish, Ukrainians, Cambodians, Armenians, blacks, Native Americans. Why a national memorial to the agony of just one very small and rapidly shrinking tile in the American mosaic?[158]

Elliot Jager asks about possible lessons Holocaust museums can teach:

The Holocaust museum business is booming. They are building bigger, better, state-of-the-art Holocaust museums. One in Wash-ington, DC, another, soon, in New York. We are not just trying to preserve the memory of the Holocaust for Jews. We are asking the world to learn the universal lessons of the Holocaust. We want our Holocaust, and we want to share it, too. Has our obsession with memorializing the Holocaust to the world at large made future genocide less likely? Plainly, the news from Africa (Rwanda, Burundi, etc.), Asia (where the fanatic communist mass murderer Pol Pot died only this year in Cambodia), Europe (where the tormentors of the Jews during the Holocaust are now the tormented in Bosnia), and many other parts of the globe demon-strates, 50 years later, that humans still practice mass murder.[159]

Daniel Silver and Raymond Scheindlin challenged the idea of constructing a Jewish museum that was to be focused exclusively on Jewish suffering:

In Washington, a memorial to the Holocaust will cast a dark shadow which cannot, of itself, provide the light of clear purpose or a real sense of the meaning of Jewish life. Such a museum will speak of death, not life, of victimization, not civilization ...[160]

Because of the Holocaust museum's narrow focus, visitors will not learn anything about the people targeted for destruction except their Holocaust experience. The result will be the perpetuation of the image of the Jews as pitiable outsiders ... Most disappointing, the Holocaust museum will confirm for its visitors a view of the Jews as suffering victims. This may be expedient in the present political climate, in which minority groups are engaged in intense competition over which one has experienced the worst Holocaust. But it is neither a healthy foundation on which to build Jewish consciousness nor a sound basis for intercommunal dialogue and understanding. In national identity as in personal life, it is best to concentrate on future possibilities rather than on past wrongs.[161]

As we can see, the major points of critique concern the possible implications of building Holocaust museums in America (specifically, the United States Holocaust Memorial, USHMM): that is, that the Holocaust could overshadow all other aspects of Jewish life and that it could erode Jewish–Gentile relations. And this would happen if Jews were to be perceived through the prism of their victimhood. In any event, the situation of the Jewish community in America in the 1980s and 1990s was changed by the Holocaust to such an extent that some of its members sought to analyse the reasons and results thereof. The issue most often debated was the role of the 'Holocaust and redemption' myth and its institutionalization. The main types of institutions whose purpose was to memorialize the Shoah were university-based Holocaust research centres, museums and other Holocaust memorials/centres. In 1979 Jacob Neusner, one of the most caustic critics of Shoah-centred Judaism, contended that he had become aware of an 'obsession with "the Holocaust" which wants to make the tragedy into the principal subject of public discourse with Jews and about Judaism'.[162] In his view, this intense interest in the Shoah was becoming quasi-religious in character; it was being treated as the focal point of discussions within American Jewry. In fact, Neusner thought that the emerging centrality of the European catastrophe in American life was in large measure an outcome of the multiplying Holocaust centres (with their own buildings, professional teachers, educational and commemorative programmes, and solemnities) that were to be established in every Jewish community. 'Such "Holocaust centers"', Neusner remarked, 'are to function like synagogues.' The only rationale for the creation of these institutions, and their unique point of interest, was just 'one chapter in the history of the Jew[s]'. He went on to note that one need not necessarily want to forget 'the unforgettable in order to judge such "centers" as nihilistic and obsessive'.[163] As the development of Holocaust-related institutions was growing apace, especially in the academy, Daniel Silver wrote in 1986: 'Centers for the study of the Holocaust dot the academic landscape and Holocaust seminars fill the academic calendar ... More university students enroll in courses on the Holocaust than in any other Jewish Studies offering.'[164]

The Shoah thus came to be *the* most distinctive – if also the most debated and controversial – component of both Jewish and non-Jewish American public life. Moreover, it has come to play a religious function as an element unifying American Jewry, as many authors maintain, and bestowing upon them the status of a special community. This specialness lies in the very fact that the nexus that binds them together is the greatest of all tragedies the Jewish people has ever lived through. It is exactly because of this dimension of Holocaust-presence, and because of the specific organization of the domain of Jewish collective memory[165] and collective symbolic acting that the Shoah started to be called the 'civil religion' of American Jews.[166] (Sometimes, as in Neusner, it is in parallel with the state of Israel, forming together the myth of 'Holocaust and redemption'. [167])

The criticisms of certain religious authorities have also been aimed at the so-called 'Holocaust theologians', including Richard L. Rubenstein and Emil L. Fackenheim. In Fackenheim's view, Auschwitz is not exclusively a place of horror, but also a place from which a 'commanding voice', as he has called it, emerges. This 'Commanding Voice of Auschwitz' is a moral–religious imperative that compels authentic Jews to oppose Hitler's plan of extermination. That is why those who can hear the voice cannot cease being Jewish; they must not quit Judaism lest Hitler be given a posthumous victory. The concept of the 'Commanding Voice of Auschwitz' was later named by Fackenheim the '614th Commandment',[168] by which he meant that to the 613 commandments traditionally recognized in Judaism, as revealed in the Torah, was added another one – the commandment of survival. If Fackenheim was criticized at all, it was mainly because he had made Auschwitz a rationale for remaining Jewish. If we accept the view that one of the core elements of Judaism is the continuity of the Jewish people, then Fackenheim's imperative is nothing less than a religious commandment which would never have been formulated if not for Hitler. That is why Fackenheim's postulates were refused by several Jewish thinkers; even among his admirers, voices of criticism were heard. In general, Fackenheim was mostly criticized for grounding Jewish future in a Holocaust past, and for formulating a religious commandment which was supposedly binding for believing as well as secular Jews. The most serious and most often-expressed reproach was that in his theory he granted a greater place to Hitler than to the prophets and traditional Jewish sources.[169]

From where, then, did the idea emerge of putting the Shoah at the centre of American Jewish life? And how did it happen that the Holocaust gained religious meaning? Many authors say that the inspiration was borrowed from Israeli Jews.[170] It is Israel that they perceive as the motherland of 'Holocaust religion', because – so they argue – in the era of the Six Day War (1967) and the Yom Kippur War (1973), the Israeli government and media were using a characteristic rhetoric in which the word 'Shoah' had a privileged status.[171] The inhabitants of Jerusalem and Tel Aviv were aware that they had to defend themselves against the attacks of the neighbouring Arab countries in order not to let another Holocaust happen. No wonder, then, that at the same time, the term 'Holocaust' came to be commonly used on the American continent – all the more because in the new, secular consciousness of American Jews, both the Shoah and Israel constitute, as it were, two pillars of faith.[172]

Thus it seems that many authors legitimately claim that the Holocaust – containing the same elements which are included in all theistic religions, except for a transcendent deity – now functions in some circles as a civil religion. It has sacred texts: the memoirs literature, films such as *Shoah* and *Schindler's List*; it has places of worship: university centres for Holocaust and genocide studies, local Holocaust museums and memorials, of which the greatest is Washington's United States Holocaust Memorial Museum; it has rituals: regular celebrations in memory of the victims, scholarly conferences and art exhibitions; it has saints: the survivors; and it has the faithful: people for whom the Holocaust constitutes the core of their identity.[173]

The phenomenon Jacob Neusner called 'Holocaustomania'[174] and its alleged religious character has been described in many different ways. But many, if not most, authors agree that the Shoah has taken too large a place in the public and intellectual sphere of American Jewry – even though in Judaism it is a religious and a cultural imperative to remember

(*Zakhor!*). Critics emphasize the fact that the narrative of Jewish death cannot replace the memory of tens of centuries of flourishing Jewish life. They are also sceptical about the efficacy of Shoah rhetoric in opposing the processes of assimilation. Phillip Lopate again remarks:

> the Holocaust has begun to replace the Bible as the new text that we must interpret. There is the danger that the 'glamor' of the Holocaust will eclipse traditional religious practice in the eyes of American Jewry – that, in effect, the Holocaust will swallow up Judaism. In the vacuum where God used to be, we are putting the Holocaust ... The desperation to hold onto the Holocaust is informed by this larger decay. Underneath these anxious injunctions never to forget, what I hear is: 'We must never forget the Holocaust because we're rapidly forgetting everything else.'[175]

The Shoah could not have become a civil religion if not for its centrality in American Jewish life and a singularly important role it plays in American culture at large.[176] On one of the first pages of his *After Tragedy and Triumph* (published in 1990), Michael Berenbaum wrote: 'The Holocaust has become a symbol central to the identity of American Jewry.'[177] Many American and Israeli Jewish intellectuals agree that what happened to American Jewry (we must resort to a generalization of sorts) is that they have absorbed the Holocaust to such an extent that it has now become their civil religion – in some cases, even the sole religion they practise. Critics of this phenomenon can be found on both extremes of the Jewish community – the anti-fundamentalist liberals and the Orthodox. The Israeli historian, Yehuda Bauer, active in the Secular Humanistic branch of Judaism, has said:

> I ... agree that the Holocaust has been misused, especially, but not solely, by the Israeli political establishment – especially, but by no means only, by the right. I agree that much of the literature, and especially the media treatment, has resulted in a trivialization of the event, which is little short of catastrophic ... I also agree that a tendency exists, especially in the United States, to turn the Holocaust into a 'civil religion', to substitute it for identification with the Jewish heritage (however that may be interpreted). And I agree that this tendency is dangerous.[178]

Deborah Lipstadt, in her article *Invoking the Holocaust*, wrote a whole section devoted to the issue of secular religion. In that section, titled *The Holocaust: A Religious Surrogate*, she claims:

Among those who have reacted negatively to the increasing emphasis on the Holocaust have been members of the Orthodox community, who believe that the Holocaust is being used as a means of fostering segments of lapsed tribalism. They contrast themselves with other segments of the Jewish community who have only recently begun to maintain an active Jewish identity. The latter are best described not as a community of the pious, but as adherents to a 'civil religion', a religion based on a shared history and tradition and not dependent on belief in an all powerful Deity. Many traditionally observant Jews ... possess a myriad of positive symbols on which to rely and they reject the suggestion that Jewish suffering might serve as an agent for the maintenance of communal cohesion. When the Holocaust becomes the focal point for preservation of Jewish tradition, it is virtually transformed into a religious symbol.[179]

It becomes clear, therefore, that the Shoah is not an 'obsession' of any particular denomination of Judaism; even if it is less likely for the devout Orthodox to turn into 'Jews defined by the Holocaust'; there are no particular borders which the *Churban*-myth, in its civil–religious aspect, could not cross. The Holocaust's omnipresence, however, has been a problem for some. That it was becoming visible, and even dominant, in almost all spheres of America's politics and cultural life – from literature, to cinema, to high school and academic education, to arts, monuments and museums – caused embarrassment among several Jewish intellectuals. The most radical critics did not hesitate to call it 'Shoah business' or 'Holocaust industry'. It is a widely shared belief that the controversial term 'Holocaust industry' was coined by Norman G. Finkelstein. In fact, by titling his book *The Holocaust Industry*, Finkelstein only popularized a shocking phrase that had long ago been employed by Paul Eric Soifer in his 1980 article, 'Remembrance and the Victims' Covenant'.[180] In 1985, on the pages of (anything but leftist) *Commentary*, Robert Alter said he saw a danger of turning the Holocaust into 'a kind of pornography of horror' and 'produc[ing] a Holocaust industry' by involving too much effort in memorializing the event.[181] It was also claimed at times that the development of all sorts of Holocaust-related institutions and cultural programmes resulted in making the Shoah into a commodity that could be sold.[182] Speaking of American Jewry, Anne Roiphe affirmed that launching a Holocaust industry was perhaps an unintentional outcome of the attempt to present the group 'as a collective witness'.[183]

Even the well-known historian and founder of the first Holocaust study centre in the United States, Yaffa Eliach, is reported to have said (as early as 1979) that America's Jews saw a 'vast educational and financial potential in the Holocaust', and that to them it was 'an instant Judaizer, shocking people back into their Jewishness'. She concluded that 'one can sadly reflect that "there is no business like Shoah business"'.[184]

2. WAS THE HOLOCAUST UNIQUELY UNIQUE?

Closely related to the question of the centrality of the Shoah is the issue of its uniqueness. This was undoubtedly one of the most controversial and most livelily debated topics among American Jewish intellectuals in the last two decades of the twentieth century. A simplified scheme would have two opposing groups: those claiming the uniqueness and incomparability of the Holocaust, and those arguing that the event, though distinct from and irreducible to any other genocide, is not incomparable. The latter group reproaches the former with the point that seeing the Shoah as unique belittles the sufferings of other groups (Armenians, Cambodians, Bosnian Muslims, etc.) and makes them appear 'less horrible'. On the other hand, the partisans of the uniqueness concept accuse the other group of betraying Jewish history and the memory of the dead by artificial and forced universalizing of Jewish suffering. One of the groups involved in the discussion includes several well-known authors gathered around the periodical titled *Shoah*: Alvin Rosenfeld, Elie Wiesel, Irving Greenberg and Emil Fackenheim. To them, as Robert Alter claims, the Shoah 'is a unique Event (the capital letter is a frequent usage) in historical time, like Sinai; and no less than the great desert theophany, it confronts us with mysteries to brood over'.[185] Indeed, Wiesel and Fackenheim are known to have argued with passion and consequence for preserving the uniqueness of the Holocaust.[186] Thus we read in Fackenheim that 'Auschwitz is the scandal of evil for evil's sake, an eruption of demonism *without analogy*; and the singling-out of Jews, ultimately, is an *unparalleled expression of* what the rabbis call *groundless hate*' (italics added).[187] Also, having formulated a concept that forbids the Jews to despair of God in the face of gas chambers, he nevertheless contends that 'no purpose, religious or non-religious, will ever be found in Auschwitz. The very attempt to find one is blasphemous.'[188]

A critique of views advocating the Holocaust's uniqueness is explicitly voiced in an article by Phillip Lopate:

It is almost as if we Jews wanted to monopolize suffering, to appropriate death as our own. But, as Irving Louis Horowitz points out, while Judaism as a way of life is special, there is no 'special nature of Jewish dying. Dying is a universal property of many peoples, cultures, and nations.' I cannot help but see this extermination pride as another variant of the Covenant: this time the Chosen People have been chosen for extraordinary suffering. As such the Holocaust seems simply another opportunity for Jewish chauvinism ... There are other reasons besides chauvinism why Jews might be loath to surrender the role of chief victim. It affords us an edge, a sort of privileged nation status in the moral honor roll, such as the one that Native American Indians have enjoyed for some time.[189]

David Stannard, probably one of the severest critics of the Holocaust uniqueness concept, speaks in a similar vein. He, too, points to the quasi-theological character of thinking demonstrated by some proponents of this idea.[190] In his analysis, Stannard sketches a brief history of this particular view. First, he contends, the uniqueness of the Shoah was seen in the sheer numbers of Jews killed by the Nazi regime. When historians questioned this assertion, another argument was proposed: the percentage of the Jewish population exterminated had allegedly been the greatest in the annals of humankind. But scholars found out that many indigenous peoples in the Americas had been destroyed by as much as 95 per cent, or even totally annihilated. The supporters of Holocaust uniqueness, as Stannard persuasively argues, then stated that it is not *how many* but *how* the Jews were killed that matters. Specifically, the speed at which the victims were murdered was to point to the incomparability of the Holocaust, 'because it destroyed more innocent people "per unit of time" than has any other mass killing event'.[191] In his work, Stannard often refers to 'the leading and certainly the most prolific advocates of the uniqueness of the Jewish Holocaust', namely the Israeli historian Yehuda Bauer and the American scholar Steven Katz:

[They] have now admitted that on every other significant point previously asserted as grounds for proclaiming the uniqueness of Jews as victims one or more other groups have at least an equal claim to recognition. But no other group, they assert, can claim that their tormentors were seized with what Bauer calls the Nazis' 'pseudo-religious, pseudo-messianic' obsession with not allowing a single Jew on the face of the earth to escape. 'To date', says Bauer, 'this has happened once, to the Jews under Nazism.'[192]

Katz took the uniqueness concept as a central dogma of his scholarship. Thus he states clearly at the outset of one of his chapters: 'The Holocaust, that is, the intentional murder of European Jewry during World War II, is historically and phenomenologically unique. No other case discussed in this book parallels it.'[193] He then briefly analyses several cases of mass killings, but in each instance he finds only marginal similarities – numbers, or some structural aspects. However, reflecting on the 'Armenian Tragedy' (he does not call it a genocide) he gives estimated numbers of the pre-First World War Armenian population and of the people killed by the Turks, which shows that at least 50 per cent of Armenians survived the massacre. After which Katz concludes: 'This is not the Holocaust.'[194] This, however, is no surprise, as he earlier remarked that 'the Holocaust is phenomenologically unique by virtue of the fact that never before has a state set out, as a matter of intentional principle and actualized policy, to annihilate physically every man, woman, and child belonging to a specific people'.[195]

Richard Rubenstein's stance on the question of uniqueness is in large measure based on his theological interpretations of the Shoah. He maintains that the extermination of European Jewry not only 'has challenged the very foundations of Jewish religious faith',[196] but has also impacted Christianity, as both religious traditions place 'enormous weight ... on the interpretation of Jewish disaster as an expression of God's justice and providence'.[197] If not for the specificity of Judeo-Christian beliefs, says Rubenstein, the Shoah would probably have never gained such persistent interest among Western intellectuals – hence his conviction 'that the religious character is responsible for the uniqueness of the Holocaust'.[198] Rubenstein argues that though historians have pointed to various similarities between the Shoah and other instances of mass murder – be it the case of Armenians, or of Stalin's purges, or of Pol Pot's Cambodia – there still remains one aspect of Nazi crime that is unlike all other genocidal actions: '*The fate of the Jews is a matter of decisive religiomythic significance in both Judaism and Christianity*. No example of mass murder other than the Holocaust has raised so directly or so insistently the question of whether it was an expression of *Heilsgeschichte*, that is, God's providential involvement in history.' (Italics in the original.)[199] The specificity and uniqueness of the Shoah, Rubenstein claims, is not only *relevant* to Christianity, it is a *troublesome* and *puzzling* question: Why did this happen in the heart of Christian Europe? And what does it reveal about Christian Churches? Rubenstein asks whether 'the Christian Church's attitude towards Jews and Judaism involve[s] it in a process that, in times of stress, can lead to the murder of Jews?' He admits, however, he must 'append a further question: Does the way Jews regard themselves religiously contribute to the terrible process?'[200]

Among those who took their stance on the question of Holocaust uniqueness, Peter Novick is perhaps one of the best-known, if controversial, scholars. In his famous, magisterial work, *The Holocaust in American Life*, Novick argues in uncompromising language:

> In Jewish discourse on the Holocaust we have not just a competition for recognition but a competition for primacy. This takes many forms. Among the most widespread and pervasive is an angry insistence on the uniqueness of the Holocaust. Insistence on its uniqueness (or denial of its uniqueness) is an intellectually empty enterprise ... The notion of uniqueness is quite vacuous ... To single out those aspects of the Holocaust that were distinctive (there certainly were such), and to ignore those aspects that it shares with other atrocities, and on the basis of this gerrymandering to declare the Holocaust unique, is an intellectual slight of hand. The assertion that the Holocaust is unique ... is, in practice, deeply offensive. What else can all of this possibly mean except 'your catastrophe, unlike ours, is ordinary; unlike ours is comprehensible; unlike ours is representable'.[201]

In an exceptionally insightful essay dedicated to the topic of Shoah consciousness, Alan Milchman and Alan Rosenberg persuasively argue that we are dealing here with a bipolar problem – one of remembering *and* forgetting the Holocaust.[202] They begin with the concept originally formulated by Edith Wyshogrod of 'the community of memory'. However, contrary to Wyshogrod's opinion that a community of memory sacralizes the mythical past and 'is based largely on nostalgia for the past', they assert that it is, rather, prospective, serves 'future transformations', and 'problematizes the present'.[203] They do not perceive both aspects of the community of memory as significant and functional, but instead they focus on its present-tense character and contend that 'a preoccupation with the past, in this case the Holocaust, is mediated by *present* concerns, and has a distinctly *political* dimension'.[204] Putting the memory of the Holocaust in Foucauldian perspective, Milchman and Rosenberg see it as a political (or politically used) issue, for 'memory is a decisive element of most political struggles'.[205] This political setting of Holocaust memory and its omnipresence in the public life compels them – or so it seems – to think over the question of the uniqueness of the Shoah. Milchman and Rosenberg say there is danger in remembering and memorializing the Holocaust as unique, for it may result in seeking respect for one's group's victim status while creating a 'distance – from the horrors perpetrated on others'.[206] A similar view was originally presented by Charles S. Maier, who claims that persistently demanding respect from others may have undesirable political consequences, though he does not say any respect is unnecessary. In his opinion, respect is not to be removed from Holocaust discourse; it is not *too much*, it is *too little* and, therefore, it should not monopolize this discourse.[207]

Maier also analyses with a critical eye one of the essential elements of the 'uniqueness question', namely the issue of comparability. His study is based on the German *Historikerstreit*, or historians' controversy that exploded in Germany in the 1980s. In the *Historikerstreit*, the most contentious problem (and, in fact, one that had ignited the discussion) was the question of whether the Shoah could legitimately be compared to any other examples of genocide or mass murder. On one hand, Maier is opposed to Ernst Nolte's concept of 'normalizing' recent German history through 'historicizing' Nazi atrocities, through comparing them to those committed by other totalitarian regimes. Maier believes that the kind of comparison which leaves no room for distinctive traits is unacceptable. And if 'any comparison ... fails to emphasize the persisting differences [it] is probably undertaken in bad faith'.[208] To his mind, comparison is of special importance only when it adds to knowledge and is based on facts; only then can it 'help reveal a wider historical process at work'.[209] Moreover, Maier believes that comparative history is not just one of the numerous branches of history as a science; it is history *tout court*. In other words, there can be no history but comparative history, for 'all history is condemned to comparison'.[210] It utilizes analogies, not to blur differences but to show events as having some traits that make them similar and other traits that make them different from one another.

Maier believes:

> Comparisons cannot be declared intrinsically valid or invalid, right or wrong. They are tools whose utility depends upon the question being posed. An open ended comparison of Soviet and Nazi prison camps is certainly a useful tool for thinking about how the two regimes resembled each other ... Any genuine comparative exercise

emphasizes uniqueness as much as similarity; it establishes what is common in contrast to what is distinctive. Ever since Aristotle, comparison has been understood to be an exercise in classificatory logic in which what is generic can be understood only in relation to what is specific. Comparison must be a two-edged sword.[211]

An issue almost identical with the question of incomparability is the one of the incomprehensibility of the Holocaust. One of the best-known advocates of this view, as many have remarked, is Elie Wiesel. A survivor, Wiesel maintains that the Holocaust's uniqueness consists in two basic facts: one, as an event it is unprecedented and unrepeat-able – it happened outside of history; two, no one who has not lived through it can know what it was. Giving an example of survivors' testimony, Rosenberg refers to Wiesel's statement 'that "whoever has not lived through it can never know it. And whoever has lived though it can never fully reveal it." '[212]

Dan Magurshak, too, has pointed out that some authors do believe the Shoah to be beyond comprehension:

> Nora Levin writes: 'The Holocaust refuses to go the way of most history, not only because of the magnitude of destruction ... but because events surrounding it are still in a very real sense humanly incomprehensible ... Indeed, comprehensibility may never be possible.' In the same vein Elie Wiesel asserts that 'Auschwitz cannot be explained' ... because 'the Holocaust transcends history'.[213]

Magurshak himself also wrestles with the notion of incompre-hensibility. Unwilling to dismiss it outright, he tries to demonstrate how incomprehensibility can be assigned to the Shoah and yet not hinder attempts to understand it. In his view, common psychological incompre-hensibility does not necessarily mean that 'the Holocaust is theoretically incomprehensible' – which is to say that the European catastrophe does not have to be seen as an utterly mysterious event, but as a fact subjected to human reasoning, though it paralyzes the human mind and psyche. It can be 'overwhelming without necessarily being incomprehen-sible'.[214] Moreover, even if the Holocaust is deemed incomprehensible, Magurshak argues, its incomprehensibility is not absolute, neither is it unique to the Shoah.[215] It is 'no more [incomprehensible] than any event in human natural history'; it can be put beside the French Revolution or some other 'complex human phenomenon [that] provides the various disciplines with an almost endless field of investigation which is, nonetheless, always open to further comprehension'.[216] Thus, even if the Holocaust is not fully understood now, it can and should be analysed in order to be thoroughly and deeply comprehended, which is a long and difficult process, but that does not imply it is ontologically impossible.

If the feature of incomprehensibility is not unique to the *Churban Europa*, then we ought not to refrain from saying what is trivial: namely, that there have been many *relatively* incomprehensible events. Accordingly, the Shoah, like many other events, is unique. First of all, it is unique in a trivial sense: it is unprecedented and unrepeatable. But so are all other occurrences noted in the annals of humanity. The Holocaust shares this notion of uniqueness with all other happenings. This is not to say, however, that the word 'unique' is to be understood as pertaining only to unrepeatable spacio-temporal circumstances which determine the historical location of any given event. Of course, this aspect of an event cannot be denied, but it is accompanied by unique social and moral features. Again, *every* event has its unique social and moral characteristics. How, therefore, is the Holocaust different from other occurrences? It has a combination of moral and social features that make it distinctive from all other events. Yet, it is not *completely* unlike other affairs in human history. Being different does not preclude its being similar. In contradistinction to what Alan Rosenberg claims, this basic level of uniqueness seems of importance, for it points to the fact that the Holocaust happened within the realm of human history and human responsibility, and not in some metaphysical space.[217] Also, it seems advisable to point to a crucial distinction between two terms often used in Holocaust-related discussions: 'unique' and 'unprecedented'. That the Jewish catastrophe was unprecedented is a historical assertion (and practically an unquestioned one); that it was unique is a metahistorical or transhistorical assertion.[218] That is why ascribing uniqueness to the Shoah may be understood as substituting metaphysical discourse for historical discourse and pure speculation for scholarly research.

If, therefore, the Holocaust is unique in a trivial sense and, as such, it is like other events, can it not be argued that it is nonetheless more than unique? Or that its uniqueness is of a special kind? Alice L. Eckardt and A. Roy Eckardt, both Christian theologians, in their book, *Long Night's Journey into Day*, have proposed to view the Shoah as *uniquely unique*. They distinguish between several categories of events that form a pyramid-like structure which has its most unique event at the peak:

We move from the surface level of repetitive events ... to the ...

level of relative uniqueness ... and finally to an ultimate level transcending other levels: to the level of incomparability or unique
uniqueness ... We see, accordingly, how any such wording as 'Is the
Holocaust unique?' is exceedingly trivial ... Instead we have to
ask, *in what senses* is the Holocaust unique? Is it indeed *uniquely*
unique? [Italics in the original.][219]

The authors make it clear that it is just to elevate the Holocaust above
the level of trivial events that they have invented the category of unique
uniqueness. What is striking is that even though asking whether the
Shoah is unique or not is for them a trivialization of the issue, they do
not hesitate to ask *in what senses* the Nazi genocide was unique. This
is an important question, for it implies that in some respects the Holocaust is unique whereas in others it is not – which is what I have argued
above. Yet the problem is that for the Eckardts, the question of 'in what
senses is it unique?' is tantamount to 'is it uniquely unique?' In terms of
logic, this makes little sense, since the former question is one of qualities
or features, while the latter is one of degree. In other words, it is one
thing to examine what features make the Jewish catastrophe unique,
and it is another thing to inquire whether, or how, its uniqueness is
unique. Alice and Roy Eckardt, however, do not see this difference and
assume that by enumerating those traits of the Holocaust that they
deem unique, they will demonstrate that it is indeed uniquely unique.[220]

What is also worth our attention is the theological framework in
which they place the Shoah. They claim it is a 'truly transcending and
metahistorical event ... an event that raises the question of *Heilsgeschichte* ('salvation history')'.[221] Following Wiesel and Fackenheim,
the Eckardts put the Holocaust in line with the Exodus and the gift of
the Torah on Mount Sinai. They go, however, a step further and say
that the Shoah, in terms of theological implications, can be compared
to the Crucifixion and the Resurrection,[222] which, to the Jewish ear,
might sound provocative. The two Christian theologians also suggest
the possibility of introducing a new method of counting years: it would
have as its 'year one' the year 1941, allegedly the beginning of the
Holocaust. The Eckardts' argument is that the Shoah has brought with
itself a total change of human history, indeed an 'ontological redirecting
of [its] course'.[223] Placed as it is in the theological perspective,
the claim of ontological novelty caused by the Holocaust may seem
outrageous, especially for the believer. For how would that ontological
redirecting be possible, if it were not decreed or permitted by the
Higher Being? This problem the Eckardts do not even touch.

Alice and Roy Eckardt's concept of unique uniqueness was critically evaluated by the Armenian American scholar, Pierre Papazian. In his view, their concept of uniqueness, as applied to the Shoah, is carried 'to an absurd extreme'.[224] He agrees that the Holocaust was a singular event, but to claim it was uniquely unique is for him unacceptable:

> the term 'uniquely unique' does injury to the English language and insults the reader ... The concept of 'unique uniqueness' denies the possibility of comparison of the Holocaust with any other case of genocide. This play on words can only be characterized as intellectual pretension devoid of meaning, although it supports Wiesel's position of incomparability and uniqueness of the Holocaust ... according to the Eckardts [the only category that fits the Holocaust] is the transhistorical or metahistorical interpretation, in which certain events are beyond being unique, and must be characterized as uniquely unique. According to this viewpoint, the Holocaust is 'an event that twists our journey through space-time by 180 degrees'. While the purpose of such a description is obviously to prove the uniqueness of the Holocaust, it also makes it sound as if the Holocaust took place in the fourth dimension, and is beyond human understanding.[225]

Papazian, certainly, does not only reflect on the Eckardts' understanding of uniqueness. He also analyses many other concepts whose purpose is to demonstrate that the Shoah is incomparable and incomprehensible, which makes it different from other acts of mass destruction. Thus he challenges Lucy Dawidowicz's assertion that no other people, save the Jews, were 'chosen' for total annihilation, let alone almost completely destroyed. He reproaches Dawidowicz with overlooking the actual fate of the Armenian people during the First World War: 'Dawidowicz's arguments fit the Armenian example so well that if she had applied them to that event she could have only concluded that the Holocaust cannot be called unique on these grounds.'[226] Papazian claims that a parallel of Hitler's plan to solve the Jewish Question through extermination would be 'the Pashas' of Turkey [attempt] to solve the Armenian Question'. And though in absolute terms the Armenian losses were not as great as those of the Jews, 'as a percentage of the total population, the Armenian nation lost fully one-half of its people, exceeding the one-third of the total Jewish population that was murdered'. If some would take offence at such an argument,

Papazian explains that 'this comparison is intended neither to belittle the Jewish loss nor to magnify the Armenian loss, but to put both in perspective'.[227]

It is hardly surprising that the Armenian scholar looks with a critical eye at what Elie Wiesel says about the Shoah. First and foremost, Papazian notices Wiesel's preoccupation with the mysteriousness and intellectual inaccessibility of the *Churban Europa*. 'Wiesel does indeed refer to the mystical quality of the Holocaust in many of his writings. "Remove the Jews from the Holocaust, and the Event loses its mystery." Since the Holocaust … refers specifically to the genocide of European Jews, removal of the Jews from the Holocaust would leave no Holocaust, let alone mystery.'[228] Papazian's argument goes on to demonstrate that 'the Armenian people suffered a destruction that also defies reason and morality, an experience that also can be said to be endowed with a religious mystery. If the Jews suffered genocide as the Chosen People, the Armenians suffered genocide as the First Christian Nation.'[229]

Gradually, it becomes clear that among the many factors that fanned the debate over the question of uniqueness, there is one that has little to do with recent historical experience, but is deeply rooted in Jewish theological tradition; it is the issue of chosenness. Lucy Dawidowicz's argument is the epitome of the kind of reasoning which sees the uniqueness of the Shoah as tragically confirming the status of the Jews as a chosen people.[230] Alice and Roy Eckardt assert that 'sometimes the claimed uniqueness of the *Shoah* is derived from the claimed uniqueness of the Jewish people', in which statement, they say, 'there is much plausibility'.[231] As is well known, the concept of election is present in traditional Jewish texts, both biblical and rabbinic.[232] Among those Jewish scholars who generally do not accept the concept of uniqueness of the Holocaust, there are some who perceive the idea as in large measure linked with the notion of election. To Ismar Schorsch, for instance, the belief that the Shoah was unique is a 'distasteful secular version of chosenness'.[233] We have to be cautious, however, and not neglect the fact that many of those who deny the Holocaust's uniqueness are simply opposed to the concept of chosenness as such.

Besides Elie Wiesel, the thinker who is probably most often associated with the idea that uniqueness of the Holocaust is a result of the election of Israel is Emil Fackenheim. As Hyam Maccoby has pointed out, what is characteristic in Fackenheim's reasoning is that in the first place, the Holocaust cannot be likened to any other 'horrific massacres, such as the Turkish massacre of the Armenians, or the sufferings of

Hiroshima'.[234] Two factors make it radically different from these events. First, those other atrocities can be rationally explained as caused by specific political circumstances; second, 'only in the case of the Jews was a people *chosen* for extermination not because of anything they did or claimed, or were thought to have done or claimed, but simply because they *were*' (italics added).[235] Moreover, what made the Holocaust unique, within and without Jewish history, as Fackenheim maintains, is that they were not only chosen to be murdered but also to be deprived of the 'normality', as it were, of human death. 'The Holocaust Kingdom', says Fackenheim, 'was a celebration of degradation as much as of death, and of death as much as of degradation.'[236] Whereas previous instances of genocide were means to achieve political and economic ends, the Holocaust, for the first time in human history, proved 'to be *the sole ultimate end*' (italics in the original). Therefore, as Fackenheim claims, even the very term 'genocide' is not appropriate as a depiction of what the Jewish catastrophe was.[237]

While the notion of uniqueness can be thought of as little more than a rhetorical figure, Fackenheim puts it into a quasi-philosophical framework, saying that 'the Holocaust is not only a unique event: it is *epoch-making*. The world, just as the Jewish world, can never be the same.' (Italics added.) The concept of the Shoah as an epoch-making event was later elaborated upon by Alan Rosenberg. For Rosenberg, the Holocaust's impact on our understanding of history is so great that it really constitutes a civilizational breach (*Zivilisationsbruch*); it marks the decline of one epoch and opens another one: it is a *caesura*. Thus, Rosenberg argues, the Holocaust possesses a 'transformational potential'.[238] Alluding to the theories of Peter Berger and Thomas Luckmann, of Anthony Giddens and also Michel Foucault, Rosenberg (in some publications together with Milchman) affirms that if the Holocaust can indeed be seen as a unique or transformational event, it is so because society perceives it as such. For no occurrence has any particular meaning in and of itself; it is we humans, or our discourses, that invest events with various meanings.

Therefore, if we understand the Shoah as marking a discontinuity, it is our structuration of the social world and our images of it that make us claim that the Shoah is a break with 'normal' history. Rosenberg convincingly argues that it is through our acts of structuration that a *potentially* transformational event can become an *actual* transformation of our thinking.[239] He does not show, however, why 'the *preliminary* question of uniqueness [of the Holocaust] ... must surely be resolved if the event itself is to be transformational' (ialics in the original).[240] We can easily imagine a situation where people could be involved in an argument over the issue of the uniqueness of the Shoah, or its being *unlike* other genocides, while still agreeing that it is, in one way or another, a transformational event. Furthermore, even if we accept, as most scholars do, the view that for the Western world the Shoah is a civilizational breach, a *novum* – indeed, a transformation – it does not imply, perforce, that people in China, Rwanda, or Haiti would share this opinion.

Also, we cannot exclude that in the future, for Western civilization or even for Judaism, the Holocaust will lose much of its current significance. Discontinuity means not only that what we think here and now is different from what our parents used to think, but also that people living in distant countries may have other transformational events. In other words, the crucial issue is not so much whether the Holocaust was or was not a unique, unprecedented, or transformational event – since any uniqueness or potential for transformation is always relative – but what uses we make of our images of the catastrophe.

Yet, for all the attractiveness and insightfulness of the concept of the Shoah as a rupture and an epoch-making, transformational event, we must agree with Rubenstein that

> the Holocaust was not a complete rupture with the values of the Western religion and Christian thought and the just-war tradition that legitimates whatever measures are necessary to combat a mortal enemy, once the Nazis succeeded in convincing a majority of Europeans that the Jews were a mortal threat to Christian civilization, it became morally acceptable for normal men and women to participate in the project of mass extermination *with a good conscience*. [Italics in the original.][241]

The statement that the alleged rupture was incomplete, however, does not only pertain to Christianity. It can also be said that the Holocaust did not break with Western post-Enlightenment philosophical tradition. It was a product of the Enlightenment, of its spirit of rationality and formalization. Which is not to say, of course, that rationality itself, or that humanism so exalted by the Renaissance and the Enlightenment, are to be blamed for the Shoah.[242] Here I shall point to two important issues. One is that we have to distinguish between two kinds of rationality: rationality for the sake of purpose and rationality for the sake of values, or *Zweckrationalität* and *Wertrationalität*, as Max Weber has called them. The other thing is that the very term 'Holocaust' implies two meanings, the first one being the fact of Nazi extermination of the Jews; the second one being what implications we claim the event has for us, and how we think of it.

That is why one has to be cautious when saying that if not for the rationality of the perpetrators, the Holocaust would never have happened; and if not for the employment of modern bureaucracy and modern technologies that made assembly-line death factories possible, the event would probably not be unique. As Rosenberg and Marcus contend, with the advent of the Holocaust, the old categories of evil became irrelevant or inapplicable to the new phenomenon of mass death. The Nazi genocide itself constitutes a new form of evil, 'a form that is structured by the calculating ideological rationality of functional reason ... It is a form of evil comprising the ultimate perversion of the Enlightenment ideal of progress.'[243]

In their book *Experiments in Thinking the Holocaust*, Rosenberg and Milchman, interpreting Blanchot and Bataille, assert that the extermination of Jews was 'the absolute event of history' and that 'Auschwitz is the reality (*le fait*), the badge (*le signe*), of man. The image of man is henceforth inseparable from a gas chamber'. Finally, they seem to agree with Philippe Lacoue-Labarthe that the Holocaust discloses the very nature of our civilization – that it is 'the revelation of the essence of the West'.[244] Now that is a proposition with which one can hardly concur. First of all, not all of the victims perished in gas chambers and crematoria; we must not ignore those who died of hunger or diseases in the ghettos. This kind of death had not been, so to speak, 'planned' by the Nazi regime; we do not even have accurate statistics about those who died this death in the ghettos. They seem not to 'fit in' with the picture of the modern machine-produced cadavers in the death camps. Apart from that, one should not overlook more than one million killed by the notorious *Einsatzgruppen*; this was not so much a 'modern' death, either. If it is argued that the Holocaust was a meticulously planned extermination, executed by way of modern methods and modern means, doesn't that imply that a large number of Jewish victims who perished outside of camp fences are not Holocaust victims? That is, of course, absurd and the authors must be aware of it, but nevertheless, their line of argument would not preclude such conclusions (as noxious as they are).

If we do agree that the functional reason (*Zweckrationalität*), in contradistinction to the moral reason (*Wertrationalität*), is in some way to be blamed for the Holocaust, we had better avoid selecting Auschwitz as the epitome of the modern machinery used to annihilate European

Jews. The assembly-line technology and the production of other modern devices are not in themselves the cause of the death of millions. Rather, we should blame the bureaucratization of our society, the dissolution of inter-human relationships, the atomization of public life. It is modern bureaucracy that has brought forth the 'desk killer' and thus technically banalized evil.[245] Richard Rubenstein briefly described how this horrific and banal, state-controlled evil was committed:

> At first, the *Reichsvereinigung* performed the bureaucratic prelim-
> inary work necessary for the later stages of the destruction process.
> Jewish statisticians informed the SS of births, deaths, and other
> demographic changes ... Jewish bureaucrats sat at their desks and
> performed the tasks assigned to them by German bureaucrats
> further up the chain of authority.[246]

One of the crucial, indeed catastrophic, stages for Europe's Jews in the accelerating Nazi bureaucratic process of extermination was depriving them of their citizenship. As stateless persons they found themselves under no legal protection. Rubenstein's conclusion is that 'the Nazis committed no crime at Auschwitz since no law or political order protected those who were first condemned to statelessness and then to the camps'.[247] We can thus infer two things from the way the Nazi regime treated the Jews: one is that it can happen in the future in any state that has at its disposal a well-functioning bureaucratic system; the second is that '*rights do not belong to men by nature*. To the extent that men have rights, they have them only as members of the polis, the political community.'[248]

In the final analysis, I concur with Alan Rosenberg that 'the question of the "uniqueness" of the Holocaust has itself become a unique question'.[249] Indeed, interpreting the destruction of European Jews has become a separate scholarly discipline, in contradistinction to historical study of the Holocaust. The issue of uniqueness thus belongs to 'Holo-caustology' rather than to historical research. It has become unique because it draws so much attention among Jews and Gentiles alike. It is now one of the most often discussed themes, not only in America and Israel but in many European countries as well. It triggers animated discussions among scholars in the humanities and in social sciences. In this sense, the Holocaust (specifically its reception and implications) is unique, for it has brought about more debates than any other event in Western history. It has tremendously influenced the way we westerners perceive politics and engage in political affairs. Last but not least, it has penetrated our everyday life, from elementary education to universities to newspapers and television. In short, it has become a unique hallmark of contemporary Western culture.

NOTES

1. See M.M. Kaplan, *Judaism as a Civilization: Toward a Reconstruction of American-Jewish Life* (1981) reprinted with an introduction by A. Eisen (Philadelphia, PA: Jewish Publication Society, 1994 [1934]).
2. 'In 1900, nearly 60 per cent of adult Jewish workers labored in blue-collar vocations. In 1933, this figure has fallen to 29 per cent nationwide (35 per cent in New York), and among second-generation Jews to 14 per cent.' H.M. Sachar, *A History of the Jews in America* (New York: Vintage Books, 1993), p.428. See also B. Lazerewitz et al., *Jewish Choices: American Jewish Denominationalism* (Albany, NY: State University of New York Press, 1998), p.25; N. Glazer, *American Judaism* (Chicago, IL: University of Chicago Press, 1957), p.81.
3. According to the religious census of 1926, there were 3,118 congregations and 1,782 synagogues in the United States, while its Jewish population counted 4.1 million. Ten years later, the figures were: 3,738 congregations, 2,851 synagogues, and the Jewish population had grown by half a million. See Glazer, *American Judaism*, p.165.
4. 'In the mid-thirties seven thousand New York City children attended these schools.' Ibid., p.87.
5. Ibid., p.85.
6. Ibid., p.89. Today, these centres are called Jewish Community Centers (JCC).
7. See E. Lederhendler, *New York Jews and the Decline of Urban Ethnicity, 1950–1970* (Syracuse, NY: Syracuse University Press, 2001), pp.10–13. The influx of the East European Jewish masses, however, was significantly diminished in the early 1920s as a result of the Immigration Act (or Johnson Act) of 1921 and 1924, which set special quota for immigrants coming to the United States. This act ought not to be viewed as an expression of anti-Semitism (which was certainly on the rise in interwar America), for it was not aimed against particular nations or ethnic groups. The quota imposed by the act referred to the immigrants' citizenship and not their ethnic background. As Henry Feingold has noted, 'the Congress that passed the restrictive immigration law of 1921 also passed the Lodge-Fish resolution confirming the promise of a Jewish national home in Palestine contained in the Balfour Declaration of 1917'. H. Feingold, *A Time for Searching: Entering the Mainstream 1920–1945* (Baltimore, MD: Johns Hopkins University Press, 1992), p.1.
8. As Chaim Waxman has observed, the economic mobility of the second-generation New York Jews enabled them to change place of residence: 'They moved out of the immigrant neighborhoods to the modern, middle-class neighborhoods ... In New York City ... there was a mass movement of Jews from Manhattan to these neighborhoods in Brooklyn and the Bronx during the 1920s and 1930s.' They settled mostly in Eastern Parkway and Flatbush in Brooklyn, and in Pelham Parkway and the Grand Concourse in the Bronx. C.I. Waxman, *America's Jews in Transition* (Philadelphia, PA: Temple University Press, 1983), p.62.
9. Glazer, *American Judaism*, p.116.
10. Nevertheless, *Yiddishkeit* was a source of secular tendencies observable in a great number of young Jews, especially 'fresh' immigrants from Eastern Europe: 'Yiddish secularism presents a unique phenomenon, combining a secularist *weltanschauung* with a religious mood ... Beginning as militant secularism in the United States in the 1890s, its proponents delighted in flaunting their violation of religious practices, as in the case of the "Yom Kippur Ball", marriage without religious ceremony or sanction, and vehement denial of the existence of God.' G. Winer, 'The Religious Dimension of Yiddish Secularism', *Judaism*, 41 (Winter 1992), p.80.
11. Hannah Arendt wrote that 'there were quite a number of families in Germany who had been baptized for generations and yet remained purely Jewish. That the converted Jew only rarely left

his family and even more rarely left his Jewish surroundings altogether, accounts for this. The Jewish family, at any rate, proved to be a more conserving force than Jewish religion.' H. Arendt, *The Origins of Totalitarianism* (San Diego and New York: Hartcourt, 1985), p.64, n.23.

12. Glazer, *American Judaism*, p.118.

13. In subsequent years he wrote two more volumes. The parts of the trilogy were titled: (1) *The International Jew: The World's Largest Foremost Problem*; (2) *Jewish Activities in the United States*; (3) *Jewish Influences in American Life*. See ibid., p.269. On the question of American anti-Semitism, see also A.J. Karp, *Haven and Home: A History of the Jews in America* (New York: Schocken Books, 1984), pp.266ff.

14. See Feingold, *Time for Searching*, p.2; E.S. Shapiro, *A Time for Healing: American Jewry Since World War II* (Baltimore, MD: Johns Hopkins University Press, 1992), p.300.

15. See Shapiro, *A Time for Healing*, pp.108, 120. Mordecai Kaplan, by many regarded as a heretic who wanted Judaism to get rid of the idea of a supernatural God, insisted: 'Interpret God as you will, provided you do so in a spirit of affirmation, but you cannot afford to ignore Him if your purpose is to cultivate a Jewish consciousness ... The God idea, in whatever form it is expressed, being universal, evidently answers to some need that is characteristic of human nature as such.' M.M. Kaplan, 'The God Idea in Judaism', in M.M. Kaplan (ed.), *The Jewish Reconstructionist Papers* (New York: Jewish Book House, 1936), pp.90f.

16. Glazer, *American Judaism*, p.123. Writing in the latter half of the 1950s, Glazer did not yet know the term 'Holocaust'. It appeared, however, in the second edition of his book, although it was not introduced throughout; it is used only in the added Chapter 9. See N. Glazer, *American Judaism*, 2nd revised edition, with a new introduction (Chicago, IL, and London: University of Chicago Press, 1989), p.172. Subsequent quotations are from the first edition.

17. Glazer, *American Judaism*, p.123.

18. Ibid., p.106.

19. As Arnold Eisen has noted, 'disenchantment with Marxism and the trauma of the war had lent religion new credibility among intellectuals, while Jews recently arrived in gentile suburbs in the postwar years found that their neighbors went to Church and believed in God and expected the Jews to do the same'. A.M. Eisen, *The Chosen People in America: A Study in Jewish Religious Ideology* (Bloomington and Indianapolis, IN: Indiana University Press, 1983), p.127; see E.S. Shapiro, 'Jewishness and the New York Intellectuals', *Judaism*, 38 (Summer 1989), p.285.

20. Ibid., p.283.

21. A similar intuition was expressed by Jacob Neusner, who affirmed that Jews 'form a coherent group in American society. They generally regard their group as religious, though doing so requires the revision of commonplace definitions of religion.' J. Neusner, *American Judaism: Adventure in Modernity* (Englewood Cliffs, NJ: Prentice Hall, 1972), p.2.

22. See P.L. Berger, 'The Desecularization of the World: A Global Overview', and J. Sacks, 'Judaism and Politics in the Modern World', in P.L. Berger (ed.), *The Desecularization of the World: Resurgent Religion and World Politics* (Washington, DC: Ethics and Public Policy Center, 1999).

23. There are, of course, other kinds of etymological interpretation of this term; the one accepted here seems, however, the most 'natural' and appropriate in explaining the socio-historical phenomenon know as religion.

24. In 1940, according to US census, a total of 1.75 million American Jews said Yiddish was their mother tongue. See Lederhendler, *New York Jews*, p.28.

25. See Glazer, *American Judaism*, p.108. There was considerable development of an Orthodox primary and secondary schooling system. In the 1930s, Orthodox all-day schools (*yeshivas* or *yeshivot*) gathered some 3,000 children, whereas in the 1950s there were around 30,000 pupils attending them. That, however, was in part due to an influx of Second World War survivors from Europe. See ibid., p.110.

26. Ibid., pp.124f. According to a 1937 survey of American rabbis (Orthodox, Conservative and Reform), 'only one-seventh of those polled professed belief in a God who created the universe, while most of the rest assented to a less personalist definition of God as the "sum total of forces which make for greater intelligence, beauty, and goodness" ... Perhaps most important of all, the rabbis were in agreement about the relative nonimportance of either theology or politics in their preaching.' Eisen, *Chosen People in America*, pp.10f; see also Glazer, *American Judaism*, p.130.

27. In Europe, the *kehillah* (or *kahal*) always functioned not only as a religious community but also as an administrative body, comprising many social institutions. In fact, it was 'a state within a state', as J.S. Woocher has observed in his *Sacred Survival: The Civil Religion of American Jews* (Bloomington, IN: Indiana University Press, 1986), p.1.
28. Here is a description of a typical American Jew and his family at the beginning of the 1960s:

    > His attitude toward religion is ... conflicting at times. In a vague, ill-defined way, the American Jew likes to think of himself as religious. Close examination would be apt to reveal, however, that what he really means is being Jewish and this in a national, cultural, or social sense. He merely considers himself a conscious Jew. When pressed for more specific evidence of 'religiosity', he is apt to reply that he supports the Temple and pays his dues. He may add further that he belongs to the Men's Club, his wife to the Sisterhood and Hadassah and, if young enough, both of them to the Mr and Mrs Club. He is proud of the fact that both he and his wife have worked hard to provide the Temple auditorium with a new piano, the kitchen with a set of new dishes, and the Hebrew School with a brand new movie projector. Yes, he supports the Temple. And he does attend services on the holidays and Yahrzeits and sometimes even on Friday nights. He would like to attend more often, but ... To compensate for the 'but', he insists on the kids regularly attending Hebrew School. He is especially proud of this endorsement of Hebrew education – an education which, it must be said in fairness to him, he never had himself – which looms especially large in view of rabbinical stress upon it.

    Lothar Kahn, 'Another Decade: The American Jew in the Sixties', *Judaism*, 10 (Spring 1961), p.107.
29. Woocher, *Sacred Survival*, pp.14f.
30. See ibid., p.17.
31. See Woocher, *Sacred Survival*, p.17.
32. Glazer gives quite a convincing description of the motivation to be religiously involved in spite of one's disinterest in the idea of God: he analyses 'that obscure process whereby a minimal relation to Judaism is established. The mental calculus seems to be as follows: Since I myself have a good traditional education, I can afford to be an agnostic or an atheist. My child won't get such an education, but he should at least get a taste of the Jewish religion.' Glazer, *American Judaism*, p.141.
33. S.M. Lipset and E. Raab, *Jews and the New American Scene* (Cambridge, MA: Harvard University Press, 1995), p.49.
34. This negative something is the strongest and ... most significant religious reality among American Jews: it is that the Jews have not stopped being Jews ... It is not that most Jews in this country submit themselves to the Jewish law; they do not. Nor can they tell you what the Jewish heritage is. But they do know it may demand something from them, and to that demand ... they will not answer No. The significance of the fact that they have not cast off the yoke is that they are prepared to be Jews, though not to be the Jews their grandfathers were.

    Glazer, *American Judaism*, p.139.
35. Ibid., p.132.
36. Exceptionally important in this regard were the 'New York Jewish intellectuals', as Lederhendler has called them, 'the creative members of New York's intellectual community'. Lederhendler, *New York Jews*, p.15; see also ibid., pp.18ff. He stresses the fact that New York played a unique role in the whole of American Jewry both in quality and quantity:

    > It is generally recognized that New York from the 1940s to the mid-1960s went through a period of cultural primacy: a time of 'intellectual ferment and artistic creation ... unsurpassed in the history of the modern city'. The editors of *Fortune Magazine* devoted their February 1960 issue to New York City and included a feature story called 'The Jewish Élan'. Noting that more Jews lived in New York than in the State of Israel, or in any other single country outside of the United States and Russia, for that matter, its author asserted: 'As no other city, New York is their home; here a Jew can be what he wants to be. Here he lives out of the shadow of his historic crisis ... And surely it can be said that Jewish élan has contributed to the city's dramatic character – its excitement [and] its originality.'

Ibid., pp.16, 36; the article Lederhendler quotes is Sam Welles's 'The Jewish *Élan*', *Fortune Magazine*, February 1960, p.134.
37. See P. Novick, *The Holocaust and Collective Memory: The American Experience* (London: Bloomsbury, 2000), pp.33f.
38. See ibid., pp.39–46.
39. Ibid., pp.1f.
40. Ibid., p.3.
41. As Novick has remarked, only an insignificant proportion of American Jews were active in the Communist Party. On the other hand, 'a great many – perhaps most – American Communists in these years were Jews. (An American Jewish Committee memorandum in the late 1940s cited a private FBI estimate that fifty to sixty per cent of Communist Party members were Jews.)' Ibid., p.93. This was surely problematic for the Jewish community at large, since if referring to the extermination of European Jews was identified with Communist inclinations, Jews would naturally avoid touching on the topic.
42. They were executed on 19 June 1953. Later on, it was found that Ethel had not spied for the Soviets, but was indicted on the false testimonies of David Greenglass and his wife.
43. Glazer, *American Judaism*, p.114.
44. Ibid., p.132.
45. Eli Lederhendler is an American Jew by birth. He was born in New York and started his scholarly career there, but afterwards he moved to Israel, where he teaches history at the Hebrew University in Jerusalem.
46. Lederhendler, *New York Jews*, p.xvii.
47. In fact, in Singer's writing we can trace some episodes that do pertain to the Holocaust. In his *Enemies*, for example, the main character, Herman Broder, had visions of the Nazis raiding New York and himself hiding in the bathroom. Herman had been saved by a Polish girl, Jadwiga, whom he later married; his Jewish lover, Masha, had survived the ghetto and concentration camp. Masha, who had started to hate God in the camp, says: 'Murdering the Jews is part of the adventure. The Jews have to be murdered, that's what God wills ... Papa always used to say that everything comes from God ... If God had allowed the death of Jews in Europe, why would he prevent a shoah from happening in America? God doesn't care about it. That's how it is.' Isaac B. Singer, *Wrogowie* [Enemies], trans. Ludmiła Melchior-Yahil (Warsaw: Amber, 1998).
48. Lederhendler, *New York Jews*, p.44.
49. H. Flanzbaum, *The Americanization of the Holocaust* (Baltimore, MD: Johns Hopkins University Press, 1999), p.1.
50. Ibid.
51. See Novick, *The Holocaust and Collective Memory*, p.103.
52. See ibid. Flanzbaum claims the film was seen by a couple of million people. See Flanzbaum, *Americanization of the Holocaust*, p.2.
53. In fact it could be heard once in the French dialogue, but was omitted in the English captions. See Novick, *Holocaust and Collective Memory*, p.103.
54. E.T. Linenthal, *Preserving Memory: The Struggle to Create America's Holocaust Museum* (New York: Columbia University Press, 2001), p.7; see also Novick, *Holocaust and Collective Memory*, p.103. See, however, views to the contrary as summarized below in note 132.
55. *Night* is still becoming more and more popularized, especially in the United States:

> Chicago chose *Night* for its second *One Book, One Chicago* program, to be read in March and discussed during National Library Week, April 14–20, 2002. The Chicago performance is part of a 14-city tour that premieres in New York City, then moves on to Boston, New Orleans, Denver, Salt Lake City, Atlanta, Chicago, Puerto Rico, Miami, Seattle, Portland, San Francisco and finally Washington, DC.

> *Elie Wiesel: Night (La Nuit)* (accessed 12 March 2004), <http://www.frenchculture.org/perfo/events/02wieselnuit.html>.

56. Eli Pfefferkorn and David H. Hirsch, 'Elie Wiesel's Wrestle with God', *Midstream*, 43 (November 1997), p.22.
57. See the website articles, 'Elie Wiesel: *Night (La Nuit)*' and 'Writer of Silence: Elie Wiesel Brought the Holocaust and its Survival to the American Public' [reprinted with permission

from *Jewish American Literature: A Norton Anthology*, published by W.W. Norton & Co.] (accessed 12 March 2004), <http://www.myjewishlearning.com/culture/literature/Overview_ Jewish_American_Literature/Jewish_American_Literature_Today/Wiesel.htm>. It is not really clear whether he started writing *Un di velt hot geshvign* before or after the meeting with Mauriac. Wiesel himself expressed contradictory opinions on this issue. In any event, there is no reason to question the fact that he began his work in 1955, after having fulfilled the vow he had made in 1945 to keep silent about the Holocaust for ten years.

58. *Elie Wiesel: Nobel Prize for Peace. Biography*, 13 January 1997 (accessed 12 March 2004), <http://www.achievement.org/autodoc/page/wie0bio-1>. More precise data is given by Cargas: 'In 1959, Hill & Wang purchased the manuscript for $100. It sold 1,046 copies in its first eighteen months on the market.' H.J. Cargas (ed.), *Telling the Tale: A Tribute to Elie Wiesel on the Occasion of His 65th Birthday* (St Louis, MO: Time Being Books, 1993), p.23; see also S.G. Freedman, *Jew vs Jew: The Struggle for the Soul of American Jewry* (New York: Simon & Schuster, 2000), p.299. Interestingly enough, when, in mid-March 2004, I sent a post to the 'H-Holocaust' listserv, asking the participants about their opinions on why people in the 1960s would be so uninterested in Wiesel's *Night* – a novel that became a best-seller some ten to twenty years later, an animated discussion started. It continued for over two weeks and drew more than twenty-five members of the list. Among those who joined in the discussion at least once were such 'big names' as Peter Novick, Lawrence Baron, Richard L. Rubenstein and Henry Greenspan, as well as other scholars in the field of Holocaust studies, and several survivors, too. Richard Rubenstein has remarked:

> among the reasons ... why *Night* began to get wider circulation in the Jewish community [only in the late 1960s] was because it was seen as the answer to *After Auschwitz*. People said that Wiesel is a survivor and a believer. His testimony is more reliable than Rubenstein's who wasn't there. However, the main reason was that for at least two decades people had been in denial. Another element in the change was the 1967 war ...

(I identify Rubenstein as the author of this quote by his permission.) One of the survivors, however, challenged Rubenstein's opinion: 'that was not entirely the main and true reason – one of many reasons was the fact that the Jewish community suffered from shock, disbelief AND a serious and justified sense of guilt. They did not help when they could have done so and when they should have done more to avoid the murders.' Upon coming to America, the person was offered medical and psychiatric help by 'a German couple ... for very little money. The wife was a baptized Jew, the husband was Lutheran. Both implored me to "forget the past, start anew" and assured me that nobody wanted to hear what I had to tell. They were right.' With that another person concurred: 'no wonder [that the] survivors did not speak out or that Wiesel's *Night* did not catch on – we were too traumatized to speak and the world did not want to know.' A similar opinion was voiced by a survivor who came to the United States in 1952: 'often in the 1950s American Jews would avoid me as some sort of pariah. I am told that my experience was not unique.' Another participant in the debate claimed:

> the common assumption that Americans were uninterested or in active denial of the Holo-caust until the 1960s flies in the face of much evidence to the contrary. It wasn't only Anne Frank who was popular in the 1950s; it was also [films such as] Hersey's *The Wall* and Uris' *Exodus*. Although called the Jewish catastrophe or extermination and not the Holocaust yet, there were many works dealing with Nazism that appeared in this period that devoted significant attention to the 'Final Solution'.

He also believes:

> [that] these [early] ways of interpreting the Holocaust may not accord with our contem-porary understandings of the event. Nevertheless, they were far more pervasive than Holocaust scholars have hitherto acknowledged. And they indicate that we shouldn't make the Eichmann Trial or the '67 War as the catalysts that shocked Americans out of their denial, but rather as events that heightened a developing interest in the Holocaust.

Commenting on this view, another 'H-Holocaust' listserv member said: 'the consciousness raising impacts of the Eichmann trial, the '67 war, and, last but not least, the late 1970s TV mini series *The Holocaust* are overly depreciated'. Someone else admitted:

> after returning from the Pacific area of the war in the latter part of 1945, I and
> many others first became acutely aware of what became known later as the Holocaust
> when reports and photographs of the events were published in the everyday press ... I am
> not Jewish. My wife is of Jewish descent, but she is of such a nature that she never has
> wanted to dwell on the catastrophe (=Shoah), or any other large catastrophe. It gives
> her more pain than she wants to bear.

Also, there were voices on the issue of the number of Holocaust-related publications in
America during the first fifteen years after the catastrophe: 'If one looks at memoir publication, for example, there were a great many published in the first 2–3 years following liberation. The numbers then drop down for three decades. It is not until the late 70s/early 80s
that one finds the number of published survivor memoirs matching the first few years following the end of the war.'
    Referring to early historical works on the Holocaust, a list member argued:

> Reitlinger's *The Final Solution* and Poliakov's *Harvest of Hate* were reviewed in schol-
> arly journals. *International Affairs*, the *American Journal of Sociology*, the *Annals of the
> American Academy of Political Science*, the *Journal of Central European Affairs*, and *So-
> ciology and Social Research* reviewed one or both of the books. *Commentary*, reviewed
> both in 1955 along with Whitney Harris's *Tyranny on Trial* and Lord Russell's *The
> Scourge of the Swastika*.

Rubenstein maintains, however, that 'obviously, books about the Holocaust were published
in the late forties and the fifties, but the fundamental question is the degree to which they
had any real impact in the Jewish or larger community. This writer can testify that they had
little.'

59. Novick, *Holocaust and Collective Memory*, p.120. Peter Novick quotes some acclaimed
    authorities in Holocaust and Jewish studies who critically assessed the *Diary* itself. Israel
    Gutman, for instance, wrote: 'Anne Frank is unlike many of the Jewish young people in the
    communities of Eastern Europe. The Dutch girl is not an organic part of Jewish national life
    and a Jewish atmosphere.' Ibid., p.119; the quote is from Israel Gutman, 'Remarks on the
    Literature of the Holocaust', *In the Dispersion*, 5–6 (Spring 1966), p.123.
60. Novick, *Holocaust and Collective Memory*, p.120.
61. 'Scientific Research in Anti-Semitism: Paper Delivered by John Slawson Executive Vice-President
    [of AJCommittee], at NCRAC [National Community Relations Advisory Council], September
    11, 1944', in AJCommittee Papers GS 10, Box 9, Anti-Semitism, 1938–60, Speeches 7, 9, 13,
    14, quoted in Novick, *Holocaust and Collective Memory*, pp.121f. Another telling fact is one
    concerning the proposal to build a Holocaust memorial in New York City. The project had
    gained the support of some prominent Jews as well as Gentiles, but still a formal endorsement
    of and financial aid from the leading Jewish organizations was needed. 'On three separate
    occasions – in 1946, 1947, and 1948 – the representatives of the NCRAC organizations,
    including the American Jewish Committee, Anti-Defamation League, and Jewish War Veterans,
    unanimously rejected the idea – and effectively vetoed the initiative'. Ibid., p.123.
62. Arthur Hertzberg wrote in an open letter to Elie Wiesel: 'In the late 1950s ... very few in
    America were much interested in either the Holocaust or Zionist ideology'. A. Hertzberg,
    Jewish Polemics (New York: Columbia University Press, 1992), p.52.
63. D.G. Myers, *Annotated Bibliography of Holocaust Writing in American-Jewish Magazines,
    1945–1952* (1999) (accessed 24 November 2003), <http://www-english.tamu.edu/pers/fac/
    myers/annotated_bib.html>. The list includes articles published in *The Jewish Spectator*,
    Commentary, *Jewish Social Studies*, *The Chicago Jewish Forum*, *The Menorah Jewish Journal*,
    and *The Reconstructionist*.
64. See Flanzbaum, *Americanization of the Holocaust*, p.1.
65. Lederhendler, *New York Jews*, p.37. The Yiddish milieus were indeed more interested in what
    was happening in Europe. Peter Novick has claimed:

> [the] Yiddish-language press had much greater coverage of the events of the Holocaust
> than the Anglo-Jewish press. It was in immigrant centers like the Lower East Side of

Manhattan and the Williamsburg section of Brooklyn that wartime memorial activity was concentrated. There is some truth to the assertion that defining oneself more as an American and less as a Jew served to diminish one's reaction to the Holocaust.

There is, however, a serious 'difficulty with explanations of the thin contemporary American Jewish response to the Holocaust which emphasize excessive Americanization and its corollary, decreased Jewish identity. The difficulty is that the same marginalization of the Holocaust in consciousness took place in the Yishuv – the Jewish community of Palestine'. Novick, *Holocaust and Collective Memory*, p.35; see B. Lang, 'Translating the Holocaust: For Whom Does One Write?', *Judaism*, 48 (Summer 1999), p.341.

66. James E. Young, 'America's Holocaust: Memory and the Politics of Identity', in Flanzbaum, *Americanization of the Holocaust*, p.69.
67. See ibid., p.70.
68. Ibid.
69. It only means that the original plans O'Dwyer had made were never realized. It does not mean, however, that there is no Holocaust memorial in New York City. In Tribecca, not far from where the WTC towers once stood, is situated the Museum of Jewish Heritage which is in part dedicated to the history of the Holocaust, but it is popularly called the New York Holocaust Museum.
70. W.B. Helmreich, 'The Impact of Holocaust Survivors on American Society: A Socio-Cultural Portrait', *Judaism*, 39 (Winter 1990), p.23.
71. 'The avoidance of Jewish theological discussion of the Holocaust reflected widespread dissatisfaction with the traditional explanation of Jewish catastrophe as a wake-up call from God occasioned by a Jewish sin.' Novick, *Holocaust and Collective Memory*, p.108.
72. Ibid., p.104.
73. Neusner, *American Judaism*, p.3.
74. Ibid., p.17.
75. See Novick, *Holocaust and Collective Memory*, pp.134–55, and R. Alter, 'Deformations of the Holocaust', *Commentary*, 71 (February 1981), p.48. Samuel Freedman, too, has noticed the importance of the two phases, though he does not mention the 1973 war in the context of rising Holocaust consciousness. See Freedman, *Jew vs Jew*, p.281.
76. Howard Sachar dedicated one chapter to this issue ('Ethnicity at the Apogee') in his *History of the Jews in America*, pp.852–62.
77. A.J. Wolf, 'The State of Jewish Belief: A Symposium', *Commentary*, 42 (August 1966), p.157.
78. Hannah Arendt said that 'for hundreds of years, [Jews] had been used to understanding their own history, rightly or wrongly, as a long story of suffering'. Arendt, *Eichmann in Jerusalem: A Report on the Banality of Evil*, revised and enlarged edition (New York: Penguin Books, 1994), p.153.
79. Y.H. Yerushalami, *Zakhor: Jewish History and Jewish Memory* (Seattle, WA, and London: University of Washington Press, 1996), Foreword by Harold Bloom, p.xiv.
80. Lederhendler, *New York Jews*, p.xvii.
81. Ibid., p.142.
82. Ibid. The shift can clearly be seen in Arendt – in the different perspectives of her two major books, *The Origins of Totalitarianism* (1951) and *Eichmann in Jerusalem* (1963). One is focused on the universal problems that totalitarianism engenders, the other on problems specific to the extermination of a particular group, European Jews. Nevertheless, Lederhendler's remark that with Hilberg and Arendt the public discourse's attention moved from the perpetrators to the victims is debatable. Both authors, however, have long been criticized – and, to some extent, rightly so – for concentrating on the murderers and not on the sufferers.
83. I do not argue that the extermination of European Jews was not touched upon by the general public in the 1940s and 1950s; it was talked about, if rarely, as a *humanitarian* catastrophe, a political issue, whereas from the 1960s on it became *the holocaust* (and later *the Holocaust*), a *Jewish* catastrophe. In short, for the first twenty years after the war, 'the Holocaust was subsumed under the "problem of evil" and did not possess any separate ontological category. From the extermination of European Jewry it was transformed into "the Holocaust" '. See Jacob Neusner, *Stranger at Home: 'The Holocaust', Zionism, and American Judaism* (Chicago, IL, and London: University of Chicago Press, 1985), pp.6, 78.
84. In the 1961 symposium titled 'My Jewish Affirmation', published by *Judaism*, twenty-one authors participated. The five questions which were to be answered by the participants dealt

with Jewish tradition, adaptation to modernity, usefulness of Jewish outlooks, Israel, and experience of a Jewish home. None of the authors used the term 'Holocaust', which is not at all surprising, for the word was still virtually never used in the context of the Second World War. On the other hand, meaningful words that could be associated with *Churban Europa* appeared only occasionally: Hitlerism (four times), Auschwitz (once), Bergen-Belsen (once), *kiddush hashem*, or sanctification of God's name by death (once), god-killing (once). Most authors were speaking of Jewish civilization, God-choosing, Heilsgeschichte, Yishuv, Bris Mileh (circumcision), Hassidism, folk and halakha, whereas the most frequently used words were: Judaism, God, Israel, Torah, religion. 'My Jewish Affirmation: A Symposium', *Judaism*, 10 (Fall 1961). That same year, the *Commentary* magazine published a symposium on 'Jewishness and the Younger Intellectuals'. Similarly to the *Judaism* symposium, none of the questions was related to the Holocaust; they concerned the following problems: (1) the change of the situation of American Jews within the last fifteen years; (2) Jewish intellectuals and what they think of socialism and Jewishness; (3) Jewish culture vis-à-vis American culture at large; (4) Jewish tradition as a source of values; (5) the possibility of conversion of one's children; (6) the State of Israel. 'Jewishness and the Younger Intellectuals: A Symposium', *Commentary*, 31 (April 1961). Therefore, it may be assumed that at that time the Holocaust had not yet visibly affected Jewish theological discourse in America.

85. Lederhendler, *New York Jews*, p.205.
86. Ibid., pp.195f. Novick asserts, agreeing with Deborah Lipstadt's opinion, that 'Kahane's repeated invocation of the Holocaust gave rise to a fear among many Jewish institutions that he seemed to appropriate the catastrophe for his organization's and his own political ends.' That is why, Novick claims, Jewish leadership 'began to talk more about the Holocaust'. *Holocaust and Collective memory*, p.174.
87. See Neusner, *Stranger at Home*, p.63.
88. Jacob Neusner believes that 'to American Jews, "never again" – referring to the slaughter of nearly six million European Jews – means that the State of Israel must not be permitted to perish'. Neusner, *American Judaism*, p.88.
89. It is usually assumed that the creation of the State of Israel was in large measure the result of the feeling of guilt and remorse of the Western world for their failure, or unwillingness, to avert the extermination of European Jews. The facts, however, as Novick maintains, contradict this claim. There is no indication that the countries that endorsed the November 1947 partition resolution of the United Nations were motivated by an alleged remorse for their complicity in the Shoah. Certainly it cannot be said that the Soviet Union and many Latin American countries wished the establishment of Israel out of a feeling of guilt. On the other hand:

     the Allied nation against which charges of guilty complicity have most often been brought, Great Britain, which had closed down immigration to Palestine before the war, did not support partition ... [Also,] there is no evidence that guilt for inaction during the Holocaust played any role in the American government's (halting and ambivalent) support of Israeli statehood. Insofar as there was any group in the American polity against which charges of complicity could be laid, it was the State Department and the Pentagon, which consistently opposed partition ... [American] Protestant churches were divided over the creation of a Jewish state. The Catholic Church – at least the Catholic press – was, on the whole, cool toward the idea.

     Novick, *The Holocaust and Collective Memory*, pp.71f. See L. Fein, *Where Are We? The Inner Life of American Jews* (New York: Harper & Row, 1988), p.74. Certainly the Christian attitude toward Israel remained practically unchanged even after the 1967 assault of Arab countries on the Jewish state. See Sachar, *History of the Jews in America*, p.844.
90. See ibid., p.845.
91. Of the relation between Israel and the Holocaust, Eugene Borowitz has written that 'one cannot understand the State of Israel today or the relations of world Jewry to it, unless one realizes the elemental nature of the decisions after Auschwitz: there will be no more Holocausts; the Jewish people must live!' E.B. Borowitz, 'Jewish Theology Faces the 1970s', *Annals of the American Academy of Political and Social Science*, 387 (January 1970), pp.24–6, quoted in Neusner, *American Judaism*, p.137.

92. Neusner, *Stranger at Home*, p.1. It is important to know that for Neusner, myth is not to be understood in the sense of illusion, but in terms of 'a story lending meaning and imparting sanctity to ordinary, every-day actions'. Ibid., p.66. With time, Israel has become one of the most important elements shaping American Jewish identity. As Norman Finkelstein has noted, the well-known editor of *Commentary*, Norman Podhoretz, recalled 'that after June 1967 Israel became "the religion of American Jews" ... Coverage of Israel in *The New York Times* increased dramatically after June 1967. The 1955 and 1965 entries for Israel in *The New York Times Index* each filled 60 column inches. The entry for Israel in 1975 ran to 260 column inches.' N.G. Finkelstein, *The Holocaust Industry: Reflections on the Exploitation of Jewish Suffering* (London and New York: Verso, 2001), pp.21f.
93. In the era of the Six Day War and the Yom Kippur War, the Israeli government and media were using a characteristic rhetoric, in which the word 'Shoah' had a privileged status. At that time the term 'Holocaust' came to be commonly used on the American continent, all the more because in the new, secular consciousness of American Jews, both the Shoah and Israel started to be seen as two pillars of faith. See David Singer, 'From Judaism to Jewishness', *Commentary*, 90 (July 1990), p.53; D. Lapin, 'What Do American Jews Believe? A Symposium', *Commentary*, 102 (August 1996), p.63; R.L. Rubenstein, *After Auschwitz: History, Theology, And Contemporary Judaism*, 2nd edition (Baltimore, MD: Johns Hopkins University Press, 1992), p.xii.
94. Neusner, *Stranger at Home*, p.87.
95. In his book, Novick analyses the problem at length and gives numerous examples of polemical enunciations of both sides:

> A victim identity was reassuringly comfortable to all sorts of Jews who found it disturbing that Jews were no longer seen as victims or underdogs; that ... through 'some sociological sleight-of-hand ... Jews have become part of the "white majority" '. [Benjamin R. Epstein, 'American Jewry in the 1970s: Security, Problems, and Strategies', in National Jewish Community Relations Advisory Council, *Papers from the 1974 Plenary Sessions*, NJCRAC Papers, Box 12, Plenary Sessions, 1974, p.7.] ... An editorial in *Tikkun* insisted that Jews weren't really white: 'In current discourse, who gets labeled "white" and who gets labeled "person of color" derives not from the color of one's skin ... but from the degree to which one has been a victim of Western colonialist oppression. By that measure, Jews have been the greatest victims of Western societies throughout the past two thousand years and must certainly be understood to be one of the "peoples of color".' ['Farrakhan's Jewish Problem', *Tikkun*, 9 (March–April 1994), p.10.] Whatever other function they serve, the yellow stars Jewish students proudly wear on Yom HaShoah are their passport to the ranks of the oppressed.

Novick, *Holocaust and Collective Memory*, p.191.

> The most often publicized conflicts in [the] realm [of victimhood] were between Jews and blacks. Those that attracted the greatest attention featured Louis Farrakhan and his merry band. 'Don't push your six million down our throats', Farrakhan said, 'when we lost 100 million.' [Penelope McMillan and Cathleen Decker, 'Israel a "Wicked Hypocrisy" – Farrakhan', *Los Angeles Times*, 15 September 1985.] 'The black Holocaust', said his aide Khalid Abdul Muhammad, 'was a hundred times worse than the so-called Jew Holocaust.' [S. Fields, 'To the Defenders of Free Speech', *Washington Times*, 2 May 1994.]

Ibid., pp.193f.

96. Lazerewitz et al., *Jewish Choices*, p.138; the authors quote M. Sklare, *Conservative Judaism: An American Movement* (New York: Schocken, 1972), p.215.
97. Neusner, *Stranger at Home*, p.62.
98. D.E. Lipstadt, 'Invoking the Holocaust', *Judaism*, 30 (Summer 1981), pp.336f.
99. Freedman, *Jew vs Jew*, p.344.
100. Novick, *Holocaust and Collective Memory*, p.190. Michael Meyer holds a similar opinion on this issue:

> Few American Jews were survivors in the literal sense. But the notion that every Jew living in the post-Holocaust age was a kind of survivor gained more and more acceptance.

> Whereas before, American Jewish identity had for most Jews been either a religiously based morality or a loose bond of ethnic solidarity, the rise in awareness of the Holocaust produced in many individuals a much more determined Jewishness.

Michael A. Meyer, 'Anti-Semitism and Jewish Identity', *Commentary*, 88 (November 1989), p.40.

In a controversial article, Zygmunt Bauman introduced the notion of *hereditary victimhood* and *aristocracy of victimhood*:

> There is something else, though, to the status of a 'victim by proxy' – one of belonging to a *sui generis* 'aristocracy of victimhood' (that is, having a *hereditary* claim to sympathy and to the ethical indulgence owed to those who suffer). That status can be, and often is, brandished as a signed-in-advance and *in blanco* certificate of moral righteousness ...

Z. Bauman, 'Hereditary Victimhood: The Holocaust's Life as a Ghost', *Tikkun*, 13 (July–August 1998), pp.35f.

101. Alvin H. Rosenfeld, 'The Americanization of the Holocaust', *Commentary*, 99 (June 1995), p.37.
102. Novick, *Holocaust and Collective Memory*, p.190.
103. D. Klinghoffer, 'What Do American Jews Believe? A Symposium', *Commentary*, 102 (August 1996), p.56.
104. Ibid.
105. Novick, *Holocaust and Collective Memory*, p.190. He also affirms that for many secular Jews the awareness of being vulnerable to persecution is at the core of their Jewish identity; see ibid., p.191.
106. If Christian anti-Semitism (or Christianity *tout court*) was viewed by some as a negative phenomenon that could, paradoxically, serve to motivate Jews to retain or renew their Jewish identity, others questioned the very idea of building Jewish identity in opposition to other groups. Michael Medved, for example, affirmed:

> the chief distinguishing characteristic of most American Jews is not what they do believe, but what they do not believe. They do not believe in Jesus as the messiah. Period. End of sentence, end of story ... Since nonacceptance of Jesus is the one common commitment that seems to unify our community, then Jews for Jesus – in contrast to Jews for Buddha or Jews for Krishna or the vastly more popular Jews for Nothing – seem to represent a unique threat to that community's core beliefs ... Of course, any group that attempts to define itself by what it rejects rather than what it affirms can enjoy only the shakiest, most uncertain existence. Seven-Up might attempt to market itself as 'Un-Cola,' but Judaism will never survive as 'Un Christianity.

Michael Medved, 'What Do American Jews Believe? A Symposium', *Commentary*, 102 (August 1996), pp.70f.

107. J. Wertheimer, 'What Do American Jews Believe? A Symposium', *Commentary*, 102 (August 1996), p.92. Compare Elliot Dorff: 'The greatest challenges arise, ironically, from the degree to which Jews have been accepted in America, to the point of intermarriage, and from the Jewish emphasis on education which has led Jews to postpone marriage, often until it is too late to have children.' Elliot N. Dorff, 'What Do American Jews Believe? A Symposium', *Commentary*, 102 (August 1996), p.30.
108. Neusner, *Stranger at Home*, p.70. Again in caustic language, Bauman, concurring with Neusner, says:

> Contrary to what they say, and think they wish, children *manqués* – the 'flawed children' – are unfit to live, and feel out of place in a world free of that possibility [of another holocaust]. They would feel more comfortable living in a world more like that other world, populated by the Jew-hating murderers who would not stop short of including them among its victims ... The flawed children of the martyrs do not live in homes; they live in fortresses.

Bauman, 'Hereditary Victimhood', p.37.
109. Glazer, *American Judaism*, p.88.

110. Novick, *Holocaust and Collective Memory*, pp.113, 175. Lipset and Raab, too, show that toward the last quarter of the twentieth century, American anti-Semitism was in decline: while in 1938 and 1939, 42 to 49 per cent of Americans held the opinion that Jews were less honest than other citizens, in a similar public opinion survey conducted in 1964, only 28 per cent kept that opinion; in 1981 and 1992 the figures were 17 and 16 per cent respectively. Also, in a 1937 survey, 46 per cent of Americans said they would vote for a Jewish presidential candidate, while in 1983 the number grew to 90 per cent. See Lipset and Raab, *Jews and the New American Scene*, pp.77f.

111. Freedman, *Jew vs Jew*, p.344.

112. Lederhendler, *New York Jews*, p.113.

113. Heilman, *Jewish Unity and Diversity*, p.37. On the other hand, among Reconstructionist rabbis polled, 100 per cent disagreed with that statement. Yet Reconstructionism constitutes only 1 per cent of American affiliated Jews. As Hannah Arendt has observed, the myth of 'eternal anti-Semitism' has become widespread among Gentile and Jewish scholars alike (not to mention 'ordinary' people). The problem with the myth, as she insists, is that it does not serve as a conclusive explanation of any event, for the very concept of eternal anti-Semitism requires critical analysis. See Arendt, *Origins of Totalitarianism*, pp.7f. As Zygmunt Bauman has noted, one of the greatest paradoxes of history is that while the Nazis 'did not manage to turn the world against the Jews', their posthumous victory may be that 'they can still dream of turning the Jews against the world'. Bauman, 'Hereditary Victimhood', p.37; see also Zygmunt Bauman, *Modernity and the Holocaust* (Ithaca, NY: Cornell University Press, 2000), p.33.

114. The Reform movement, however, in a document issued by its Central Conference of American Rabbis (CCAR), 'declare[d] that the child of *one* Jewish parent is under the presumption of Jewish descent. This presumption of the Jewish status of the offspring of *any* mixed marriage is to be established through appropriate and timely public and formal acts of identification with the Jewish faith and people.' (Italics added.) A similar stance, too, was accepted by the Reconstructionists. See Richard A. Hirsh, 'Jewish Identity and Patrilineal: Some Second Thoughts', *The Reconstructionist*, 49 (March 1984), pp.25f.

115. See J. Yaffe, *The American Jews: Portrait of a Split Personality* (New York: Random House, 1968), p.81.

116. See Glazer, *American Judaism*, pp.3–5. Glazer says he uses 'the word nation to refer to a group of people who feel they have a common identity and a common cultural heritage, who may feel they are of common descent, who may speak a common language, who may inhabit a contiguous stretch of territory, and who may on occasion form a nation-state'. He employs the terms nation, nationality, national group, people and race interchangeably. The very notion of 'ethnicity' has also been questioned in regard to American Jewry – Lipset and Raab claim that the term has become too much blurred and politically loaded (used by various racial groups in their struggle for political privileges). Therefore, the authors suggest employing the term 'tribalism' instead of 'ethnicity'; the purpose of so doing is 'to deromanticize the pervasive term "ethnic" '. They also contend that the word 'tribal' 'just describes the more cohesive rather than the nostalgic edge of ethnicity'. They are, however, aware that it is a highly controversial notion, for 'the use [of the term] often shocks and draws resistance just because it so starkly signifies group solidarity and particularism'. Lipset and Raab, *Jews and the New American Scene*, pp.49–51. And it is exactly because of the term's controversial potential that it will not be employed in the present study.

117. Lipset and Raab, *Jews and the New American Scene*, p.49. See also Robert Goldenberg, 'Is There an "Essence of Judaism" After All?', *Judaism*, 38 (Winter 1989), p.27.

118. Fein, *Where Are We?*, p.62.

119. 'Judaism is, in large measure, a historical creation of the way Jews have lived; while the way Jews have lived, and the way they live today, is, in large measure, a creation of Judaism. It is impossible to divide the two.' Glazer, *American Judaism*, pp.6f; see H. Putnam, 'Judaism and Jewish Identity', in D.T. Goldberg and M. Krausz (eds.), *Jewish Identity* (Philadelphia, PA: Temple University Press, 1993), p.109.

120. Glazer, *American Judaism*, p.69.

121. There is, however, yet another understanding of 'Jewishness', one proposed by Michael Krausz. Being a follower of social constructivism (and determinism), his major premise is

that 'there is no essence of the Jewish people as such ... Thus, the questions, What is a Jew? or What is Jewishness? are misconceived if they are understood essentialistically and should be recast.' Krausz opts for a descriptive and evolutionary comprehension of Jewishness. Thus, to him Jewishness is '*a set of characteristic positions in which certain people are cast or ascribed – by themselves and by others*' (italics in the original). Finally, he distinguishes between 'Jewishness-by-descent' (that is, by birth) and 'Jewishness-by-assent' (that is, by self-identification). Krausz, 'On Being Jewish', in Goldberg and Krausz (eds), *Jewish Identity*, p.266.

122. Before the war, many leftist Jewish intellectuals in America maintained that Jewish identity has to do in the first place with social issues. Sydney Hook, for instance, believed that 'the essence of [American Jewish] identity lies not in language, custom, literature, religion, history, or nationality, but in the affinity of American Jewish culture for democratic, secular, and egalitarian "values" '. Shapiro, *Time for Healing*, p.289. That is perhaps why East European Jews regarded America to be 'un-kosher' (*trefa* land). See ibid., p.291.

123. Berger claims that 'by and large, religious communities have survived and even flourished to the degree that they have *not* tried to adapt themselves to the alleged requirements of a secularized world ... Experiments with secularized religion have generally failed; religious movements with beliefs and practices dripping with reactionary supernaturalism ... have widely succeeded.' (Italics in the original.) Berger, 'Desecularization of the World', p.4. This is evidently not true with regard to American Jews. Secular religion of American Jewry was in no way an experiment. It has been, and still is, a spontaneous development of their way of life. As for the decline in the belief in God, what American Jews have undergone is similar to the experience of Jews in most European countries. According to a 1990 survey, the percentage of Europeans who believe in God is relatively low: France – 57 per cent; Italy – 83 per cent; Ireland – 96 per cent (Northern Ireland – 95 per cent); Great Britain – 71 per cent; West Germany – 63 per cent; Denmark – 64 per cent; Sweden – 15 per cent: the (West) European average being 70 per cent. Yet, contrary to the religious pattern of Europe, which is 'believing without belonging', the Jewish pattern in America is 'belonging without believing'. See Grace Davie, 'Europe: The Exception That Proves the Rule?', in Berger, 'Desecularization of the World', pp.68–71.

124. C.S. Liebman, *Aspects of the Religious Behaviour of American Jews* (New York: Ktav Publishing House, 1974), pp.189f.

125. Kaplan, 'The God Idea in Judaism', p.88. His vision of Judaism was much too traditional for the Reform and those he called Secular-Culturalists. The Orthodox, however, condemned him as a heretic:

> In June [of 1945], as New York City prepared a gigantic homecoming parade for General Dwight Eisenhower to celebrate the Allies' defeat of Hitler's Germany, the Union of Orthodox Rabbis of the US and Canada unanimously voted to ban the newly published Reconstructionist *Sabbath Prayer Book*. After the vote, a young rabbi stood up and ceremoniously burned the book. The burning, eerily reminiscent of the Nazi book-burnings that preceded Hitler's rise to power, climaxed a reading that proclaimed *herem* (excommunication) against Rabbi Mordechai M. Kaplan for expressing 'atheism, heresy, and disbelief in the basic tenets of Judaism' in the prayer book introduction and for altering traditional prayer texts to implement those 'heresies'. Kaplan's assertions that 'the Jews are not a chosen race ... [and] that the Torah is a human document and not supernaturally inspired' were the principal reasons for the Union members' unanimous action.

G.B. Driesen, 'Revisiting the Chosen People', *The Reconstructionist*, 60 (Fall 1995), p.78.

126. Kaplan, 'The God Idea in Judaism', p.91.

127. See William H. Frelick, 'Mordecai Kaplan's Idea of God', *The Reconstructionist*, 46 (November 1980), p.7; Richard A. Hirsh, 'The Nuances of Chosenness: A Reconstructionist Approach', *The Reconstructionist*, 50 (September 1984), p.8.

128. See Liebman, *Aspects of the Religious Behaviour*, p.199.

129. Mordecai M. Kaplan, 'The State of Jewish Belief: A Symposium', *Commentary*, 42 (August 1966), p.108.

130. See Hirsh, 'Nuances of Chosenness', p.8.

131. Kaplan, *Judaism as a Civilization*, p.181.
132. Jacob Neusner, for example, asks:

> Which, then: ethnic group or religious minority? If the former, why? If the latter, how? Individuals in the ethnic group are bound to raise religious questions, and if the answers do not come from Judaism, they will come from somewhere else – and this the ethnic group cannot endure ... This disintegration of the archaic religious and ethnic unity of the 'holy people' seems to me the most important Jewish testimony about what it means to be modern.

Neusner, *Stranger at Home*, p.48.
133. Liebman, *Aspects of the Religious Behaviour*, p.282.
134. Kaplan, *Judaism as a Civilization*, p.178.
135. In a national survey on Jewish beliefs, conducted in 1969, most Reform, Conservative and Reconstructionist rabbis disagreed strongly, or somewhat, that Judaism is rather a religion than a culture or civilization (that is, they consider Judaism mostly a culture and civilization). Also, lay synagogue presidents of all Jewish denominations said they disagreed to some extent with this view. See Liebman, *Aspects of the Religious Behaviour*, p.262. By way of conclusion, Liebman contends:

> in most instances ... laymen (except for the Orthodox) were in greater agreement with Reconstructionist rabbis than with the rabbis of their own denominations. Reconstructionist rabbis, in turn, are indeed Reconstructionist in their acceptance of the major outlines of Kaplan's position. The question then arises why, if most Jews adopt positions congruent with Reconstructionism, they neither affiliate with the movement nor identify themselves with the movement.

Ibid., p.269. In search of answers to this question, Liebman finally proposes an interesting theory claiming that American Judaism functions on two levels: one is *folk religion*, the other *elite religion*:

> Folk religion can be thought of as the *popular* religious culture. The elite religion is the ritual, belief, and doctrine which the acknowledged religious leaders teach to be religion ... For many people folk religion permits a more intimate religious expression and experience. It may in fact integrate them into organizational channels of the elite religion. Folk religion is not necessarily more primitive than elite religion ... its very lack of interest in ideological or doctrinal consistency makes it more flexible than elite religion ... The absence of an articulated position in folk religion ... does not mean that intellectuals will necessarily find it less attractive than elite religion ... The folk religion cut across Conservative, Reform, and many nonreligious organizational lines.

Ibid., pp.276–9 (italics in the original). This brief sociological sketch makes it quite clear that Reconstructionism is just an organized, intellectually elaborated form of folk religion; indeed, it is a unique sociological phenomenon: folk religion formulated in elitist terms. And herein lies the answer to Liebman's question: 'the very nature of folk religion makes it unsuitable for elitist formulation. In an elitist formulation folk religion is often unrecognizable for the folk.' Ibid., pp.279f. There is yet another possible solution to Liebman's problem of why so few people identify themselves as Reconstructionists if most of them hold Reconstructionist views. It is that Reconstructionism

> may be a religion by a sociologist's standards, but it is not quite a religion by American standards of what religion ought to be. After all, it denies belief in a supernatural God. The fact that most American Jews do so, too, is immaterial. For most Jews their denial is a personal attitude; but affiliation with a synagogue which accepts their own theology will cause them embarrassment. Synagogue affiliation is more than a private act. It is public identification with a major American religion, and the *American* thing to do. [Italics in the original.]

Ibid., p.281.

136. 'The Emergence of Jewish Cultural Identity', *Jewish Culture News*, Spring 2003 (accessed 2 July 2003) (pdf document), <www.jewishculture.org.jcn>.
137. Neusner, *American Judaism*, p.94.
138. See ibid., p.95. Some even believe that the modern type of 'fluctuating' identity based on personal decisions rather than on religious authority is to be blamed for the allegedly progressing dissolution of Jewry in the contemporary world:

> Having thus acquired religious freedom, as well as material success and social status, the generality of Jews, of their own free choice, have, since the Emancipation, willfully behaved in a sinful or otherwise blameworthy manner that is destroying the Jewish collectivity. In brief, the generality of Jews is itself responsible for the *silent holocaust*. Among the noteworthy items in the establishment's bill of particulars against the generality of Jews are the following: Jews, in the main, do not attend the services of the establishment religious institutions.

> A.J. Reines, 'Ontology, Demography, and the Silent Holocaust', *Judaism*, 38 (Fall 1989), p.483 (italics added).

139. Sherry Israel wrote an extremely interesting passage on the issue of choosing identities:

> The title of Waters' book, *Ethnic Options*, should strike us as ironic. How can ethnicity be an *option*? Isn't it a *given*, like the year you were born? The short answer is, no. Using data from the 1980 US census question on ethnic ancestry and following up with extensive personal interviews, Waters found that today's Americans of white, European ancestry pick and choose their ethnic identities – taking on, giving up, combining. The operative principle is personal preference, not inheritance. Here is the flavor: Q. 'What about your husband's ancestry?' A. 'He would have answered Russian Jew and English and Scottish on the census form. He really likes his Russian Jew part. We have a *mezuzah* on the front door. He converted to Catholicism when he married me. He grew up with his mother, and she was Baptist, so he was kind of raised in that tradition. But he likes his Russian Jew part more, he feels closer to being Catholic, and that part goes together more. They are kind of similar.' ... It is identity without obligations. It functions in what I would call a decorative way. It gives *a sense of belonging to something besides the great mass American culture*, but in a way that does not violate the principle of individual choice.

> S. Israel, 'Ethnicity, Geography and Jewish Community', *The Reconstructionist*, 60 (Spring 1995), p.15 (italics added).

140. As Michael Krausz has observed, tradition is by definition exposed to change and constant reformulation, as was the case with the 'talmudic and midrashic tradition of perpetual interpretation and reinterpretation'. Krausz, 'On Being Jewish', in Goldberg and Krausz (eds), *Jewish Identity*, p.274.
141. Leon Goldstein says 'there may be a multiplicity of "whys" [why someone is Jewish] but there is only one Jewishness'. However, if we accept Krausz's concept of Jewishness-by-descent and Jewishness-by-assent, we can agree that there is only one Jewishness-by-descent, but not that there is only one Jewishness-by-assent (or by choice). See L.J. Goldstein, 'Thoughts on Jewish Identity', in Goldberg and Krausz (eds), *Jewish Identity*, p.86.
142. Berel Lang says we ought to ask, 'What *are* Jewish identity?' (Italics in the original). B. Lang, 'The Phenomenal-Noumenal Jew: Three Antinomies of Jewish Identity', in Goldberg and Krausz (eds), *Jewish Identity*, p.279.
143. Fein, *Where Are We?*, pp.62f.
144. Ibid., pp.63, 69.
145. Linenthal, *Preserving Memory*, p.11.
146. M. Berenbaum, *After Tragedy and Triumph: Essays in Modern Jewish Thought and the American Experience* (Cambridge: Cambridge University Press, 1990), p.4.
147. Novick claims:

> Jewish college students who had shown no interest in other academic courses with Jewish subject matter oversubscribed offerings on the Holocaust. Supply responded to demand, and the number of such courses rapidly multiplied throughout the seventies. According to one (possibly inflated) estimate, they were being offered at more than seven hundred

colleges by 1978 ... programs related to the Holocaust showed a capacity to pull in Jews with an otherwise marginal Jewish identity. These, of course, were precisely the people who were the object of 'survival anxiety'.

... In 1974 ... the body that coordinated the work of various Jewish organizations, the National Jewish Community Relations Advisory Council, asked member agencies to sponsor Holocaust Day observances around the country, promote teaching of the Holocaust in schools, and include the Holocaust as a priority item in Jewish–Christian dialogue.

Novick, *The Holocaust and Collective Memory*, pp.187f; 318, n.21. In the latter citation, Novick summarizes the view of J.J. Goldberg, *Jewish Power: Inside the American Jewish Establishment* (Reading, MA: 1996), p.191. Schoenfeld claims that 'if in 1981 there were 93 courses being offered on the subject in American and Canadian institutions of higher learning, ten years later that figure had nearly doubled, and has continued to grow throughout the 90s'. Gabriel Schoenfeld, 'Auschwitz and the Professors', *Commentary*, 105 (June 1998), p.42. It can be argued that whereas Novick overestimated the number of universities offering Holocaust courses in the latter half of the 1970s, Schoenfeld underrated that number. The information Berenbaum provides seems to be the most reliable. Thus, by a conservative estimate, in the early 1980s there were at least 200 university and college courses on the Shoah taught in the United States. And this was most probably due to the emerging salience of the Holocaust in the awareness of Americans after 1978.

148. See Linenthal, *Preserving Memory*, p.20.
149. The legal basis for the creation of the commission was the president's executive order 12093 issued on 1 November 1978. The commission's suggestion to create a Holocaust *museum* was formally accepted through executive order 12169 on 26 October 1979. See P.E. Soifer, 'Remembrance and the Victims' Covenant', *The Reconstructionist*, 46 (April 1980), p.19; Linenthal, *Preserving Memory*, p.23. The political background of this decision, as some authors claim, was the Carter administration's intent (known as early as 1977) to sell F-15 bombers to Egypt and Saudi Arabia. Also, Carter had spoken earlier in favour of the idea of a Palestinian homeland and allegedly wanted to show the American Jewish constituency that he was well disposed towards them, too. See ibid., pp.17f; Berenbaum, *After Tragedy and Triumph*, pp.5, 41. 'Early in Jimmy Carter's presidency, Stuart Eizenstat and several other Jewish aids had suggested the building of a Holocaust memorial on federal land, but the idea went nowhere until 1978, when there was trouble over the sale of F-15s to the Saudi Arabia.' E. Norden, 'Yes and No to the Holocaust Museums', *Commentary*, 96 (August 1993), p.26. A similar opinion is held by Young; see his 'America's Holocaust', pp.72f. According to Peter Novick, 'when the American Israel Public Affairs Committee (AIPAC) was lobbying against the sale of American aircraft to Saudi Arabia, it sent a copy of the novel based on the TV miniseries *Holocaust* to every member of Congress'. Novick, *Holocaust and Collective Memory*, p.156.
150. Public Papers of the President of the United States: Jimmy Carter, 1978, (Washington, DC, 1979), p.813, quoted in Novick, *Holocaust and Collective Memory*, p.216.
151. Of these four events, the clearest link can be noticed between the television mini-series *Holocaust* and the President's Commission: 'on the thirtieth anniversary of the creation of Israel on May 1, 1978, two weeks after *Holocaust* had been aired on national television, President Jimmy Carter announced the creation of a commission to recommend a national Holocaust memorial'. A. Mintz, *Popular Culture and the Shaping of Holocaust Memory in America* (Seattle, WA: University of Washington Press, 2001), p.26.
152. History reconstitutes itself in memory ... The tide of Americanization cannot easily be avoided ... For Jews to solidify the place of the Holocaust within Jewish consciousness, they must establish its importance for the American people as a whole. The process cannot be reversed for the decision has already been made. By sharing our experience with the world, we have transformed it and it, in turn, has changed us.

M. Berenbaum, 'The Nativization of the Holocaust', *Judaism*, 35 (Fall 1986), p.457.
153. See Neusner, *Stranger at Home*, p.89, and Alter, 'Deformations of the Holocaust', p.53. The article mentioned was published in the *National Review* on 3 August 1979. On this topic see also Mintz, *Popular Culture*, p.23.

154. To Elie Wiesel the film was 'misleading, complacent, dangerous'. What made it still more controversial was that it was interrupted several times by commercials advertising chemicals used for exterminating rats and insects (Wiesel is quoted in Flanzbaum, *Americanization of the Holocaust*, p.5).
155. In his own view, it was unfortunate that there was no 'commission created to memorialize the Armenian massacres of World War I (the first major act of genocide in this century) [and] the Nazi war against the Poles, Russians, South Slavs, Slovaks, and other people deemed by the racist *Wissenschaft* to be subhuman'. Neusner, *Stranger at Home*, p.85.
156. A.J. Wolf, 'The Shoah in America', *Judaism*, 48 (Fall 1999), p.494. Howard Husock argued that building the Holocaust Museum on Washington's Mall could be seen as asking 'for a guarantee of safety based [on] history of special victimization'. Even if this were to incite sympathy, he claims, such feelings do not bring about political order; instead, it might 'set a precedent of particularism'. H. Husock, 'Red, White, and Jew: Holocaust Museum on the Mall', *Tikkun*, 5 (July–August 1990), p.92.
157. P. Lopate, 'Resistance to the Holocaust', in 'Distance from the Holocaust: A Symposium', *Tikkun*, 4 (May–June 1989), pp.59f. It is also worthwhile considering that 'when plans for the US Holocaust Memorial Museum in Washington were being proposed, the objection was raised from Israel that the appropriate site for such commemoration was in Israel, not in Washington or, for that matter, any place in the United States (or anywhere other than in Israel)'. Lang, 'Translating the Holocaust', p.342.
158. Norden, 'Yes and No to the Holocaust Museums', p.26.
159. E. Jager, 'Take Back the Holocaust', *Midstream*, 44 (July–August 1998), p.27.
160. D.J. Silver, 'Choose Life', *Judaism*, 35 (Fall 1986), p.466.
161. R.P. Scheindlin, 'Museum of Death, Museum of Life', *Tikkun*, 8 (November–December 1993), p.86.
162. Neusner, *Stranger at Home*, p.85. See also Jean-Marc Dreyfus, 'Comment l'Amérique s'est identifiée à la Shoah', *Le Débat*, 130 (May–August 2004), pp.31–4.
163. Neusner, *Stranger at Home*, p.85.
164. Silver, 'Choose Life', p.460. Reviewing Novick's book for *Commentary*, David Roskies asks:

> Is there not something deeply troubling about an American Jewish community that has been spending exponentially more money erecting monuments to the dead than to educating its young, or about the proliferation of Holocaust courses that teach about the Jews only as a community marked for destruction, and then often in the context of a competition for victim status in today's multicultural America?

And the answer he gives is, yes. D.G. Roskies, 'Group Memory', *Commentary*, 108 (September 1999), p.64.

165. This term was coined by Maurice Halbwachs. Alan Rosenberg, however, proposes to replace it by 'social memory', or 'cultural memory', as more relevant to the contemporary situation. See A. Milchman and A. Rosenberg, 'Remembering and Forgetting: The Social Construction of a Community of Memory of the Holocaust', in A. Rosenberg, J.R. Watson and D. Linke (eds), *Contemporary Portrayals of Auschwitz: Philosophical Challenges* (Amherst, NY: Humanity Books, 2000), p.261.
166. See Lipstadt, 'Invoking the Holocaust', p.338. Robert Alter has called the Holocaust the 'new "civil religion" of American Jewry'. Alter, 'Deformations of the Holocaust', p.53. Jacob Neusner is even more explicit on this issue: 'What we have done is to make the murder of the Jews of Europe into one of the principal components of the civil religion of American Jews. That is the religion expressed on neutral, nonreligious occasions, to make sense of and celebrate our community, its distinctiveness, its program, its demands upon ourselves.' J. Neusner, 'Beyond Catastrophe, Before Redemption', *The Reconstructionist*, 46 (April 1980), pp.7f.
167. My answer to the question of whether there is a religious aspect in the way the Holocaust is being commemorated and ritualized is the same as I gave in discussing the 'secular religion' issue. If a social phenomenon bears with it a potential for group identity building, and it actualizes the potential, it is a religious phenomenon – in the specific sense of the word expounded above. A more difficult question, however, would be one regarding the difference

between twentieth-century American Judaism as a 'secular religion' and the Holocaust as a 'civil religion'. At this stage of my research, I find it hardly possible to provide credible, objective criteria for making such a differentiation. What I can say is that I intuitively distinguish between the two things on the basis of their origin. Thus, the etiology of secular American Judaism is revealed in the complex and long-lasting process of secularization of traditional Jewish faith (with its idea of a supernatural deity). As for the Holocaust's function as a civil (or civic) religion, it appeared on the *public* scene of American life as a cult of memory of American Jewish citizens, as a way of emphasizing their Jewishness by taking advantage of their American citizenship, their civic rights. Therefore, if some sort of Jewishness can be created through focusing on Jewish catastrophe, it gets transformed into a new collective identity (which implies creation of new values, too). Moreover, the centrality and the cult-like character of the Shoah within the American Jewish community was a specific addendum to the already existing all-American civil religion.

168. E.L. Fackenheim, *God's Presence in History: Jewish Affirmations and Philosophical Reflections* (New York: New York University Press, 1970), p.84.

169. Even among his admirers he has been taken to task for exaggerating the significance that the Holocaust poses for Jewish theology, for overemphasizing its historical uniqueness, or for seeming to ground all prospect of future Jewish salvation in the Holocaust itself. Thus in a 1971 review of *God's Presence in History*, Michael Wyschogrod contended in response to Fackenheim that 'If there is hope after the Holocaust, it is because, to those who believe, the voices of the Prophets speak more loudly than did Hitler, and because the divine promise sweeps over the crematoria and silences the voice of Auschwitz.'

Robert M. Seltzer, 'Judaism According to Emil Fackenheim', *Commentary*, 86 (September 1988), p.33. See also David Berger, 'What Do American Jews Believe? A Symposium', *Commentary*, 102 (August 1996), p.20.

170. 'Torah of our day is the story, effectively captured by the Israeli version of the same civil religion, of *Shoah u'gevurah*, Holocaust and heroism.' Neusner, 'Beyond Catastrophe, Before Redemption', p.8. See Berenbaum, 'Nativization of the Holocaust', p.449; Milchman and Rosenberg, 'Remembering and Forgetting', p.259.

171. See Singer, 'From Judaism to Jewishness', p.53.

172. See Lapin, 'What Do American Jews Believe? (August 1996), p.63, and Rubenstein, *After Auschwitz*, p.xii.

173. David Roskies interprets – somewhat ironically – Peter Novick's view in the following way:

American Jews who themselves have abandoned any but the most rudimentary religious practices, and are as fuzzy in their grasp of history as their fellow non-Jewish Americans, have created an entire surrogate religion around the Holocaust, complete with saints (survivors), scripture (*Schindler's List*), and shrines (those ubiquitous museums). A community more secure, and more affluent, than Jews have ever been in all of history has given itself over to an utterly irrational scenario of destruction and victimization, in disregard of political reality and to the detriment of its own best interests and values.

Roskies, 'Group Memory', p.63. See Novick, *Holocaust and Collective Memory*, pp.11, 199–201, 212, 225, 269, 274, 280.

174. Neusner, 'Beyond Catastrophe, Before Redemption', p.9.

175. Lopate, 'Resistance to the Holocaust', pp.63f.

176. According to Elliot Jager, 'Holocaust museums and memorials dot our landscape, schools use the Holocaust to teach tolerance, celebrated Hollywood directors make Holocaust movies for popular consumption ... At least eight states have adopted Holocaust curriculums.' Jager, 'Take Back the Holocaust', p.27.

177. Berenbaum, *After Tragedy and Triumph*, p.4. What Berenbaum admits with caution, Bauman puts bluntly and with overemphasis: 'the status of the "Holocaust children", that is of hereditary victim, is open to every Jew, whatever his or her parents might have been "doing in the war" (in fact, embracing this status has turned for many into their main vehicle of Jewish self-definition)'. Bauman, 'Hereditary Victimhood', p.36.

178. Y. Bauer, 'A Critique of Phillip Lopate: Don't Resist', in 'A Distance from the Holocaust: A Symposium', *Tikkun*, 4 (May–June 1989), p.65; see Alter, 'Deformations of the Holocaust',

p.53. Yet not all authors who commented on this subject shared the concern about the possible trivialization of the Holocaust if it were to become the civil religion of American Jews. Howard Husock, for instance, thought that what was, in fact, dangerous was that the elevation of Holocaust cult to the heights of the sacred sphere of the American nation would 'undermine a civil religion that has served American Jews so well that now we take it for granted'. Husock, 'Red, White, and Jew', p.32. It is worthwhile noting that, in his address to the participants of the national conference on 'Shoah Remembrance: Contemporary Portrayals', held in Łódź, Poland, on 12–14 May 2003, the Israeli ambassador Szewach Weiss asserted that 'the Holocaust is a religion. It has all the traits and symbols of religion. It is a world religion ... The Holocaust is a religion of morality. As an antithesis of fascism, it is a religion of tolerance ... What binds us, Israelis, and ours the world over, is the religion of the Holocaust. It is the only religion of the righteous.' Henryk Grynberg seems to be quite close to Weiss's opinion: 'The rabbis complain that the Holocaust has become the religion of the Jews. And this is in fact how things really are, for trauma is the religion of the Jews. It binds them together, confers an identity upon them.' H. Grynberg, *Monolog polsko-żydowski* [A Polish-Jewish Monologue] (Wołowiec: Wydawnictwo Czarne, 2003), p.70. Compare Elie Wiesel's enunciation: 'I may sound arrogant, but I believe that only the memory of what happened to our people can save the world now.' E. Wiesel, 'Some Questions That Remain Open', in A. Cohen et al. (eds), *Comprehending the Holocaust: Historical and Literary Research* (Frankfurt/Main: Verlag Peter Lang, 1988), p.18.

179. Lipstadt, 'Invoking the Holocaust', p.338.
180. Soifer, 'Remembrance and the Victims' Covenant', p.19.
181. R. Alter, 'Vistas of Annihilation', *Commentary*, 79 (January 1985), p.39. Speaking of memory and history, Charles S. Maier argued that there is what he called 'the memory industry, that is Holocaust commemoration'. C.S. Maier, 'A Surfeit of Memory? Reflections on History, Melancholy and Denial', *History and Memory: Studies in Representation of the Past*, 5 (Fall– Winter 1993), p.143.
182. See Alter, 'Deformations of the Holocaust', p.54; A. Roiphe, 'The Politics of Anger', *Tikkun*, 1 (1986), p.18; A.H. Rosenfeld, 'Letters', *Commentary*, 100 (September 1995), p.11. Gershon Mamlak wrote in a clearly provocative way: 'we dismembered the Holocaust to allow a *feast* over the ashes of the martyrs and over the memories of the survivors' (Italics in the original). G. Mamlak, 'The Holocaust: Commodity?', *Midstream*, 29 (April 1983), p.15. Arnold Wolf, writing about his own experience in teaching at Yale and about Anti-Defamation League activities in Connecticut, said: 'There is a clientele for Holocaust studies, which excludes other alternatives and which is producing, counterproductively, a sense that this is what we are in the business of doing ... It seems to me the Holocaust is being sold – it is not being taught.' Arnold Wolf, 'The Centrality of the Holocaust Is a Mistake', in Berenbaum, *After Tragedy and Triumph*, pp.44f.
183. Roiphe, 'The Politics of Anger', p.18.
184. Cited in Linenthal, *Preserving Memory*, p.13.
185. Alter, 'Deformations of the Holocaust', p.50.
186. However, Wiesel probably slightly modified his view on uniqueness after learning about the genocide of Indians in Paraguay. See E. Wiesel, 'Now We Know', in R. Arens (ed.), *Genocide in Paraguay* (Philadelphia, PA: Temple University Press, 1976), pp.165f, quoted in D.E. Stannard, 'Uniqueness as Denial: The Politics of Genocide Scholarship', in A.S. Rosenbaum (ed.), *Is the Holocaust Unique? Perspectives on Comparative Genocide* (Boulder, CO: Westview Press, 1996), p.197.
187. E.L. Fackenheim, *The Jewish Return into History: Reflections on the Age of Auschwitz and a New Jerusalem* (New York: Schocken Books, 1978), p.29. He continues on page 30: 'all comparisons are odious or irrelevant. This is what makes Jewish religious existence today unique, without support from analogies anywhere in the past.'
188. Ibid., p.29.
189. Lopate, 'Resistance to the Holocaust', p.61.
190. 'We are concerned with a small industry of Holocaust hagiographers arguing for the uniqueness of the Jewish experience with all the energy and ingenuity of theological zealots.' Stannard, 'Uniqueness as Denial', p.193.

191. Ibid., p.172.
192. Ibid., p.183. Quotations from Bauer excerpted from Yehuda Bauer, 'Is the Holocaust Explicable', in Y. Bauer et al. (eds), *Remembering for the Future: Working Papers and Addenda* (Oxford: Pergamon Press, 1989), vol. 2, p.1970, and Y. Bauer, *The Holocaust in Historical Perspective* (Seattle, WA: University of Washington Press, 1978), p.38.
193. S.T. Katz, 'The Uniqueness of the Holocaust: The Historical Dimension', in Rosenbaum (ed.), *Is the Holocaust Unique?*, p.19. This kind of reasoning is said to be typical of the Holocaust uniqueness advocates: 'They began with conclusions, peered through their facts, and came back in a circle to the same conclusions', which appears as 'advocacy masquerading as objectivity'. Stephen J. Gould, *The Mismeasure of Man* (New York: W.W. Norton, 1981), p.85, quoted in Stannard, 'Uniqueness as Denial', p.190.
194. Katz, 'Uniqueness of the Holocaust', p.36. Stannard strongly opposes this view.
195. Ibid., p.19. Stannard provides data questioning these claims. Among other things, he points out that out of some 2,000 distinctive indigenous peoples dwelling in the pre-Columbian Americas, only about 500 are officially recognized by the United States government as separate ethnic groups living within its boundaries. See Stannard, 'Uniqueness as Denial', pp.180f, 184f, 197. He also harshly criticizes the general concept of denying the status of genocide to other than Jewish tragedies: 'When advocates of the allegedly unique suffering of Jews during the Holocaust *themselves* participate in denial of *other* historical genocides – *and such denial is inextricably interwoven with the very claim of uniqueness* – they thereby actively participate in making it much easier for those other genocides to be repeated.' Ibid., p.197; see D.E. Stannard, 'The Dangers of Calling the Holocaust Unique', *Chronicle of Higher Education*, 2 August 1996, p.2B. According to Rubenstein, 'the Turkish massacre of about one million Armenians during World War I, [was] perhaps the first full-fledged attempt by a modern state to practice disciplined, methodically organized genocide'. Richard L. Rubenstein, *The Cunning of History: Mass Death and the American Future* (New York: Harper & Row, 1975), p.11.
196. Rubenstein, *Cunning of History*, p.3.
197. Richard L. Rubenstein, 'Religion and the Uniqueness of the Holocaust', in Rosenbaum (ed.), *Is the Holocaust Unique?*, p.12.
198. Ibid., p.13. Rubenstein shares this view with Yehuda Bauer, who claims that one of the two elements that make the Holocaust unique is 'the quasi-religious, apocalyptic ideology that motivated the murder' – the other element being that it was a 'planned total annihilation of a national or ethnic group'. Y. Bauer, 'Whose Holocaust?' *Midstream*, 26 (November 1980), p.45.
199. Rubenstein, *After Auschwitz*, p.161.
200. Ibid., p.13. In *The Cunning of History*, Rubenstein further elaborates on the role of Jews themselves in the developing process of extermination. See Rubenstein, *The Cunning of History*, pp.68, 72.
201. Novick, *Holocaust and Collective Memory*, p.9.
202. See Milchman and Rosenberg, 'Remembering and Forgetting', p.253.
203. Ibid., p.252.
204. Ibid., p.253.
205. Ibid., p.255.
206. Ibid., p.257.
207. See Maier, 'Surfeit of Memory?' p.145. As an example of denying due respect to the Holocaust, Maier refers to the so-called revisionist historians.
208. C.S. Maier, *The Unmasterable Past: History, Holocaust, and German National Identity* (Cambridge, MA: Harvard University Press, 1997), p.70.
209. Ibid., p.69.
210. Ibid., p.99.
211. Ibid., pp.83f.
212. A. Rosenberg, 'Crisis in Knowing and Understanding the Holocaust', in A. Rosenberg and G.E. Myers, (eds.), *Echoes from the Holocaust: Philosophical Reflections on a Dark Time* (Philadelphia, PA: Temple University Press: 1988), p.386.

213. D. Magurshak, 'The "Incomprehensibility" of the Holocaust: Tightening Up Some Loose Usage', *Judaism*, 29 (Spring 1980), p.233.
214. Ibid., p.235.
215. See ibid., p.236.
216. Ibid., pp.238–42.
217. Rosenberg argues that seeing the Shoah as merely unrepeatable or unusual 'is clearly a "trivialization" of the "uniqueness question" '. It is difficult to imagine, however, how the Holocaust can be put in the context of other historical events, as Rosenberg does, without first being described as an event that in fact *can* be placed inside history. Therefore, from the methodological viewpoint, the statement that in a trivial sense the Holocaust is both unique and normal' is a legitimate one. To be sure, analysing the different approaches to the issue of uniqueness and universality of the Shoah, Rosenberg proposes an interesting trichotomic scheme: he distinguishes between the trivialists, the absolutists and the contextualists. Of course, he sees himself as belonging to the middle-of-the-road group – that is, the contextualists. This is justified, for he accepts (if only implicitly) some of the trivialists' tenets, without at the same time rejecting all implications of the absolutists' reasoning. See A. Rosenberg, 'Was the Holocaust Unique? A Peculiar Question', in I. Walliman and M.N. Dobkowski (eds), *Genocide and the Modern Age: Etiology and Case Studies of Mass Death* (Westport, CT: Greenwood Press, 1987), pp.149f. For the Polish edition, see A. Milchman and A. Rosenberg, *Eksperymenty w myśleniu o Holokauście: Auschwitz, Nowoczesność i Filozofia* (Warsaw: Wydawnictwo Naukowe Scholar, 2003), pp.96, 99.
218. See B. Lang, 'The Concept of Genocide', *Philosophical Forum*, 16 (Fall–Winter 1984–85), p.4.
219. A.L. Eckardt and A.R. Eckardt, *Long Night's Journey into Day: A Revised Retrospective on the Holocaust* (Detroit, MI: Wayne State University Press, 1988), p.55.
220. They quote H.J. Zimmels, *The Echo of the Nazi Holocaust in Rabbinic Literature*, where the author gives a list of characteristics that make the Holocaust unique, including the very nature of atrocity, the employment of modern technologies, the number of countries that had fallen under the Nazi extermination policy and the impossibility of finding refuge. They fail to see, however, that all of these features, in one way or another, can be ascribed to other instances of mass murder or persecution. Even the most unique feature, which was the use of modern technologies in order to kill off millions of people, is only relatively unique, since what was used in the First World War was also modern in the 1910s; also, what was used by the Inquisition or during the Wars of Religion was modern at the time when it was happening. See Eckardt and Eckardt, *Long Night's Journey,* p.56.
221. Ibid., p.54.
222. See ibid.
223. Ibid.
224. P. Papazian, 'A "Unique Uniqueness"?', *Midstream*, 30 (April 1984), p.16.
225. Ibid., pp.16f.
226. Ibid., p.15.
227. Ibid.
228. Ibid., p.17. On mystery as a factor in shaping the uniqueness discourse, Phillip Lopate wrote:

> The hostility toward anything that questions the uniqueness of the Holocaust can now be seen as part of a deeper tendency to view all of Jewish history as unique, to read that history selectively and use it only insofar as it promotes a redemptive script. Thus, the Holocaust's 'mystery' must be asserted over and over, in the same way as was the 'mystery' of Jewish survival through the ages, in order to yield the single explanation that God 'wants' the Jewish people to live and is protecting them. Being a secular, fallen Jew with a taste for rationalism and history, I cannot help but regard such providential interpretations as mumbo jumbo.

Lopate, 'Resistance to the Holocaust', p.64.
229. Papazian, 'A "Unique Uniqueness"?', p.15.
230. This issue will be further elaborated in the second part of this book, in the analysis of interviews.

231. Eckardt and Eckardt, *Long Night's Journey*, p.57.
232. ' "Rabbi Chananya son of Akashya used to say, the Holy One, blessed be He, wished to render Israel more worthy. Therefore, he provided them with much Torah and commandments." Or [again we read in the Bible]: "You only have I known of all the families of the earth; therefore I shall visit upon you all your iniquities." ' A. Lichtenstein, 'The State of Jewish Belief: A Symposium', *Commentary*, 42 (August 1966), p.114. It is worthwhile noting that the latter passage (Amos 3: 2) was one of the texts that incited Richard Rubenstein to dismiss the concept of chosenness. His reasoning was that if divine election meant condemnation, the concept was harmful and should be rejected. He claimed that '*as long as we continue to hold to the doctrine of the election of Israel, we will leave ourselves open to the theology* [according to which] *because the Jews are God's chosen People and yet failed to keep God's Law, God sent Hitler to punish them*'. Rubenstein, *After Auschwitz*, p.13 (italics in the original).
233. I. Schorsch, 'The Holocaust and Jewish Survival', *Midstream*, 27 (January 1981), p.39. On the notion of election, Harold Schulweis has offered a provocative comment:

> 'Chosen people' is an example of a doctrine believed to be of divine origin which can no longer be accepted in the light of our experience and ethics. The doctrine presupposes a super-personal deity whose inscrutable will chose to inform a particular group of His truth and ways. To be exclusively chosen by God is to have a special metaphysical status. Such supernatural selection remains inviolate. The elected may be punished for not properly witnessing to the truths it is specially given, but its status as elect remains eternal. Under no conditions will a people admit that its election has been nullified, and no prophet has dared so to proclaim even in the midst of his fiercest denunciation of Israel. While one can understand the psychological value of such belief during years of isolation and humiliation, one cannot on such pragmatic grounds justify its morality or truth.

Harold M. Schulweis, 'The State of Jewish Belief: A Symposium', *Commentary*, 42 (August 1966), p.140. See also A. Eisen, 'Kaplan and Chosenness: A Historical View', *The Reconstructionist*, 50 (September 1984), p.13. In two symposia on Jewish belief, published in *Commentary* in 1966 and 1996 respectively, many other authors spoke at length on the issue of chosenness. Some advocated its traditional meaning (Aharon Lichtenstein, M.D. Tendler, Herbert Weiner, Peter Knobel, David Novak and Emil L. Fackenheim); others proposed to rid it of its exclusionist character or to give it an ethical sense of obligation and responsibility, rather than being better or unlike Gentiles (Jacob B. Agus, Solomon B. Freehof, Arthur Green and Francine Klagsburn). Still others saw it as basically irrelevant or even offensive (Ira Eisenstein and David M. Gordis). See 'The State of Jewish Belief: A Symposium', *Commentary*, 42 (August 1966); 'What Do American Jews Believe: A Symposium', *Commentary*, 102 (August 1996); 'Jewishness and the Younger Intellectuals: A Symposium', *Commentary*, 31 (April 1961); 'The "Chosen People" Reconsidered: A Symposium', *Reconstructionist*, 50 (September 1984).
234. H. Maccoby, 'Theologian of the Holocaust', *Commentary*, 74 (December 1982), p.34.
235. Ibid.
236. Fackenheim, *Jewish Return into History*, p.278.
237. See ibid.
238. See Rosenberg, 'Was the Holocaust Unique?' p.150; A. Rosenberg and P. Marcus, 'The Holocaust as a Test of Philosophy', in Rosenberg and Myers (eds), *Echoes from the Holocaust*, p.203.
239. See Rosenberg, 'Was the Holocaust Unique?' Unfortunately, Rosenberg does not offer us any help in discerning which events do contain a transformational potential – unless it is only the Shoah that is such an event.
240. Ibid.
241. Rubenstein, *After Auschwitz*, p.183.
242. This statement is clearly incompatible with the views of some postmodern philosophers on the topic.
243. Rosenberg and Marcus, 'Holocaust as a Test of Philosophy', p.216.
244. Milchman and Rosenberg, *Eksperymenty w myśleniu o Holokauście*, p.58; see A. Milchman

and A. Rosenberg, 'The Need for Philosophy to Confront the Holocaust as a Transformational Event', *Dialogue and Universalism*, 13, 3–4 (2003), pp.66f.

245. I agree with Rosenberg and Marcus, who say that 'by banal evil we mean evil that is done
by "normal" ordinary people, as part of their everyday routine more or less detached from the
overall evil effect of their usual bureaucratic activities'. 'Holocaust as a Test of Philosophy',
p.216.

246. Rubenstein, *The Cunning of History*, p.73.

247. Ibid., p.87.

248. Ibid., p.89.

249. Rosenberg, 'Was the Holocaust Unique?', p.145.

The Shoah as a Challenge to Jewish Faith

1. TRADITIONAL INTERPRETATIONS OF *CHURBAN EUROPA*

According to traditional Jewish doctrine, the history of the Jewish people, though generally linear, runs cyclically through three stages: '*churban, galut, geula – destruction, exile, redemption*, and no event requires new categories of definition.'[1] It implies that the term *churban* is a generic one; it refers to all those events in Jewish history that were unimaginable in horror and disastrous in their outcomes. Thus, *churbanot* (plural form of *churban*) are: the destruction of the First and the Second Temples in Jerusalem (*Churban Beit Hamikdash*, 586 BCE, 70 CE), remembered each year on *Tishah B'Av*, the Crusades (eleventh to thirteenth centuries), the expulsion of the Jews from Spain (1492) and the Chmielnicki massacres (1648–49). The question is whether these *churbanot*, and specifically the last one, the total destruction of European Jewry, referred to by most Orthodox thinkers as the *Churban Europa*, are just points in the developing Jewish history or have a particular theological meaning and purpose.

In traditional Judaism, all Jewish history is pregnant with religious sense; it unfolds divine plans for Israel. Though Jews live among the nations of the world, their history has its origin and finds its consummation beyond the common secular reality. The same could be said of the most recent history; thus the famous Lithuanian rabbi, Reb Elchonon Bunim Wasserman, speaking in the late 1930s, claimed that 'all the events of contemporary Jewish history are beyond the laws of the natural course of human history'.[2] Therefore, the only explanation of the occurrences that he witnessed could be found in the Torah. What is more, he saw the Torah not only as a text helpful in explaining particular events, but also as a source of survival. What he and most Orthodox Jews call *Torah Judaism* was therefore perceived as a golden means for the Jewish people to ensure safety and well-being. On the other hand, abandoning the study and practice of the Torah accounted for all Jewish suffering, including the difficult plight of European Jewry in the 1930s.[3]

What, therefore, does the Torah teach, according to Orthodox thinkers, about *churbanot* and, more widely, about suffering? First and foremost, it must be underscored that none of these cases of destruction can be considered in separation from the others, especially the demolition of the Temple. So, if we reflect on the Shoah, we ought to bear in mind that our understanding of this event 'must begin with works written 2,500 years ago. Yirmiyahu the Prophet [Jeremiah] had written *"Hashem* [God] *destroyed without mercy"*,[4] regarding the destruction of the First *Beis Hamikdash.* Yet, this *pasuk* [verse] has been understood to extend beyond that *Churban* to include *Churban* in all times. The *Churban* of the *Beis Hamikdash* becomes the paradigm for all future *Churbanos'*.[5]

Thus, whenever the Jewish people faced an enormous tragedy, each such instance was to be seen in the context of all the preceding catastrophes, beginning with the first and the paradigmatic one, the destruction of the Jerusalem Temple. Accordingly, each particular destruction should not be viewed in isolation but, on the contrary, should be put in the context of the covenant and be understood as an element in the continuum that was commenced at Sinai.[6] This covenantal framework is not surprising when reflecting on the evil and catastrophe which have befallen the Jews throughout the ages. According to traditional Jewish theology, suffering is not regarded as a reality from outside their history and relationship with God; it is an inseparable aspect of the covenant. What is more, it is the essence of any *churban* that it must be decreed by God, whose will it is to lead his people to achieve particular goals by way of *churbanot.*[7] Weinberg argues that during the Shoah, most Jews failed to see their fate on the continuum of their destiny. *Klal Yisrael,* the nation of Israel, forgot, as it were, that whatever happens to them, happens as part of their 'ongoing relationship with G-d'. It is his firm belief that 'never since the *Churban* of nineteen hundred years ago has it been so abundantly clear that all that had occurred is the workings of the direct hand of G-d'.[8] Seen from the perspective of Jewish tradition, this is not as shocking as it may sound at first. For in Judaism (at least in its traditional teaching), God becomes known through history, as well as personal and collective experience, rather than through intellectual speculation.[9]

But how are we to understand the claim that any event we witness is a sign of the direct hand of God? Is this to be understood literally? Maybe not in the physical sense, but certainly in terms of theological interpretation, everything is willed or permitted by God. Everything has its place in the divine scheme of things:

> The Torah directs us to view history as the unfolding of the Divine plan: History is the metamorphosis of man through the stages of destruction and redemption, continuing toward his final redemption in the days of Moshiach [Messiah]. And all such events, the redemptions *and the destructions*, are perceived as fundamental testimony to the presence of G-d in this world. [Italics added.][10]

What is more, suffering and catastrophe are so much part of the divine presence among the Jewish people, Mordechai Gifter continues, that it is almost indispensable for the feeling of closeness of God. Attempting to find the meaning of the Holocaust, the Orthodox theologian contends that 'if, Heaven forbid, *Hashem* would have forsaken us, this *Churban* could never have occurred. The *Churban* itself is evidence and testimony to the fact that "we have a Father in Heaven".'[11]

How, then, is it possible to view God as the ultimate author of all events, *including mass destruction*, and at the same time maintain that *all* these events are expressions of covenant and of the faithfulness of God? Many rabbis wrestled with this problem during wartime. One of the most revered of them was the Hassidic rebbe of Piaseczno, Kalonymos Kalmish Shapira, whose sermons given in the Warsaw ghetto were collected and edited under the title *Esh Kodesh* (*Sacred Fire*).[12] Although he believed that anything that Jews experience is a way in which divine presence is made manifest, at times he had, if not doubts, then at least troubling questions. On the one hand, he maintained that the ever more intense suffering of the Jewish people – 'the suffering of loved ones and the suffering of all Israel – is a sign that they are experiencing the manifest revelation of God's sovereignty'.[13] Yet, on the other hand, he was concerned about the immensity of evil that had befallen the Jews, and especially disturbing was the fact that the most pious of his compatriots were the easiest target for the perpetrators and therefore suffered the most severe losses. It was his conviction that what was happening before his eyes was divine punishment. What troubled him was that the whole 'Torah world' was in danger of total extinction:

Everything God does to us – even when, God forbid, He is punishing us – is for the good. There are times, however, when we are smitten not only with physical suffering but also with things that, God forbid, distance us from Him, blessed be He ... In times such as this, God forbid, uneasy doubts may arise within us, asking how it is possible that even now God's intention is for our benefit. If it were for the good, surely He would be punishing us with things that draw us closer to Him, and not with the annihilation of the Torah ... A person is never able to tell whether what is happening to him is a curse or an event. All that he can say is that it looks like a curse ... [However] what God is doing with us is for the good of Israel.[14]

In many places Shapira expresses both excruciating pain and a longing and hope for salvation from oppression. He says prayer is becoming hardly possible, not only because it is forbidden, but also because it is difficult to pray amidst such unimaginable suffering.[15] He reveals not only his own pain, but the pain of 'the Jewish people, children of the King, [who] are in great distress', as well.[16] In all his reflections and exegesis of Torah and Talmud passages, he seeks to find confirmation of his belief that everything Jews face is God's doing, and that all that happens to them has a reason and a meaning.

In a lengthy passage on the issue of truth, he rejects the concept of truth as existing *a se* and *per se*, or independently of God. The very idea of intrinsic truth is to him an instance of idolatry, for it questions divine commandments. Only what God commands is true, and all that is true is such only because it is commanded by him. Therefore, the idea *aseitas* and *perseitas* of truth, Shapira claims, flies in the face of the basic tenets of Judaism, namely that God is the source of everything, which implies that he is also the source of truth. It seems that what Shapira is interested in, while discussing the problem of truth, is not the philosophical question of the origin and nature of truth, but the nature of the events he witnesses. He attempts to find a way to reconcile the cruelty he can see with his eyes with the faith he has in his heart. Thus he focuses on the issue of the 'legitimacy' of what is happening. What he sees is undeniable; what he and all Jews experience is simply true. Therefore, if he is not to wind up in utter dualism, or even schizophrenia, he cannot let the realm of truth be separated from the realm of the divine. His conclusion is that all truth comes from God, which implies that all he truly experiences comes from God, too; thus it must have some meaning, if not for people then at least for God himself. 'Any truth that exists in the world is only true because God commanded it so, and wanted it so.' If it was done by God's will, then it is inscrutable and inaccessible for human intellect: 'We do not measure truth and righteousness with our minds, nor do we stop and ponder upon God, God forbid. We do not ask if this is how it should or should not be, or whether something is or is not true.'[17]

All this leads him to assert (or, rather, he leads his reasoning in such a manner that the assertion becomes possible) that the incomprehensible horror that has befallen the Jewish people is part of the divine truth: that it belongs to divine plans which are right:

> The will of God, blessed be He, is true and right, and even when we are tortured, God forbid, we do not deliberate. What is happening may not meet with our approval, but it does not depend upon our approval, and so we do not merely dismiss the problem as unanswerable, explaining that we cannot reconcile it because it is beyond our grasp ... There is no such thing as intrinsic truth; there is only God's will and His deeds, and these are the truth ... We Jews know that ... the real truth is that all judgements depend solely upon Your righteousness.[18]

With the passage of time, however, the enormity of suffering and affliction became practically unbearable, even for the pious. Their way of expressing extreme pain and exhaustion, in most cases, was not outright rebellion, but cries for mercy. Accordingly, on 3 October 1940, Kalonymos Shapira wrote: 'How could you bear to hear our pain and not have mercy, God forbid? You hear our voice: "Please be not deaf to [our] plea for well-being." '[19] What is even more striking, in a gloss to a passage written in August 1941, Shapira remarked that in the time he had given the sermon 'it was at least possible to lament ... to worry about the survivors, and to grieve for the future'. During the course of a year, however, the situation had changed dramatically. 'This was no longer the case', he said, 'now at the end of 1942, when the holy congregations have been annihilated in a radical excision.'[20] In that situation, even grief and planning a renewal of the destroyed world was barely possible. The only resort was to turn to 'God [who] will have mercy and save us in the blink of an eye ... Please, O God, have mercy; please do not delay rescuing us.'[21]

A similar attitude can be found in Rabbi Ephraim Oshry's *Responsa from the Holocaust*, where he says that 'it ... seemed appropriate that all of us accept upon ourselves some form of penance and implore

G-d to have mercy on His people and to tell Satan, "Enough!" '.[22] Like many other Orthodox authors, Oshry also believed that whatever happened to the Jews, it must have been willed by God and should be thanked for: 'Just as one must bless G-d for the good that He gives us, so must one bless G-d for the evil that He unleashes upon us. Instead of yielding to despair, we must wait for G-d's assistance.'[23] Moreover, waiting for salvation from evil – one may infer from his writings – was parallel to expecting God to rebuke the wrongdoers: 'May the G-d of vengeance avenge Himself against the evildoers who oppressed His people, tortured His righteous ones, and murdered His pure ones!'[24]

It seems that almost all interpretations of the Shoah given by Orthodox scholars revolve around the question of *why?* – though the problem is not always expressed explicitly. Despite the fact that they know the whole Torah and Talmud, they ask, Why did this happen to the Jews – to the people of God? The question, especially if uttered by Orthodox and Hassidic rabbis, comprises, in fact, two parts: Why did it happen to the Jews? and Why did the spiritual and study centres of Judaism suffer the most?[25] Thus, Rabbi Eliyahu Eliezer Dessler asked: 'Why did G-d permit the destruction of Torah centers and allow Torah scholars and teachers of Torah to be ruthlessly murdered?'[26] 'How could a Merciful G-d have allowed that to happen? What can justify the brutality inflicted upon the Six Million?'[27] 'The unprecedented bloodletting and barbarism raise excruciatingly difficult questions of *hashkafah* [view]: How could G-d allow it to happen? What sins could have justified such punishment? Why was the cream of religious Jewry decimated when the principal sinners were surely found elsewhere?'[28]

The answers most of these authors give deal with God's justice and loving kindness. In other words, if the Jewish people have to endure *churbanot*, this must be seen as a sign of divine righteousness and concern for the chosen nation. Rabbi Shapira explains:

> everything happens at the hand of God [who] does not execute judgment without justice, God forbid. This is fundamental. It is one of the Thirteen Principles of the Jewish Faith ... 'I believe without a doubt that the Creator, blessed be His name, rewards those who observe His commandments and punishes those who violate them.' ... Also ... as is written in the *Tanya*: 'If a person ... sees why this particular punishment was justly dealt him, he will not complain, God forbid. On the contrary, he will assume that just as God has punished him he will nurture him when he repents of his sins.' Aside from that, sufferings are *hester panim*,

concealment of the Divine Face. When a person perceives within his suffering the Hand of God, and His justice and truth, he abolishes the *hester* (concealment).[29]

We might be somewhat surprised to read that these Jewish theologians speak of punishment and repentance from sins. What sins? – one may ask. Do the Orthodox thinkers really believe the Holocaust could have been divine punishment? It seems that there is little room within Orthodoxy[30] for any other explanation of *Churban Europa* than 'just punishment'. Most Orthodox Jews and Hassidim are prone to interpret the Shoah in terms of *mipnei hataeinu* – because of our sins were we punished. The very notion of *hester panim* is immediately linked with punishment. For we read in Isaiah 59:2: 'Your sinful acts have alienated you from your God; your sins have made him turn his face away [*histiru fanim*] and not listen to your prayers.' Strangely enough, Norman Lamm accepts the concept of *hester panim*, though he criticizes Orthodox thinkers for referring to the concept of punishment for sins:

> Almost all those (few) Orthodox thinkers who have ventured into this area at all offer variations of the *mi-pnei hata'einu* ('because of our sins') thesis ... They see the Holocaust as punishment for Israel's sins ... [However,] they use the words *u-mi-pnei hata'einu*, 'because of our sins', when they really mean to say *u-mi-pnei hata'eihem*, 'because of *their* sins'! In the past, every case of interpreting a disaster as the result of sin was one in which the interpreter included himself in the group that was guilty ... Today, in trying to explain the greatest of all disasters ever to befall us, small minded people blame others, not themselves ... In sum, if we ask, if we may resort to the *mi-pnei hata'einu* rationale for the Holocaust, my answer is a resounding no – indeed, six million times no! [Italics in the original.][31]

It is quite clear why Lamm challenges the concept of *mi-pnei hata'einu*. But why in its place he offers 'the conceptual framework ...of *Hester Panim*'[32] is much less comprehensible. He asks: What is the cause of the hiding of God's face? His answer is that 'sin brings in its wake punishment, the acme of which is *Hester Panim*; the turning aside of God's face is worse than any punishment He metes out to us directly'.[33] Instead of acknowledging the straightforward idea of punishment for sins, he chooses to embrace the vague, symbolic term, the meaning of which is nonetheless virtually identical with the concept he rejects. A more coherent position is taken by David Weiss Halivni, who opposes the notion of 'God's hidden face' just because it entails punishment for sins.[34]

Coming back to the disturbing question of 'why', we should remark that several authors point out that the question is simply misconceived. Rabbi Soloveitchik, for example, argues that pondering on human life, we can look at it from two different perspectives, and see in it either fate or destiny. In the world of fate, one is an object and 'asks a theoretical–metaphysical question regarding evil',[35] which leads one to no answers. This type of question begins with 'Why?' The problem here is, as Soloveitchik contends, that the 'why' questions turn human beings into passive objects, whereas the right way to ask questions is to ask freely, knowing one's worth, and inquiring about one's destiny and obligations. Although the difference between the notions of fate and destiny seems only verbal or rhetorical, we can infer that Soloveitchik's real point is to distinguish between two general outlooks. One is: Why did this happen to me? The other is: What can I do with what happened to me? Needless to say, it is the latter question that Soloveitchik deems worth considering. He claims that 'the fundamental question is: What obligation does suffering impose upon man?' In his opinion, the Halakhic way of life motivates people to transform their fate into destiny, which leads not to causal or teleological speculations on suffering, but to 'the rectification of suffering'.[36] Therefore, we see that Soloveitchik's argumentation is meta-ethical in its nature (it deals with ethics). He does not inquire about the human condition or the origin of evil. His is the problem of acting-as-response-to-suffering. Interpreting the case of Job, he puts his views in an unambiguous way. He describes an imaginary situation where God speaks to Job 'as a man of destiny'. There is one thing he must remember:

> You will never understand the secret of 'why', you will never comprehend the cause, or telos, of suffering. But there is one thing that you *are* obliged to know: the principle of mending one's afflictions. If you can elevate yourself via your afflictions to a rank that you had hitherto not attained, then know full well that these afflictions were intended as a means for mending both your soul and your spirit. [Italics in the original.][37]

Another example of methodological approach to the 'why' question can be found in Bernard Maza's theology. Although what he focuses on could be labelled by Soloveitchik 'teleological thinking', Maza is interested in the moral implications of – and conclusions to be drawn by – the sufferer from his affliction.[38] To Maza, the problem with the 'why' questions lies with the direction in which they point. He claims that biblical literature gives many examples of dialogues between great Jewish leaders and God, where the human partner did not ask 'Why?', but 'To what effect?' The direction of the question was just the opposite to these troubling questions most people have been asking after the Holocaust. Thus, Maza argues, the question directed to God should not be: 'What caused you to act in such a manner?', but rather 'To what purpose have you acted in such a manner?'[39]

At first, the distinction Maza makes seems clear, and of course logical, but a closer look reveals that the difference between the two questions is only rhetorical. Whereas, methodologically, the question concerning causes is not identical with the one concerning purpose, what we are interested in here is the moral weight of the problem. Thus, what moral difference might there be between what caused God to act in a given way, on the one hand, and the effect of the acting that he willed, on the other? The answer is: none. For what we can call the effect or purpose of any divine action is the cause of this action. To be sure, classical Jewish (or any other theistic) theology always perceives the purposes of God's deeds as the motivating force of his acting. What is more, even if we accepted the formal distinction between cause and purpose, there still remains the question, as Maza honestly admits, of the commensurability of means in relation to expected results. So the new excruciating problem is: 'Why did the Almighty choose to permit the Shoah to be the instrument to achieve the desired effect?'[40] This, however, is an *absolutely unanswerable question* for theologians, philosophers and sociologists.[41] And for many a believing person this may be indeed a stumbling block.

Some Orthodox authors even claim that any question of 'why' is a wrong one. It is a question that emerges out of the depths of our modern, or postmodern, culture. Our secularized thinking makes the 'why' questions unavoidable, and the opinion that there can be questions without answers is ridiculed or deemed unsatisfactory. As Nosson Scherman has noted, 'we are living in an age that is not prepared to accept anything without a full explanation'.[42] Many authors maintain that the problems Jews have with accounting for Auschwitz are exactly an outcome of the secular, over-intellectualized mentality. Jews have been saturated with western thinking, and that is why they have lost their clarity of insight, their self-awareness and the conviction of being covenanted to God.[43]

That is why they pose the wrong questions and finally have 'failed to recognize instinctively that this *Churban* has also its place in the continuity of [the Jewish people's] destiny'.[44] Some even go as far as to argue that the Jewish psyche must be separated from the intellect of the western nations:

> If the [European] *Churban* has any instruction for us, it is that we must stop revering the alien intellectual. Our entire sense of awe for the heritage of western civilization has left us with a malaise of religious insecurity and weak posture. It is long overdue that we begin to regain our balance and spiritual pride ... The emphasis [should be put on] the need to eliminate from our individual and communal psyches the false notion that *Vernunft*[45] and *Wissenschaft* of other nations possess moral virtue. Our sense of awe and our devotion, after the *Churban*, must turn *exclusively inward to our culture and our heritage*.[46] [Italics in the original.]

Yet we should not assume that any kind of reasoning, even in the traditional sense, is removed from the visions and concepts of Orthodox scholars; what they do is employ the basic, universal modes of reasoning *within* the limits of their theological traditions. It is a sui generis reason, a halakhic *Vernunft*. Halakhah, the Jewish law, sets the demarcation line of accepted theorizing, and produces what might be called *Wissenschaft des Orthodoxes Judentums*,[47] or science of Orthodox Judaism. In other words, traditional – even fundamentalist – Judaism has its own scholarship, which is not necessarily limited to biblical stories as well as mythical and mystical texts of Kaballa. It is this inner intellectual framework, and its specific methodology, that constitutes the realm of speculation of the Orthodox Jew. The man who functions within this domain, who uses his intellect for the purpose of explaining the reality in terms that are comprehensible and *acceptable* to himself and his peers, Soloveitchik calls *Halakhic man*.[48] Who is Halakhic man? To put it briefly, he is a person that is neither *homo religiosus* nor cognitive man in separation from one another, but is both simultaneously. From the standpoint of the basic tenets of his world view, he is *homo religiosus*, yet seen from the perspective of his life activities and his way of thinking, he is cognitive man. In his reasoning, Halakhic man's point of departure is the belief in the God of Israel and in his Torah (both written and oral); his methodology, however, is the obverse of that of *homo religiosus*. The latter starts with this world only to arrive at the transcendent world, while the former starts with the divine realm and ends up with the mundane, instead of fleeing it.[49]

We can, therefore, argue that what most Orthodox scholars say about the *Churban Europa* is, to a large extent, an example of the thinking of Halakhic man. They use pure instrumental reason in order to find theological, Halakhic explanations of the events they witness. The data they analyse is the historic-material world perceived with human senses and the spiritual world of Torah, Talmud and other rabbinic sources. The tool they use is reason, though it is limited by the boundaries of their basic beliefs: God, covenant, tradition.

The fundamental historiosophic concept of Judaism is that whatever happens, happens by the will of God. Each and every event, be it natural or human-made, has its place in the divine scheme of things. Therefore, all occurrences must be explainable within the biblical–rabbinic theological system. Any interpretation that the system sanctions is thus acceptable. That is why traditional (non-modern) Orthodox thinkers virtually always explain suffering in terms of just punishment for sins, 'for he whom Hashem [God] loves He reproves and He appeases as a father does his son'.[50] Even if a person experiences some kind of evil only for pedagogic or therapeutic reasons, the conclusion seems obvious: something must have been wrong with the person, s/he must have committed some, if only minor, transgression of the law, or his/her character must have had some flaw. In any case, the evil that befell the person was just a consequence of the evil the person had had in him/herself:

> Rabbi Avrohom Grodzenski (who was killed in the Grodno Ghetto) made a list of specific *aveiros* [sins] that in his view brought down G-d's wrath; but that is only of secondary importance. The primary point made must be that one way or another the destruction was a Divine corrective action for a long standing accumulation of shortcomings on the part of *Klal Yisroel* [the nation of Israel] over the ages ... A 'corrective action' for [these shortcomings] was a brutal, massive rejection of Jewry by the most powerful of Western nations ... This terrible suffering was *Bikrovei Ekodeish* [sanctification of God through his people] before the eyes of humankind as a whole ... And the purest, the saintliest, the most learned innocent were included in this terrifying enactment of *Bikrovei Ekodeish*.[51]

The above passage signals several problems I have not touched upon so far: namely, specific sins as the cause of the Holocaust as an alleged punishment; *churban* as a corrective action; and God's sanctification through his people. As to the first issue, many prominent Orthodox and/or Hassidic thinkers pointed to particular ways of behaviour of the Jews or of particular Jewish groups as being the cause of the Shoah.

As the Maggid of Kelm maintained, the Shoah was punishment for the creation of the Reform movement in the nineteenth century by Abraham Geiger. 'Because of this sin', the Maggid said, 'another law will emerge from Germany. It will say that every Jew, without exception, must die.'[52] Yoel Moshe Teitelbaum, known as the Satmarer Rebbe, saw the transgression elsewhere. It was his conviction that

> the Zionists were responsible for the tragedy of the six million. The arrogance of the nationalistic self-determination in trying to build a Jewish state caused the great destruction. The fact that so many Zionists were secularists, nonbelievers, only made matters worse. They violated the injunction to remain passive, refrain from interfering in the divinely preordained plans of redemption, and to await the miraculous coming of the Messiah. Hence, the Zionists are guilty, and all the Jewish people suffered because of their sins.[53]

Another Orthodox scholar held that the sin was socialism: 'Because of the upsurge of the greatest defection from Torah in history, which was expressed in Poland by materialism, virulent anti-nationalism, and Bundism (radical anti-religious socialism), God's plan finally relieved them of all freewill and sent Hitler's demons to end the existence of the communities.'[54]

Another author saw the danger in the possibility that the Eastern European Jews would not make spiritual progress gradually, on a step-by-step basis, and therefore could go astray from the Torah. Hence, this reasoning continues, God had immediately to intervene with measures he deemed proper and efficient – a corrective action. The diagnosis was that

> there is no alternative but to proceed as the physician who advises a dangerously ill man to undergo surgery ... It becomes mandatory to perform an extremely dangerous operation ... the removal of spiritual guides and influences, and the destruction of a sound, stimulating environment, for they are only means for the attainment of spirituality. The hazardous operation of removing the

righteous who aid and support *Hashem's* service had to be undertaken.[55]

Yet there are those who claim that no one is entitled to adjudge that the Holocaust was brought about by anyone else's faults. For it is one thing to assert that the catastrophe was an expression of divine justice or even retribution, and it is another thing to say that any particular transgression occasioned the *Churban Europa*. Yitzchak Hutner contends that the destruction 'of European Jewry was [indeed] a *tochachah* phenomenon, an enactment of the admonishment and rebuke which *Klal Yisrael* carries upon its shoulders as an integral part of being the *Am Hanivchar*, G-d's chosen ones'.[56] Hutner underscores that *tochachah* – the warning of rebuke and of divine pedagogy-by-punishment – is undetachable from Judaism; it is 'a built-in aspect' of the Jewish people. In spite of the element of rebuke, however, he admonishes his compatriots: 'we have no right to interpret these events [of catastrophe] as any kind of *specific punishment for specific sins*' (italics in the original).[57]

The last of the three aspects mentioned above is the issue of the sanctification of God. In the summer of 1942, Kalonymos Shapira wrote:

> There is suffering we endure individually for our sins, or pangs of love that soften and purify us. In all of this, God merely suffers with us. But then there is suffering in which we merely suffer with him, so to speak – suffering for the sanctification of God's name ... The chief suffering is really for God's sake, and because of Him we are ennobled and exalted by this sort of pain.[58]

What is in a way striking in Shapira is that he argues that suffering has the power to wash out sins. This purifying, indeed salvific,[59] character of suffering is traditionally stressed by Christian theologians, but in Judaism affliction was hardly ever seen as possessing any positive value. It seems that Shapira was somehow forced by external circumstances to invest suffering with the meaning of purification and sacrifice. He claims that when a Jew is stricken with pain, then his 'suffering washes away sins and he is crying out to God, [and] this also is counted as a sacrifice'.[60]

Perhaps the most stunning words uttered by an Orthodx rabbi during the war were those said by Elchonon Wasserman at the point when he knew he would not survive:

> Apparently they consider us *tzaddikim* in Heaven, for we were

chosen to atone for *Klal Yisroel* with our lives* ... If so, we must
repent completely here and now ... We must realize that
our sacrifices will be more pleasing if accompanied by repentance,
and we shall thereby save the lives of our brothers and sisters in
America. Let none of us think an impure thought which would
render us unfit as a korban [offering].**[61]

The situation to which Wasserman alludes is exactly what most
Jewish religious thinkers have called *kiddush hashem*, the sanctification
of God's name. Indeed, it is an important category in Jewish theology
of suffering. Having its biblical basis in Leviticus, *kiddush hashem* is the
way a Jew becomes a martyr – when s/he gives his/her life for God's
sake. According to this commandment, a Jew should rather die than
renounce his/her faith. This particular death, death as the price paid
for one's faithfulness, is considered in Judaism as the highest way of
sanctifying the divine name. Many rabbis and Hassidic leaders are
known to have summoned their disciples during the war to be prepared
to freely give their lives for God. They considered it as the most lofty
and, at the same time, self-evident way of confirming their faith.[62]
Many of them even taught their close ones and yeshivah students what
particular religious formula to say at the moment of death. Elchonon
Wasserman, for example, 'was teaching his son Reb Naftali the blessing
to be recited when giving one's life for *Kiddush Hashem*'. When he
himself faced imminent death, those who saw him then 'all received
the same clear impression, that of a great leader of Israel preparing to
offer his life for the sanctification of G-d's Name'.[63]

2. FROM RUBENSTEIN TO GREENBERG: IN SEARCH OF RADICAL RESPONSES TO THE SHOAH

In order to comprehend the background of the Holocaust debate
which has been one of the central themes of the public discourse in
America since the end of the 1970s, it is advisable to look at its
beginnings before the Vietnam War. It seems legitimate to say that the
question of God vis-à-vis the Holocaust was not really a problematic
one for American Jewish thinkers until the 1960s. Of course, this does
not mean that no one had pointed earlier to the paradox of the
unimaginable suffering of the Jewish people as confronted with the
biblical teaching of the faithful and merciful (*rahamim*) God, who,
according to the Torah, had entered in covenant with Israel. As is
widely known, this question was posed in Elie Wiesel's novel *Night*,

which was first published in Yiddish in 1956 in South America and then translated into French (1958) and English (1960). It was Wiesel, coming from a family of pious Hassidim and having survived the Shoah, who formulated the metaphorical thesis of God's agony. That was his reaction to what he saw one day in Auschwitz: a little boy, whose body was hanging on a camp gallows and who could not die because he was too light:

> For more than half an hour he stayed there [on the gallows], struggling between life and death, dying in slow agony under our yes. And we had to look him full in the face. He was still alive when I passed in front of him. His tongue was still red, his eyes were not yet glazed. Behind me, I heard the same man asking: 'Where is God now?' And I heard a voice within me answering him: 'Where is He? Here He is – He is hanging here on this gallows ...'.[64]

This, however, does not mean that Wiesel became an atheist in the camp. Although he admits he will never forget the children whose bodies were turned into smoke 'beneath a silent blue sky [and the] flames which consumed [my] faith forever [and] those moments which murdered [my] God and ... soul',[65] he nevertheless claims: 'I did not doubt God's existence, but I doubted His absolute justice.'[66] Thus, Wiesel's words seem to be just a literary metaphor, an accusation he will be disavowing and coming back to all through his life.

RICHARD L. RUBENSTEIN: CULTURAL DEATH OF GOD

Wiesel's voice was understood as a cry of despair, not a calm statement. It did not provoke an immediate discussion either in the circles of Jewish theologians and philosophers or amongst the general public.[67] The first scholarly works that gave rise to an intellectual storm in academia, authored by a graduate of the Jewish Theological Seminary of America and of Harvard University, Richard L. Rubenstein, were published in the 1960s. In his early writings he had already employed the term 'death of God', which was coined by Nietzsche and which was to become the leading slogan of the generation of young, radical Christian theologians. The question of religious appraisal of the genocide of European Jews was formulated in a clear, sharp and explicit way from the very onset, only to become a sore point later, a real controversy that brought about animated polemics between different theological and political factions.

At first, Rubenstein referred only to the philosophical postulates of Friedrich Nietzsche and Paul Tillich (the latter he called the father of all radical theologians). He was more engaged in philosophy than in theology *sensu stricto*. After all, in his best-known book *After Auschwitz*, he contends that, as a matter of fact, contemporary theology has become anthropology, as it tells not as much about God as it does about man.[68] He also admits having been significantly influenced by European existentialism and psychoanalysis.[69]

It should not be overlooked that Rubenstein started writing on the question of God and human existence roughly at the same time as the Christian death-of-God theologians (Hamilton and Altizer's *Radical Theology and the Death of God*[70]) and before the English publication of Elie Wiesel's *Night*, which makes him one of the pioneers of the death-of-God theology. In two articles published in 1959 in *The Reconstructionist*, Rubenstein discussed the issue of faith in God vis-à-vis existential anxiety (*Urangst*).[71] I will now examine some important points already discussed in these two early publications.

It seems that, though focusing at that time mainly on the subject of existential anxiety, he saw the significant implications of current historical events. One particular event that started to play an ever more important role in his writing was the European genocide (at that time he never used the term 'Holocaust'). Rubenstein believes that life experience, even for those having no idea of Nietzschean interpretations, drives the believer to affirm that 'the old God of Jewish patriarchal monotheism [is] dead beyond all hope of resurrection'.[72] This contention is the crucial issue not only in the articles discussed here, but also in Rubenstein's subsequent writings, where his thought evolved and finally proved to be the only well-elaborated Jewish post-Holocaust theology.

But why is this particular God dead? And how is this particular God different from other God(s)? Rubenstein argues that we live 'in an epoch of historical change, catastrophe and rebirth of greater scope than any which has befallen the Jewish community since the times of Vespasian, Trajan and Hadrian'.[73] Like most critical, radical thinkers, Rubenstein sees history and a given context of human life as decisive determinants of people's views and feelings. Their situatedness – *Sitz im Leben* – determines their way of perceiving things and reflecting on them. Part of that life context is the finitude of life itself – which causes existential anxiety, an ineradicable fear of great loss, the loss of the self.[74] Hence it follows that the post-Second World War situatedness of

Jewish people makes the *Urangst*, experienced to some extent by all human beings, even stronger – for life has proved so unimaginably cheap, devoid of dignity, and its finitude so tangible.

In traditional Judaism, however, God was always a powerful God, one that had entered human history through saving and covenanting Israel. As the Jewish concept of deity comprises the idea of life-giving, life has been very much cherished in Judaism. The Jewish God, while he can inspire fear and awe before the Godhead itself, anaesthetizes his people, as it were, so that they are not conquered by fear. The traditional God of Judaism is redeemer, Lord of history who intervenes in history, who acts with a strong hand, and who is faithful to the people Israel. In short, it is a God who is both merciful and mighty. This idea of God, then, as Rubenstein points out, has turned out to be false. The idea of a transcendent, personal, acting God is a dead idea:

> It is certainly possible to understand God as the primal ground of existence out of which we arise and to which we return. Yet the God who is the ground is not the transcendent Father-God of Jewish patriarchal monotheism. Though many still believe in the Father-God, they do so out of personal need and inclination rather than out of a disciplined confrontation of the issues of human evil and human freedom. For those who face these issues the Father-God is not only the enemy of genuine freedom but is either involved in evil or lacks the power to control it. Because of this he is for us a dead God. Even the leap of faith will not and cannot resurrect this dead God.[75]

Another aspect of traditional Jewish doctrine that Rubenstein challenges is the idea of punishment for sins. Certainly he does not yet oppose the biblical idea of God, but the vision of the rabbis.[76] In an article published in *The Reconstructionist*, his critique is aimed rather at the rabbinical teaching of divine retribution for trespasses, which he finds untenable:

> The myth that once upon a time God gave His people laws and commandments, but that they sinfully rejected them and were subjected to the hideous retaliatory punishment of exile and disaster ... can be described as the core myth of traditional rabbinic Judaism. It pervades rabbinic thought, as even a cursory examination of the sources will reveal. It is clearly insupportable as a living faith for the modern Jew. Rabbinic theology permits no other interpretation of Jewish disaster. In *Midrash* and *Aggada*

misfortune is always interpreted as God's retaliation for sinful conduct. In literally hundreds of rabbinic interpretations, events which the Bible treats merely as misfortune are interpreted by the rabbis as God's punishment for prior sins. The logic of rabbinic theology is as inescapable as it is unacceptable.[77]

In 1966 Richard Rubenstein took part in a symposium that was published in a special issue of *Commentary* magazine, which included a lengthy debate on the views and beliefs of contemporary Jews.[78] The thirty-eight American rabbis who gave their contributions came from different Jewish denominations. Each of them presented brief answers to five questions, one of which dealt with the death-of-God theology. The participants were asked whether, in their opinion, the concept widely discussed by Christian thinkers was of any significance to Judaism. The very fact of asking the question shows how much agitation it must have caused within American academia.

Less than half of the participants in the debate believed that the death-of-God theology was not relevant in any way to the problems of Judaism, or that it was relevant but only to a certain extent. For instance, the well-known Orthodox Jewish theologian Eliezer Berkovits contended:

> The 'God is dead' question is a direct outgrowth of the Christian promise to man. Christianity promised redemption through a self-sacrificial act of God. The sacrifice was made, but all historic experience has gone to show that the promise has not been kept ... The question's relevance to Judaism I see in the fact that among the untold abominations of human history, the murder of six million Jews in the heart of Christian Europe has been one of the most abominable. For me this proves that *that* God is indeed dead.[79]

Looking at the death-of-God concept, many thinkers point to two of its different aspects: the first is the declaration of the death of 'the messenger-boy God', or the anachronistic image of the divine;[80] the second – and more important, as the authors say – is the problem of the individual's existential experience, in which there is no space for the supranatural – the kind of experience wherein God is absent. But what particular experiences do they have in mind? Only a minority of the participants mention Auschwitz in the context of the existential death of God. What does that mean in terms of anthropology? Or more precisely: What does it say about the anthropology of those who did not deem the Holocaust an event important enough to comment upon? One might suppose that for a great many Jewish thinkers who took part in the 1966 symposium, the time of reflection on the Shoah, the time of intellectual deliberation about the not-so-distant history, had not yet come. For there were only five discussants, including Rubenstein, who confronted the death-of-God problem with Auschwitz. Others seemingly did not think the death camps had anything to do with the death of God.

There was, however, yet another interesting voice, in addition to Rubenstein and Berkovits cited above, that merits our attention. One of the most inspiring features in the *Commentary* symposium was authored by Emil L. Fackenheim. At the outset of his article, he contends that Christian death-of-God theologians, in their reflections, rarely speak about the gas chambers of Auschwitz; and that is perhaps why it is so easy for them to view the twentieth century as a time when man matures and becomes free. In Fackenheim's opinion, the gaining of freedom by humans is not the only possible interpretation of the death-of-God issue. Another way of understanding this concept may be illustrated by the assertion 'that modern man is *incapable* of hearing the word of God *even if he listens*'.[81] It seems, therefore, that at that time, even Fackenheim did not perceive the extermination of European Jews as the essence of the death-of-God question.[82] Insofar as he was interested in radical theological theories, he was preoccupied with the relation between the death of God experienced in the existence of the secular Jew who no longer needed the God-hypothesis on one hand, and the classical teachings of Judaism on the other. For him, as well as for the majority of Jewish theologians in the mid-1960s, Auschwitz was just one more problem to be interpreted, but not an event requiring a thorough rethinking of the God-idea contained in Judaism. Up to that time, one might conclude, the Holocaust had not triggered a need to transvaluate religious values and beliefs.

It was also in 1966 that Richard L. Rubenstein published his now-famous book, *After Auschwitz: Radical Theology and Contemporary Judaism*. This piece of work earned him the name of the first (and so far the only) Jewish death-of-God theologian.[83] But what exactly does it mean in practice? Is Rubenstein an agnostic, an atheist, or is he an atheistic theologian, for that matter? The latter expression seems truer, but only if it is spelled 'a-theistic' – which implies that in Rubenstein's theology the traditional, personal God is in a way absent. His is a *theology* without the *theos* of the Jewish tradition. That, however, does not mean that he is not concerned about the problem of God: only that what he calls 'God' is alien to theism. Hence, it is of utmost importance now to see what Rubenstein understands by the 'death of God' and whether he really claims God is dead.

In the first edition of *After Auschwitz* he asserts: 'God really died at Auschwitz. This does not mean that God is not the beginning and will not be the end. It does mean that nothing in human choice, decision, value, or meaning can any longer have vertical reference to transcendent standards. We are alone in a silent, unfeeling cosmos.'[84] God is not simply dead, for, as Rubenstein explains later, his death is *complete*: the God of monotheism is dead 'beyond all hope of resurrection'.[85] Yet in this context the notion of death is not used with its commonplace meaning. For 'No man can really say that God is dead. How can we know that?' What we can say, however, is that 'we live in the time of the "death of God"'. This is more a statement about man and his culture than about God. The death of God is a cultural fact.'[86] Let us have an attentive look at the very phrase 'death of God'. Is seems to be a *contradictio in adiecto*: the very idea of God rules out any possibility whatsoever of the death of deity. In other words, mortality is no divine attribute within the Judeo-Christian religious tradition.[87] Christianity, however, accepts the concept of God's death in Christ – but that's obviously an idea totally alien to Judaism. '*God simply doesn't die in Judaism*', says Rubenstein (italics in the original).[88] Nevertheless, he feels compelled to use the term 'the *death of God*' as an accurate description of the state of society he lives in. American Jews share with Christians the same cultural situatedness, they co-shape and participate in the same society. Thus, even if estranged 'from the symbolism of the cross', Rubenstein believes he 'must use these words of alien origin and connotation',[89] for he finds death-of-God theology to be closer to his 'own theological writing' than 'any other movement in Christian theology'.[90] He shares with Christian thinkers their analysis of the decidedly secular character of contemporary culture. Rubenstein also concurs with them that 'ours is the time of the death of God'.[91]

He also mentions the radical thinkers who influenced his views on life and human predicament; after reading Freud, Sartre, Hegel, Dostoevski, Melville and, notably, Nietzsche, he can no longer retain the traditional idea of God. As noted earlier, Rubenstein was to a large extent impacted by his teacher and the 'father' of all radical theologians, Paul Tillich. But where he parts company with Tillich, and also with Thomas Altizer, is his interpretation of Nietzsche. The two Christian thinkers read Nietzsche as the one who rebelled against the tyranny of God as a being superior to human beings, arguing by the same token that for human freedom such a concept of God is simply insupportable. Rubenstein, in contradistinction to them, points to a passage in Nietzsche's *Gay Science*, where the Madman enters a church and sings his *Requiem aeternam deo*, as if he were inside God's own sepulchre. 'After Nietzsche', Rubenstein concludes, 'it is impossible to avoid his language to express the total absence of God from our experience.'[92] The difference I am trying to sketch here lies mostly in emphasis: Whereas Tillich and other Christian death-of-God theologians dwell on the problem of man's freedom allegedly jeopardized by the idea of a theistic God, Rubenstein underscores the tragic situation of humans who are staring at the empty space where God once was, and are horrified by that emptiness.

But is it only philosophical speculations – however compelling and cogent – that have laid the foundation for Rubenstein's rejection of theism? How did this empty space appear in his theological experience? And last, but not least, what is the relation between his general existential pessimism and Auschwitz? (Michael L. Morgan is to some extent right to have argued that Rubenstein does not give a satisfying explanation of what the very term Auschwitz denotes and how it led him to object the idea of a theistic God.[93]) Rubenstein contends that while for Tillich and Altizer, what compelled them to wish for the death of the theistic God was human freedom, for him 'the problem of human freedom was far less important than the problem of divine justice and theodicy. Moreover, I never "willed" the death of God; I sadly found the idea of such a God lacking in credibility in the face of the Holocaust.'[94] Now it becomes clear why Rubenstein's book is entitled *After Auschwitz* and not *After Nietzsche*. The death of the God of patriarchal monotheism is not willed – it is inescapable after the destruction of the European Jews. This catastrophe appears to Rubenstein as the ultimate question of ultimate concern, the incarnation of *Urangst*: what paralyzes his mind is now not only 'What is my origin and my destiny?', but also 'Why was there a Holocaust?' The latter, however, is not so much a question of 'why' as it is a question of 'what now?' Thus Rubenstein appears as the first person ever to inquire about the implications of the Holocaust for the realm of human thought.

It seems appropriate now to try to investigate just how and when Rubenstein faced the Auschwitz-event and felt compelled to respond to it in his writing. Before Auschwitz became a symbol for Rubenstein and many other thinkers, he had been seriously affected by 'reports of the capture of the camp at Majdanek, Poland ... in the fall of 1944'.[95] It was the High Holy Days season, and during that time he served as a student rabbi in Tupelo, Mississippi, where he was supposed to give a sermon. It was exactly then that he learned about the details of the almost Auschwitz-like camp at the outskirts of Lublin in south-eastern Poland: 'The image that made it impossible for me to regard the slaughter as an abstraction was the discovery of six hundred thousand pairs of ownerless shoes at the camp. The absence of the owners was a haunting presence I could not obliterate from my mind.' Even though he was thousands of miles away from the place of mass murder, he 'could no longer offer the gathering congregation the age-old assurance that all was well, nor could [he] celebrate the triumph of order over disorder, rule over misrule, nomos over chaos'.[96] He even had to write his sermon anew, changing it significantly, for he was not able to speak on the faith in progress and human perfectibility, so typical of Reform Judaism. Moreover, he was not capable of 'regard[ing] the doctrine that there was a God who had chosen Israel as his peculiar people as having even a shred of credibility. Chosen for what? – for Majdanek and Auschwitz?'[97] He finally came to the conclusion that, 'There was no all-powerful judge. No power in the universe had the slightest concern for the hopes, yearnings, or aspirations of human beings.'[98]

This was his first encounter with the catastrophe. Richard Rubenstein was then in his twenties, a young rabbinical student at the Hebrew Union College in Cincinnati. Another significant event took place fifteen years later, when he was a rabbi and a scholar. During his visit to West Germany he met Dean Heinrich Grüber[99] of the Evangelical Church of East and West Berlin. He had previously talked with many German clergymen, most of whom were convinced that God is involved in a special kind of relationship with the people Israel, and that whatever happens to the latter is the will of God. To these opinions Rubenstein would always reply that the unavoidable consequence of such reasoning must be the assertion that 'God really wanted the Jewish people to be exterminated by Hitler.'[100] What was unusual about the meeting with Dean Grüber was that he proved to be the only one of Rubenstein's interlocutors not to withdraw from the dangerous proposition. On the contrary, he tried to avoid inconsistency whatever the result. To Rubenstein's question, whether he believed that it was

God's will that the Nazis had exterminated European Jews, Dean Grüber answered: 'For Thy sake are we slaughtered every day' (Psalm 44:22)'. He added: 'For some reason, it was part of God's plan that the Jews died. God demands our death daily. He is the Lord, He is the Master; all is in His keeping and ordering.'[101] At face value, Grüber's reasoning might seem just an example of typical Christian theology of providence and of obedient acceptance of God's will. The moral weight of such thinking, however, is much more far-reaching:

> Grüber likened Hitler to Nebuchadnezzar as the 'rod of God's anger'. In effect, Grüber asserted that God sent Hitler to punish the Jews at Auschwitz *because Israel, God's chosen people, had sinned and nothing can happen to the Jews save that which God intended* ... Although Grüber did not identify the offense for which Israel had been punished, there is little reason to doubt that he regarded Jewish misfortune as Christian thinkers have throughout most of history. In fact, Grüber's colleagues in the German Evangelical Church meeting in Darmstadt in 1948, three years after the *Shoah*, asserted that the Holocaust was a divine punishment visited upon the Jews and, in a spirit of brotherhood, called upon the Jews to cease their rejection and continuing crucifixion of Jesus Christ. [Italics in the original.][102]

One might suppose that, while the 1944 event in Tupelo was rather existential in character, the meeting in Berlin had a specifically theological overtone and was perhaps intellectually more challenging to Rubenstein as a rabbi, though both events were an immediate confrontation with the problem of God and Auschwitz:

> The interview [with Grüber] pushed me to a theological point of no return: If I truly believed in God as the omnipotent author of the historical drama and in Israel as His Chosen People, I had no choice but to accept Dean Grüber's conclusion that Hitler unwittingly acted as God's agent in committing six million Jews to slaughter. *I could not believe in such a God, nor could I believe in Israel as the Chosen People of God after Auschwitz* ... After the death camps, the doctrine of Israel's election is in any event a thoroughly distasteful pill to swallow. Jews do not need these doctrines to remain a religious community. [Italics added.][103]

If Morgan was right only up to a point in arguing that Rubenstein does not make it clear what he means when he uses the term

'Auschwitz', and what kind of link there is between Auschwitz and rejection of the God of patriarchal monotheism, it is because he seems not to be satisfied with Rubenstein's reasoning. After all, even scholars experience sometimes something that might be called *illuminatio*. In Rubenstein, however, it was probably a negative illumination; he referred to it at some point as 'the dark night of the soul'. The content of this negative illumination is the very confrontation with the death camps. Such confrontation is no intellectual aphasia, but is hardly expressible in a purely speculative language, either. To be sure, Rubenstein does explain why Auschwitz means to him a radical breach within Jewish faith, a chasm that separates the 'before' from the 'after'. It makes the Jewish (and Christian) God – the Lord of history – utterly unreal, or ideal in terms of his non-existence beyond the realm of ideas. The question of 'why', quasi-automatically asked in the face of catastrophes like the Shoah, remains a disturbing one, but rather in the sense of a cry of rebellion. The real question, as I have noted above, pertains to the problem of the post-Holocaust present. It demands a response – and Rubenstein's failure to retain the biblical–rabbinic God-concept is just that: it is a response to Auschwitz. That Rubenstein responds to a radical event in a radical way is not surprising. Rather, what should be surprising are attempts at 'explaining Auschwitz away' in a traditional – and by the same token inadequate – way.[104] That is what traditional theology, both Jewish and Christian, does; and Rubenstein is unable to accept it. If he were to 'reconcile' Auschwitz with the monotheistic idea of a benevolent and all-powerful God, he would have to consciously carry out a *reduction of cognitive dissonance*. He analyses at length the applicability of Leon Festinger's theory of cognitive dissonance for theology and comes to the conclusion that what theology actually does is chiefly to help people to manage cognitive dissonance by reducing it.

But what exactly is cognitive dissonance theory, and is it applicable in our context? According to Festinger, cognitive dissonance occurs whenever an individual or a group finds two elements of their knowledge (cognition) inconsistent with one another. It is the very experience of inconsistency that Festinger calls dissonance, whereas by the term *cognition* he means 'any knowledge, opinion, or belief about the environment, about oneself, or about one's behavior'.[105] If two elements of cognition – 'knowledges', in Festinger's parlance – do not contradict each other, they are in a consonant relation. A cognition can exemplify 'knowledge about oneself, what one does, what one feels, what one wants or desires, what one is',[106] but it can also refer to areas of human mentality that are not usually associated with the word *knowledge* – this might be mere views or a set of opinions. For 'a person does not hold an opinion unless he thinks it is correct, and so, psychologically, it is not different from a "knowledge". That same is true of beliefs, values, or attitudes, which function as "knowledges" for our purposes.'[107]

Put more formally then, 'two elements [of cognition] are in a dissonant relation if, considering these two alone, the obverse of one element would follow from the other ... *x* and *y* are dissonant if not-*x* follows from *y*'.[108] Such a situation may occur when new information reaches a person who has so far held views standing in opposition to the newly acquired knowledge. As a result, tension arises and the individual is psychologically motivated to change either of the opposing elements in order to reduce the tension. As Rubenstein explains:

> Dissonance reduction strategy has been used frequently by groups that have experienced unanticipated, traumatic misfortune but who nevertheless believe an all powerful, beneficent deity guides their destiny. *Self-accusation and introjected guilt can permit a group to retain a belief in the existence and goodness of its deity ...* This dissonance-reducing function can be especially important in cultures, such as our own, in which the dominant religious institutions affirm that God is both the Creator and the ultimate actor in the drama of history. [Italics in the original.][109]

The single most important word in the above-quoted passage is the conjunctive *and*. It is crucial in the phrases where Rubenstein argues that people believe God exists AND is good AND is all-powerful; that he is the Creator AND the ultimate actor in history. Let us now confront this concept of God with the Holocaust and apply to it Festinger's theory in its formal shape. Assume our *concept* of God is *x*, while the event of the Holocaust is *y*. Are the two elements of cognition – the one being a belief or opinion, the other being knowledge about a factual event – in a dissonant relation? If God is good, is the Creator, and acts in history, then the Shoah – an attempted, and to a large extent realized, annihilation of European Jews, this God's chosen people – stands in opposition to that idea of God. Hence, from *not*-this-concept-of-God (not-*x*) it follows that the Holocaust was possible and in fact happened (*y*). Or, we can have it the other way round: from *not*-Holocaust (not-*y*) it follows that this-concept-of-God is valid (*x*). The '*not*-Holocaust' affirmation, however, obviously defies the reality. Thus, what we are left with is the first proposition: the Holocaust did happen; therefore, our concept of God, in its hitherto existing form, is untenable. We then have an actual cognitive dissonance which most people, including professional theologians, will probably attempt to reduce. Professor Rubenstein's conviction is that 'the underlying purpose of much of Holocaust scholarship is [this] dissonance reduction'.[110]

What are the most frequent and typical strategies of this 'Holocaust-dissonance reduction'? In Festinger's theory, a successful management of cognitive dissonance demands a change in one of the cognition elements – either its elimination or its modification. In the issue under discussion, it is thinkable to change the troublesome elements of the God-concept. This, of course, would entail objection to one of God's attributes: either his goodness, or his involvement in human history, or his might, which would be a rather painful operation (as is mostly the case with changing an existentially significant opinion one has held through one's lifetime[111]). Exactly this kind of strategy was applied by the well-known German-born Jewish philosopher Hans Jonas. He questions the traditional idea of God, whom he calls 'the Lord of *History*', but who 'remained silent' during the Second World War.[112] According to Jonas:

> after Auschwitz, we can assert with greater force than ever before that an omnipotent deity would have to be either not good or ... totally unintelligible. But if God is to be intelligible in some manner and to some extent ... then his goodness must be compatible with the existence of evil, and this it is only if he is not *all* powerful ... God was silent. And there I say, or my myth says, not because he chose not to, but because he *could* not intervene did he not intervene.[113]

Arthur A. Cohen's view is, in this respect, similar. He, too, claims that God is not the one who intervenes in history but the one who teaches humans how to constructively engage in history. Cohen claims that 'God is not the strategist of our particularities or of our historical condition, but rather the mystery of our futurity, always our *posse*, never our acts.'[114] However, though God is not the immediate director of history, he is not utterly divorced from it or indifferent to it, either.[115] The divine is, rather a 'filament within the historical',[116] but as such it is 'a precarious conductor always intimately linked to the historical ... and always separate from it, since the historical is the domain of human freedom'. Although Cohen strives to hold to the traditional vision of God as at least *mysteriously* present in history, and at the same time attempts to show that God actually does not create history, his concept is not convincing, if only because it is unclear and unnecessarily complicated. Cohen's God-teacher, therefore, is not only impotent (his teaching seems to have little influence upon humanity) but is totally beyond reproach. And this is perhaps what Cohen was aiming at: explaining away God's silence (this is perhaps the real *tremendum* of the Holocaust[117]), taking all responsibility off God, absolving him of any fault. Thus he saved God as such by sacrificing his dialogical relatedness to humankind: Cohen contends that God does not communicate with people through history, and if he does speak at all, it is not his speaking but our hearing that appears in our minds.[118] (Rubenstein is right to observe that in this context Cohen's theology resembles Berkovits's, but it is my contention that both Cohen and Berkovits are equal in their lack of clarity and consistency in this respect.)

The easiest way to reduce the tension in discussion would be to state that there is no tension whatsoever between the Shoah and God: in other words, to deny there is a problem. Outright rejection of the Holocaust-dissonance question was the reaction of some of the Orthodox thinkers whose argumentation I have presented in the previous chapter.[119] Certainly, the denial-of-the-problem reaction, particularly in the form of indirect repression, is not only typical of people emotionally and intellectually shaped by a fundamentalist religiosity. Those who come from liberal religious circles, too, construct their argumentation in such a manner that it does not disturb the fundamental element of their world view, which is their belief in the existence of a good God-Creator. In other words, they try to absolve God of responsibility for the fate of humans. This is, perhaps, what motivates Peter Knobel, a Reform rabbi: 'The Holocaust is for me the equivalent of our exile in Egypt – a frightening example of how human evil when unchecked threatens not only our existence but God's existence as well. It has reinforced my belief in partnership between God and humankind and the special role which our faith plays in encouraging others to remain believers.'[120]

David M. Gordis, president of the Hebrew College in Boston, deems both the Holocaust and the establishment of the state of Israel as events of utmost importance for contemporary Jews. He claims, however, that these facts

> have not had an impact ... on my religious or theological positions.

God is not responsible for evil, even the depths of depravity represented by the Holocaust. God is not responsible for historical achievements, even those as notable as the reestablishment of the state of Israel. Both of these events have intensified my sense of Jewish identity and had a role in shaping it. Neither has created a theological crisis or generated a 'eureka' experience.[121]

What is underscored in both quotations is the conviction that the Shoah not only does not trigger religious rebellion, it reinforces the foundation of faith; it also gives a stronger awareness of one's religious and ethnic background. Moreover, the process of relieving God of his responsibility seems symbolic (a concept which is more vividly seen in Gordis). The transmittal of responsibility from God to man seems understandable from the point of view of purely secular logic but not so comprehensible from the point of view of Jewish theology. Here we are facing an unsolvable problem, since the Rabbis themselves have not decided what kind of response to give it. The unanswered question is to what extent God bears responsibility for history, which also implies responsibility for human acts. All authors commenting on the topic support their stance with suitable citations from the Torah, the Prophets or the Talmud. If, however, the contention that the divine enters the history of man, as is maintained in numerous places in the Bible, is still accepted and agreed upon in Judaism, than the unavoidable question arises: Whether and why did God allow the extermination of Jews?

Peter Knobel, mentioning the exile in Egypt, does not mention the fact that this period in the history of the Hebrew tribes was ended by a spectacular Exodus. That event, in the biblical narrative as well as in the commentaries of later interpreters, is considered as the constitutive event for the people Israel, which is to this day remembered and is retold during the Pesach Seder.[122] Other intellectuals, however, do point the Exodus from Egypt as a fact that cannot be neglected in the debate on the Shoah. Thus, John Fisher inquires: 'If God did intervene at the Exodus, why did He not do so at Auschwitz?'[123] This question is a legitimate one from the point of view of the religious system of Judaism. For the classical Jewish historiosophy has claimed that God can and does intervene in history – if not in the history of all humankind, at least in that of the people Israel. That is why it is affirmed sometimes that the very 'Jewish existence bears eloquent testimony to the God of history and to His presence.'[124] Fisher says that one of the proofs of the Absolute's presence in history is the re-establishment of the state of Israel. This political fact he even calls a 'modern day miracle',[125] not to be ignored in the Holocaust discussion, because this fact 'stands as the outstanding example of Jewish survival in history and thus testifies loudly to God's "miraculous" guidance in history. It helps us understand God's role in history that includes the Holocaust, and it gives us hope for the future.'[126] Opposed to this argumentation is the opinion of David Weiss Halivni: 'There are those who connect the Holocaust and the state of Israel – as though God somehow compensated us for the children who were gassed. I do not.'[127]

Lewis Feuer admits that, in terms of historical causality, it is possible to come to the conclusion that if not for the Shoah, the Jewish state would not have been established in 1948. However, he adds immediately: 'Who would dare say that the creation of the state of Israel was worth an Auschwitz, a Treblinka, a Maidanek?'[128] This seems to be a rhetorical question, but is not. Feuer says that in a sociological survey focused on the topic of the Holocaust, 6 per cent of the survivors interviewed deemed the creation of Israel as worth 'the sacrifice of the Six Millions' [*sic*] of human beings.[129]

If Fisher talks of the 'miracle' of the *statehood* of Israel, others ask why, earlier on, did a miracle not prevent the destruction of the *people* of Israel? In other words: Why did the Holocaust become sort of 'a negative miracle'? It is again Lewis Feuer who argues, this time in a somewhat ironic manner, that a 'negative miracle ... would constitute evidence for God's absence or withdrawal from history, if not the actual intrusion of a dualistic anti-God, the Devil'.[130] Some thinkers do not even deem it sensible to talk of the Shoah in relation to the state of Israel. Ismar Schorsch, for example, considers futile the kind of theological discourse which oscillates between victories and failures in the history of Israel. In his view, to interpret these events at one time as God's presence, and at other times as God's absence, is intellectually poor.[131]

Quite often in this particular context, some authors introduce the 'human freedom' argument. This is exactly the question raised in one of *Tikkun*'s editorials. The editors argue that from the moment of revelation on – that is, from the investiture of the Torah (*Torah min ha-shamayim*) – God has begun to withdraw from the world. The process of divine 'contraction' (*tzimtzum*) is meant to enable humans to be free. Thanks to the self-limitation of divine activity in the world, humanity gains a chance to shape its history by itself. Freedom of men and women, the *Tikkun* editors maintain, is unthinkable if God is involved in every particular event of their lives.[132] The anthropology of freedom is undoubtedly one of the characteristic traits of the *Tikkun's* board of editors' worldview. In the introductory note to a symposium on the Shoah, published in this journal, the editors declare: 'Tikkun has argued for a version of Judaism that sees God as having given human beings the possibility of moral insight (Torah) and the freedom to make their own errors and sin their own sins (even at the cost of allowing a Holocaust to take place).'[133] But is such a concept really philosophically tenable? Is it consistent in itself? If God should not – as the argument goes – interfere with every single and trivial fact occurring in history, it might be inferred from this assumption that he could impact at least some affairs. Thus, is the Holocaust one of these unimportant things that God is not to be concerned about? Furthermore, is human freedom, for which the Shoah is allegedly a reasonable price, not just freedom for the chosen ones – for those who have survived or who were born after the war? Accepting this view would mean that the millions who paid with their own lives to prove, as it were, the factual freedom exercised by others, are themselves deprived of the privilege those others can enjoy. But even if freedom could serve, hypothetically, to explain evil, it is incapable of explaining the existence of the victim.[134] Therefore, this kind of anthropology seems to justify the Holocaust in the spirit of the Hegelian law of history which provides each and every event with a *raison d'être*, because all of them are supposed to lead to the consummation of history.

The human freedom argument, however, seems unconvincing to some of the intellectuals involved in the Holocaust debate. Kenneth Seeskin is one of the unpersuaded:

> The Children of Israel were saved when God parted the Red Sea. But who would argue that the Egyptians were not allowed to exercise freedom in pursuing them across it? In principle, the lives of six million Jews might have been saved without robbing anyone of his freedom. There are even accounts indicating that many Jews failed to resist the Nazis because they believed that such a rescue was inevitable.[135]

We have seen thus far how various authors try to reduce Holocaust-dissonance by either modifying one of the cognition elements involved in it or by objecting to the very statement that there is dissonance here. This apparently confirms Rubenstein's diagnosis of Shoah debate: namely, that it is in large measure engaged in reducing the dissonance. What Rubenstein, however, does not see is perhaps that he himself is attempting to get rid of the puzzling contradiction between the biblical–rabbinic God-idea and the event of the Holocaust. What he ends up with is not dissonance reduction but, what should be underscored, *dissonance elimination*. If, as Festinger has observed, the process of reducing a cognitive dissonance may prove to be a painful one – it may even entail a loss in one's harmonious life – how much more painful can it be to resolutely eliminate a dissonance? This process has to do with our situatedness in the world, with how we internalize the world, how we transform it into an image which we store in ourselves. Alan Rosenberg has aptly pointed out that 'each person's way of being in the world is relatively fixed – and serves as a protection against the anxieties of the unknown ... [Thus] [t]o give up a world in which one's life makes sense means undergoing great loss.'[136]

We now come to one of the most important and inspiring of Rubenstein's utterances. It is not shocking that he rejects the biblical God, but that he does it so honestly, thoroughly and painfully. The death of the Jewish God is for him a great loss. This is more vividly seen in the second edition of *After Auschwitz*, where Rubenstein elucidates what he means by the death of God and why he does not consider himself an atheist,[137] and in what respect he changed the views that he had presented in 1966. Although he no longer strongly believes the cosmos to be 'cold, silent, unfeeling', he still maintains an utterly fundamental opinion on God and the Holocaust. He repeats in the second edition what he had already stated in the 1966 *Commentary* symposium and in the first edition of his acclaimed book:

> I believe the greatest single challenge to modern Judaism arises out of the question of God and the death camps. I am amazed at the silence of contemporary theologians on this most crucial and agonizing of all Jewish issues. How can Jews believe in an omnipotent, beneficent God after Auschwitz? Traditional Jewish theology maintains that God is the ultimate, omnipotent actor in the historical drama. It has interpreted every major catastrophe in Jewish history as God's punishment of a sinful Israel. I fail to see how this position can be maintained without regarding Hitler and the SS as instruments of God's will.[138]

What brings together the two editions of *After Auschwitz* is not, however, just paralyzing questions but radical answers:

1. the idea of God of the 'biblical and rabbinic mainstream', i.e. the 'God of History', is no longer credible[139]

2. 'rejection of the notion that the Jews are in any sense a people either chosen or rejected by God'.[140]

One can imagine that this was no easy solution for a Jew to accept. Indeed, Rubenstein confesses that denial 'of the biblical God and the doctrine of the Chosen People was a step of extraordinary seriousness for a rabbi and Jewish theologian'.[141] As a result, concluding the chapter titled 'Death-of-God Theology and Judaism', he affirms: 'Unlike Altizer, I cannot rejoice in the death of God. *If I am a death-of-God theologian, it is with a cry of agony.*' (Italics added.)[142] From this phrase one can infer that Rubenstein's experience testifies to Festinger's contention that dissonance reduction entails great loss. Rubenstein's, however, is no mere psychological reduction but complete elimination of dissonance.[143] Perhaps he would not describe his own theologizing as dissonance elimination, but this is what it really is: a complete, grounded change of *Weltanschauung*. Rubenstein is certainly by no means the only one to have come to such radical conclusions. Irrefutable doubts, rebellion, or radical denial of God brought about by the Shoah are also experiences shared by many other Jewish thinkers and/or clergy, who, after pondering over the Holocaust, became convinced that God does not exist, or at least that there is no such God as he is described in the biblical narrative. Almost every time, in such circumstances, a person who makes the decision to change their world view is aware of breaking the continuity of the forefathers' tradition. This exactly is the case of the Reform rabbi from Alabama, Steven Jacobs:

> [The] Holocaust has shattered forever and all time the easy acceptance of Jewish religious thinking that is most particularly identified with thinking about God ... [It has] forced me to – *re-think* – the entire process of my Jewish identity ... I no longer believe as my Grandfather, killed by the Nazis, believed; I reject the God that my Father rejected because that God, too, died in those same camps, along with our family and our historical ideas ... I no longer pray to a Commander God because I do not believe that this concept is accurately reflective of either the God of the Jewish People or of the historical experience of the Jewish People ... I must (1) *rethink* my understanding of God, God's supposed relationship with humanity ... and (2) *rethink* and, therefore, redefine this whole concept of 'commandments'. [Italics in the original.][144]

A similar process of rethinking his former standpoint could probably be observed in Rubenstein. As a result of his confrontation with the event of Auschwitz, Rubenstein's traditional Jewish theology of history becomes transformed into non-traditional, Spinozian, Jewish philosophy. Hence, he does not focus on seeking God in history, for he knows God is absent from it, but on formulating such an idea of the divine that would conform to his conviction about the tragic predicament of human beings. It is not really obvious whether this transformation is Rubenstein's last word, for his final chapter is titled 'God after the Death-of-God'. Rubenstein argues that the classic radical theology is wrong in its assertion that God is factually dead. What can be meaningful in such an assertion, he claims, is that the very act of uttering the phrase 'God is dead' reveals a great deal about the one who says it. In other words, radical theologians communicate much about themselves but not necessarily about God. This, in turn, confirms Rubenstein's thesis that theology is just a specific kind of anthropology. Hence, 'It is more precise to assert that *we live in the time of the death of God* than to declare "God is dead". *The death of God is a cultural fact. We shall never know whether it is more than that.*' (Italics in the original.)[145] Thus the death of God would be tantamount to a novel revelation of the dramatic human predicament.

What kind of God, then, is left for Rubenstein after the death of God? It is a non-theistic God that does not compel him to become an atheist. Rubenstein, a non-theistic non-atheist, so to speak, claims that the only idea of God acceptable to him after Auschwitz has been found in mysticism and pantheism.[146] There are several sources of the inspiration he finds in those religious currents. As to the latter, Rubenstein has been deeply influenced by oriental religions with their non-personal, totalizing conceptions of deity. The most pre-eminent single idea that has cast a spell on him is the Buddhist notion of *Nothingness*. At this point, Rubenstein – though usually both a theologian and philosopher – becomes a mystical philosopher: he can say *nothing* about God save that he is no-thing. Yet God's name is not nothing but Nothingness (the state of being no-thing). Since, however, the divine is not devoid of some kind of sanctity, he calls it Holy Nothingness, *das Heilige Nichts*.[147] In Rubenstein, the non-objectifiable character of the Holy Nothingness is interpreted, paradoxically, as fullness, or *plenum*. The Nothingness-as-Fullness concept is, according to Rubenstein, similar to the idea of *En-Sof*, the limitless, an idea he discovered in Kabbalistic mysticism. 'God, thus designated, is regarded as the ground and source of all existence', not a void or emptiness but 'a *plenum* so rich that all existence derives from it. God as the "Nothing" is not absence of being, but superfluity of being.'[148] With the idea of divinity as the 'Ground of Being' Rubenstein is, of course, indebted to Paul Tillich. Tillich's *Urgrund* is the concept that fits well with the *En-Sof* of Jewish Kabbalists, as well as with Paul of Tarsus's vision of 'all in all' unity. Rubenstein's mystical pantheism invites him to yearn for a final unification of *all*-things, of the whole 'cosmic *galut* or exile ... with primordial source, the Aboriginal *Urgrund*' (italics in the original).[149] Here, interestingly (if not surprisingly) enough, his philosophy takes on an eschatological shade.

There is yet another source of mystical inspiration that plays a certain role in Rubenstein's theology, especially in the first edition of *After Auschwitz*. It is what he calls 'nature paganism'.[150] In this context he refers to the gods of Canaan and the Mediterranean cults of the Earth Goddess – the Holy Mother.[151] Rubenstein seems to be fascinated by the priestly structure of these pagan cults as well as their bacchanalian mood. He, too, underscores the power of immanentism and mysticism in nature paganism. In his opinion, 'pagan sanity' fits the human condition more naturally, as it were, than the 'atheistic Christian apocalypticism' of Altizer. As a matter of fact, paganism is triumphant in the hearts of men and women, both in Judaism and Christianity, for the symbols and rituals these two religions use are 'instrumentalities whereby the decisive crises of life can be celebrated and shared ... Birth, adolescence, marriage, and death demand religious celebration. At such times we are far less interested in prophetic proclamations than in cultic acts.'[152] This does not mean, however, that Rubenstein is opposed to ethics, especially ethics incarnated in some kind of law. For him, perhaps the best way to avoid chaos and anomie is to follow religious law: all the more so that we live in times of gods but of no God – that is why 'religious law is more necessary for us than ever'.[153]

It is, however, to a certain extent disappointing how Rubenstein, concluding the final chapter, describes his overall religious outlook. On one of the last pages of the book, we read: 'I often expressed my deepest religious feelings by saying that *omnipotent Nothingness is Lord of all creation*. This affirmation of mystical faith seems to offer a concise way of synthesizing mystical, dialectical, psychoanalytic, and archaic insights concerning God as the ground, content, and final destiny of all things.' (Italics in the original.)[154] Of course, Rubenstein is free to hold any kind of religious beliefs, and those beliefs should be respected, yet such a syncretic mixture seems less than original for a thinker of his stature. Not that syncretism cannot be interesting, but in light of the aforementioned expression, some of Rubenstein's clear-cut, innovative and highly inspiring ideas become, in a way, muted.

ELIEZER BERKOVITS: HESTER PANIM

At the other theological extreme in interpreting the God-image in light of the Shoah, we have Eliezer Berkovits. An Orthodox Jew, Berkovits had been given a rather traditional education in Berlin's Hildesheimer Rabbinical Seminary. His deep immersion in the biblical-rabbinic narrative has presumably shaped his view on history. In fact, his concept of history is a derivative of his religious beliefs. For him, covenant is the key category of Judaism.[155] Israel's covenant with God, according to the Bible, is a historical event. If the covenant is viewed as a paradigm of the Jews' relationship with God, then, generally speaking, any event in Israel's history is an encounter with the divine. In the whole of Berkovits's reasoning, this idea seems to be of great relevance. According to the Orthodox rabbinic doctrine, God is a person who intervenes in history and affects its course.[156] Berkovits accepts this stance, though, confronted with the Holocaust, it can have dramatic consequences. That God enters history is, however, too general a statement. Berkovits, following traditional Jewish teaching, does not believe that divine presence is manifested in history at large – it is within the history of Israel that it proves really visible:

> God's unconvincing presence in history is testified to through the survival of Israel. All God's miracles occur outside of history. When God acts with manifest power, history is at a standstill. The only exception is the historic reality of Israel ... There is no other witness that God is present in history but the history of the Jewish people ... Half a billion Christians prove nothing about God's presence in history.[157]

Berkovits maintains that God simply *is* the God of history.[158] Moreover, he reproaches the post-Auschwitz theologians, claiming that they are naively radical in their rejection or elimination of God from history.[159] He underscores the fact that for biblical prophets the vision of God is always one of the God of history. In the prophetic books, God's providence is factual and observable in history – not only in the history of Israel, but that of other nations, too. If whatever happens within the human world must somehow be in accord with divine plans, then how is evil experienced by the righteous to be explained? Berkovits joins Jeremiah and Habakkuk in asking, 'Wherefore doeth the way of the wicked prosper?[160] Wherefore lookest Thou, when they deal treacherously / And holdest Thy peace, when the wicked swalloweth up / The man that is more righteous than he?'[161] If, therefore, God does act in history – and is said to be just – then, 'The facts do not fit the theory. This, of course, is the key theme of the Book of Job.'[162] Interestingly enough, in a chapter titled 'Job's brother', Berkovits honestly presents a radical diagnosis of the present-day situation: the death camp experience has led many a Jew to a crisis of faith. And the questions 'Where was God all the time? How could he countenance the infliction of such suffering and degradation of helpless millions, among them untold numbers of innocent children?' have become essential, not only to the survivors, but to other Jewish people, too: 'The faith of many [of them] was choked in the smoke of the crematoria.'[163] Berkovits knows this problem is not totally new; it is the latest example of the theologically embarrassing question of theodicy. Its old formulation – *unde malum*? – is modified so that it is relevant to the present-day historical circumstances and to the current religious consciousness of men and women. Therefore, the question now reads: How to absolve God of the guilt of indifference in the face of the Holocaust? Of course, Berkovits himself does not ask this question; what he does, however, throughout the entire book, is seek answers to the question.

It is worthwhile noticing that, despite the fact that the figure of Job is recalled on innumerable occasions in Holocaust literature, the story of Job has seemingly never been overtly rejected as an explanation of evil. No suffering of the innocent can be justified as God's test of one's faithfulness. To do so is obscene; it is a scandal that defies human moral intuition. To condemn a single person, or a whole family as in the Book of Job, to suffering and/or death only to try another person's faith is to destroy any viable morality. Such a stance would entail a vision of God for whom some individuals are subjects to be respected, whereas others are mere objects to be used as instruments. Moral reason could not stand that. On the other hand, if, assuming that Job's affliction was God's test, we wanted to construct the generalization argument, we would have to ask: What if God decided to so try every right and decent person? Then, his/her affliction would have to be considered unjust punishment – punishment for being just – *poena sine peccato*, punishment without sin.

Berkovits is well aware that his God of history was absent from the death camps, that he remained silent and hidden. 'Millions were looking for him – in vain.'[164] But 'absent' is probably not the right word here. Although he admits there exists the *problem* of 'the absence of God', Berkovits does not believe it is absence *sensu stricto*, for the term seems to him loaded with meanings given to it by radical theologians. God is not so much absent as in hiding. Berkovits cannot overlook the fact that the rabbis did not speak of God's absence, either, but spoke of his silence.[165] *El Mistater*, 'the hiding God is present; though man is unaware of him. He is present in his hiddenness.'[166] Berkovits assumes, after Isaiah, that hiddenness is an attribute of God.[167] Hence, he comes to the conclusion that God's presence in history is not as self-evident as traditional theology would have it. It remains and must remain in large measure unconvincing.[168] Thus we have to ask why God remained hidden and silent while his creatures were being exterminated. As we have seen, for Berkovits, God's actions in history are mostly – if not uniquely – present in the fate of his people Israel. The question then becomes much harsher and puzzling: *Why did the God of Israel allow this to happen to his holy people?*

Berkovits finds answers to both questions in two different realms: one is philosophical anthropology, the other Jewish theology. In search for philosophical explanations he resorts to the concept of human freedom. He argues that freedom is a condition *sine qua non* of human engagement in and responsibility for history. Deity is the warrant of man's freedom and responsibility. And by granting him the gift of freedom, God at the same time shows his trust for human responsibility, even if the record of man's deeds in history leaves much to be desired:[169]

> [Man] must have freedom of choice and freedom of decision. And his freedom must be respected by God himself ... Man can be frightened; but he cannot be bludgeoned into goodness. If God did not respect man's freedom to choose his course in personal responsibility, not only would the moral good and evil be abolished from the earth, but man himself would go with them. For freedom and responsibility are the very essence of man. Without them man is not human. If there is to be man, he must be allowed to make his choices in freedom. If he has such freedom, he will use it. Using it, he will often use it wrongly; he will decide for the wrong alternative. As he does so, there will be suffering for the innocent.[170]

Similarly to what we have seen in one of *Tikkun*'s editorials, Berkovits, too, makes a high point of the anthropology of freedom. This even seems to be the point of departure for his theology of history. History is what it is, not because God has failed, but because man is free. But why does a free human being have to suffer? Is freedom tantamount to suffering? In trying to solve this problem, Berkovits has recourse to what he calls 'the paradox of divine providence'.[171] We thus come again to the prophets' vexing question: Why do the righteous perish while the wicked prosper? The answer lies nowhere else than in human freedom, or rather in the relation between God's might and his creatures' freedom. Employing theological categories, Berkovits affirms that God is waiting (self-limiting his power to punish)[172] for the sinner to return to him; he is waiting for the sinner's repentance (*teshuvah*). Therefore, this very attribute of God – forbearance with the wicked – makes for violence, persecution, and suffering of the weak. It is just because God is patient, Berkovits believes, that 'he must turn a deaf ear to the anguished cries of the violated'.[173] This conclusion, to be sure, does not provide comfort or consolation for Berkovits. With some sadness in tone, he says that 'it is the tragic paradox of faith that God's direct concern for the wrongdoer should be directly responsible for so much pain and sorrow on earth'.[174] So long as people use their freedom for evil ends, Berkovits contends, the patient God is in exile. The state of divine exile – *Galut haShekhinah*[175] – is what humans perceive as divine absence. In point of fact, however, God does not withdraw from history – he only hides his face.

The idea of the hidden face of God (*hester panim*) has been one of the most accepted explicatory categories employed in Jewish theology in the context of great catastrophes. It had been useful to explain away the destruction of the two Temples and the expulsion of Jews from Spain. The concept has proved fitting and effective also in Jewish post-Holocaust thought, at least to some scholars, including Eliezer Berkovits. In the opinion of William Orbach, Berkovits attributes to man the responsibility for the situation in which humanity is separated from God by a veil of silence. It is human beings who possess the power to cause the eclipse of God's countenance.[176] Berkovits himself, however, is very equivocal on this issue and lacks consistence. In effect, for one thing, there are numerous passages to be found in his *Faith After the Holocaust*, where he states that man is the only actor in the *theatrum mundi*, which makes him the principal author of total evil (*hastrat panim*, in theological terms). What is more, he argues that if God were to enter history with his material power, he would destroy history. For another, he claims that human history would be unthinkable without God's presence, and that the divine cannot retreat from this world if humankind is to survive.[177] As we can see, Berkovits's attempts to save both God's caring relation to humankind and human beings' real freedom lead practically nowhere. His reasoning is quite often emotional, but lacks consequence. Of course, as a theologian he can always say he is dealing with paradoxes of faith. But if a thinker, theologian or otherwise, is to gain any credibility, s/he should considerably limit the use of the word 'paradox'.

Although the *hester panim* doctrine is usually not rejected by believer-philosophers, some of them find it unacceptable. David Weiss Halivni, for instance, strongly opposes this explanation of the Shoah. He does so on the grounds of the biblical context in which the expression appears. Weiss Halivni maintains that the 'hidden face' teaching is based on the doctrine of punishment for sins – which is rarely noticed by other scholars. He refers to a passage in Deuteronomy, where God's hiding is a sign of divine fury: 'Then my anger shall be kindled against them on that day, and I will forsake them, and I will hide my face from them'.[178] For that reason, Weiss Halivni does not consider the whole concept morally suitable to provide any explanation for the Holocaust.

Berkovits is well aware of the problems that the passage from Deuteronomy entails; nevertheless, he does not reject the idea of *hester panim*. Instead, he quotes a fragment from Psalm 44 which illustrates a situation where God is hiding his countenance while innocent people are murdered.[179] In fact, however, in Judaism, the oldest tradition of explaining evil almost always saw it as punishment for individual or group transgressions. The Hebrew expression that constitutes the core of *punishment theology* reads as follows: *mipnei hataeinu galinu mearzeinu*, we were exiled because of our sins. To Berkovits, the way of thinking about suffering as retribution from God for sins committed is unacceptable. Taking into consideration the whole history of Jewish suffering, he claims, leaves no room for such an explanation of evil. That all violence and oppression experienced by Jews over the ages were due to their unfaithfulness to the covenant is for him an obscene idea. However, he does not completely rule out the very possibility of punishment for sins; there is evil that may be regarded as due punishment, but that all suffering is caused by actual sins – that view Berkovits finds outrageous.[180]

The concept of *hester panim* is not Berkovits's last word. To his credit, he seems not to be content with easy or safe theological explications that he can work out for himself on the basis of biblical doctrine. In spite of having analysed selected passages from the Bible and the rabbis, he does not come to the conclusion that God can be regarded as bearing no responsibility at all for the Shoah:

> Not for a single moment shall we entertain the idea that what happened to European Jewry was divine punishment for any sins committed by them. It was injustice absolute. It was injustice countenanced by God. But if we hold onto our faith in a personal God, such absolute injustice cannot be a mere mishap in the divine scheme of things. Somehow there must be room for it in the scheme, in which case the ultimate responsibility for this ultimate evil must be God's ... As Isaiah saw clearly, God as the only creator is also the creator of evil.[181]

Berkovits sees this situation, and that of all Jews after the Holocaust, as a new incarnation of Job's dilemma: the Jew who has faith in God cannot help but accuse God of tolerating injustice and being indifferent toward his chosen people. He distinguishes between such an accusation deeply rooted in faith, and what he calls a simple solution to the crisis engendered by the death camps. He depicts the simple-solution reaction in terms of cutting 'the Gordian knot with the classical formula: "There is no justice and there is no judge!" '[182] It is not only present-day advocates of the death-of-God concept who suggest this kind of a solution, but several 'radical theologians of old Israel',[183] such as Elisha ben Abuyah, a Talmudic scholar who could not find a better explanation for the issue of theodicy than the assertion that God does not exist.

Berkovits admits that if there is in his generation a real challenge to the theistic world view, it is the most extreme and excruciating experience that emerges out of the death camps. Auschwitz constitutes a crisis for Jewish life and faith. Indeed, he feels empathy with both those who have clung onto their faith in God after having gone through the Holocaust and those who have rejected God. He himself cannot deny the existence of the divine, as he had not been in the camps, and there are many who had been there and still remained believers. On the other hand, he cannot accept what happened in the war years 'in awesome submission to the will of God',[184] for there were Jews who lost their faith. He feels incapable of either accepting or rejecting God because he did not live through the Shoah. Nevertheless, he finds it 'easier to understand the loss of faith in the "Kz" than the faith preserved and affirmed. The faith affirmed was superhuman; the loss of faith – in those circumstances – human. Since I am only human, what is human is nearer to me than the superhuman.'[185]

The tension that is so clearly demonstrated in the passage on faith preserved and lost is perhaps the very specific feature of Berkovits's book. Most often he does not want to take sides. His is a stance that finds its best expression in the tension itself. He is not 'in between'; he feels compelled to accept two apparently contradictory views, be they belief and unbelief (save when the latter is proclaimed by atheist non-survivors), God present in history and God exiled from history, man responsible for the course of this-worldly matters as a free creature and God responsible for man's world as his creator. Yes, this is his paradoxical framework outside which he cannot function.

Berkovits's reasoning is an excellent illustration of what Jacob Neusner has dubbed the 'myth of Holocaust and redemption'.[186] This kind of thinking focuses on two major events of twentieth-century Jewish history, namely the Holocaust and the establishment of the state of Israel. Although Berkovits is very much troubled by the challenge of *Churban Europa*, he finds cause for great optimism in the return of the Jewish people to the land of Israel.[187] One last citation will serve as an epitome of his persistent philosophic-historical vagueness (if not dualism):

> the Holocaust is not all of Jewish history, nor is it its final chapter ... it did not become the Final Solution as was planned by the powers of darkness ... Yet all this does not exonerate God for all the suffering of the innocent in history. God is responsible for having created a world in which man is free to make history ... It is not a willingness to forgive the unheard cries of millions, but a trust that in God the tragedy of man may find its transformation.[188]
>
> The overwhelming majority of [Jews] experienced the recent confrontation between the state of Israel and the Arab nations as a moment of messianic history. It was an event not on the purely man-made level of history, but one that took place in conformity with the divine plan. Especially in the land of Israel the widest section of the population were convinced that 'this is God's doing; it is marvelous in our eyes'.[189]

Although God is still responsible for the kind of beings we are – free human beings – it is man that *freely chose to commit the Holocaust*.

On the other hand, the establishment of the state of Israel is part of the divine plan. Of course, it would be unthinkable for Berkovits to say that the Shoah was God's doing, but he would have come to such a conclusion had he put his reasoning to a test similar to Rubenstein's: If Israel's history is a realization of divine plans, then Hitler was God's instrument.

EMIL L. FACKENHEIM: A NEW COMMANDMENT

The Holocaust theologian who is probably the most often quoted and the best-known is Emil L. Fackenheim. Born in Germany, incarcerated in Sachsenhausen for some time in 1938, he emigrated to Canada, where he spent most of his lifetime as professor of philosophy in Toronto.[190] He became famous as a scholar who made the Holocaust one of the foci of his thought when he published his *Quest for Past and Future* in 1968. The book opens with an essay in which Fackenheim analyses the situation in Jewish philosophy and theology in America in the first two decades after the war. He is close to Rubenstein when he observes that most of American philosophy is liberal, melioristic thinking fed by the hope engendered in the Enlightenment. Whereas Europe was dominated by pessimism and atheistic existentialism, America was under the spell of pervasive optimism – optimism which was grounded not in God, but in man. That kind of euphoria was ubiquitous in religious thought, too.[191] Fackenheim noticed that American Judaism was also deeply influenced by the liberal philosophy of the nineteenth and early twentieth centuries. Jews considered themselves as members of a religion called 'ethical monotheism', which has lost the living God and which, as a wit once put it, could easily be mistaken 'for members of the *Kant-Gesellschaft*'. (Italics in the original.)[192] In short, speaking from the middle of a crisis, Fackenheim asserts that the contemporary Jew (1) is a universalist; (2) is a secularist (in so far as s/he is engaged in the politics of society); (3) finds his/her Jewish particularity important (for even a non-believing Jew has to deal with religion if s/he cares about the future); the Jew of today, either in America or in Israel, the two main Jewish centres, 'is at home in the modern world', though s/he lives in the post-Holocaust world.[193]

Fackenheim himself, however, could not take on the role of yet another philosophy-producer who would entertain the reader with an optimistic, self-assured view of man and the world. It was obvious to him that the European catastrophe was a central event for him as a thinker, and a Jewish one. He was convinced that 'the Jewish theologian of today cannot continue to believe, or continue to engage in theological thought, as though the events associated with the dread name of Auschwitz had not occurred'.[194]

For Fackenheim, the death camps were an explosion of a wholly new, alien world, indeed a new planet. 'The Holocaust Kingdom' or 'Planet Auschwitz', as he has called the Jewish catastrophe, constitutes a real 'anti-world'.[195] This utter newness, as it were, of the Holocaust is what makes it unique. The uniqueness of the Auschwitz-event, especially in religious terms, lies in the fact that it is unlike other events which were usually subject to interpretation and explanation. As such, the Holocaust not only cannot be rationally explained (for to seek an explanation of an unexplainable event is logically absurd), but is also devoid of any religious significance – 'no religious meaning will ever be found in Auschwitz, for the very attempt to find it is blasphemy'.[196] Theological interpretation is to be excluded because it always attempts to find meanings and purposes in things – and Fackenheim is persuaded that the Shoah is theologically meaningless and purposeless. As comparing different historical events is most often a way of trying to understand them, comparison, too, is to be rejected as 'odious or irrelevant'.[197] Thus, the event that is both logically and theo-logically inexplicable, is also historically unique, unprecedented; it has had no precedent either in Jewish history or in history at large. Therefore the Shoah is an 'epoch-making' event.[198] But, if it is an epoch-making event, Fackenheim claims, we cannot leave the Holocaust beyond the realm of human reflection. For to refrain from interpretation does not mean to refrain from every kind of intellectual reception. In Fackenheim's opinion, the only acceptable attempt to intellectually deal with this event is to seek a response to it. He argues that while it is impossible to find in the Holocaust anything that could be deemed meaningful, it is at the same time unavoidable to try to respond to it. Any authentic response, however, must meet certain criteria: it must be respectful of millions of innocent victims, including children; it must not view the victims as martyrs; and – last but not least – it 'must be rid totally of any *appearance* of being an explanation.' (Italics in the original.)[199]

An authentic response to the European catastrophe given by an authentic Jew[200] must be worked out as a confrontation with the Shoah. Fackenheim excludes, however, two of the possible reactions that might arise out of such a confrontation: on the one hand, through remembering the Shoah, we cannot turn our life into death;

on the other, it is unacceptable to affirm life 'at the price of forgetting Auschwitz'.[201]

The single response to the Shoah that Fackenheim criticized most
severely is the death-of-God theology. To begin with, Fackenheim
analyses the Christian radical thinkers, such as Thomas J.J. Altizer, who
reject the possibility of the existence of a real God on philosophical
grounds. For them the idea of a living God is nothing more than an
illusion – it has nothing to do with a factual being. Thus, what they call
the death of God, Fackenheim believes, is not the death of God, but
death of the belief in him. He also points to the fact that for most of
those thinkers, the death of God is, too, a condition *sine qua non* of
human freedom and autonomy. He sees this attitude unambiguously
phrased already by Nietzsche: 'the Nietzschean death of God is not a
limited and contingent event which is without permanent or universal
effect. In this event *God dies away into man*, leaving man both forever
Godless and endowed with a wholly new freedom.' (Italics in the
original.)[202] Though Fackenheim refers to Rubenstein explicitly only
on rare occasions,[203] he does have in mind Rubenstein's theology when
he criticizes the radical thinkers. In concurrence with Rubenstein,
however, he remarks that the very term 'death of God' is absolutely
un-Jewish, that it has emerged from a Christian milieu. For even in
Nietzsche, the proclamation of the death of God has strictly Christian
overtones, not to mention in Tillich, Altizer and others. What Fackenheim apparently overlooks is the fact that Rubenstein does not
celebrate the death of the biblical God, but, on the contrary, mourns it,
since for him this death is a great and inexorable loss. Thus Fackenheim does away with the death-of-God concept as merely a metaphor
pertaining to belief in God. He claims the Nietzschean death of God is
a real challenge to Judaism and Christianity, but completely ignores the
problems raised by Rubenstein, namely his assertion that after
Auschwitz the biblical–rabbinic idea of God has lost credibility on
account of its existential irrelevance.

The crucial issue, however, is what kind of response to the Shoah
Fackenheim proposes himself. His is a completely novel solution, truly
original in its very formulation as an additional commandment. In its
original version his response is not yet presented as an additional commandment per se, it is a commanding voice. Though this is perhaps the
best-known phrase of all Holocaust literature, few authors cite it
at length even if they comment on it. Let us, then, quote the whole
passage in which Fackenheim expounds his stance:

I believe that whereas no redeeming voice is heard at Auschwitz, a commanding voice is heard, and that it is being heard with increasing clarity. *Jews are not permitted to hand Hitler posthumous victories.* Jews are commanded to survive as Jews, lest their people perish. They are commanded to remember the victims of Auschwitz, lest their memory perish. They are forbidden to despair of God, lest Judaism perish. They are forbidden to despair of the world as the domain of God, lest the world be handed over to the forces of Auschwitz. For a Jew to break this commandment would be to do the unthinkable – to respond to Hitler by doing his work. [Italics in the original.][204]

Later on, basing his argument on the rabbinic tradition that says there are 613 commandments in the Bible, Fackenheim called this *commanding voice* the *614th commandment*.[205] This, however, was only a minor modification of his concept and one that did not alter its very content: in his *To Mend the World*, Fackenheim uses both terms interchangeably.[206] Our task now will be to analyse this commandment in order to find out whether – and, if so, in what respect – it is an (authentic) response to the Holocaust.

First of all, we should explore the very nature of this commandment: What is it that makes it a commandment? Whose is the voice? And to whom does it speak? In the Torah, commandments are concrete laws given by God to Moses, and through Moses to the Jewish people. Thus, a commandment always originates with God and is an expression of his will. God, as it were, reveals himself through his commandments. But can it be legitimately argued that the same happened in Auschwitz? Did God reveal himself in any way in Auschwitz? Was he – we must ask the ever-recurring question – present in the death camps? And is it possible at all to believe in a self-revealing deity in the twentieth century?[207]

While trying to find Fackenheim's answers to this significant question, we will see how, in fact, he attempts to explain the Holocaust – what the event really was and what theological interpretation can be given to it. According to Fackenheim, Judaism's conception of divinity is such that it is presence, and a commanding presence. In the human–divine encounter there is no room for fear or hope on the human side, for such feelings would render human freedom heteronomous. The divine commanding presence needs absolute freedom as a partner – '*freedom to accept or reject the divine commanding Presence as a whole, and for its own sake – that is for no other reason that that it* is *that Presence*' (italics in the original).[208] Nevertheless, Fackenheim is well aware of the fact that his idealistic vision of human freedom accepting the divine commanding presence is barely tenable in a world that has seen so many catastrophes, of which the most paralyzing, at least for the Western mind, is the Nazi Holocaust. He knows that many people are no longer capable of believing in a caring, benevolent deity; in their opinion such a deity simply does not exist. Fackenheim argues, however, that 'this view reflects a complete lack of understanding of the nature of religious faith in general and Biblical faith in particular. Biblical faith – and I mean both Jewish and Christian – is never destroyed by tragedy but only tested by it'.[209] From the existential standpoint, it matters very little whether faith is destroyed or *only* tested if the events a person faces are excruciating. Whether eventually one's faith will be ruined or survive the test can be known only ex post. At the very moment of *the test* – let us continue with this terminology – it cannot be known whether it is *only* a test or something more than that.

Thus, Fackenheim's assertion seems rather fideistic and dogmatic. Moreover, his contention simply stands in contradiction with day-to-day experience; after all it is not so rare that believing Jews and Christians lose their faith in the biblical God. Yet to say that is trivial. Fackenheim surely knows that such things happen: he knows it very well. If he, then, says biblical faith cannot be destroyed, he does so purposefully. He is preparing the ground for his *commanding voice* concept. For it would be naive to expect people to listen to the voice if they no longer believe in the Commander. Thus, Fackenheim announces, as it were, the good news: 'Your faith is not destroyed, for it cannot be destroyed; you have been put to a test, but you must persevere.' One might imagine this is the commanding voice he claims to have heard whereas others have not. Here Fackenheim presents himself as a rabbinic–prophetic scholar. He is a prophet who he can hear more than ordinary people and he announces the news revealed to him. But he is like an ancient rabbi, one of the law-makers, too, for he formulates a new commandment. (Of course, it is understood that the commanding voice comes from on high, while Fackenheim only gives it a shape.)[210]

Although God is neither provable not refutable,[211] religious faith in God, Fackenheim affirms, is '*empirically verifiable* ... [and] *nothing empirical can possibly refute it*' (italics in the original).[212] He refers to the Psalmist's situation when he experiences oppression and faces death. The danger is so great that the Psalmist feels as if God has hidden his face. Yet the Psalmist – and Fackenheim – hope for brighter days to come: God has hidden his face 'only for a while; and He will turn His face back to man again'. Then Fackenheim presents us with a scheme of interpretation which, it might be inferred, serves as a model explanation – yes, explanation – of evil. It is the oldest possible type of theodicy: what is good comes from God, what is bad comes from no-one-knows-where. 'Good fortune ... reveals the hand of God; bad fortune, if it is not a matter of just punishment, teaches that God's ways are unintelligible, not that that are no ways of God. A full heart ... indicates the Divine Presence; an empty heart bespeaks not the non-existence or unconcern of God, but merely His temporary absence.'[213] The biblical God, however, is at least capable of being present. As the God of Israel, he 'is a present God', *tout court*. 'He and the God-hypothesis' of the *philosophes* 'have nothing in common'.[214] Fackenheim honestly admits that, to the secularist, the biblical–rabbinic God is still a hypothesis, only it serves to offer an explanation not of the physical world, but of the religious experience.[215]

Following Fackenheim's argumentation, one gains the impression that he himself is not persuaded by his own reasoning. Perhaps that is why his last resort in trying to find answers to why God was silent at Auschwitz (and, by the same token, in trying to understand that silence), is the old idea of *hester panim* in a slightly modified, Buberian shape. He instructs 'adherents of Biblical faith [that they] should always have regarded times of external or internal darkness not as evidence against God, but rather – to use Martin Buber's expression – as evidence of an "eclipse of God" '.[216] It is clear that what Fackenheim seeks is to absolve God of any responsibility for the catastrophe.[217] For, according to Buber's vision, the eclipse is something that happened not to God, but *between* God and human beings. It is thus legitimate to conclude that God's presence during the Holocaust was non-existent, not real, or at least unexperienceable. As his presence could not have been felt, hence it follows he could not have revealed himself either; ergo, he did not command anything. Even relying on Jewish religious tradition which accepts struggling with God, one might argue that God had no right to command anything at Auschwitz, either during or after the war, for he was not there, he let his countenance be *eclipsed*. Fackenheim encourages other religious Jews to wrestle with God 'in however revolutionary ways',[218] but he himself remains surprisingly calm and to a certain extent divorced from the problem of historic-theological scandal of the Holocaust.

Fackenheim, obviously, would not concur with this conclusion. His faith is based on a belief in a transcendent God and a supernatural revelation. Fackenheim's faith, and along with it all religious thinking, all theology, is incapable of finding a meaning in the Shoah, and stands in awe before that event. Yet that faith cannot be destroyed – whatever the circumstances, however high the price. From the outset of his reflections, Fackenheim was not ready to test his God-idea against the historical-existential evidence, though he agrees that human faith can be tested in the fire of crematoria. But even if the Holocaust does challenge his view of God as all-powerful and caring, still the core of his traditional Jewish theology is left untouched. The idea of the God of Israel, the one who entered in covenant with the Jewish people, who is the saviour of Israel, is not questioned. It is as if Fackenheim as a philosopher did experience some problems when confronting the Shoah, whereas Fackenheim as a Jew did not. Thus the 614th commandment emerges from the catastrophe as a religious call to remain faithful to the God of Israel. The voice conveying the commandment is the voice of God, who, if he 'is a God of history He must be a God of contemporary secular history also'.[219] Unfortunately, to the detriment of his theology, Fackenheim does not demonstrate how God is present in secular history. His concept of presence could arguably be called a modern version of Tertullian's *credo quia absurdum*. Although the God of Israel kept silent and hid his face during the Holocaust, this very event was purportedly revelatory in character. Moreover, it proved to be comparable with the Sinai-event.[220] In this particular context – one of Sinai and revelation – Fackenheim asks whether the critical question for the Jew of today is the question of Jewish survival and unity:

> Throughout the ages the religious Jew was a witness to God. After Auschwitz even the most secularist of Jews bears witness, by the mere affirmation of his Jewishness, against the devil ... Jewish survival after Auschwitz is not one relative ideal among others but rather an imperative which brooks no compromise ... Jewish opposition to Auschwitz cannot be grasped in terms of humanly created ideals but only as an *imposed commandment*. And the Jewish secularist, no less than the believer, is *absolutely singled out* by a Voice as truly *other* than man-made ideals – an imperative as truly *given* – as was the voice of Sinai. [Italics in the original.][221]

We now see why the Holocaust is an epoch-making event: because it is Sinai-like. It comprises a renewed revelation, a renewed covenant;

otherwise, the commanding voice of Auschwitz would be far from similar to that of Sinai. There are, however, several differences between the two events: Sinai was preceded by the exodus (first salvation, then revelation), while the Shoah was followed by the establishment of the state of Israel (first annihilation, then political rebirth); and no less important a fact is that in the Shoah, there was no Moses, unless Fackenheim himself is to be considered the new Moses. Last but not least, there were witnesses to both events. Fackenheim, following Judah Halevi, gives credit to 600,000 witnesses present at Sinai,[222] but seems to ignore six million Jewish victim-witnesses who were present at numerous camps and in countless ghettos. I do not intend to instrumentalize millions of lost lives, but their disappearance from the face of the earth cannot be excluded from the experience of modern man; the empty place that is left after them, the space that is saturated with cold, divine silence, must not be overlooked or hushed in order to sustain any belief, religious or otherwise. Fackenheim does not want to think of the extermination of European Jews in terms of anti-testimony. On the contrary, he argues that the secular Jew is forbidden 'to use Auschwitz as an additional weapon wherewith to deny [God] ... The secularist Jew, who has all along lost Sinai and now hears the Voice of Auschwitz, cannot abuse that Voice as a means to destroy four thousand years of Jewish believing testimony.'[223] Thus, both believing and non-believing Jews are obliged to listen to and obey the commanding voice of Auschwitz; the former because of his faith, the latter in spite of his disbelief. For Jews are all called to unity, and their unity will make for their survival as Jews.

Therefore, Fackenheim now seems to take the survivalist stance: he is not so much concerned with the future of Jewish faith as he is with the continuity of the Jews as a people. To that end he summons all Jews to foster unity – unity in obeying the commanding voice of Auschwitz as a new Sinai voice. Of course, there is nothing wrong in calling for unity and survival (even understood as a value in itself), but would that be unthinkable or unfeasible without the Holocaust? Is not the 4,000-year-old tradition worth being sustained and developed because of the potential it has in itself? And, finally, is not Fackenheim trying to prove that his faith continues *despite* the Holocaust?[224] One can have the impression that most of the strong expressions he employs are but poetic rhetoric: that although he claims we cannot live and think as though there was no Holocaust, he is, in fact, constructing his theology, as it were, *without Auschwitz,* or at least *muffling the*

scream of Auschwitz and transforming it into the voice of Auschwitz.
What is more, Fackenheim's concept ascribes to the Holocaust the
central integrating role that was once played by the Exodus, which
psychologically can be dire to bear – for a salvific event is now
replaced by total destruction. In the final analysis, one might conclude
that what Fackenheim does, even if he does not actually realize it, is point
to Hitler as the single most significant personage for contemporary Jewry
– indeed, a motivating force for Jews striving to preserve their identity.
Certainly that is an outcome Fackenheim would not wish; nevertheless,
it troubles many critical minds exploring his scholarship.[225]

IRVING GREENBERG: MOMENT FAITHS AND A NEW COVENANT

Of the four authors whose ideas are presented in this chapter, Irving
Greenberg was the last to publish his *magnum opus* on the Holocaust.
His 'Cloud of Smoke, Pillar of Fire'[226] (not 'magnum' in volume, but
rather in approach) came out in 1977 – that is, after Richard Rubenstein's *After Auschwitz* and *The Cunning of History*, as well as after
Emil Fackenheim's *Quest for Past and Future* and *God's Presence in
History*. Though Greenberg refers to both scholars and shares with
them the view of the centrality of the Holocaust, he does not merely
respond to them. His is a completely independent way of thinking; if
it does depend on anything, it is an event from his youth:

> Greenberg's love for *clal Yisrael*, the Jewish people, was instilled
> in him in the learned Orthodox household in which he was raised
> in Brooklyn. Once, several years after World War II, when he was
> a teenager passing through an intensely religious phase, he made
> some highly critical comments about American Jews' irreligiosity.
> His staunchly Orthodox father was angered by his words: 'You
> dare to attack Jews in the name of God? Tell me – of these two
> [God and the Jewish people], who should be more ashamed of
> their behavior over the last decade?'[227]

The words uttered by Greenberg's father were not wasted on him:
his theology would become centred on the Shoah and would aim to
find viable responses to the event. Analysing his major piece, I intend
to demonstrate how he perceives the present religious situation of
Judaism (and Christianity) and what conclusions he reaches on
confronting both religions with the European catastrophe. Greenberg
concurs with the three previously mentioned authors on two principal

points: firstly, that religious thinking cannot go on as if the Holocaust had not happened (as was the case after 1945, he claims); secondly, that the Nazi genocide has put Judaism and Jewish existence into question.[228]

One of the most stunning and thought-provoking remarks Irving Greenberg has ever made is what he called, in 'Cloud of Smoke, Pillar of Fire', his 'working principle'. It says that 'no statement, theological or otherwise, should be made that would not be credible in the presence of the burning children'.[229] It is so eye-opening, even revolutionary, that it long seemed sensible to me to present Greenberg's argumentation in an inverted way, as it were: that is, to first show the basic tenets of his thinking, and then to reveal Greenberg's working principle as the most pointed and challenging thesis – indeed, the keystone of his theological system. Upon thorough analysis, however, it proved to be practically unfeasible. And it is not only that one has to take other people's statements for what they are. If a working principle is so powerful and pregnant with meaning, it can sometimes be interpreted as an important thesis of an author. Yet with Greenberg's concept of response to the Holocaust, this would be of no help either. It is obvious that the main theses in any theory or system, if that system is to be innerly coherent, have to be confronted with one another so as to see whether they form a whole. Greenberg's principle should be subjected to the same procedure. But what exactly is the meaning of his proposition? On the face of it, it is about credibility, or whether a statement is intellectually tenable – here: in the presence of the burning children. It seems, however, that it is not intellectual perspective that is at stake: rather, the crux of the matter is the moral credibility of a given statement – when confronted with the Shoah. Therefore, it is indeed important to take the working principle as a methodological tool with which to test Greenberg's own system.

Greenberg emphasizes several times that the Holocaust constitutes a 'radical counter-testimony to Judaism and Christianity',[230] and specifically to both religions' idea of God and their theology of sin. That the Shoah directly brings into question these two conceptions constitutes the present crisis of faith. But Greenberg means no abstract crisis; instead, he sees it as a 'crisis of biblical faith'.[231] Paradoxically, however, the dilemma has its source in the Bible itself, in both the Hebrew Scriptures and the New Testament. Greenberg dismisses the traditional Jewish concept of *mipnei hataeinu* – we were punished for our sins – as well as the Christian interpretations which put the blame for the catastrophe on the alleged Jewish rejection of the Messiah.

He gives a few examples of how Christian theology during and after the Nazi genocide remained insensitive to the fate of the Jewish people. Thus, the Catholic Archbishop Kametko of the Slovak town of Nitra was to reply in the following way to the local rabbi who came to him to plead for intervention against the deportations of the Jews of Slovakia:

> It is not just a matter of deportation. You will not die there of hunger and disease. They will slaughter all of you there, old and young alike, women and children, at once – it is the punishment that you deserve for the death of our Lord the Redeemer, Jesus Christ – you have only one solution. Come over to our religion and I will work to annul this decree.[232]

Equally shocking a reaction was that of the German Evangelical Conference held at Darmstadt in 1948, where its members 'proclaimed that the terrible Jewish suffering in the Holocaust was a divine visitation and a call to the Jews to cease their rejection and ongoing crucifixion of Christ'.[233]

Greenberg is no less caustic in evaluating certain Jewish thinkers who 'sought ... to explain destruction as a visitation for evil':

> To account for the Holocaust as God's punishment of Israel for its sins is to betray and mock the agony of the victims. Now that they have been cruelly tortured and killed, boiled into soap, their hair made into pillows and their bones into fertilizer, their unknown graves and the very fact of their death denied to them [by Holocaust deniers], the theologian would inflict on them the only indignity left: that is, insistence that it was done because of their sins.[234]

The crisis of biblical faith also touches the central concept of Judaism, which is that God acted historically in entering into covenant (*brit*) with the Jewish people. It is, too, the covenant that is one of the core elements of Greenberg's thought – how to live it after the Shoah. He does not question the very facticity of *brit*. Rather, he contends that God failed to keep the covenant,[235] if only because of his impotence. Greenberg also refers to the rabbis who affirmed that the prophets Jeremiah and Daniel refused to speak of God in terms of power and awe because of the destruction of the Temple. 'The line between the repudiation of the God of the covenant and the Daniel–Jeremiah reaction is so thin that repudiation must be seen as an authentic reaction even if we reject it. There is a faithfulness in rejection; serious theism must be troubled after such an event.'[236]

Theism is in trouble indeed; theistic faith, so Greenberg maintains, is really endangered by the Shoah; it may even have lost (some) of its credibility.[237] The danger is real because the Jewish and Christian historical sensitivity must not ignore this event if it is to speak to contemporary men and women. And for our generation – at least for many of its members – the horrors of the death camps convey an upsetting message: God had deserted his people. The very divine–human covenant thus proved to be broken – and the rupture is due to the Holocaust. But to say this would be euphemistic; it is God who broke the covenant by his non-action during the catastrophe. What happened, in fact, during the Shoah was that the more religious and observant a Jew, the more s/he was vulnerable to Nazi violence. At the same time, those who were assimilated and less involved in traditional Judaism found it easier to avoid death. Hence, it follows that for those who faithfully abided by the covenant 'the reward for ... loyalty was that such Jews were more likely to be killed'.[238] Therefore, if there can be any covenant at all, it is only thinkable as a *voluntary covenant* of the Jewish people who remained faithful.[239]

Reflecting on the lively dispute over God's alleged absence or presence in history, Michael Oppenheim seeks to draw conclusions by formulating an argument that might be called *evolutionary covenant theory*. Following Irving Greenberg, he contends that the traditional biblical paradigm, rooted in covenant theology, had ceased being relevant after the double destruction of the Jerusalem Temple. 'In response to this catastrophe, the Rabbis rethought some of the basic concepts of Judaism. They recognized that God no longer directly intervened in history, which left that stage open to human initiative and responsibility.'[240] In this way the covenant gained a more balanced character – the divine and the human roles came to be perceived as complementary and equal to one another. Since then, besides the written Torah (*Torah min ha-shamayim*), an important function will have been performed by the oral Torah (*Torah she-be'al peh*): that is, by the Talmud. Oppenheim believes, however, that the destruction of the European Jews has brought an end to the paradigm modified by the rabbis, so that now it will have to be re-modified. He then concludes that the Holocaust 'demonstrated that God is more hidden/limited than the Rabbis had believed. History and the movement toward redemption is now given over to human efforts to an even greater extent. Correspondingly, the Jewish people have become the "senior partner" in the covenantal enterprise.'[241]

Notwithstanding the fact that the covenant is *broken*, the *senior partner* has rebuilt it so the covenant is now *whole* again.[242] One has to ask, however, if the once-broken covenant has had any impact on the God-idea. Is the Jewish God still the same? For we can imagine a situation where the covenant (its voluntarist version) would be upheld by the Jewish people, who are aware not that the other party is not engaged in the partnership, but simply that there is no other party. Greenberg takes such a hypothesis into account when he comments on Rubenstein:

> [He] made the extremely powerful statement ... that, in the light of the Shoah, 'God is dead', i.e., the only messiah is death. My response was that, logically, he was probably right. But religion and theology are based on life, not logic ... Basically, the Jewish people did not react as Rubenstein argued ... Traditional notions of God are wounded by the Shoah, but the awareness of God and the covenant was renewed.[243]

From this passage one could infer that God can be logically dead, but he is *theo*-logically alive – which necessarily means that in declaring whether God is (living) or not, Greenberg resorts to faith in the divine. Of course, logically, this kind of reasoning would fall under the blame of explaining *idem per idem*, but theologically the argument is coherent – faith is the basis of all theological concepts and interpretations. But is faith itself unaffected by the Shoah? Can one – can Greenberg – steadfastly believe in God? Is *faith after Auschwitz* not an oxymoron? Certainly, these questions are also troubling and vexing for Greenberg himself. He does deem it sensible to ask 'whether even those who believe after such an event dare talk about a God who loves and cares without making a mockery of those who suffered'.[244] How can the believers talk of God who is caring? On the other hand, how can they not talk about such a God – whom they find in the *Tanach*?[245] How can their faith survive Auschwitz? Greenberg, attempting to answer these questions, refers to the category of 'dialectical faith'. This notion, however, probably does not fit best in this context, for dialectical faith would mean faith and anti-faith together forming some sort of synthesis, and it is difficult to see how belief in a deity could be 'reconciled' with its opposition. Thus, if we have the tension between belief and unbelief – and this is an insurmountable tension – it is better to use the term 'moment faiths', as Greenberg does.[246]

The idea of moment faiths flows, as it were, from a deep existential experience of confronting Auschwitz. Greenberg seems to argue that one cannot be immersed in one's belief and seriously face the death camps. Nevertheless, he maintains, like Fackenheim, that Auschwitz has the same revelational potential as did Sinai.[247] If this is so, what is the revelation of the death camps? Is it only a negative revelation, one demonstrating the ultimate crisis of faith? It seems that for Greenberg the Holocaust revelation is twofold: it unveils both the crisis and the rebirth of faith. Thence the concept of moment faiths: at one time the Shoah reveals destroyed, empty faith; at another it shows rebuilt faith (tantamount to rebuilt covenant). In constructing his concept, Greenberg also finds inspiration in Buber's notion of 'moment gods' which assumes that passing feelings and awareness of divine presence are interspersed with moments of mere awareness of one's day-to-day, physical existence.[248] In contradistinction to Buber, Greenberg, in his concept, finds room for torment and anxiety. His moment faiths are moments when

> vision[s] of redemption are ... interspersed with times when the flames and smoke of the burning children blot out faith – though it flickers again ... This ends the easy dichotomy of atheist/theist, the confusion of faith with doctrine or demonstration ... The difference between the skeptic and the believer is *frequency of faith*, and not certitude of position. The rejection of the unbeliever by the believer is literally the denial or attempted suppression of what is within oneself. The ability to live with moment faith is the ability to live with pluralism and without the self-flattering, ethnocentric solutions which wrap religion, or make it a source of hatred for the other. [Italics added.][249]

In this passage, we notice two important propositions: (1) that faith, though burnt out together with the burning children, flickers again; (2) that the first proposition implies *Aufhebung*, or sublation, of the atheist/theist dichotomy.[250] Why does faith become non-existent – if, indeed, it does so? It is because – so Greenberg seems to argue – the divine presence is non-existent in the awareness of those who look, with the eyes of their mind, at the burning children. God is absent from their consciousness; thus faith is blotted out too. However, the fact that the SS-men were compelled by Himmler to believe in a Higher Being – 'I insist that members of the SS must believe in God'[251] – makes the belief in God even more problematic, as Greenberg claims. God-fearing SS-men thus bear witness against the belief in God. Yet, curiously, right on the next page Greenberg, analysing a biblical story, states that 'Amalek could not attack the weak and those who lagged behind because Amalek did not "fear God".'[252] He then continues to assert that people cannot kill unless they deny beforehand all limits set by God.[253] And that is exactly what Himmler and his men did: most of them, while believers in some sort of Higher Being, nevertheless abolished all allegedly divine law while affirming the need for a belief in the divine. This contradiction reveals that the category of fear of/belief in God has little to do with ethics. In fact, in 'Cloud of Smoke, Pillar of fire', Greenberg overlooks the issue of ethics; faith is the key point of his reflections.[254]

So, as we have seen, even faith is difficult to speak about, for it is faith and non-faith at once. It is common to the believer and to the atheist alike, the only difference being its frequency. It is to his credit that Greenberg remarks the artificiality of the two-centuries-old dichotomy of atheist/theist. But this is true in only one respect: the borderline between the theist and the atheist is vanishing in the existential experience. In other words, the existential atheist may at times be close to being a believer in his/her wish for God to exist. Yet the same cannot be said of the philosophical atheist, for whom any deity is logically impossible. What is more, for some modern atheist thinkers, such as Altizer and Hamilton, God's non-existence is liberating, a source of joy, because, to them, human freedom demands that there be no God. Between this kind of an atheist and a traditional believer there seems to be no visible affinity. In any case, Greenberg is right in insisting that the believer and the non-believer – whom I call the existential non-believer – ask the same questions of ultimate concern. Where they differ is in the answers they give. The believer, like Greenberg, will say that even though God might have broken the covenant, 'I believe that God was in Auschwitz. I believe that God was in the gas chambers with the Jewish people.'[255] Yet s/he does not claim that God was present there historically: rather, that his presence was purely theological. Greenberg does not concur with the view that God either condemned the Jews to die in those chambers or destroyed the chambers and liberated his people.[256] This purely theological, anti-historical presence, it can be argued, is imperative in nature: God must have been there – otherwise there would be no dialectical faith, only the perpetual moments of non-faith.

The existential non-believer, however, answers that the divine absence was absolute, the human pain unimaginable, and so faith would be scandalous. S/he may mourn the dead God while still longing for a living and faithful God, but be unable to assert God *is*. This is very different from 'a celebration of the death of God or of secular man', which is, in Greenberg's opinion, 'collaboration with ... the demons of Auschwitz'.[257]

Let us, then, ask the critical question: Is there any constructive response to the troublesome tension between belief and unbelief, between God and the Holocaust? Or is the opposition inescapable and insurmountable? Is there anything in Jewish life that can serve as counter-weight to the Shoah? According to Greenberg, we can seek relevant responses to the tragedy of mass death in theological recreation of the image of God, and in political recreation of Israel. The post-Holocaust image of God must be one that is woven out of silence. Such an image of God will redirect the thoughts of men and women beyond the image itself – toward the transcendent. To turn the human mind to transcendence – mute and distant, as it seems – is 'the only statement about God that one can make'.[258] Words are not only inappropriate here, they are even impossible, for our religious language is paralyzed; muteness of the re-formed image of God entails muteness on the part of human beings. It is worthwhile mentioning, too, that Greenberg admits there is some mystery in the way the atheist shows his/her 'reverence for the image of God'.[259] The atheist, since s/he cannot speak with the language of faith, uses the languages of acts. His/her reverence for the image of God must then signify the way s/he deals with other people, which means reverence for God's image present in human beings. The non-be-liever, Greenberg argues, denies s/he respects God's image because s/he is the true believer whose faith is totally inward; thus such a person is one of the *lamed-vovniks* – the thirty-six righteous who support the world in its existence.[260]

As regards the state of Israel, Greenberg perceives it as an historical fact of uttermost theological significance. Its very re-establishment and continuing existence is a counter-testimony to Auschwitz:

> Israel's faith in the God of history demands that an unprecedented event of destruction be matched by an unprecedented act of redemption, and this has happened ... almost all Jews acknowledge this phenomenon ... and it touches their lives. Studies show that the number of those who affirm this phenomenon as central (even if in nontheological categories) has grown from year to year; that its impact is now almost universal among those who will acknowledge themselves as Jews ... The whole Jewish people is caught between immersion in nihilism and immersion in redemption – both are present in immediate experience, and not just

historical memory ... Biblical theology already suggested that the
time would come when consciousness of God out of the restoration
of Israel would outweigh consciousness of God out of the Exodus.[261]

In the final analysis, Greenberg's argumentation, with regard to the idea
of dialectical response to the catastrophe, is coherent in its structure.
He has clearly stated that the Holocaust may not be used for any
particular ends or instrumentalized so as to support propaganda. And
he has consistently abided by this postulate. This methodological rule
found its perfect consummation in the 'moment faiths' concept wherein
Greenberg's dialectical approach plays a crucial role. In its entirety,
Greenberg's response to the Shoah is neither a spiritualist, dogmatic
faith in the God of history, nor an encouragement to rebel against and
deny the divine. In his view, life between these two polar experiences
– he honestly gives examples of both extremes – is possible; it is even
presented as a model of modern responses to God.[262] Yet, in another
respect, his response proved inconsequential. Greenberg's most shocking and disturbing claim, introduced as a working principle, remained
but a half-fulfilled call. To propose that no statement should be made
unless it could be uttered in the presence of the burning children was
to set an unusually high standard. Greenberg, however, has kept this
standard only to a certain extent. For to say that the post-Holocaust
man experiences both moments of faith and non-faith apparently does
not violate the principle, but to contend that God *was* in Auschwitz, or
that the act of Nazi genocide would be 'matched' by the political rebirth
of Israel, does sound like a mockery, although certainly not intended.
Though Greenberg asks: 'Why is it not a permanent destruction of faith
to be in the presence of the murdered children?', one of the answers
he offers is that the event of the Exodus is at times 're-enacted and
present'.[263] However, that the re-establishment of the state Israel should
be perceived as a new Exodus seems both theologically and historically
dubious. First of all, there was no Exodus *during* the Shoah; it is
unthinkable to argue that the time when one-third of European Jews
survived while a majority was annihilated was an Exodus-like event.[264]
And among the religious Jews the percentage of loss was considerably
higher. Secondly, as we shall see in the next chapter, the political
process that led to the establishment of the state of Israel had little to
do with the European catastrophe. That is simply a powerful myth,
widespread both within and without the Jewish people. Though the
myth is instrumental in shaping present-day Jewish identities, it has
barely any ground in reality.

But if some of Greenberg's statements do not stand up to his own working principle, what should be said of much Christian theology, if put to the test of Greenberg's postulate?

In closing, it can be argued that the four authors discussed above not only have ignited a Holocaust debate in America, but have also left an ineffaceable mark on it. To their credit, it must be said that all tried to find adequate responses to the catastrophe. Rubenstein and Greenberg even sought to introduce new ways of thinking into Judaism. They were all persuaded that contemporary Judaism could not avoid the confrontation with Auschwitz. Characteristically, they also saw a link between the Holocaust and the creation of the state of Israel, which illustrates the phenomenon that Jacob Neusner has labelled 'the myth of Holocaust and redemption'. Yet Neusner is not right to assert that after the Second World War, Jews 'did not write new prayers or holy books, create new theologies, or develop new religious ideas and institutions'.[265] In any event, this observation is not applicable to the authors considered in the present chapter. Richard Rubenstein and Irving Greenberg especially have presented not only radically new but thought-provoking and even revolutionary ideas. Theirs are the new holy books. It is my conviction that these two scholars offered the most radical – and honest – responses to the Shoah. Rubenstein's concept of the cultural death of God, though heretical or blasphemous to some, seems to be the farthest-reaching theological conclusion that a Jewish thinker could give without at the same time denying his Jewish identity. His rejection of the biblical idea of God, along with simultaneous acceptance of the functional value of religion and myth with its psychological potential, is indeed an attractive, inspiring conception. Also, his view that we should learn how to speak of religion in the time of no God can prove to be a viable proposal for the modern man who has lost his/her God, but still needs a community with which to share life experiences. Irving Greenberg, no less original a thinker, should be praised chiefly for his working principle – saying that each assertion which cannot be credible in the presence of the burning children had better not be uttered at all. Though Greenberg himself might have failed to abide by this rule – at least with regard to some of his theses – it still remains an extremely powerful postulate, one that does not lose any credibility in the face of the crematoria. The same can probably be said about his idea of the broken (if partially rebuilt) covenant.

As to Emil Fackenheim and Eliezer Berkovits, although both attempted to give responses to the Shoah, neither of them has left the confines of a traditional, biblical–rabbinic theological framework. Fackenheim asserted that no religious meaning can be found in the death camps and that explanations thereof would be, in fact, odious. He also contended that even after the Holocaust, faith cannot be destroyed; it can only be tested by God, whose face may be temp-orarily eclipsed. His idea of the commanding voice of Auschwitz is an intriguing one, and has found numerous followers, but upon closer analysis it turns out to be devoid of spiritual depth; eventually it is a survivalist version of the religious commandment. Besides that, it makes the Holocaust the central motivating force of the Jewish people in their struggle for identity and demographic survival. Eliezer Berkovits, like Fackenheim, uses the ancient notion of *hester panim* and its modern Buberian version, the eclipse of God, in order to explain the Shoah. Incredible as it seems, what they are both doing, in spite of claiming the opposite, is seeking how to explain Auschwitz in light of more or less traditional Jewish theology. Yet it should be emphasized that Berkovits does notice the inevitability of disbelief after the catastrophe, for, having experienced the Shoah, it is even more human to lose faith than to retain it. For Berkovits, however, the most authentic Jewish response to the problem is to rebel against God, to wrestle with him – yet nevertheless believe in him.

NOTES

1. Y. Hutner, '"Holocaust": A Rosh Yeshivah's Response', in N. Wolpin (ed.), *A Path Through the Ashes: Penetrating Analyses and Inspiring Stories of the Holocaust from a Torah Perspective* (New York: Mesorah Publications, 1986), p.53.
2. Elchonon Wasserman, cited in Y. Rudomin, *The Second World War and Jewish Education in America: The Fall and Rise of Orthodoxy* (dissertation published on the website of the Jewish Professionals Institute) (accessed 17 February 2004), <http://www.jpi.org/holocaust/ hlchp3a.htm>). Elchonon Wasserman was born in 1874 in Birz, Lithuania. He was considered the most outstanding student of the renowned Talmudic *chacham* (sage), Chofetz Chaim. In 1921, Reb Elchonon was offered the post of the *Rosh Yeshivah* (head of yeshivah) in Baranovitch, where he stayed until the outbreak of the Second World War. He was killed by the Germans in 1941.
3. See ibid.
4. Lamentations 2:2.
5. M. Gifter, 'A Path Though the Ashes: Some Thoughts on Teaching the Holocaust', in Wolpin, (ed.), *A Path Through the Ashes*, p.58.
6. See Y. Weinberg, 'The Destruction of European Jewry: A Churban of Singular Dimensions', in Wolpin, *Path Through the Ashes*, p.70.
7. 'The fundamental concept of *Churban* is that it is a decree issued by *Hashem* for the achievement of an ultimate purpose.' Gifter, 'Path Through the Ashes', p.61.
8. Weinberg, 'Destruction of European Jewry', p.71.

9. See A. Shafran, 'Great Thinkers and Their Hangups', in *A Manual of Jewish Belief (A Guide to Real Judaism) for the Thinking Individual*, 25 December 2002 (accessed 17 February 2004), <http://www.vtc.net/~cdgoldin/r'avi/jewthink09.htm>. This stance, underscoring *feeling*, *experience* and *theological perspection*, rather than intellect, is based on Yehudah Halevi's views, as opposed to Moses Maimonides' stress on reason:

> According to Maimonides, the *telos* of Halakhah is to create ideal conditions for the realization of intellectual love of God ... It is [his] understanding of the universality and importance of philosophy which led to Maimonides' attempt to integrate philosophic knowledge with his own tradition ... What makes Maimonidean philosophy perennially significant is his attempt to explain Jewish particularity in the light of his acceptance of the universal way of reason.

D. Hartman, *Maimonides: Torah and Philosophic Quest* (Philadelphia, PA: Jewish Publication Society, 1986), pp.104, 139f. See also I. Husik, *A History of Mediaeval Jewish Philosophy* (New York: Atheneum, 1973), pp.243–5.

10. Gifter, 'Path Through the Ashes', p.57. The common belief that all things belong to some divine scheme is plainly expressed in Yitzchak Hutner: 'As we delve more deeply into the Torah view of these awesome events, we shall find that they certainly are not coincidental, but reflect the greater cosmic plan of the Creator of the Universe.' Hutner, ' "Holocaust": A Rosh Yeshivah's Response', p.44.

11. Gifter, 'Path Through the Ashes', p.62.

12. Rabbi K.K. Shapira, *Sacred Fire: Torah from the Years of Fury 1939–1942*, edited by D. Miller and translated by J.H. Worch (Northvale, NJ: Jason Aronson, 2000).

13. Ibid., p.6 (14–15 September 1939).

14. Ibid, p.83 (13 April 1940).

15. See ibid., p.108 (15 June 1940).

16. Ibid., p.131 (3 October 1940).

17. Ibid., p.132 (3 October 1940).

18. Ibid., pp.132f.

19. Ibid., p.131. Square brackets in the original.

20. Ibid., p.209 (gloss to a sermon given on 16 August 1941).

21. Ibid.

22. E. Oshry, *Responsa from the Holocaust* (New York: Judaica Press, 2001), p.9.

23. Ibid., p.79.

24. Ibid., p.42. According to Rabbi Soloveitchik, the concept of God avenging Jewish blood has biblical roots: 'it is God's wish that the blood of the Jewish children reciting the *Shemoneh Esreh** be avenged. When God smote Egypt, He wished thereby to demonstrate that Jewish blood always has claimants.' J.B. Soloveitchik, 'Kol Dodi Dofek: It Is the Voice of My Beloved That Knocketh', in B.H. Rosenberg and F. Heuman (eds), *Theological and Halakhic Reflections on the Holocaust*, (Hoboken, NJ: Ktav Publishing House, 1992), p.74. (*Shemoneh Esreh is a prayer consisting of eighteen benedictions; it constitutes part of the three daily prayers.)

25. The latter question, in a slightly modified version, is perhaps one of the most puzzling questions for all people of all times: Why do the just suffer? As Norman Lamm has put it: 'from Job to the sages of the Talmud, from Maimonides to Luria to the Besht [Baal Shem Tov], there is only one constant, and that is the question of *tzaddik ve-ra lo*, the righteous who is afflicted with evil ... The question remains the Question of Questions for Judaism.' N. Lamm, 'The Face of God: Thoughts on the Holocaust', in Rosenberg and Heuman (eds), *Theological and Halakhic Reflections*, p.119.

26. E.E. Dessler, 'The Loss of Europe's Torah Center: A Lesson for Our Generation', in Wolpin (ed.), *Path Through the Ashes*, p.26.

27. A. Wolf, '... Questions Without Answers ... Faith Without Questions ...', in Wolpin (ed.), *Path Through the Ashes*, p.32.

28. N. Scherman, 'An Understanding of the Holocaust in the Light of Moshe Prager's "Sparks of Glory" ', in Wolpin (ed.), *Path Through the Ashes*, p.92.

29. Shapira, *Sacred Fire*, p.210 (23 August 1941).

30. In this chapter, when I use the term 'Orthodoxy', I mean the branch of Orthodox Judaism that is centred around *Agudath Israel*, the leading American Jewish organization gathering both Orthodox rabbis and laity. This part of the Orthodox movement should be distinguished from the Neo-Orthodoxy.
31. Lamm, 'The Face of God', pp.121, 125.
32. Ibid., p.126.
33. Ibid., p.127.
34. 'I have not made any use of the concept of "the hiding of God's face" (*hester panim*) that is so prevalent in the literature of Holocaust theology ... I reject this notion, because ... the hiding of God's face arises as a consequence of sin [Deuteronomy 31:17f].' D. Weiss Halivni, 'Prayer in the Shoah', *Judaism*, 50 (Summer 2001), p.283. Weiss Halivni is indeed right in stating that the 'hidden face' concept is prevalent in Shoah literature. Tellingly, Rabbi Shapira wrote in 1940: 'the Jewish people ... can take the revealed Face of God representing Love and Mercy and turn it into *Hester Panim*, which is by definition a punishment'. Shapira, *Sacred Fire*, p.198 (15 June 1940).
35. Soloveitchik, 'Kol Dodi Dofek', p.54.
36. Ibid., p.58.
37. Ibid., p.59.
38. In fact, it is strange that Soloveitchik uses the terms 'cause' and 'telos' interchangeably. He rejects, however, any deliberation over causes, and concentrates on the telos of suffering. The same can be seen in Maza: they both inquire about the possible meanings of suffering and obligations of the afflicted person – which is nothing else but seeking answers to the question: What is the telos of this?
39. B. Maza, 'Why?', in S.L. Jacobs (ed.), *Contemporary Jewish Religious Responses to the Shoah* (Lanham, MD, New York and London: University Press of America, 1993), p.152.
40. Ibid.
41. Though this chapter examines theological propositions, the purpose of the present work is to analyse religious phenomena from the standpoint of sociology and philosophy, *not speculative theology*. Therefore, I shall not investigate in detail the numerous theoretical deliberations on the problem by theologians.
42. Scherman, 'Understanding of the Holocaust', p.92.
43. See Weinberg, 'Destruction of European Jewry', p.71.
44. Ibid. See Shapira, *Sacred Fire*, p.8 (14–15 September 1939).
45. In the original, probably because of a typing error, the word is misspelled: *Vernunft*.
46. Y. Perlow, 'Our Generation: Churban Plus-One', in Wolpin (ed.), *Path Through the Ashes*, pp.77f. It could be argued that the more fundamentalist Orthodox thinkers would agree with Perlow's stance. On the other hand, it should be noted that this view stands in opposition to many classical Jewish texts, and especially to the Maimonidean tradition.
47. As opposed to the *Wissenschaft des Judentums*, the modernized version of Judaism that appeared in Germany in the eighteenth and nineteenth centuries.
48.   When halakhic man approaches reality, he comes with his Torah, given to him from Sinai in hand. He orients himself to the world by means of fixed statutes and firm principles. An entire corpus of precepts and laws guides him along the path leading to existence. Halakhic man, well furnished with rules, judgments, and fundamenta principles, draws near the world with an a priori relation. ... Halakhic man ... desires to coordinate the a priori concept with the a posteriori phenomenon.

    J.B. Soloveitchik, *Halakhic Man*, translated by L. Kaplan (Philadelphia, PA: Jewish Publication Society, 1983), pp.19f.
49.   The only difference between *homo religiosus* and halakhic man is a change of courses they travel in opposite directions ... *Homo religiousus*, dissatisfied, disappointed, and unhappy, craves to rise up from the vale of tears, from concrete reality, and aspires to climb to the mountain of the Lord ... Halakhic man, on the contrary, longs to bring transcendence down into this valley of the shadow of death.

    Ibid., p.40.
50. Proverbs 3:12.

51. A. Scheinman, 'Bikrovei Ekodeish: The Six Million Kedoshim', in Wolpin (ed.), *Path Though the Ashes*, pp.100f. The phrase *Bikrovei Ekodeish* means literally: 'I will become sanctified through my close ones.' Ibid., p.99. There are, however, dissenters from this opinion. Yaakov Feitman, for instance, holds that 'the ideological "right" agonizes over the alleged "sins" of this or that community which led to God's wrath ... In Torah circles, the Nazi ogre is almost erased from the picture. We are taught to accept and to learn to repent from the past – and indeed, this is an essential part of the pattern of Jewish history.' Y. Feitman, 'The Master Race and the Chosen People: A Look at the Nazi Ideology in a Torah Light', in Wolpin (ed.), *Path Through the Ashes*, p.109.
52. Maggid of Kelm, cited in Wolf, '... Questions Without Answers', p.37.
53. Precis of Teitelbaum's views on Jewish guilt vis-à-vis the Holocaust. Lamm, 'The Face of God', p.121.
54. Rabbi Avigdor Miller quoted in Lamm, 'The Face of God', p.122.
55. Dessler, 'The Loss of Europe's Torah Center', p.30.
56. Hutner, '"Holocaust": A Rosh Yeshivah's Response', p.54.
57. Ibid.
58. Shapira, *Sacred Fire*, p.334 (11 July 1942). The Hebrew term translated as 'the sanctification of God's name' is *kiddush hashem*.
59. 'All suffering turns into true salvation and redemption in every respect.' Ibid., p.12 (16 September 1939).
60. Ibid., p.136 (5 October 1940). In fact, according to Shapira, 'sacrifices are referred to as "bread of God" because just as bread gives a person strength, so our sacrifices give, as it were, strength to God'. Ibid. What is more, a few lines later, he even says: 'we are lucky to have you chastise us'. Why is chastisement considered to be luck? Can anyone be happy about enduring pain? Paradoxically, Shapira seems to say yes. But there is nothing close to masochism in what he claims, for he has a specific theory about the nature of pain suffered by holy people. As he maintains, there is an oral tradition according to which 'anyone martyred for the sanctification of God's name feels no pain at all'. Ibid., p.11 (16 September 1939). How is that possible?

> The author of the *Arvei Nachal* explains that when a person is consumed with passion and the desire to die for the sanctification of God's name, all his senses are elevated beyond the physical plane of existence into the highest realms, the world of thought ... The person's feelings and sensations are muted, his physical body is silenced ... a person who is suffering needs to remember that the pain is washing away his sins and purifying him so that he can draw closer to God.

Ibid.
61. A. Sorasky, *Reb Elchonon: The Life and Ideals of Rabbi Elchonon Bunim Wasserman of Baranovitch*, edited by N. Scherman and M. Zlotowitz, translated [from Hebrew] by E.S. Wasserman and L. Oschry (New York: Mesorah Publications, 1982), p.410.

> * In other sources, this phrase is translated as 'with our bodies' (in the Yiddish original the text reads 'with our proper persons'). See Perlow, 'Our Generation', pp.80f.
> ** The last quoted sentence is taken from Perlow, 'Our Generation', p.81.

62. Many such histories are described in the volume *The Unconquerable Spirit: Vignettes of the Jewish Religious Spirit the Nazis Could Not Destroy*, edited and translated by G. Hirschler, compiled by S. Zuker (New York: Zachor Institute, 1981).
63. Sorasky, *Reb Elchonon*, pp.408f.
64. E. Wiesel, *Night*, in *The Night Trilogy* (New York: Hill & Wang, 1987), pp.71f.
65. Ibid., p.43.
66. Ibid., p.53.
67. Immediately after the Second World War:

> most Jews ... were in fact agnostics, who had abandoned belief in a God who punishes and rewards. They joined synagogues in order to find a satisfactory niche in a culture that accepted Jews as part of the Protestant–Catholic–Jew triad: 'To raise a cry against the God who tolerated such an enormity would expose the full extent of Jewish unbelief to

Christian America, thereby undermining Judaism's status as one of America's equivalent faiths.'

P. Novick, *The Holocaust and Collective Memory: The American Experience* (London: Bloomsbury, 2000), p.109. In this passage, Novick cites E. Borowitz, 'Rethinking Our Holocaust Consciousness', *Judaism*, 40 (Fall 1991), p.390.

68. 'Contemporary theology reveals less about God than it does about the kind of men we are. It is largely an anthropological discipline. Today's theologian ... has more in common with the poet and the creative artist than with the metaphysician and the physical scientist.' R.L. Rubenstein, *After Auschwitz: History, Theology, And Contemporary Judaism*, 2nd edition (Baltimore, MD: Johns Hopkins University Press, 1992), p.xx.

69. See ibid., p.xxi.

70. T.J.J. Altizer and W. Hamilton, *Radical Theology and the Death of God* (Indianapolis, IN: Bobbs-Merrill Co., 1966). The book is a collection of articles published by both authors in the years 1959–66.

71. See R.L. Rubenstein, 'The Symbols of Judaism and Religious Existentialism', *The Reconstructionist*, 25 (1 May 1959). This article was included in the first edition of *After Auschwitz* under the title 'The Symbols of Judaism and the Death of God'. It was originally presented as a paper at a conference in Middlebury, Vermont, in 1955. See R.L. Rubenstein, 'The Vocation of the Modern Rabbi', *The Reconstructionist*, 25 (27 November 1959).

72. Rubenstein, 'Symbols of Judaism and Religious Existentialism', p.13.

73. Rubenstein, 'Vocation of the Modern Rabbi', p.8.

74. Rubenstein, 'Symbols of Judaism and Religious Existentialism', p.15.

75. Ibid., p.18.

76. As I shall demonstrate in this chapter, Rubenstein also rejects (in his *After Auschwitz*) the God-concept of the Bible.

77. Rubenstein, 'Vocation of the Modern Rabbi', p.9.

78. 'The State of Jewish Belief: A Symposium', *Commentary*, 42 (August 1966), pp.71–160. This article was then incorporated into *After Auschwitz*. The symposium will be cited subsequently as 'The State of Jewish Belief'.

79. E. Berkovits, 'The State of Jewish Belief', pp.79f.

80. See M.N. Eisendrath, 'The State of Jewish Belief', p.84; I. Eisenstein, 'The State of Jewish Belief', p.86.

81. E.L. Fackenheim, 'The State of Jewish Belief', p.89.

82. 'Emil Fackenheim, who later became an important "Holocaust theologian", recalled his earlier avoidance of the issue. "One does not have to be either an enemy of the Jews or an indifferent Jew in order to change the subject when the Holocaust comes up .... I once did the same thing ... The cause was a hidden fear that if a Jew faced up to the scandal truly, fully, honestly, the result would be despair of Judaism."' E.L. Fackenheim, 'Jew of Fidelity', in H.J. Cargas (ed.), *Telling the Tale: A Tribute to Elie Wiesel on the Occasion of His 65th Birthday* (St Louis, MO: Time Being Books, 1993), p.308.

83. 'My interpretation of the Holocaust and the return to Israel in the first edition of *After Auschwitz* was initially regarded as a distinctively Jewish expression of death-of-God theology. Indeed, I saw it as such myself.' Rubenstein, *After Auschwitz*, p.xii.

84. R.L. Rubenstein, *After Auschwitz: Radical Theology and Contemporary Judaism*, 1st edition (Indianapolis, IN: Bobbs-Merrill, 1966), p.224.

85. Ibid., p.227.

86. Ibid., p.153.

87. Though the notion of 'Judeo-Christian' tradition is questioned by some Jewish thinkers (e.g. Jacob Neusner and Eliezer Berkovits), Rubenstein uses it several times – quite naturally, as it were – throughout his book. He does so because he seemingly notices many similarities between the Jewish and the Christian concepts of the election of Israel, the idea of covenant, and the view of history as the arena of God's salvific interventions. See, for example, Rubenstein, *After Auschwitz*, pp.xvi, 43, 294.

88. Ibid., p.249.

89. Ibid.

90. Ibid., p.251.
91. Ibid.
92. Ibid., p.250.
93. See M.L. Morgan, *Beyond Auschwitz: Post-Holocaust Jewish Thought in America* (New York: Oxford University Press, 2001), p.62.
94. Rubenstein, *After Auschwitz*, p.248. We have seen, however, that freedom, especially in early Rubenstein, was not really unimportant. In the first edition of *After Auschwitz*, he wrote that only those 'ignoring the questions of God and human freedom and God and human evil' (p.238) can believe in the transcendent God of patriarchal monotheism. Also, one has the impression that in the 1950s and 1960s, Rubenstein was much more under the spell of Tillich than when he was preparing the second edition of his book:

> Tillich insists that the God of theism (that is, a personal God) is dead and deserved to die. He claims that a God who stands above all human activity and who controls the cosmos is ultimately the enemy of human self-fulfillment ... Tillich praises the German philosopher Nietzsche who proclaimed that God is dead. Tillich claims the theistic God is dead and deserved to die because He opposes human freedom. When Tillich's contention that a personal God is the enemy of freedom is compared with Erich Fromm's analysis of the types of human personality which an authoritarian conception of deity either reflected or engendered, *it becomes apparent that human moral autonomy is incompatible with the traditional conception of a personal God.*

Rubenstein, *After Auschwitz*, 1st edition, p.87 (italics added); see also Rubenstein, 'Symbols of Judaism and Religious Existentialism', p.18.
95. R.L. Rubenstein, *Power Struggle: An Autobiographical Confession* (Lanham, MD: University Press of America, 1986), p.65.
96. Ibid.
97. Ibid., p.66.
98. Ibid.
99. During the war, Dean Grüber was involved in an underground movement whose task was to help the Jews; for that he was sent to Dachau and barely survived. In 1961 he was *the only German* to testify against Adolf Eichmann during his trial in Jerusalem. He was also one of the two non-Jewish witnesses for the prosecution. See Rubenstein, *After Auschwitz*, pp.5f; H. Arendt, *Eichmann in Jerusalem: A Report on the Banality of Evil*, revised and enlarged edition (New York: Penguin Books, 1994), pp.129–31.
100. Rubenstein, *After Auschwitz*, p.8.
101. Ibid., p.9.
102. Ibid., p.169.
103. Ibid., pp.3, 20. Besides Richard Rubenstein, there are many other thinkers who are resolutely opposed to interpreting the Holocaust in terms of either divine plan or divine anger. For example, Kenneth Seeskin has said: 'To suggest that the horrors of Auschwitz were part of God's providence and, therefore, contain a disguised moral truth is to speak of the Holy One as if He were a monster. God was not present in Hitler's plan to exterminate the Jews – directly, indirectly, or anything else. The SS was not the rod of God's anger.' K.R. Seeskin, 'The Reality of Radical Evil', *Judaism*, 29 (Fall 1980), p.450.
104. Later on I shall try to demonstrate how this manner of theologizing can be seen in the work of Eliezer Berkovits and, to a lesser extent, in Emil L. Fackenheim.
105. L. Festinger, *A Theory of Cognitive Dissonance* (Stanford, CA: Stanford University Press, 1962), p.3.
106. Ibid., p.9.
107. Ibid., pp.9f.
108. Ibid., p.13.
109. Rubenstein, *After Auschwitz*, pp.85f.
110. Ibid., p.86.
111. See Festinger, *Theory of Cognitive Dissonance*, p.25.
112. See H. Jonas, 'The Concept of God after Auschwitz: A Jewish Voice', in A. Rosenberg and G.E. Myers (eds), *Echoes from the Holocaust: Philosophical Reflections on a Dark Time*

(Philadelphia, PA: Temple University Press, 1988), pp.294, 302.

113. Ibid., pp.301f.

114. A.A. Cohen, *The Tremendum: A Theological Interpretation of the Holocaust* (New York: Crossroad, 1981), p.97.

115. To use Cohen's own metaphor, 'The world is the divine *scenum*, the mime theater where only the passivity of God's essence is displayed.' Ibid., p.92.

116. Ibid., p.97.

117. One must say, to his credit, that in *The Tremendum* Cohen at least admits that the Shoah constitutes a real challenge to Judaism. In his earlier work, however, he maintained that reading Dubnow, Ahad Ha-Am, and Montefiore, 'One realizes ... that nothing has really changed; that with six million Jews dead and the State of Israel reborn, Jews continue to wonder ... about the proper relations between Zion and the Diaspora, about the pre-eminence or subordination of the spirit and the moral law in Jewish life.' Arthur A. Cohen, *The Natural and the Supernatural Jew* (New York: Pantheon Books, 1963), p.63. What is more, in *The Tremendum* he agrees with Rubenstein's critique of Cohen's 1963 book: 'Richard Rubenstein was right. I had ignored Auschwitz, imagining that somehow I had escaped ... For nearly a generation I could not speak of Auschwitz for I had no language that tolerated the immensity of the wound.' Cohen, *Tremendum*, pp.36f.

118. See ibid., p.97.

119. Rubenstein, too, is of the opinion that 'many important Jewish religious authorities have emphatically rejected the idea that the occurrence of the Holocaust is in any way inconsistent with the traditional Jewish conception of divinity'. Rubenstein, *After Auschwitz*, p.159.

120. P. Knobel, 'What Do American Jews Believe? A Symposium', *Commentary*, 102 (August 1996), p.57. This symposium will be subsequently cited as 'What Do American Jews Believe?'

121. D.M. Gordis, 'What Do American Jews Believe?', p.41.

122. The solemn supper shared in the first evening of the Pesach festival.

123. J. Fisher, 'God After the Holocaust: An Attempted Reconciliation', *Judaism*, 32 (Summer 1983), p.320.

124. Ibid., p.318.

125. Ibid.

126. Ibid.

127. Weiss Halivni, 'What Do American Jews Believe?', p.48.

128. L.S. Feuer, 'The Reasoning of Holocaust Theology', *Judaism*, 35 (Spring 1986), p.203.

129. Ibid., p.201; see R.R. Brenner, *The Faith and Doubt of Holocaust Survivors* (New York: Free Press, 1980), p.242.

130. Brenner, *Faith and Doubt of Holocaust Survivors*, p.199. The term 'a negative miracle' is also used by Phillip Lopate in his article, 'Resistance to the Holocaust', in 'Distance from the Holocaust: A Symposium', *Tikkun*, 4 (May–June 1989), p.64.

131. I. Schorsch, 'The Holocaust and Jewish Survival', *Midstream*, 27 (January 1981), p.41. A good example of the reasoning Schorsch criticizes may be the statement of Susan Last Stone: 'In contrast to the Holocaust, the overriding theme of which is the absence of God, the existence of the state of Israel in the face of great odds and the dramatic ingathering of exiles have provided me with a sense of the hand of God acting in history.' S. Last Stone, 'What Do American Jews Believe?', p.87.

132.   After that moment of revelation ... God begins to contract Her/His presence in the world, in order to allow for human freedom. What Kabbalists and Hasidim described as *tzimzum*, the contraction of God, is the process by which God chooses not to intervene in history, so that human beings have the opportunity to shape their own destiny. The claim that human beings are shaped in God's image is a Biblical claim that human beings are free to respond to God's call and command, but that *freedom requires that God not be involved in shaping every particular historical event*, or in secretly guiding the world so that it comes out God's way.

    Editorial, 'God and History', *Tikkun*, 2 (February 1987), p.9 (italics added).

133. Editors' Introduction to 'A Distance From the Holocaust: A Symposium', *Tikkun*, 4 (May–

June 1989), p.45. A similar opinion as to the price of freedom was uttered by Elliot N. Dorff. He also believes that, from the philosophical point of view, the suffering of a child dying of leukaemia can be much less easily reconciled with the idea of a benevolent God than the Holocaust. E.N. Dorff, 'What Do American Jews Believe?', p.30.

134. Judith Plaskow says she has 'always found the "free will defense" powerful and explaining the origins of moral evil, but it does nothing to explain the victims of evil, and for the same reason, it is useless to explain physical evil'. 'The Problem of Evil: A Conversation', *The Reconstructionist*, 57 (Spring 1992), p.17.

135. Seeskin, 'Reality of Radical Evil', p.451. Freedom as a value is not always so much cherished in Jewish liturgical tradition. In the *Emet ve-Emunah* prayer, recited after the *Shema* during evening service, the participants give thanks to God, 'who wrought for us miracles and vengeance (*neqamah*) upon Pharaoh'. See E.L. Friedland, 'O God of Vengeance, Appear!', *Judaism*, 37 (Winter 1988), p.73.

136. A. Rosenberg, 'Crisis in Knowing and Understanding the Holocaust', in Rosenberg and Myers (eds), *Echoes from the Holocaust*, p.382. See Festinger, *A Theory of Cognitive Dissonance*, p.25.

137. He states overtly in several places that he is not an atheist. See Rubenstein, *After Auschwitz*, pp.171, 172 and 237f.

138. Ibid., p.171.

139. Ibid., pp.172, 175. That Rubenstein rejected the biblical–rabbinic deity, however, does not mean he did not need religion. In contradistinction to Dietrich Bonhoeffer, whose critical problem was how to speak of God in an irreligious age, Rubenstein asks 'how to speak of religion in an age of the absence of God'. Ibid., p.174. The religious element of existence, so Rubenstein argues, is present in many people who cannot accept such an idea of God that would compel them to interpret the Nazi genocide and other humanitarian catastrophes as parts of God's 'providential way ... leading humanity to its final redemption. [These] thoughtful men and women find this idea too great a strain on their credulity. Their experience of the death of God rests upon their loss of faith in the transcendent God of History, *but not necessarily upon the loss of the sense of the sacred*'. Ibid., p.294 (italics added).

140. Ibid., p.172. Rubenstein criticizes Arthur Cohen for his acceptance of the doctrine of election after the Holocaust. Indeed, Cohen affirms with much certainty in tone that '[t]he death camps ended forever one argument of history – whether the Jews are a chosen people. They are chosen unmistakably, extremely, utterly.' Cohen, *Tremendum*, p.11.

141. Rubenstein, *After Auschwitz*, p.173.

142. Ibid., p.264.

143. While writing the passage on the theory of cognitive dissonance reduction, Rubenstein probably did not think of himself as willing to reduce the Holocaust-dissonance. What he arrived at was rather total elimination of this dissonance, and – it must be said to his credit – he did it fairly convincingly.

144. S.L. Jacobs, '(If) There Is No "Commander"? ... There Are No "Commandments!"', *Judaism*, 37 (Summer 1988), pp.323f. See Brenner, *Faith and Doubt of Holocaust Survivors*, p.111, where the author quotes one of his interviewees: 'I'll tell you why I lost my faith in God in the Holocaust. Because if God exists then he's a monster. And Hitler was God's deputy on earth. Do you want me to believe that? I'd rather be an atheist.' Most Jewish intellectuals who deal professionally, as it were, with the Shoah, and who reject the existence of God on the grounds of his radical alienation from the catastrophe, are born in America and did not personally experience the trauma that survivors did. The following quotation will perfectly illustrate this:

> Perhaps one of the most scathing criticisms of Rubenstein was delivered by Elie Wiesel. 'How strange that the philosophy denying God came not from the survivors. Those who came out with the so-called God is dead theology, not one of them had been in Auschwitz. Those who had, never said it. I have my problems with God, believe me. I have my anger and I have my quarrels and I have my nightmares. But my dispute, my bewilderment, my astonishment is with men. I did not understand how men could be so "barbarian".'

> Fisher, 'God After the Holocaust', p.311.

145. Rubenstein, *After Auschwitz*, p.250. Elsewhere he puts it the following way: '*It must be*

stressed ... that the death of God is not something that has happened to God. It is a *cultural* event experienced by men and women, many of whom remain faithful members of their religious communities.' Ibid., p.294 (italics in the original).

146. See ibid., p.174.
147. See ibid., p.298.
148. Ibid.
149. Ibid., p.304.
150. Ibid., p.175.
151. See ibid., pp.259–61. It is worthwhile to emphasize that Rubenstein's view on Israel's earth paganism has changed over the years. He believes that

> the old earth goddess has reappeared in Eretz Israel and that her principal, though by no means only, worshippers are to be found among those religious Jews for whom settlement of the land is the overriding religious obligation, regardless of practical consequences. In 1966 I looked favorably upon the possible revival of paganism in the land of Israel. Today, I have become ambivalent about it.

Ibid., p.232.
152. Ibid., p.260.
153. Ibid., p.261.
154. Ibid., p.305.
155. See E. Berkovits, *Faith after the Holocaust* (New York: Ktav Publishing House, 1973), p.148.
156. See Hirschler (ed. and trans.), *Unconquerable Spirit*, p.xiii.
157. Ibid., p.114. Rubenstein, too, is well aware of the fact that, according to the Bible and rabbinical literature, 'God is regarded as uniquely involved in the history and destiny of Israel.' Rubenstein, *After Auschwitz*, p.157.
158. 'Never in the long history of the Jewish people has there lived a generation of Jews, having experienced so much degradation and humiliation as ours, that has also been granted such a rich measure of encouragement by the God of history as ours.' Berkovits, *Faith After the Holocaust*, p.86.
159. See ibid., p.88. In this context he quotes, several times, Thomas J.J. Altizer, William Hamilton and Harvey Cox. Although Richard Rubenstein's name is never mentioned throughout the book, Berkovits obviously alludes in this passage to Rubenstein's objection to the biblical idea of deity. In some other places Berkovits's distaste for radical theologians is unambiguous, too.
160. Jeremiah 12:1.
161. Habakkuk 1:13.
162. Berkovits, *Faith after the Holocaust*, p.93.
163. Ibid., p.67. Indeed, in Berkovits's view, 'for our generation Auschwitz represents the supreme crisis of faith. It would be tantamount to a spiritual tragedy if it were otherwise. After the Holocaust Israel's first religious responsibility is to "reason" with God and – if need be – to wrestle with Him.' Ibid., p.68.
164. Ibid., p.69.
165. See ibid., p.98.
166. Ibid., p.64.
167. 'God's hiding himself is an attribute of the God of Israel, who is the Savior. In some mysterious way, the God who hides himself is the God who saves.' Ibid., p.101.
168. See ibid., pp.107, 114.
169. See ibid., p.61.
170. Ibid., p.107. According to Berkovits, the propensity of human beings to misuse their freedom is an inescapable trait of human condition: 'Neither the Nazis nor the Germans were a race different from the generality of mankind. Only because humankind is what it is could what happened happen.' Eliezer Berkovits, *Crisis and Faith* (New York: Sanhedrin Press, 1976), p.4. On the other hand, he blames Western civilization especially as it 'revealed the bankruptcy of its spirit ... [i]n the ghettos and the concentration camps'. Ibid., p.5.
171. Berkovits, *Faith after the Holocaust*, p.106.
172. In his description of God's handling of people, Berkovits applies categories similar to those used by Hans Jonas and Arthur A. Cohen. Whereas Cohen and Jonas speak of divine impotence, Berkovits believes God is mighty in his renunciation of might. See ibid., p.109.

173. Ibid., p.106.
174. Ibid.
175. See Berkovits, *Crisis and Faith*, p.155. Berkovits coins the term 'cosmic exile', which denotes the exile of divine purposes until they are fully realized in the universe, and in particular in human history.
176. See W. Orbach, 'The Four Faces of God: Toward a Theology of Powerlessness', *Judaism*, 32 (Spring 1983), p.245. Orbach also likens Berkovits to Buber, who named the destruction of the European Jews, somewhat poetically, as the *eclipse of God*.
177.   If man is to act on his own responsibility, without being continually overawed by divine supremacy, God must absent himself from history ... If man is not to perish at the hand of man ... God must not withdraw his providence from his creation. He must be present in history. That man may be, God must absent himself; that man may not perish in the tragic absurdity of his own making, God must remain present. The God of history must be present and absent concurrently. He hides his presence.

    Berkovits, *Faith after the Holocaust*, p.107. 'God cannot be present in history through manifest material power. Such presence would destroy history. History is the arena for human responsibility and its product. ... *Yet he is present in history. He reveals his presence in the survival of his people Israel*.' Ibid., p.109 (italics added).
178. Deuteronomy 31:17. Weiss Halivni also quotes Isaiah 59:1–2: 'Look, the Lord's hand is not too weak to deliver you; his ear is not too deaf to hear you. But your sinful acts have alienated you from your God; your sins have made him turn his face away [*histiru fanim*] and not listen to your prayers.' Weiss Halivni, 'Prayer in the Shoah', p.283.
179. 'All this is come upon us; yet we have not forgotten Thee, / Neither have we been false to Thy covenant. ... / We are accounted as sheep for the slaughter. / Awake, why sleepest Thou, O Lord? ... / Wherefore hidest Thou Thy face[?]' Psalm 44:18, 23, 25. See Berkovits, *Faith after the Holocaust*, p.95.
180. See ibid., p.94.
181. Ibid., p.89. He also quotes the Talmud: 'Rabbi Akiba said: God created the righteous and he created the wicked; he created Gan Eden (Paradise) and he created Gehenna.' Ibid., p.102.
182. Ibid., p.70.
183. Ibid., p.97. Another well-known Jewish atheist was Hiwi of Balkhu, who lived in the ninth century CE.
184. Ibid., p.4.
185. Ibid.
186. J. Neusner, *Stranger at Home: 'The Holocaust', Zionism, and American Judaism* (Chicago, IL, and London: University of Chicago Press, 1985), p.1.
187. Berkovits made aliyah (Hebrew term for settling in Israel by a Jew) in the 1980s.
188. Berkovits, *Faith after the Holocaust*, p.136.
189. Ibid., p.153.
190. Fackenheim emigrated to Israel in the early 1980s. He died in Jerusalem in September 2003.
191. See E.L. Fackenheim, *Quest for Past and Future* (Boston, MA: Beacon Press, 1968), p.7.
192. Ibid., p.14.
193. See E.L. Fackenheim, *The Jewish Return into History: Reflections on the Age of Auschwitz and a New Jerusalem* (New York: Schocken Books, 1978), p.20.
194. Fackenheim, *Quest for Past and Future*, p.17.
195. E.L. Fackenheim, *To Mend the World: Foundations of Post-Holocaust Jewish Thought* (Bloomington, IN: Indiana University Press, 1994), p.xxxvii.
196. Fackenheim, *Quest for Past and Future*, p.18.
197. Ibid., p.19; see Fackenheim, *To Mend the World*, pp.11–13.
198. See Fackenheim, *Jewish Return into History*, p.279.
199. Ibid., p.281.
200. For the idea of 'authenticity', Fackenheim is indebted to Martin Heidegger. Yet he does not offer a clear explanation of the term when he speaks of authentic Jews or authentic responses: we do not know who an authentic Jew is, and what makes a response to the Holocaust inauthentic. It seems that most opinions that do not concur with his own are to

be thought of as inauthentic. Perhaps the only passage from which we can gain some idea of Fackenheim's notion of 'authenticity' is the rather vague contention that 'the heart of every *authentic* response to the Holocaust – religious and secularist, Jewish and non-Jewish – is a commitment to the autonomy and security of the state of Israel'. Ibid., p.283 (italics in the original). If this view is to be taken seriously, then he has replaced methodological criteria with political ones.

201. Ibid., p.22.
202. E.L. Fackenheim, *God's Presence in History: Jewish Affirmations and Philosophical Reflections* (New York: New York University Press, 1970), p.51.
203. '"Holocaust theology" has been moving toward two extremes – a "God-is-dead" kind of despair, and a faith for which, having been "with God in hell", either nothing has happened or all is mended.' Fackenheim, *To Mend the World*, p.309. In a note pertaining to this passage, Fackenheim says: 'The most influential expression in the first extreme is Richard Rubenstein's *After Auschwitz*.' He claims that the other extreme is represented by Eliezer Berkovits, whose theology, 'though deeply shaken by the Holocaust, is not altered in consequence'. Ibid. Jacob Neusner makes a pointed remark on Fackenheim's treatment of Rubenstein: 'His most prominent critic, Emil Fackenheim ... in much of his writing rarely alludes to Rubenstein by name, and when he does, it is to compare Rubenstein to Nazis'. Neusner, *Stranger at Home*, p.71.
204. Fackenheim, *Quest for Past and Future*, p.20. This passage was part of the article 'Jewish Faith and the Holocaust', published in *Commentary* in 1967. Fackenheim ignores, however, the fact that for some people Auschwitz makes any commandment irrelevant, as Steven Jacobs claims.
205. See Fackenheim, *Jewish Return into History*, p.22.
206. See Fackenheim, *To Mend the World*, pp.299f.
207. See Fackenheim, *Quest for Past and Future*, p.125.
208. Ibid., p.220.
209. Ibid., p.229.
210. Jacob Neusner is only partly right to argue that 'One may compare Rubenstein's mode of thought to the first-century apocalyptic visionaries, Fackenheim's to that of the rabbis of the same period', but he probably underestimates the latter's prophetic inclination in declaring that the divine voice could be heard once again – and this in the concentration camps. As to Rubenstein, he is probably more priestly than apocalyptic- or rabbinic-oriented. See Neusner, *Stranger at Home*, p.74.
211. See Fackenheim, *Quest for Past and Future*, p.235.
212. Ibid., p.231.
213. Ibid.
214. Fackenheim, *God's Presence in History*, p.40.
215. See ibid., p.42.
216. Fackenheim, *Quest for Past and Future*, p.231.
217. One of the thinkers who oppose Buber's, and all his followers', concept is Arthur Hertzberg, who affirms:

> I have never found a way to absolve God of the crime of Auschwitz ... I find no help in those who say that He is a limited Power who encourages humanity to do good but is not responsible for the pain and evil in the world ... The most elegant version of this idea – that God is not responsible for evil, and especially not for the ultimate evil of the Holocaust – was fashioned by Martin Buber in his *Eclipse of God* ... But, as I once screamed at Buber himself in his home in Jerusalem, what right had God to go away, or to permit Himself to be eclipsed, while my grandfather and all of my mother's brothers and sister and their children were being murdered?

A. Hertzberg, *Jewish Polemics* (New York: Columbia University Press, 1992), p.243.
218. Fackenheim, *God's Presence in History*, p.88.
219. Ibid., p.46.
220. 'Elie Wiesel has compared the Holocaust with Sinai in revelatory significance – and expressed the fear that we are not listening.' Ibid., p.84.

221. Ibid., pp.82f.
222. See Fackenheim, *Quest for Past and Future*, p.136.
223. Fackenheim, *God's Presence in History*, pp.88f.
224. See Neusner, *Stranger at Home*, p.74.
225. For an outline of critical opinions on Fackenheim's theology see R.M. Seltzer, 'Judaism According to Emil Fackenheim', *Commentary*, 86 (September 1988), p.33; D. Berger, 'What Do American Jews Believe?', p.20.
226. I. Greenberg, 'Cloud of Smoke, Pillar of Fire: Judaism, Christianity, and Modernity after the Holocaust', in E. Fleischner (ed.), *Auschwitz: Beginning of a New Era? Reflections on the Holocaust* (New York: Ktav Publishing House, 1977). In Greenberg's own opinion, this is, 'The most important piece that I ever wrote on the Holocaust'. Irving Greenberg, *Living in the Image of God: Jewish Teachings to Perfect the World: Conversations with Rabbi Irving Greenberg as Conducted by Shalom Freedman* (Northvale, NJ: Jason Aronson, 1998), p.233.
227. J. Telushkin, 'Foreword', in Greenberg, *Living in the Image of God*, p.xx. Greenberg studied at Yeshiva Etz Chaim in Boro Park, Yeshiva University High School and Musar Yeshiva Bais Josef.
228. See Greenberg, *Living in the Image of God*, pp.54f; Greenberg, 'Cloud of Smoke, Pillar of Fire', p.8.
229. See Greenberg, 'Cloud of Smoke, Pillar of Fire', p.23. A similar view is echoed in Dan Magurshak: 'Believers in Israel's God of history or in the Christian God of the resurrection have often asked how God – omnipotent, omniscient, benevolent – could let the children burn under the blue and empty sky.' D. Magurshak, 'The "Incomprehensibility" of the Holocaust: Tightening Up Some Loose Usage', *Judaism*, 29 (Spring 1980), p.237.
230. Greenberg, 'Cloud of Smoke, Pillar of Fire', pp.9, 41.
231. Ibid., p.33.
232. Ibid., pp.11f.
233. Ibid., p.13.
234. Ibid., p.25.
235. '[He] did not keep His share of the covenant in defending His people in this generation.' Ibid., p.33.
236. Ibid.
237. See ibid., p.30.
238. Greenberg, *Living in the Image of God*, p.56.
239. See Telushkin, 'Forword', p.xxii.
240. M. Oppenheim, 'Irving Greenberg and the Jewish Dialectic of Hope', *Judaism*, 49 (Spring 2000), p.195.
241. Ibid. Greenberg himself, however, is slightly ambiguous on this point. On one hand, he maintains that man has grown mature, and that, 'The interpretive rules have changed as the covenantal rules have changed, and humans have taken on more responsibility'; on the other, he still believes that divine providence (*hashgachah*) accompanies people in every moment of their lives, and God 'now acts primarily ... through human activity'. Thus it is not clear whether human acts are human acts tout court, or God's acts through humans. Greenberg, *Living in the Image of God*, pp.38f.
242. See ibid., p.56.
243. Ibid., p.236.
244. Greenberg, 'Cloud of Smoke, Pillar of Fire', p.11.
245. The Hebrew Bible – acronym for *Torah + Neviim + Ketuvim = TaNaK* (Pentateuch, Prophets, and (other) Writings).
246. Greenberg, 'Cloud of Smoke, Pillar of Fire', p.27.
247. Greenberg, *Living in the Image of God*, p.231.
248. See Greenberg, 'Cloud of Smoke, Pillar of Fire', p.27.
249. Ibid.
250. In his view, 'Neither classical theism nor atheism is adequate to incorporate the incommensurability of the Holocaust; neither produced a consistently proper response; neither is credible alone – in the presence of the burning children.' Ibid., p.26.
251. Ibid., p.46; Greenberg quotes R. Manvell, *SS and Gestapo* (New York: Ballantine, 1969), p.109.

252. Ibid., p.47.
253. See ibid.
254. That does not mean he completely ignores the topic in his scholarship. His *Living in the Image of God* is in large measure dedicated to ethical issues.
255. Greenberg, *Living in the Image of God*, p.39.
256. See ibid.
257. Greenberg, 'Cloud of Smoke, Pillar of Fire', p.50.
258. Ibid., p.42.
259. Ibid., p.48.
260. See ibid. In Hebrew, the letters 'lamed' (L) and 'vov' (V) denote the number 36. The *lamed-vovnik* concept is one of the most basic ideas of Jewish mysticism.
261. Ibid., p.32.
262. See ibid., p.28.
263. Ibid., pp.27f.
264. Greenberg claims that the recreation of the State of Israel is the 'fundamental act of life and meaning' for the Jew after the Second World War, and acknowledgement of this fact is a *sine qua non* condition of an authentic theological comprehension of Israel. See ibid., p.43.
265. Neusner, *Stranger at Home*, p.65.

CHAPTER THREE

Being Jewish In Post-War Poland

1. BACK TO LIFE IN POLAND?

In late 1944, large parts of Eastern Poland had already been liberated by the Red Army, and numbers of Jews started to return to their pre-war homes. Thousands had survived in hiding or in the camps. Also, trainloads of Jewish repatriates from the Soviet Union (including Belarus, Ukraine, the Baltic republics, European and Asian parts of Russia, Kazakhstan and Uzbekistan) were coming to their old homeland. By the summer of 1946, around 150,000 Jewish refugees from the East had registered with local Jewish committees in Poland. Those who had survived the war on the German-occupied Polish territory in principle had forged 'Aryan' IDs with Polish names, or had no documents whatsoever (specifically those hidden by non-Jewish families and children).

Having gone through an unimaginable gehenna of German anti-Jewish policy, which was tantamount to a death sentence for anybody who was born a Jew, and having also experienced Polish anti-Semitism – blackmailing, denouncing and sometimes even murdering Jews – the survivors often wanted to keep their assumed Polish identities. For many of them the choice was so much easier because before the war they had been completely assimilated. At times they even did not know any Yiddish, had what they called 'a good, Aryan look' and thus found it almost natural to stick to their new, typically Polish names.

The story of the eastern refugees was a different one. While in the USSR, they had not been in a situation requiring name changes. In most cases they had been given Soviet passports but retained their pre-war family names. Those returning from the Soviet Union and those who had survived on Polish soil hoped to recover their houses, their workshops, their smaller or bigger businesses, and to find relatives. But it all turned out to be barely possible. Most of their family members had long been dead – they died of hunger or diseases in the ghettos, were killed in the camps or, in some cases, murdered by their neighbours. Coming to their home towns and villages, no one greeted them, no one waited for them, and almost no one was even happy with their return.

The houses and the moveable property they had left, when fleeing the Germans, had been taken over by Polish families. It would be a rare case when a former Jewish owner of a house or a farm would get back their property. Sometimes they were 'advised' to leave town unless they wanted to face problems; others got beaten up, or were seriously injured or even killed. In 1945 and 1946 it was not unusual for a Jew in Poland to be thrown out from a running train or to be dragged out from it when it stopped. Many were robbed or killed. It is estimated that by mid-1946, between 1,500 and 2,000 Jews had been killed in Poland.[1] Even though the assumption that in each and every instance they were killed because they were Jews would be difficult to prove, it is more than probable that the victims' ethnic origin played a major role in these incidents.

Among the Jews who came from the East, a large proportion constituted those who had left their property in what had been Poland before the war but was now incorporated into the new Soviet republics: Belarus and Ukraine. They knew they would never be recompensed for that. The Polish (communist) government directed them to the western territories of Lower Silesia (Dolny Śląsk) and far to the north of new Poland: Szczecin and Koszalin, lands given to Poland due to the Yalta agreement of February 1945. Jewish repatriates settled down in Wrocław (Breslau), Wałbrzych, Dzierżoniów, Bielawa, Gdańsk, Olsztyn, Poznań, Bydgoszcz, Włocławek and Katowice, but also in former centres of Jewish life: Warsaw, Łódź (Lodz), Kraków, Lublin, Częstochowa, Tarnów, and Przemyśl.

Altogether, between September 1944 and mid-1946, approximately 150,000 Polish Jews came to Poland from the USSR.[2] The number of those who survived the war under German occupation of Poland – either in the camps or 'on forged Aryan papers' – is estimated at between 50,000 and 100,000 (including Jewish children in Catholic monasteries). Between mid-1944 and mid-1946, the approximate number of Jews living within the boundaries of post-Yalta Poland was between 260,000 and 280,000. A more exact number cannot be given, because during that period full trains were still coming from the USSR, while thousands were leaving Poland for Israel or western European countries, many of them thanks to Brikha – an organization that helped Jews to reach Israel illegally.[3]

Jewish life in smaller towns, however, did not see a rebirth. One of the reasons for that was the hostility of the local Polish population, who threatened to kill Jewish repatriates and even actually murdered some. That is why, in 1945 and 1946, thousands of Jews were leaving small towns and moving to cities such as Warsaw, Łódź or Cracow. But even there they could not feel safe, which became all too obvious after the Cracow pogrom of 1945 and the Kielce pogrom of 1946. Whether Jews could really recreate Jewish life in Poland after the war became an extremely problematic issue. Too many of them perished at the hand of Poles for the whole community to be able to look at Poland as a safe haven.

The question of Jewish identity was one that certainly existed in the early post-war years, though it would be publically discussed only tacitly. The higher the level of discussion, the less frequently the issue would be raised, and for various reasons. First and foremost, the Polish society at large did not seem to be happy to see so many of their Jewish neighbours coming back home (although close to 90 per cent of Polish Jews perished in the Holocaust). People who, during the war, wanted to hide the fact that they were Jewish, continued the same survival strategy after 1945. Being Jewish was not something one would like to reveal to others, certainly not to Gentiles.

Secondly, Jewish identity soon became a 'political issue' – as it was called in those days. Since a visible number of Jews, specifically those coming from the Soviet Union, saw the new regime as an opportunity to introduce genuine social equality (for some it was also a way to obtain well-paid and relatively high-prestige positions in the party or in the broader public administration apparatus), revealing one's Jewish identity was deemed unwise, or at least the very fact of being a Jew was thought to be of no relevance. That was also because the communist ideology intended to introduce a new concept of citizen: an individual whose particular ethnic background was unimportant or could even be perceived as an obstacle on the road to the new social order. The new society was to be not only classless but also devoid of national, cultural and religious differences. In short, questions such as 'Who is a Jew?', 'What does it mean to be Jewish?' or 'How to be Jewish?' were hardly ever asked in public in the first post-war years.[4] The situation changed, however, when Jewish children born in the late 1940s started going to school. This topic will be analysed in more detail further on in this chapter.

It must also be said that initially there was no public debate on being Jewish in Poland. And quite understandably, for what seemed to be of the highest importance was still searching for relatives, trying to find a place to live and work, and, for a significant part of the Jewish population, struggling with the question: 'Leave Poland or stay?' Very few Jewish authors would ponder on the issue in press publications or books. It should be stressed firmly that Jewish identity as a subject of intellectual debates, particularly analysed from a sociological perspective, was virtually non-existent after the war. Up until the 1980s, this topic was generally avoided by scholars, Jews and non-Jews alike. It must be difficult for people from Western Europe, and for American Jews specifically, to imagine how this was possible. The issue of Jewish identity in all its aspects – from assimilation to religious affiliation, to secularization, to the tension between Judaism and Jewishness – was present in so many public debates on the American continent that it seems unthinkable that a similar process was not observed in Poland.

And yet, questions such as 'Who's Jewish and who's not?', and what were the social consequences of being a Jew – all this did stir up discussions in post-war Poland, as is evidenced in a number of memoirs, press articles and, to some extent, in Jewish organizations' documents. But again, there were a number of isolated opinions expressed here and there, rather than a regular scholarly debate. Definitely it was not a subject of scientific research – which, of course, makes the current analysis difficult. Therefore, what materials can be referred to? How are we to narrate or summarize a debate, an intellectual process, that never really took place? The very difficulty lies in obtaining reliable data – this could be illustrated by the fact that during the first forty years after its launching, *The Bulletin of the Jewish Historical Institute* in Warsaw was almost totally uninterested in issues pertaining to Jewish identities. For one thing, this is understandable since it was by definition focused on the historical aspect of Jewish existence in Poland, and specifically on documenting and analysing wartime materials. For another, it was the only Jewish scholarly periodical until the fall of communism, and hence one could expect a broader interest in Jewish topics, including the social and psychological aspects of Jewish post-war life. There are many articles in the *Bulletin* covering the Warsaw Ghetto uprising, life in other ghettos and the camps, and also studies on mediaeval Polish Jewry.

2. JEWISH IDENTITY VS COMMUNIST IDEOLOGY

The language used in papers published in the 1950s and 1960s perfectly reflected the political climate of the day. In an article titled 'An Exhibition on the Occasion of the 10th Anniversary of the Warsaw Ghetto Uprising', Artur Rutkowski wrote not only about the Jewish military effort, but also about 'the genocidal Hitlerite-American imperialism' and 'its war crimes (e.g. in Korea)'.[5] What is much more interesting, however, is the very approach to Jewish suffering – and to the

Jewish fate in general – as part of the overall historical condition of the Polish society. In his introductory remarks, Rutkowski mentions two previous exhibitions, organized in 1948 and 1950. The former was called 'The Martyrology and the Combat of Jews in Poland under Hitlerite Occupation', while the latter 'was dedicated to the participation of Polish Jews in the fight of the Polish nation for a national and social liberation'.[6] Rutkowski critically assesses the 1948 exhibition as being flawed with 'a generally mistaken concept of one-sided sublimation, bathing in pain, as well as representing the martyrology and combat of the Jewish population in Poland in an isolated way and divorced from the broad situation in the country and from the general plan of the occupying power to destroy the whole Polish nation'.[7]

Rutkowski went on to argue that the said exhibition artificially distinguished between Jewish fate and that of the Polish society at large, and failed to see the combat 'of all antifascist forces in the country (including in the ghettos) [unified] against the Hitlerite invader [in fighting] for a free, independent, socialist Poland'.[8]

It is exceptionally interesting to see how the communist ideology of classless society was translated into historical discourse and how it affected, explicitly, the concept of a distinctive Jewish identity. From Rutkowski's paper, and from the general 'political line' of the *Bulletin*, it stems that picturing the Jewish community and the Jewish identity as unequivocally distinct from the Polish background was undesired, questionable or even suspect. Rutkowski underscores the fact that in the 1953 exhibition, 'the genocidal character of German fascism was portrayed through a selection of documents concerning the general plan of destroying Jews, Poles, Slavs'.[9] He then enumerates several Nazi instructions, orders, reports and speeches (including ones signed by Hitler, Himmler, Goebbels, Goering, Eichmann, Heydrich, Frank and Globocnik), to conclude that these provide 'firm evidence of the genocidal plans of the Hitlerite [regime] regarding Poland, the Polish nation, and the Jewish people'.

One cannot help asking the question: Why would the editorial board of the only Jewish scholarly periodical in post-1945 Poland want to downplay the Jewish specificity of wartime suffering and combat? Why did they make all that effort to almost water down the Jewish experience and present Jews as just one of the many social groups targeted by the German criminal policy? The answer is not at all obvious. Saying that it was part of the 'classless society' concept reveals just one side of the coin. The other side is no less relevant for this study, and it is the awareness of the stereotype of 'Jewish communism' which was not only alive and kicking, but also became significantly strengthened during and right after the war.

Another factor that should be taken into account here is the impact of anti-Semitism on the post-war identity of Polish Jews. Most of the survivors and those who spent wartime in the USSR had had some experience of anti-Semitic attitudes from before the war. But it was during the war that the relations between Poles and Jews became even more complicated and ambiguous. Most survivors are fully aware of the significance of the help they had received from their Polish saviours; nevertheless, many also stress their fear that they might have been denounced by Poles to the German authorities. Despite the lack of scholarly works focused on analysing the affect of anti-Semitism on Jewish identities in Poland in the 1940s and 1950s, there are a number of testimonies, scattered in various books, memoirs and professional literature.

In her pioneering work on survivors' Jewish identities, *The Holocaust and Identity*, Małgorzata Melchior mentioned the omnipresent danger and the feeling of insecurity as the daily bread of Jews with so-called forged 'Aryan papers', who feared that their Jewish identity could be uncovered by Poles, specifically by the Polish blue police (supervised by the German civil authorities but allowed to keep its pre-war Polish uniforms) or by ordinary blackmailers. She writes: 'Many Survivors recall that one had to beware of the Poles in the first place as it was easier for them than for Germans to recognize a Jew in an unknown passer-by or a neighbour.'[10] Her interviewees confessed they had been afraid not (only) of the Germans but of the Poles (too); that walking on the streets or riding on a tram, they had been watching every single gesture and look of the people surrounding them. That was part of their survival strategy, in which constantly asking who's a friend and who's a foe was vital, and looking at Poles with suspicion was natural, automatic and unavoidable.[11] On the other hand, as some survivors admit, at times they could also encounter threats from Jewish Gestapo collaborators.[12]

This ambivalence of being helped by Poles and fearing Polish blackmailers was still present during and after the 1944 Warsaw Uprising and after 1945. Parts of east-central Poland had been liberated in the latter half of 1944, and Jews coming out of hiding had to face post-war Polish anti-Semitism. Those coming back to their homes were unwelcome, at best. Jews in general were perceived as supporters of the communist regime imposed by the Soviets. All this experience of anti-Semitism or dislike for the Jews expressed by common people, joined with traditional scapegoating of Jews as being responsible for all of Poland's ills – here of installing communism – could not have left the Jewish people unaffected.

The highly controversial and sensitive issue of the Jewish share in supporting communism in terms of ideology, as well as by joining the party apparatus, including its security police, needs to be addressed: on one hand, for reasons of historical fairness, but on the other hand, because the survivors themselves saw it as relevant to their life histories, and political and cultural choices. What is much more important, however, is how their children perceived the parents' involvement with communism. In numerous publications issued over the last twenty years, these grown-up children of survivors courageously take up the task of describing their lives in early communist Poland of the late 1940s, the 1950s, and well into the 1960s. They discuss family customs, their upbringing, their school days, and contacts with other Jewish families but also with their Polish friends. They talk about Jewish communists and Polish anti-Semites in a unique effort to reject the prevailing social taboos and to rise above political correctness.

In his *Poland and the Jews: Reflections of a Polish Polish Jew*, a work of rare intellectual depth and honesty, Stanisław Krajewski, a prominent member of – and a person frequently representing – the community of Polish Jews, analyses at length the complex story of Jewish involvement in communism. It is a widely acknowledged fact, to which Krajewski also refers, that identifying Jews with communism was common in pre-war Poland, and it only intensified in the years following the outbreak of the Second World War. Without exculpating the anti-Semitic labelling of communism as Jewish by definition, Krajewski shows the historical context that could have contributed to fanning this prejudice: 'It is a fact that many Jews, like other minorities in the same territories [in eastern Poland], spent little time mourning the passing of a Polish state in which they felt like second-class citizens.'[13] He also underscores the ignorance of the Polish population regarding the suffering of Jews under the Soviet regime:

> They looked on the change in power with a certain hope, and in some cases with enthusiasm – positions that they could never have dreamed about in Poland, in administration or the military, for instance, now became accessible to them. For Poles this was treason ... [But] Jews shared the woes of the time: they constituted 30% of the Polish citizens deported eastward into the Russian interior. Some Jews were happy to be out of Hitler's reach. Yet it is also a fact that Poles are unaware that thousands of Jews refused to accept Soviet passports early in the war and asked permission to return to the territory occupied by the Germans.[14]

It can be argued that the experience of the Soviet occupation of eastern Poland had significantly helped in strengthening the 'Jewish communism' stereotype. Even though a number of Jews rejected the system, and many fell victim to the NKVD alongside the Poles. However, the factor that proved even more decisive in this regard was that part of the Jewish population supported the communist regime after the war, and Jews constituted what is believed to be a disproportionate share in the higher echelons of the party and its security police apparatus. Krajewski contends that 'Once the war had ended, the accusation about "Jewish communism" took on substance as a result of the widespread participation by Jews in the newly-created system of rule that had been imposed on the country.'[15] At the same time, he points out that Jews did not join the ranks of the regime administration as Jews but as communists. In other words, they participated in the system not because they were Jewish but because of the political views they held.[16]

Nevertheless, the very fact of Jewish involvement in communism is a uniquely contentious and sensitive question. This can be observed not only on pages written by historians and journalists but in testimonies of the survivors' children as well. Stanisław Krajewski claims in a sincere and straightforward way that 'the role of Jewish communists in the framework of the Jewish history [is] highly emotional'. And if it 'is seen as part of the comprehensive Jewish history, it follows that in our century, in Eastern Europe, Jews were not only among the oppressed, but were also among the oppressors'.[17] But of course not all Jewish communists (or any other communists in general) were oppressors *sensu stricto*. Perhaps most were either deluded by the communist ideology or attracted by the mere possibility of becoming part of the 'elite', or both: 'In Poland, immediately after the Second World War, most Jewish organizations were pro-communist; they saw communists as the force that can bring security and stability. To be a Jew was sometimes an advantage for those ready to make careers in the emerging communist system.'[18]

Yet it cannot be taken for granted that Polish communist authorities were pro-Jewish or well disposed toward the Jewish community by definition. Jewish leaders saw much anti-Semitism as still present not only in the Polish population at large but also in the Communist Party ranks. Bernard Mark, director of the Jewish Historical Institute in the 1950s, referred in his diary to the numerous instances of removing Jews from important positions in the state apparatus as well as from industry. He also remarked that in many criminal cases where Jews were the victims, the prosecutors would express anti-Semitic attitudes and claim that the victimized Jews were not and would never become Poles.[19]

As has been mentioned above, many of those whose childhood fell in the 1950s and 1960s remember how their parents and acquaintances found a way to get along in the post-war Polish society, and – in several cases – that they were perceived as the ones 'well established' in the regime. In a book published in 2008, Joanna Wiszniewicz collected twenty-seven interviews with Polish Jews (some of whom had emigrated from Poland in or after 1968).[20] One of the interviewees, Marta Petrusewicz, confessed:

> We were born after the war in downtown [Warsaw]: my friends and I. They were children of my parents' friends – [coming] from that milieu of prewar communist Jews ... and we, their children, were going together to the military–communist kindergarten, used to go together on vacation to special government-run summer resorts, and went together to the TPD[21] Gottwald elementary school. [It was] the famous '14' – the school of the 'red bourgeoisie' (the Stalinist one). In my class all children were actually children of government ministers or vice-ministers, many of their fathers had office cars and a chauffeur at their disposal, we lived in comfortable apartments run by a housekeeper.
>
> Did I know that many of my schoolmates and kids from the kindergarten were Jewish? No ... but for me the problem of Jewishness and otherness didn't exist for a long time ... All the children I knew were nonbelieving, just as I were, or were Jewish, just like me (with no real awareness of being Jewish though).[22]

In many other stories gathered by Wiszniewicz, memories of parents' communist involvement come back constantly. One has the impression the experience of talking about their memories has a purifying or therapeutic effect on the interviewees. They often narrate how their parents had been persecuted even before the war; they sometimes talk about the parents' childhood in the Soviet Union,[23] and recall their parents praising communism and the People's Republic of Poland as the best possible Poland.[24] Some even claim that their parents bear, to a certain extent, responsibility for installing in Poland a political system that utilized violence and oppression.[25] One person admitted that her father had worked in the secret police (UB); when she later realized what it meant, it became a singularly painful issue for her, to the extent that 'until now I redden at a mere recollection of my father's past and that this past confirmed the stereotype of "Jewish communism" '.[26]

But communism is neither the only nor the predominant topic of these accounts. It is paralleled by stories of the absence of religious faith. To many of Wiszniewicz's interviewees, being divorced from organized religion and any kind of religious faith was self-evident. It was part of their identity. As one of them put it, '"being a nonbeliever" was closely related in my mind with "being a Pole of Jewish descent" '.[27] 'A-religiosity was as it were a second part of my identity',[28] said Leon Rozenbaum. And yet another person, Małgosia Tal, remembered that her parents had been explicit in this regard, saying: 'as communists we reject the Jewish religion, since every religion divides the society'.[29]

Probably the most important element in Wiszniewicz's interviewees' accounts is their early experience of Jewishness or, in some cases, an absence of Jewish awareness. It was not very rare for Jewish children born in the 1940s (both during and after the war) to be unaware of their ethnic identity. No wonder then, that in the very first sentence of the first interview, we read:

> I didn't know that I was Jewish. I was baptized, took the first communion, and in the third grade, when religion was introduced to schools (in 1956), my father made me go to those lessons. About the same time something happened to my schoolmates. They started to keep away from me. They said I was Jewish and that before the war my parents had had a different – a Jewish – family name.[30]

The little Jewish boy complained about it to his parents. They were appalled at what their son had experienced but did not tell him about his origin. Similar stories can be multiplied by the thousands.

Yet, in most cases, Jewish children simply knew they were Jewish. In one way or another they would find out about it. Sometimes the very fact of 'being Jewish' was never mentioned at home, but at some point in time the children became aware that they were part of a Jewish family.[31] In many cases, although everybody knew they were Jewish, the topic and the very word 'Jew' was to be avoided. Recalling her childhood, Ewa said: 'I've known since I was a child that we do not talk aloud about the fact that we're Jewish. We do not talk aloud. The word "Jew," by the way, was hardly ever used in my home – we used the characteristic expression: *ex nostris*.'[32] At the same time, Ewa finds it difficult to define those '*ex nostris*'. In her memory they were those who knew foreign languages and could live in just any country. 'This was not cosmopolitanism. But certainly a kind of lack of rootedness, and a lack of feeling at home in the traditional Polish culture.' In short, she says, 'they were Jewish intelligentsia people visiting my parents'.[33] Paradoxically, she was 'officially informed' – as she put it – that she was Jewish only at the age of 10. Her father did not explain to her 'at all what it means "to be Jewish"; he only said: "We are Jews and it may happen that other people will say so about you." '[34]

In many families, being Jewish was so natural that it was hardly ever mentioned by the parents. Luba Tarczyńska remembers her childhood in Szczecin. Jewish identity was for her 'something normal, natural but there was no content to it, it was linked with no tradition, no holiday observance or synagogue ... If not for the fact that my brothers would hear on the streets: "You Moshke, you this or that", there wouldn't have been any Jewishness at all in our home!'[35] Being Jewish was just a fact of life – for Luba and many other children who attended Jewish schools or TPD schools where children from Jewish families were a majority. 'Our "contentless" Jewishness was for us all the more natural that the school we went to – TPD school no. 5 ... without religious instruction – had mostly Jewish children. And in my class pure blood Polish kids could be counted on one hand.'[36]

Being Jewish and talking about it were two different things, even in predominantly Jewish milieus. Bronka Karst claims she would talk about Jewishness and the past with her friends. They would meet after school, party together, hold anti-regime conversations and sing anti-regime songs: 'most of the people I was meeting with at that time were Jewish ... But it was only after high school finals that I and Bożena realized everybody in our pack was Jewish.'[37]

In the 1950s and 1960s, for many young Jews – including those interviewed by Wiszniewicz – an important experience affecting their ethnic awareness was the Jewish Socio-Cultural Society, or TSKŻ (Towarzystwo Społeczno Kulturalne Żydów).[38] Both those for whom being Jewish was an important part of their lives, and those who had only marginal knowledge of what it could mean, were very attracted to the organization. The TSKŻ-run weekly meetings as well as summer camps made it possible for them to taste Jewish identity, as it were, and to live in a Jewish community where being a Jew was nothing to be ashamed of, nothing to hide – on the contrary, it was deemed natural, worthwhile talking about and being proud of. This is how Leon Rozenbaum saw it:

> Being in a Jewish environment was a very important part of my life. Beginning in the sixth grade of elementary school, every

Saturday and Sunday I used to go to the TSKŻ-Club ... and I would go to the summer camps since I was seven. There, among Jewish youth, I felt well, at ease. Jewish communists who organized all that perfectly understood that it was important for Jewish children to have an opportunity to be together, just with their own group.

Also, they wanted the kids to maintain a certain Jewish awareness as well as an awareness of the Yiddish culture ... they had a sentiment for that culture, and some sort of continuation of that seemed important to them. So, during those summer camps Jewish children, who in their majority did not know Yiddish, were learning Yiddish songs and taking Yiddish lessons.[39]

Rozenbaum remarked that TSKŻ had also an 'a-religious' touch, which seems obvious, since it was a purely secular organization and wished to keep with the official party line, and therefore it could not propagate anything that would even allude to religion. That not withstanding, in practice TSKŻ managed to maintain a clearly Jewish character in what it preached and what it offered culturally:

Despite that a-religious approach, our summer-camp Jewishness had a lot of authenticity in it ... Many Jewish songs had nothing to do with religion, so in that TSKŻ type of Jewishness conveyed to the youth there was this taste of Jewish culture, and that was for many of us an important – for most probably the only – contact with the spirit of Jewish culture ... By the way, in all that communist concept of TSKŻ as a Jewish society, there was enormous inconsistency since it had been devised as a continuation of the Yevsektsya – the Jewish section of the Bolshevik (and later Soviet) party propaganda division whose task was to propagate communism among Jews and drag them away from the Jewish tradition. Yet TSKŻ was doing exactly the opposite – bringing to life those Jewish sentiments, which was a contradiction of the initial idea.[40]

A number of the people Wiszniewicz interviewed claimed that anti-Semitism, to some degree, also played a role in shaping their Jewish identity. Not infrequently, they would hear unpleasant comments about Jews in general, or be mocked by their Polish mates just because they were Jewish. In some cases the experience of anti-Semitism caused a deeper trauma and led to a true fear of living among Poles. A really astounding example of how great a problem it was can be found in Marek's story:

In Niemcza all Jews would stick together. 'Cos they were afraid.

My parents too: they would tremble to think that the Poles could kill them. 'Cos the pro-London underground[41] had supposedly been shooting Jews in the forests (as my mother said), so the kids had always to be guarded, always to be close by. We even had to have typically non-Jewish names! ... In '49, when we moved from Niemcza to Legnica ... my mother would still warn us: 'Watch out! Legnica is a Catholic town and the Poles are prejudiced against other faiths and Jews!' ... so every so often the children would yell at me: 'He's a kike, he's a kike.'[42]

Anti-Semitism in post-war Poland was so overwhelming that it became part of Jewish life and Jewish identity. Considering its presence in Polish society in the 1930s and during the war, it was probably not perceived as something unexpected, but having gone through the gehenna of the Holocaust, it must have been very painful for Polish Jews after 1945. Anti-Semitism was experienced not only by adults at work, in the shops and on the streets, it also affected the children. On one hand, they had suffered a lot from their schoolmates and the children with whom they played. On the other hand, they had been taught by their parents to be always vigilant, to be careful and never to show ostentatiously that they were Jewish. This mixture of personal experience and advice given by grown-ups led to creating a picture of Poles as people who were by definition unfriendly, suspicious and ill-willed, or even hating Jews. And there definitely was some ground for maintaining this kind of opinion.

No wonder, then, that a negative picture of the Poles became so ingrained in Jews – at least a certain number of them – as to see in Poles no good qualities. Michał Fajersztajn's confession seems to be an example of this socio-psychological phenomenon. Describing an unexpectedly nice experience where Poles had been involved, he said: 'I had no idea whatsoever that Poles could be such wonderful people. Very sociable, very helpful and friendly – just like we in our Jewish school. I hadn't known that before. I was shocked to see Poles with whom I could make such good friends!'[43]

However important the general social climate in post-war Poland would have been, the main focus of this study is the impact of the Shoah on Jewish identity strategies. Did the awareness of the almost total destruction of European Jewry affect the way they behaved, thought of themselves as Jews, shaped their identities? Did it influence their identification choices – whether they wanted to continue being Jewish (whether or not it was a return to pre-war Jewishness is another question) or decided to become 'typical' (not hyphenated) Poles. This issue is yet another blank space in post-1945 studies on Polish Jewry. Two major sociological works, one by Irena Hurwic-Nowakowska, the second one by Iwona Irwin-Zarecka, though providing plenty of information otherwise unavailable, almost completely omit that subject. Why was that so? It is not an easy question to answer. Hurwic-Nowakowska's research was conducted between 1947 and 1950, while both books were published in the latter half of the 1980s. At that time Polish scholars were not sensitive enough to issues of the impact of the Holocaust upon Jewish identities on the sociological and societal level. In the United States the problem had already been subject to scholarly analysis for some twenty years, but in Poland – and more broadly in all of the Soviet Bloc – the Jews and the Holocaust were topics usually passed over in silence. However amazing this might seem, in this particular field there is nothing to refer to, no study, no first-hand source to quote.

Before analysing the interviews carried out for this study, let us once again refer to Joanna Wiszniewicz's book, in which her informants mention the topic of the Holocaust on several occasions. First of all, it has to be emphasized that this particular subject does not come up excessively often. It is not even one of the leading topics in their memoirs. They do talk about the Shoah but only in passing, it seems, as if it were too obvious to mention. To be sure, it was not only a matter of historical facts but, more importantly, of family experience. Therefore Holocaust awareness was self-evident, though not always talked about overtly.[44]

Thus, an interviewee identified as Henia, who lived in the former ghetto area, declared:

> In our yard they were building a kindergarten and an excavator happened to dig in the cellars where there were corpses from the ghetto! And some kids would throw stones at them and shout 'Lousy Jews, Jews!' So you grow up with that awareness all the time ... that the family had perished, that we live on graves, that dad cries at night – the tragedy was always somewhere near me, and not only at home! For you also had the literature ... and my father talking with my mother about Polish antisemitism – that there was no room for us in Poland, that we had to leave, that Poland is not our homeland, and that Poles did the Kilece pogrom .... And the Holocaust also meant that my father wanted always to protect us.[45]

Another interviewee, Małgosia Tal, said she had to know the names of the children from the family who had not survived the war, and she was treated as someone special just because her very birth countered

Hitler's plan.[46] Many others confirmed that the Holocaust was occasionally mentioned in their family talks.[47] In several cases, however, they had the impression that their parents had avoided the topic of the Shoah.[48] Some of them also observed that though during the TSKŻ Jewish summer camps they could learn a lot about Jewish folklore and literature, the Holocaust was virtually never mentioned. Rather, the children themselves would share stories of their parents – how they had managed to survive, where they had been hiding, and so forth.[49] A few interviewees admitted that one or both of their parents had been obsessed with the Shoah in a way that affected their everyday life. Lena, for instance, said that when, after graduating from the university, she had bought an old baroque closet, her father simply flew into a fury: 'When running away, will you bear the closet on your back?! For this money you could have bought two gold rings, and a gold ring can always be exchanged for bread.'[50]

3. FORCED EMIGRATION AND REDISCOVERING JEWISH IDENTITY: THE SECOND GENERATION COMING OF AGE

Polish Jews started emigrating soon after the liberation of Poland[51] (summer 1944 – spring 1945) or upon their arrival from the Soviet Union. Initially, the emigration was not forced. For one, the new Polish administration operated as a makeshift structure, with very limited tools at hand to control society. Leaving the country, therefore, was not a difficult task and those who were planning to emigrate faced almost no obstacles. For another, the communist authorities had an agreement with the CKŻP which guaranteed free passage of Jews willing to leave Poland. The borders with Czecholslovakia and the Soviet Zone (of occupied Germany) were not closely watched. As has been mentioned above, Brikha was instrumental in helping Jewish emigrants reach (often illegally) Palestine. But the communist regime often changed its position vis-à-vis leaving Poland by Polish citizens in general and Jews specifically. At certain periods it was virtually impossible to get a passport, even for declared Zionists who stated overtly they did not see any future for themselves in Poland. That, for example, was the case of a prominent Jewish activist from Lower Silesia – Jakub Egit.[52]

The second great, organized wave of emigration started in the summer of 1946, triggered by the Kielce pogrom. For most Jews living in Poland, though they had been well aware that anti-Semitism still existed, this came as a complete shock. A large number of those who felt Jewish, and to whom Jewish identity was self-evident, decided to leave Poland.[53] This was followed by another wave of emigration in 1949–50. By 1951, between 150,000 and 170,000 Jews had emigrated from Poland. During 1956 and 1957, another 40,000 left the country, while between 1957 and 1967 over 500 Jews emigrated every year.[54] The reasons for emigrating were manifold: fear of religiously motivated anti-Semitism and discrimination by local authorities, fear of anti-Jewish violence, perceiving Poland as a Jewish graveyard, experiencing growing problems with free religious observance,[55] the desire to live in Israel (Zionists), and – in not a few cases – opposition to the communist regime. A great majority of those who left Poland by 1967 did so of their own volition, which does not necessarily mean they were always happy about it.[56]

Those who stayed in Poland had to adjust to the reality, creating what could be likened to the pre-war Bund vision of Polish Jewry: 'a secular, "anti-Zionist", Yiddish culture', as Konstanty Gebert put it. 'Out of conviction or for convenience, most Jews chose assimilation, hiding their Jewish identity to a degree that legitimizes the use of the term "the new Marranos".'[57] That was the rule. But there were, of course, exceptions, even most unlikely ones, as in the case of Grażyna Pawlak, whose non-Jewish father had helped her mother during the war. Her childhood recollections are clear: 'In the home we were raised in a very normal way, which is our Jewishness was something utterly normal. My father used to talk about it far more than my mother did, because for her it was too painful. My father learned Yiddish to talk with my mother. In that way he wanted to save a part of her home.'[58]

The anti-Semitic purge launched by the Communist Party in March 1968 introduced a total change in terms of emigration. Leaving Poland was no longer made difficult by the regime, as far as the Jews were concerned; they were advised, urged or even forced to emigrate. And once and for all – that is why they had to relinquish Polish citizenship and were given so-called 'one-way' passports, in which it was clearly stated that the bearer thereof was 'not a Polish citizen'. The anti-Semitic campaign affected not only party members (the leaders maintained it was simply meant to rid the party of 'Zionist and reactionary elements') but also Jews occupying mid- and upper-level posts in public administration, the army, state-owned companies, education and the healthcare system. As early as 1964, the Ministry of the Interior prepared the 'Jewish list', which included also converts and mixed marriages.[59] Since 1960, the Head Political Office of the Polish Army under General Wojciech Jaruzelski (the same who introduced martial law in 1981) had been drawing up a list of 'suspect' officers, mainly Jews. As Śpiewak sees it, this was something unprecedented in post-war European history, with state authorities, the press and the whole bureaucratic apparatus engaged in identifying Jews – using racist criteria.[60]

The 1967 Six Day War was only a pretext for the Polish Communist Party for launching its anti-Semitic campaign. The campaign could certainly go unpunished, since the whole Soviet Bloc, at Moscow's wish, condemned Israel as an 'aggressor'. However, an internal party friction began much earlier, between the so-called cosmopolites and patriots, presumably at the beginning of the 1960s, and certainly after 1956.[61] The developments in the Middle East had an impact not only on Poland's foreign policy but on domestic issues, as well. Those who had been hiding their Jewish identity for the past twenty years, raising their children as just Polish, even converting to Catholicism, were now identified as Jews, stigmatized,[62] and told they were 'undesirable elements in People's Poland'.

The anti-Semitic campaign also affected Jewish institutional life. In the late 1960s and early 1970s all Jewish schools were closed, as well as the Jewish publishing house Idisz Buch, Jewish youth clubs and the Joint Distribution Committee. The only ones to have been permitted to function were the Jewish Historical Institute, the State Jewish Theater, the Jewish Socio-Cultural Society and the Religious Union of Mosaic Faith.[63]

To many, being stigmatized as Jewish was an almost everyday experience as early as 1956, when religious education was introduced to public schools. Jewish children who, in their mass, did not attend those lessons, were automatically singled out and mocked by their mates.[64] But in the 1950s and up until 1968, it was not a kind of anti-Semitism that would literally ruin their lives and make staying in Poland hardly bearable. As a result of the so-called March events, and specifically of Secretary Gomułka's anti-Semitic speech on 12 March, the word 'Jew' became tantamount to 'Zionist traitor', 'foreign element', 'the fifth column', and the like. It had a tremendous impact on Polish Jews, particularly on those who did not want to be Jews or did not even know they were Jewish.

Most of those to whom Jewish identity had been attributed (rightly or not) had to face a difficult choice: leave Poland or stay? Although there was a group for which emigration was an option and the decision to apply for a 'one-way' passport came relatively easily, for most of those targeted by the 'anti-Zionist' propaganda it was an excruciating experience. What was at stake, however, was not only the physical act of leaving the country of their birth and parting with relatives and acquaintances. Far more than that – it was also a decision that had a

deep psychological and political aspect, for leaving Poland in that
particular context would have meant submission to the oppressing communist regime and acknowledging that being Jewish had always been
more important than being Polish. The end result would have been:
yes, you are right in throwing us away from the country. This is how
Konstatnty Gebert views the situation:

> Those [Jews] who stayed [after 1968] believed that emigration
> was admitting a defeat, that it was declaring that all their lives had
> been based on illusions. Moreover, coming back to Jewishness was
> not possible for them, since they had accepted their Polish identity
> not under compulsion but out of their free will; in many cases it
> had been a choice made by their parents. 'Becoming a Jew' meant
> for them not only assuming an alien identity but also confirming
> the anti-Semites' charges, namely that they had never been Poles
> 'for real'.[65]

This predicament affected whole families, not only grown-ups. It was
not unusual for the authorities to try to coerce parents, together with
their teenage children, and children in their 20s, to leave the country.
The rationale behind that was obvious: the children will sometimes pres-
surize the parents, and if they do not succeed in convincing them to leave,
the children will be able to decide for themselves. In fact, hundreds of
university students and probably as many high school students made
the heartrending decision to leave Poland and their parents. Whatever
the decision, what all the political, social and family context meant for
them was being left 'in an undefined abyss. For them, too, 1968
became a turning point. They began that year as students, their identity
was not yet mature. When their Jewish origin had been "unmasked",
they had no other choice but to accept inside themselves both Polishness from the home, and Jewishness imposed by the outer world.'[66] If,
in the late 1940s and in 1956–57, those who decided to emigrate were
Jewish and felt Jewish and for the most part wanted to live Jewish lives,
those forced to emigrate after March 1968 were completely assimilated
– to such an extent that their Jewish identity was either symbolic, or
nonexistent. Not infrequently, their children as well as friends and
acquaintances had no idea whatsoever that they had anything to do
with Jewishness. They were people who, a few months or years earlier,
would never have considered leaving Poland, and certainly not because
of their Jewish background.[67] And those 'non-Jewish Jews', Polish
citizens who, for various reasons, had disregarded their ethnic origin,

were now identified as Jewish on the grounds of Nurenberg-like state policy of communist Poland. Even the so-called 'old communists', who strongly believed in internationalism, who identified with Poland and the Polish way of communism, were made to leave the country (most of them having been earlier expelled from the party).

It seems obvious now, just as it did forty years ago, that forcing people into 'being Jewish' was almost always equal to depriving them of their Polish identity. It was yet another proof that the century-long stereotype of 'Pole–Catholic', now accompanied by that of Pole–communist, was still prevailing. Polish identity was unipolar – but only in a certain aspect: one was 'entitled' to be Polish as long as one's ethnic background was not 'stained' with a Jewish (or German, Romani, Russian) ingredient. That ethnic exclusivism led to a situation where being identified as a Jew became tantamount to losing Polish identity – or rather being stripped of it. Analysing the March 1968 events in Poland, Paweł Śpiewak refers to Aleksander Hertz's concept of 'depolonization',[68] or a process whose end result was becoming a non-Pole, here – against one's will.[69] In other words, after 1968, the moment your Jewish identity was discovered (or imposed upon you), in the eyes of the party apparatus and, to a large extent, of the overall state administration, you were no longer a 'real' Pole. Just a Polish-speaking Jew.

Forced emigration of Polish Jews lasted some time, until the early 1970s. What followed was a gradual disappearance of the Jewish presence in Poland. The Jewish community entered a period of hibernation. The term 'community', however, is probably the least fitting here, as what little remained of Polish Jewry could certainly not be called a community. Sheer numbers cannot reveal the whole truth: while it was a group well over 10,000 strong, its social cohesion was almost unnoticeable. One of the few things they shared was the feeling of rejection and alienation, as well as the experience of 'having gone through' the anti-Semitic campaign, but also, paradoxically, having overcome the hostile communist regime policy. The very fact that – in the middle of the 1970s – they were still in Poland, testified to their victory: they had not succumbed to the brutal battue of the chauvinistic communist regime. Thus, they did not form a community; rather, they were a number of more or less scattered individuals, perhaps sometimes bound by professional interests or fear of anti-Semitism.

At first glance, that may hardly seem a positive experience, but its consequences were yet to be discovered. On one hand, Jewish community life became virtually non-existent. Jewish organizations functioned only on paper, and many of them were even disbanded. The Jewish presence in Poland was becoming barely visible. With the exception of *The Bulletin of the Jewish Historical Institute* and *Dos Yiddishe Vort/Słowo żydowskie* – a Yiddish-Polish periodical published by the communist-dominated TSKŻ[70] – there was no Jewish press. Yet on the other hand, that state-sponsored anti-Semitism triggered a phenomenon unprecedented in the history of Polish Jews: some of those for whom 'Jewish origin' had come as a revelation of sorts, or had been discovered anew, saw it as something worthy of interest and attention. Initially a shock and a mixture of painful emotions, the (re)discovery of Jewishness turned out to be a new opening, a breakthrough in their lives. For a steadily growing group of Polish Jews, then in their early twenties, it was a time of learning about and coming back to their Jewishness.

Indeed, the very question of what being Jewish means, and what the content of Jewish identity is, became a focal point of debates run by this new Jewish milieu that was still *in statu nascendi*. In the latter half of the 1970s, some kind of leadership was starting to crystallize within the new Jewish group. It included Stanisław Krajewski and Konstanty Gebert. In 1979 they created the Jewish Flying University (Żydowski Uniwersytet Latający, ŻUL).[71] A number of them were also involved in the Committee for the Defense of Workers (Komitet Obrony Robotników, KOR), founded in 1976.[72]

Although throughout the 1970s the Jewish community as such was in a state of stagnation, in the latter half of the decade a few dozen Polish Jews became more and more active both in various anti-regime movements[73] and in reviving Jewishness. Their participation in 'the underground' also had an effect on Polish–Jewish relations, specifically during 1980 and 1981 – the 'Solidarity' period. Since some Solidarity activists were Jewish, the movement took a more open approach towards ethnic minorities. That, however, was not self-evident, nor was it easy in practice, as the climate initially prevailing within Solidarity had some nationalist and manifestly Catholic tones. That is why it was at first quite unpopular with some Polish Jews, particularly with the elderly members of the Religious Union of Mosaic Faith and the TSKŻ, both of which – as Krajewski maintains – were to a significant degree dependent on the regime, and thus kept at distance from Solidarity.[74] That primitive tendency, though, was overcome, *inter alia* thanks to the Jewish Solidarity members (among whom were those active in the Jewish Flying University). They contributed to the fact that 'Solidarity's' political programme included ideas countering anti-Semitism and other kinds of social discrimination and exclusion.[75] It is worthwhile noting that on 7 October 1981, the first Countrywide Convention of (Solidarity) Delegates in Gdańsk adopted a Resolution on national minorities which positively affected the Jews, among others.[76]

Paradoxically, the relations between the state and the Jewish community were improving, although the regime still maintained its hardline anti-democratic policy.[77] In December 1981, the communist authorities allowed the Joint to return to Poland and started issuing permits for restoring Jewish cemeteries and renovating buildings used for religious purposes. That very year, a Citizens' Committee for the Protection of Jewish Cemeteries and Historical Monuments in Poland (Społeczny Komitet Opieki nad Cmentarzami i Zabytkami Kultury Żydowskiej w Polsce) was created. The members of the committee included Jews and non-Jews alike. Since 1982, Polish Radio has been regularly broadcasting programmes on Jewish topics; these programmes are aired on the eve of Passover, Shavuot, Rosh Hashana and Yom Kippur. What is more, on 19 April 1983, the Polish government transferred the Nożyk Synagogue in Warsaw (whose renovation had been paid with state money) to the Religious Union of Mosaic Faith.[78]

4. WHO'S MORE JEWISH? OUT OF THE SHADOW OF THE SHOAH?

The Jewish community was thus gradually coming back to life, and the process gained momentum in the latter half of the 1980s. In 1984 and 1988 the Union organized two conventions and an extraordinary general assembly (July 1988). In 1985, Warsaw and Cracow saw their first bar mitzvahs, after thirty and thirty-five years respectively. Four years later, the Union hired Polish-born – but long living in Israel – Pinchas Menachem Joskowicz as Chief Rabbi of Poland, and Warsaw Jews participated in the first traditional Jewish wedding ceremony since 1960.[79]

Two important events took place in the 1990s. Firstly, in 1992, the Relgious Union of Mosaic Faith was renamed the Union of Jewish Religious Communities (Związek Gmin Wyznaniowych Żydowskich, ZGWŻ), which meant that what had before been called a 'congregation' was now dubbed a 'community' or kehilla (Hebrew). In 1993, ZGWŻ adopted a new constitution. Also, in 1997 the Polish Sejm (Parliament) passed a law on the relationship of the Polish state to the Union of Jewish Religious Communities, which enabled the latter to file claims on the restitution of pre-war Jewish communal property. That same year, the Union decided that non-Halakhic Jews could be accepted in Jewish religious communities. It was a breakthrough decision, as it meant meeting the wishes of a numerous group of young Polish Jews (or Poles of Jewish origin).[80]

As there was more and more authenticity in Jewish communal activity, younger-generation and middle-aged Jews were becoming attracted to various Jewish organizations: religious communities, the reinvigorated TSKŻ, student organizations (set up in 1992), the Jewish Forum (1993) and the like. However significant this could have been for the Jewish presence in Poland, the growing numbers of participants in Jewish life involved new problems regarding basic issues: Who is a Jew? What is Jewish identity? Who is to determine Jewish identity? What is the relationship between Judiasm and Jewishness? Such questions as these abounded in the reappearing community. But there were also plenty of answers. And since a number of 'neophytes' joined ranks with some of the Orthodox old guard, a tendency arose to adopt a rather strict Talmudic interpretation of the Jewish law, including liturgical issues. The fiercest debates were over observing holidays and the rules of kashrut, as well as the role and position of women in religious communities.[81]

To the older generation of Jews, that new social phenomenon came as a shock. It was something that could not have been predicted – so their first reaction was one of being disturbed and bothered.[82] Some were even looking at the newcomers with suspicion and scorn:

> Our home-made Jewishness, oftentimes full of contradictions, did not seem authentic to them. That was briefly expressed by Marek Edelman, the last living commander of the Warsaw Ghetto Uprising.[83] He said to me: 'You're forgeries, literary fiction. Jews are dead and you have invented yourselves looking for originality and exoticism. [But] in reality you simply don't exist.' There was some truth to it but with years passing it is becoming less and less true.[84]

It is an undisputed fact that since the recovery by Poland of political (and, to a large degree, societal) freedom in 1989, ethnic and religious minorities have had more space to discuss their identities and more courage to be present in public life. This phenomenon is perhaps best epitomized by Polish Jews. Of course, the lively debates that are referred to here did not start on the day after the first free elections. It took a while before the Jewish community could feel secure and at the same time open enough to allow any public debates to take place. On the other hand, for the thousands of Poles of Jewish descent, it was not that easy to start talking about their double identity. Not all of them were willing to reveal their Jewish origins, and many just did not care about it, whereas others were waiting for the situation to develop. In the spring of 1997, the first issue of *Midrasz* appeared – the first Jewish monthly magazine to be published after the political transformation[85] – and it was clear that the editorial board, chaired by Konstatnty Gebert, had, at the top of its list of priorities, issues pertaining to Jewish identity and Jewish presence in Poland.

The identity debate triggered by *Midrasz* seemed to have been long awaited by many. Poland had regained its political and economic stability; it was soon to become a member of NATO and its accession to the European Union had been a wish shared by both decision-makers and a majority of the society at large. A number of topics of social and/or cultural import were being discussed. It was a time in Poland when people had mostly come to terms with a new political and economic system based on meritocracy. Issues of ethnic identity and cultural diversity were becoming more visible and more salient. It is no wonder, then, that the *Midrasz* discussion soon caught fire. People with Jewish roots, young and old, men and women, with or without formal Jewish affiliation, saw fit to express their views. For many of them it was a unique opportunity to get involved in a process that would possibly affect the shape of a future Jewish community. They wanted to be part of that and not to learn that things had been decided when it was too late to change them.

From the very onset, the debate revolved around the question of what could be called 'the authenticity of identity'. Some would tend to define it in religious terms, others underscored the cultural aspect. The identity of 'old' Jews was confronted with that of the 'new', although 'old' did not mean religious or more traditional, and 'new' did not mean more liberal – quite the contrary. In many respects the new and younger community members – at least a number of them – tended to be more rigid and more focused on Halakhic regulations than a lot of the old Jews. So the divide was not so much between the generations as it was between specific concepts or philosophies of Jewishness. To put it briefly: for some, Jewishness meant just being Jewish (with no need for a definition), while for others Jewishness was inextricable from Judaism, which implied the application of religious/legal terms in determining who's (really) Jewish and who's not.

In an anonymous letter from a young Warsaw Jew, published in *Midrasz*, a number of reasons are given for why joining the Jewish community was not always seen as an option to be taken seriously. That young person claims he never had 'an intent or a wish [to join the community] and ... came to the conclusion that joining it would be something artificial, decided under pressure from the milieu'.[86] He says his Jewishness has always been to him a given, something self-evident and natural:

> [The Jewish milieu] has never been ... to me an attraction coming from the outside world ... It's been something obvious that ... has to a considerable degree shaped my way of seeing the world. In my family, Jewishness was something obvious, though from a traditional, religious viewpoint it was a mediocre Jewishness ... I never needed – like many people of my generation did – to confirm my authenticity by signing up one day for a youth organization with the word 'Jews' in its name or by going to synagogue from time to time ... I respect my ancestors' tradition but take the world of religion as foreign, not-mine, and religion as such I see as a possible threat to my identity and not as its fundament.[87]

Another anonymous person writes, also in a letter to *Midrasz*, that he knows only a few Jews who always, filling out a form, would state unambiguously they are Jewish, who 'never had a Christmas tree and whose parents didn't forget to tell them they are Jews and that they should be proud of that'.[88] As to the identity of the young Jews, he sees it this way:

> [They] assume their Jewishness rivalling one another in who's got more Jewish blood, who's got a 'better' look, who's more Orthodox on the outside. On Jewish meetings they wear Jewish jewelery all over as if willing to impress their friends ... They're stiff and lacking common sense. It seems they have invented their identity in order not to become unnoticeable in the crowd of shapeless peers so similar to them ... I leave aside those 'unaffiliated' who don't feel like getting enrolled in any organizations, who often don't need any signboard, and who, using their own interesting manners, seek their way.[89]

In the same issue of *Midrasz*, the editors included a symposium on Jewish identity titled 'Seven Voices'. Though coming from just a few respondents who offered sometimes only a page-long text, it is an invaluable source of knowledge about the present-day problems of Polish Jews. Stanisław Krajewski's story is a good example of how assimilation affected those Jewish families for whom Jewishness became rather a fact to be known than a reality that was lived, celebrated and nurtured. He calls his childhood 'typical for assimilated Jews, specifically for those caught by the communist idea'. He also underscores the importance of justice, 'sensitivity to antisemitism but also to any kind of discrimination' and mentions as characteristic to Jews of his generation 'a lack of any family in Poland, no ties with the Church ... and at the same time emphasizing Polishness'.[90] He then goes on to express his current view and experience of Jewishness: 'The core of my understanding of Jewishness is Judaism, traditions defined as religious ... Yet, the fact that other Jews think otherwise does not arouse grudge in me.'[91] He then adds that 'having gone the way of de-assimilation has not decreased my Polishness. Polish intelligentsia remains my primary reference point.'[92]

Another person contributing to the symposium, Antonina Połoniecka, joins in to claim that Judaism is a determining element of her identity: 'my strongest tie is with the Jewish religion, and it's that above all that makes me think I'm a Jewess. This awareness led me to marry a Jew and send my sixteen-year-old son Ryszard to settle in Israel.'[93]

A singularly moving voice in the debate is that of Ethel Szyc. Lublin-born, now an actress of the Jewish Theatre in Warsaw, she depicts in a poetic way what Jewishness means to her – starting with childhood in early post-war Poland and passing on to her adult life:

> Jewish identity is to me:
> – my only, most tender, always by my side mayn yiddishe mame ...
> – waiting for my father coming back from the prayer house ...
> – the wonderful melody of Yiddish in which we used to talk with neighbors and acquaintances ...
> – a shock after visiting Majdanek and the discovery of the Holocaust
> – questions, feelings about the Tragedy
> – tears, tears, pain, it could have been me but it was my uncles, aunts, grandparents, everybody.[94]

She then continues on a different note, saying how she feels about present-day Polish Jews:

> Jewishness brings me closer to those who didn't survive the Holocaust. It distances me from those for whom Judaism is an opportunity to make a career, money, or is a form of psycho-therapy ... It distances me from those to whom the words shabbat, kosher,

kippa sounded a few years ago like Chinese, and a pork chop tasted delicious, and now they dare instruct me what it means to 'live a Jewish life' ... It fills me with terror to think that in a few years their children will tell my son he's not Jewish and there's no room for him here.[95]

In a brief report from a breakthrough meeting (a 'round table', one might say) of Polish Jews devoted to the subject of identity, organized by *Midrasz* at the TSKŻ premises in Warsaw on 20 October 1999, Piotr Paziński[96] showed a whole variety of views held by Jews from all walks of life. He quoted not only Jewish community members but also those unaffiliated yet feeling Jewish and willing to say out loud how they saw the changes Polish Jewry was undergoing. As could have been expected, not everybody was happy with the social and religious transformation of the community, specifically with the attempts to strictly define what is and what is not Jewish identity:

> Who gave you the right to decide what [denomination] the syna-gogue in Warsaw is to be? – Kazimiera Szczuka asked a rhetoric question, seconded by Bożena Umińska of ŻIH [the Jewish His-torical Institute]: – I'm a Jewess, I've always been Jewish and always felt like a stranger. I won't go to the synagogue. That I'd have to climb up the balcony simply humiliates me. There is not just one Jewish awareness – Umińska added. They are many.[97]

In most speeches presented in the symposium, as in most articles published earlier and before, in *Midrasz* and in other periodicals, the subject of the Shoah does not come up as a central one. It is not silenced, nor is it omitted or avoided, but it is certainly not over-emphasized. As Helena Datner put it, 'the shadow of the war' did not prevail in her home but 'it was present. On my desk there were photographs of my murdered stepsisters ... I used to say to myself that because of that memory I am and I have to be Jewish.'[98] In Ethel Szyc we saw that awareness of the Holocaust can be one of the fundamental aspects of Jewish identity; in a way the murdered Jews may seems closer to one's experience of Jewishness than the present-day appearance of a community one is not attracted to. Even if that phrasing is somewhat poetical, it does contain something real, undeniable and undisputable – one's own feelings about, and a life-long story of, Jewishness lived the way one sees fit.

The reality of the Shoah and its effect upon survivors is also present in Bogdan Wojdowski's writing. Because of the Shoah he is confronted with the question: 'How to be Jewish?'[99] Wojdowski does not hastily come up with answers. Above all, he sees the difficult predicament of the Jew, even of a survivor most likely to be taken for a winner. But to Wojdowski 'The Jewish survivor, against appearances, finds himself at the position of an alienation that is more profound than ever in history.'[100] The survivor is alienated because s/he is no longer protected by the community and is vulnerable to the blows of anti-Semitism. Not sure whether race, language, or ethnicity are factors that bring Jews together, Wojdowski makes use of the term 'civilization': 'Judaism is a civilization based on the tradition of faith … Never spreading our religious beliefs, we must be bound by a singular force and that is why we have maintained distinction despite the destructive practices used against us.'[101]

There are more voices in which the notes of insecurity, vulnerability – and the need to overcome them – sound clearly. What is of utmost interest for this study is when these issues appear in the context of the Holocaust. In an interview conducted by Elżbieta Kossewska, Abraham Burg explains how he sees Holocaust narrative and remembrance. In a general, opening remark, Burg says: 'We Jews are a society incapable of getting rid of fear. All our politics is a politics of fear.'[102] What are the manifestations of this fear? To Burg it is, among other things, preoccupation with the Holocaust. He says he has 'lost' five of his six sons due to excessive Holocaust education and specifically as a result of their participation in the March of the Living. In his eyes, the trauma of the Holocaust can sometimes be an impediment to the Jewish people, and he claims that 'We can't be settling accounts with the whole world from the perspective of the Holocaust.'[103] Burg is well aware, nevertheless, of the reasons why the Shoah has come to occupy such a prominent place in the Jewish psyche. It is insecurity, he contends, that is a crucial aspect of Jewish identity – even in America which has a six-million-strong Jewish diaspora, and where any feeling of ethnicity-based fear by Jews does not find much ground.[104]

The way the March of the Living had been organized prior to 1998 also came under the critique of many Polish Jews. What they opposed was both centring Jewish identity around the Holocaust and strengthening the stereotype of 'us against them', 'the whole world against Jews/Israelis'. Konstanty Gebert provides a good example of that way of thinking:

> One has the impression that the existence in Poland of young Jews was distorting the picture: Poland is to be exclusively the place of

death. True, during the March whistles can be heard and stones are being thrown. That is ignominious. But it is not only Polish antisemitism that is to be blamed for that. Also the disdain which the participants are being taught ... 'You will hate them for participating in the atrocities' ... It is true – Poland still has not come to terms with the guilt of blackmail. But the guilt for the Shoah is not upon the Poles. And the teaching of hatred on the way to graves[105] is a blasphemy. These words cannot be tolerated nor justified. They insult us, Polish Jews, no less than other members of the Polish society against whom they are aimed.[106]

In 1998, Konstanty Gebert (writing under his pen name Dawid Warszawski) maintained his critical view of the March: 'Its organizers want the participants to become convinced that Poland and Europe – means death, while Israel – resurrection ... This negation of the diaspora, this hostility towards the Jews who have chosen to stay in Europe, strikes us, European Jews, and insults us.'[107]

In summing up this chapter, it must be said that Holocaust awareness does not seem to be a factor overshadowing all others in shaping the identity of Polish Jews, however unexpected this might sound. Of course, as has been shown in numerous examples, the Shoah is and will be a major point of reference for generations of Jews living in Poland. The very historical specificity of the Polish land makes any voluntary neglect of the Holocaust unthinkable. The extermination of millions of Jews – Polish and others – took place on German-occupied Polish soil and this will always be remembered in Poland. This will always remain part of Jewish identity and probably will have a more visible effect on their lives than the *Churban Beis Hamikdash*, if only because its historical aspect is far better known and more palpable.[108] Yet, as we have seen, the Jewish debate in Poland has started evolving into a debate of a living community focused on its day-to-day business. Present-day Polish Jews seem to be more interested in understanding what it means to be Jewish in the twenty-first century: in developing alternative (non Orthodox, or not-strictly-Orthodox) ways of living a Jewish life.

What is more, Polish Jewry is not a homogenous group of people sharing the same image of and feelings about Judaism and Jewishness. Tendencies to autonomously define one's Jewish identity for oneself rather than letting other factors (external subjects, for example institutions or religiously interpreted texts) provide those definitions are becoming ever more visible. That, however, in contradistinction to the case of America, does not lead to the creation of secular religion of sorts, one that is focused on the Holocaust. Furthermore, the relative distance from institutional religion and theological thinking does not result in assuming a Shoah-centred Jewish identity, either. To put it briefly, the Holocaust is probably too obvious and still all too present historically for Polish Jews to be preoccupied with it; however, there are many other events which do play an important role in shaping Jewish identities in Poland: the Jedwabne massacre; the Kielce pogrom; the 1968 anti-Semitic purges; wrestling with the Jewish participation in establishing and perpetuating the communist regime; the Jewish presence in Solidarity and the democratic opposition in general; and Jewish contribution to public life in contemporary Poland – including arts, the academia and politics. The Holocaust is most certainly a Jewish topic, but definitely not 'the' Jewish topic.

Jewishness is thus more a question of identification than of identity: more an active, dynamic entity than one that is passive and taken for granted. As such, it has become a pick-and-choose way of depicting oneself. Yes – depicting, and not defining. This will be also seen in the analysis of interviews with Warsaw Jews that follows.

NOTES

1. See J. Adelson, 'W Polsce zwanej ludową', in J. Tomaszewski (ed.), *Najnowsze dzieje Żydów w Polsce* (Warsaw: PWN, 1993), p.424; see also K. Kersten, *Polacy – Żydzi – komunizm: Anatomia półprawd* (Warsaw: Nezależna Oficyna Wydawnicza, 1992); A. Bańkowska, A. Jarzębowska, M. Siek, 'Morderstwa Żydów w latach 1944–1946 na terenie Polski na podstawie kwerendy w zbiorze 301 (Relacja z Zagłady w Archiwum Żydowskiego Instytutu Historycznego)', *Jewish History Quarterly* 3 (September 2009), pp.356–60. The greatest post-war pogrom of all took place in Kielce, on 4 July 1946, where forty-two Jews were murdered by Poles. In 1945 there were pogroms in Kraków, Lublin, Chełm, Radom, Częstochowa, Rzeszów. Leżajsk and Tarnogród. See A. Cała and H. Datner-Śpiewak, *Dzieje Żydów w Polsce 1944–1968: Teksty źródłowe* (Warsaw: Żydowski Instytut Historyczny, 1997), p.17. As Dawid Warszawski (pen name of Konstanty Gebert) underscores, unfortunately Poland was not the only place where Jews were killed after the war; he also mentions a pogrom in Minsk (in the Bielorussian Soviet Republic, today the capital of Bielorus), minor pogroms in other Bielorussian and Ukrainian towns, in Hungary and Slovakia, and a huge pogrom in British-controlled Libya, which took the lives of no fewer than 167 Jews. See Dawid Warszawski, 'Mieszkając na ziemi popiołów', *Polis*, 27 (April 1998), p.19; on this topic see also S. Epstein, *Cyclical Patterns In Antisemitism: The Dynamics of Anti-Jewish Violence in Western Countries Since the 1950s* (Jerusalem: SICSA, 1993).
2. See N. Aleksiun, *Dokąd dalej? Ruch syjonistyczny w Polsce (1944–1950)* (Warsaw: Trio, 2002), pp.63–9.
3. See ibid., p.68.
4. That general party line downplaying all possible social differentiation notwithstanding, Jewish institutional life enjoyed some kind of autonomy immediately after the war. As Ewa Koźmińska-Frejlak has observed, 'The years 1944–49 were a period of a fairly sovereign existence of the Jewish community in Poland: there were Jewish political parties with their respective youth organizations, Jewish press was published in large quantities – in Polish,

Yiddish and Hebrew, there were Jewish religious communities, Yiddish and Hebrew language schools, social organizations, sports clubs and so on.' Ewa Frejlak-Koźmińska, 'Poland as the Motherland of the Jews: Jewish Strategies of Making Postwar Poland a Home', *Kultura i Społeczeństwo*, 43, 1 (January–March 1999), p.127.

5. Artur Rutkowski, 'An Exhibition on the Occasion of the 10th Anniversary of the Warsaw Ghetto Uprising', *Biuletyn Żydowskiego Instytutu Historycznego* 6–7 (April–September 1953), p.222.
6. Ibid., p.218.
7. Ibid., p.219.
8. Ibid., pp.219f.
9. Ibid., p.222.
10. Małgorzata Melchior, *Zagłada a tożsamość: Polscy Żydzi ocaleni 'na aryjskich papierach': Analiza doświadczenia biograficznego* (Warsaw: IFiS PAN, 2004), p.161.
11. See ibid., pp.161–8.
12. See ibid., p.168.
13. S. Krajewski, *Poland and the Jews: Reflections of a Polish Polish Jew* (Kraków: Wydawnictwo Austeria 2005), p.88f.
14. Ibid., p.89.
15. Ibid; see also Kersten, *Polacy – Żydzi – komunizm*, pp.83f.
16. See Krajewski, *Poland and the Jews*, p.89. It should also be noted that many of the Jews who left Poland at the end of the 1940s did so partially because they opposed the political system. In addition, some of those who chose to stay in the country more or less overtly rejected Stalinism and refused to take part in installing the Soviet-controlled rule, as was the case of Bund, the Jewish socialist party, that decided to disband rather than to join the new Polish United Workers' Party (Polska Zjednoczona Partia Robotnicza or PZPR).
17. Ibid., p.119.
18. Ibid., pp.120f. In the early post-war years, the Polish Workers' Party (Polska Partia Robotnicza or PPR) members in the Central Committee of Polish Jews (Centralny Komitet Żydów Polskich or CKŻP) were former member of the pre-war Polish Communist Party (Polska Partia Komunistyczna or KKP). Communist leaders, including Jewish ones, thought that sooner or later all Jewish parties whose political programme was not compatible with that of PPR (later PZPR) would have to be disbanded. Communist control over Polish Jewry become clearly visible during the First Convention of Jewish Delegates, held on 26 and 27 February 1949. Out of 254 delegates, 169 represented PZPR. In the newly elected CKŻP leadership (*prezydium*) six members represented PZPR; two Poaley Zion; one Mizrachi; one Ichud; while one was unaffiliated. In April of the same year, the CKŻP chairman, Adolf Berman, a Zionist, was replaced by Grzegorz Smolar of PZPR. The regional Jewish committees were allowed to exist but their role was defined as serving 'to build socialism in Poland', as Szymon Zachariasz, a Jewish member of the PZPR leadership, put it. See A. Grabski and G. Berendt, *Między emigracją a trwaniem: Syjoniści i komuniści żydowscy w Polsce po Holocauście* (Warsaw: Żydowski Instytut Historyczny, 2003), pp.17f, 172–4.
19. B. Mark, 'Dziennik (Grudzień 1965 – luty 1966)', *Jewish History Quarterly*, 2, 226 (June 2008), pp.173, 179, 188.
20. J. Wiszniewicz, *Życie przecięte: Opowieści pokolenia Marca* (Wołowiec: Wydawnictwo Czarne, 2008).
21. TPD – Towarzystwo Przyjaciół Dzieci (Society of the Friends of Children): an organization promoting secular education, it ran public schools attended generally by children of parents who were non-religious and/or were active in the communist movement.
22. Wiszniewicz, *Życie przecięte*, p.35.
23. See ibid., pp.54, 56.
24. See ibid., p.115.
25. See ibid., pp.116f.
26. Ibid., p.178.
27. Ibid., p.152. See also pp.63, 120f, 128, 254, 261.
28. Ibid., p.113.
29. Ibid., p.105.
30. Ibid., p.19.
31. This was the case of Bronka Karst, who said: 'At home we never talked about Jewishness.

Someday [my father] realized I "knew", and I realized that he knew (that I "knew") – and that's it. No conversation.' Ibid., p.47.

32. Ibid., p.53.
33. Ibid., pp.53f.
34. Ibid., p.58.
35. Ibid., p.261.
36. Ibid., p.262.
37. Ibid., p.49.
38. In 1950, the Central Committee of Polish Jews (Centralny Komitet Żydów Polskich or CKŻP) was transformed into the Jewish Socio-Cultural Society (TSKŻ).
39. Wiszniewicz, *Życie przecięte*, p.120; see also p.496f.
40. Wiszniewicz, *Życie przecięte*, pp.120f.
41. Partisan groups, some of which operated till the early 1950s, opposing the communist regime and considering the London-based Polish government-in-exile to be the only legal authority.
42. Wiszniewicz, *Życie przecięte*, p.161.
43. Ibid., p.246.
44. See J. Wiszniewicz, 'Pierwsze powojenne pokolenie polskich Żydów: Rodzicielski przekaz pamięci Holocaustu a tożsamość żydowska', *Biuletyn Żydowskiego Instytutu Historycznego*, 191 (September 1999), pp.40–7.
45. Wiszniewicz, *Życie przecięte*, p.84.
46. See ibid., p.97.
47. See ibid., pp.21, 129, 138, 193, 320.
48. Ibid., p.60.
49. See ibid., p.106.
50. Ibid., p.184.
51. When the Soviet and Polish Armies entered the western territories of former Poland and continued westward to Wrocław (Breslau) and the Oder River, among Jewish inhabitants there were also German Jews who had lived there before the war. Most of them experienced discrimination from the Soviet and then Polish military and civil administration. By 1946 almost all of them had left Poland for Germany. See B. Szaynok, *Ludność żydowska na Dolnym Śląsku 1945–1950* (Wrocław: Wydawnictwo Uniwersytetu Wrocławskiego, 2000), pp.42f, 55f.
52. See ibid., pp.190f. In September 1949, the Ministry of Public Administration officially allowed Jews to leave Poland. It was assumed that Jewish communists would 'encourage' Zionists to emigrate but then the authorities took a more radical step: they disbanded Zionist parties (starting with Ichud on 1 January 1950), putting the Zionists in a situation where emigration seemed the only option. Very often, however, decisions on whether or not to permit a particular person to emigrate were biased, or based on opinions of prominent party members or security police instructions. See Grabski and Berendt, *Między emigracją a trwaniem*, pp.178–91.
53. The situation was indeed very complex. In the first post-war years, the mainstream Jewish establishment was in principle opposed to mass emigration. At a 1946 meeting of the Polish Workers' Party (PPR) section of the Regional Jewish Committee (WKŻ) in Lower Silesia, one of its leading activists, Jakub Wasserstrum, affirmed:

> We hear about mass emigration of Jews from Poland, even the working element ... The Zionist propaganda ... making use of the slightest manifestations of anti-Semitism ... is persuading the Jewish populace that there is no room for Jews in Poland ... We have nothing against leaving [Poland] by the unproductive element, hostile towards the democratic Poland ... [Yet] It is our task to pull the Zionists and force them to take a stand against this panic at general meetings.

Szaynok, *Ludność żydowska na Dolnym Śląsku,* pp.96f; see also Grabski and Berendt, *Między emigracją a trwaniem*, pp.21, 53.
54. At the same time, thousands of Jewish repatriates were coming to Poland, thanks to a Polish-Soviet government agreement. Many of them decided to emigrate to Israel or elsewhere. The period 1956–57 is often referred to as the 'Thaw', a name alluding to Ilya Erenburg's novel. It was then, for example, that the Jewish Joint Distribution Committee was readmitted to Poland after its offices had been closed in the late 1940s.

55. In August 1949, Jewish religious communities, called congregations, gathered to form the Religious Union of Mosaic Faith (Związek Religijny Wyznania Mojżeszowego or ZRWM). The Union was totally submitted to state control and received scant government subsidies. Between 1947 and 1949 there were about eighty Jewish religious congregations in Poland, with twenty-five rabbis and thirty-eight synagogues, as well as several dozen prayerhouses. According to information provided by the congregations, approximately 50 per cent of Poland's Jews practised Judaism at the end of the 1940s. See Cała and Datner-Śpiewak, *Dzieje Żydów w Polsce*, p.238.

56. See P. Śpiewak, 'Szok Marcowy', *Polis*, 27 (April 1998), p.11.

57. K. Gebert, 'Tożsamości Żydów w Polsce: "Nowa", "Dawna" i "Wysnuta z wypbraźni"', pp.45f.

58. G. Pawlak, 'Historia opowiedziana', an interview with Grażyna S. Pawlak, *Polis*, 21 (March 1997), p.95.

59. See Śpiewak, 'Szok Marcowy', p.10. The number of mixed marriages must have been considerable at that time. In a 1963 article published in *Biuletyn Żydowskiego Instytutu Historycznego*, figures were given with regard to the percentage of mixed marriages within the Jewish population of Poland. By 1939 the figure was around 6 per cent, between 1940 and 1944 it was 37.8 per cent, and in 1945 and afterwards it was 42.3 per cent. It could be surmised that in the late 1960s, the percentage of mixed marriages stood at approximately 50 percent. See Sz. Bronsztejn, 'Badania ankietowe ludności żydowskiej Dolnego Śląska, *Biuletyn Żydowskiego Instytutu Historycznego*, 47–48 (October–December 1963), p.77.

60. See Śpiewak, 'Szok Marcowy', p.10. This anti-Jewish mood predominated also in the academe. One of its results was a tendency to downplay Jewish suffering and losses during the Second World War. For example, when the eighth volume of the *Great Universal Encyclopaedia* was being prepared (issued in 1966), in the entry on 'Hitlerite concentration camps', information was provided that 99 per cent of the inmates of those camps were Jews. That triggered a whole campaign against the editorial board, which was subsequently dismissed. A new entry was printed and sent to those who had subscribed to the encyclopedia. It read: 'extermination camps served the purpose of biological destruction of the Polish nation ... they were also used as a tool for a planned extermination of the Jewish population'. F. Tych, *Długi cień Zagłady* (Warsaw: ŻIH, 1999), p.75.

61. See ibid.

62. More on stigmatizing Jews in M. Melchior, 'What Does the Holocaust Tell Sociologists? Identity as a Stigma', in S. Rejak (ed.), *Thinking after the Holocaust: Voices from Poland* (Warsaw and Cracow: Muza, 2008), pp.77–106.

63. See K. Paszko, *Polacy i Żydzi w dialogu w latach 1979–1997* (Warsaw: PWN, 2006), p.60.

64. See Bielecki, 'Szok Marcowy', p.12.

65. Gebert, 'Tożsamości Żydów w Polsce', p.46.

66. Ibid.

67. See Śpiewak, 'Szok Marcowy', p.11.

68. See ibid.

69. 'Jewishness was in the first place a psychological problem – it was a stigma of strangeness and lesser value, forced upon with no possibility of choosing and almost against one's will.' Gebert, 'Tożsamości Żydów w Polsce', p.47.

70. In a paper written in the mid-1980s and published in 1989 in the USA, 'Solidarity and Martial Law: The Jewish Dimension', *Studium Papers*, 13, 2 (April 1989), Stanisław Krajewski wrote: 'The TSKŻ is led by communists for whom the faithful representation of the current party line is no less important than the problems of Jews.' Krajewski, *Poland and the Jews*, p.149.

71. The idea to form a group focused on studying Jewish tradition and rediscovering its members' Jewish identity was born during a seminar for young psychologists organized in 1979. Some of the participants in the meeting saw their Jewish origin as a psychological problem to work through. Soon they were joined by a number of Jewish and non-Jewish friends, and together, that same year, they established an informal body dubbed the Jewish Flying University. The founders and core members of ŻUL included Konstanty Gebert, Stanisław Krajewski, Monika Krajewska, Ryszarda Zachariasz, Barbara Kawalec, Roman Gren, Alina Cała, Zbigniew Targielski and Jan Jagielski. The group was not an organization in any sense: its members would meet clandestinely in their own apartments and there was no formal membership. The meetings were devoted to presentations by members of the group and occasionally by invited lecturers. Around thirty people would take part in the meetings, with more than a half of

them only sporadically. However, in 1980–81, when Solidarity was gaining popularity and the communist authorities seemed to allow for more social freedom, some of the ŻUL members were even considering the possibility of formally registering the group as a society or foundation. That idea never materialized, especially because after the declaration of martial law in December 1981, almost all civil and social liberties were significantly limited. ŻUL continued its (underground) existence till some time in the mid-1980s.

72. Most people active in ŻUL did not radically change their identity, they remained 'Poles of Jewish origin' ... Others started experimenting with various forms of nonreligious Jewish identity, which, for instance, took the shape of initiating efforts to save Jewish monuments in Poland, learning Yiddish, or giving lectures on Jewish topics to non-Jewish groups. Some of them, more active ones, became religious.

Gebert, 'Tożsamości Żydów w Polsce', p.47.

73. See ibid.
74. See Krajewski, *Poland and the Jews*, p.150.
75. 'Statements condemning anti-Semitism were not infrequent in Solidarity bulletins. Usually they were specifically aimed at the activities of such groups as the Grunwald Patriotic Union, which parroted the propaganda of 1968.' Krajewski, *Poland and the Jews*, p.143.
76. See Paszko, *Polacy i Żydzi w dialogu*, p.62.
77. See Krajewski, *Poland and the Jews*, pp.150f. Even at the end of the 1980s, a visible pro-communist tendency within the TSKŻ could be observed. Gebert recounts a story in which one of the young 'new' Jews asked why the organization was so inactive in nourishing Jewish tradition. He was told that 'the anniversary of the October [Bolshevik] Revolution had been celebrated. It is [also] considered a little triumph that lately ham has not been served on Fridays at the TSKŻ resort house.' Gebert, 'Tożsamości Żydów w Polsce', p.48.
78. See Paszko, *Polacy i Żydzi w dialogu*, pp.62f.
79. See ibid., p.65. That rebirth of Jewish community and Jewish identity in Poland throughout the 1980s had a visible effect on Jewish youth: 'The young people consciously don't want to emigrate, because they feel very Polish and Jewish together. They feel close to the tradition of Polish Jewry.' S. North, 'Poland Rediscovers its Jews: An Interview with Malgorzata Niezabitowska', *The Reconstructionist*, 53 (July–August 1988), p.20.
80. See Paszko, *Polacy i Żydzi w dialogu*, p.70. For more on the issue of Halakhic Jews, see also K. Gebert, 'Otworzyć synagogę?' [Should the Synagogue be Opened?], *Midrasz*, 2, 2 (June 1997), pp.8ff.
81. In the early 1990s, during one of the Lauder Foundation sponsored summer camps, a group of teens sat long into the night talking with an American rabbi. When he was about to close the meeting, one of the girls said: 'Can't you see that we're the next generation of Jewish mothers in this country? We have to know everything.' Gebert, 'Tożsamości Żydów w Polsce', p.49.
82. See Gebert, 'Tożsamości Żydów w Polsce', pp.47f.
83. Marek Edelman died on 31 October 2009 at the age of 90.
84. Gebert, 'Tożsamości Żydów w Polsce', p.48.
85. It was the first Jewish monthly for a general audience. In 1992, *Jidełe*, a Jewish children's magazine, first appeared.
86. [Anonymous], 'Dlaczego nie wstępuję do gminy?', *Midrasz*, 2, 2 (June 1997), p.9.
87. Ibid.
88. [Anonymous], 'Od rozproszenia do poszukiwań. Kilka osobistych pytań na temat żydowskiej tożsamości', *Midrasz*, 5, 5 (September 1997), p.4.
89. Ibid., p.5.
90. S. Krajewski, 'Przymierze obowiązuje', in a symposium, 'Siedem głosów', *Midrasz*, 5, 5 (September 1997), p.8.
91. Ibid.
92. Ibid.
93. A. Połoniecka, 'Przynależę do narodu', in a symposium, 'Siedem głosów', *Midrasz*, 5, 5 (September 1997), p.9.
94. E. Szyc, 'Gdzie Byłeś?', in a symposium, 'Siedem głosów', *Midrasz*, 5, 5 (September 1997), p.10.
95. Ibid.
96. Today editor-in-chief of *Midrasz*.
97. P. Paziński, 'Kafka ważniejszy od Tory?', *Midrasz*, 31, 11 (November 1999), p.40.

98. H. Datner, 'Przez tę pamięć', in a symposium, 'Siedem głosów', *Midrasz*, 5, 5 (September 1997), p.6.
99. B. Wojdowski, 'Judaizm jako los', *Puls*, 62 (May–June 1993), p.61.
100. Ibid. It is also quite typical for the generation of children of survivors to feel alienated, although for more complex reasons. The case of children born to mixed marriages seems to be even more difficult and painful. Thus Wojdowski continues:

> We are different and we stay lonely in this otherness. We don't have a place where to feel at home. We've been different since childhood ... It turned out that our father or mother was Jewish (rarely both of them, for we often come from mixed marriages). They had gone through the hell of the Shoah. They told us about it ... And nothing seemed to be like it had been before ... Our identity is not homogenous ... We see the world as hostile, uninhabited, alien, menacing, or we judge ourselves in an equally pessimistic way.

Ibid.
101. Wojdowski, 'Judaizm jako los', pp.70f.
102. A. Burg, 'Postsyjonista? Z Abrahamem Burgiem rozmawia Elżbieta Kossewska', *Więź*, 11–12 (601–2) (November–December 2008), p.77. Stanisław Krajewski believes that 'There is probably Jewish oversensitivity, looking with suspicion at every critical remark.' S. Krajewski, 'Schematy: Z dr. Stanisławem Krajewskim rozmawia Agnieszka Niezgoda', *Polis*, 27 (April 1998), p.8.
103. Burg, 'Postsyjonista?', p.79. In a similar context, Krajewski uses the term 'triumphalism of pain' and says it can sometimes be applied in a situation where Jews, because of all the evil they have suffered, may have a 'feeling of moral superiority'. See Krajewski, 'Schematy', p.9.
104. See Burg, 'Postsyjonista?', p.78.
105. Allusion to the brochure distributed by the International March of the Living (IMoL), authored by the president of the IMoL, Abraham Hirshson. The brochure included the text cited. Its circulation was stopped a year later due to protests from Polish Jews and Polish diplomats.
106. K. Gebert, 'Marsz Żywych', *Midrasz*, 2, 2 (June 1997), p.15.
107. Warszawski, 'Mieszkając na ziemi popiołów', p.20.
108. As early as the 1980s, opinions were voiced in America that Holocaust imagery, and Holocaust studies specifically, were starting to dominate the Jewish world at the cost of all other chapters of Jewish history. That, of course, was not the case in the Poland of Jaruzelski. At the turn of the twenty-first century, however, things have begun to change. Some Polish Jews point to the fact that Jewish life has indeed been marginalized and, to many Jews (mostly American and Israeli), Jewish death on Polish soil is the only association they have with Poland. Compare Edward Alexander's view vis-à-vis the Holocaust and American Jews: 'Within just the past year I can recall a dozen people, every one of them deeply committed to Jewish intellectual or communal or religious life, telling me that they were sick and tired of the subject of the Holocaust and resented the central place it has begun to occupy in Jewish learning and life, to say nothing of the Jewish moral imagination. Two of them, a rabbi and a seminary professor, complained that Holocaust studies had become a "convenient" substitute for "real" Jewish learning, i.e., for study of Torah. Several others ... found something suspect in the consuming desire of people ignorant of how the Jews lived to learn how it was that they all died.' E. Alexander, 'Stealing the Holocaust', *Midstream*, 26 (November 1980), p.46.

PART 2

Comparative Analysis of Interviews Conducted with Polish and American Jews

CHAPTER FOUR

Being Jewish as a Challenge

1. PROFILES OF THE SAMPLES OF POLISH AND AMERICAN JEWS

PROFILE OF THE SAMPLE OF POLISH JEWS

Included in the Polish group are twenty-four men (eight of whom are survivors) and twenty-five women (nine of whom are survivors). Of those who are survivors, eight lived (at least for some time) in ghettos; three were incarcerated in extermination or labour camps. Three people survived the war in the Soviet Union and came to Poland only after the liberation. Two respondents were born to Polish Jewish families outside Poland (one in Russia and one in Austria). Thirty-six people have lived in Warsaw at least from the time they were 14. The breakdown of their educational background is as follows: twenty-nine interviewees have a university degree, five have a doctorate, two have had only elementary education, two graduated from high school and three from vocational high school. Twenty-one respondents are affiliated with the Orthodox Synagogue, twenty-nine are members of the Jewish Socio-Cultural Society (Towarzystwo Społeczno-Kulturalne Żydów), five belong to the Jewish Forum, six belong to the Jewish Veterans' Organization (Stowarzyszenie Żydów Kombatantów i Osób Poszkodowanych przez Trzecią Rzeszę), six are members of the 'Children of the Holocaust' group ('Dzieci Holocaustu'), and one person is a member of the Polish Union of Jewish Students (Polska Unia Studentów Żydowskich). Twenty-two respondents are members of more than one Jewish organization, while six people have no Jewish affiliation whatsoever.

The first question all interviewees were asked concerned their Jewish identity.[1] Therefore, at the outset of this chapter, I shall present a brief overview of how they saw their Jewishness. Almost all of them, when answering the first question, referred to their Jewish family, especially their parents. They said that having Jewish ancestors was an important or even the most essential element defining their identity. The following response, given by a 74-year-old man, is to some extent typical of one half of the group:

I am a Jew by birth because I come from a Jewish family. Both my parents were Jewish, my grandparents were Jewish. Hence my descent is certain, there is no doubt about it. My attachment to Jewishness was particularly strengthened the moment I started to attend school. In Warsaw, there was a public school, sponsored by the state, but run by the Jewish Community. And then Jewishness started to consolidate in me, for when I was a child I used to live in a Polish quarter, in the Old Town, on Podwale Street, not far from the Castle Square. I lived in an environment where there were few Jews. Yet I learned about Jewishness thanks to the fact that my parents acknowledged the tradition, the holidays, but they were not Orthodox Jews, they were partly Polonized Jews. [PL 6m]

Yet not all people interviewed had been aware of their Jewish roots from the very beginning. Some of them only learned about it when they were 5, 6, 12, 13, 14, 'when I was a little boy', 'when I was an adolescent', after 1968, or even in the 1990s when some of them were over 30 years of age. A woman born in 1951 said she had Jewish parents and grandparents 'and that was mainly it. I learned I was Jewish at the age of twelve when my parents sent me to a Jewish summer camp.' [PL 40f] A man of 49 said he had found out about his origin when visiting his aunt in Lodz: 'She asked whether I knew that my mom was a Jew ... I learned many things from that aunt. Only later did I find out from my conversations with my mom that her whole family perished.' [PL 11m] It was then, at the age of 14–15, that he realized what the number on his mother's forearm was.

It is noteworthy that the year 1968 had significant consequences for many Polish Jews, not only for adults, but for their children, too. At least four of my respondents stated unambiguously that the anti-Semitic propaganda of 1968 had a tremendous impact on their Jewish identity – they simply learned they were Jewish.[2] Many others were reminded of their descent no matter how much they had wanted to forget it. As Iwona Irwin-Zarecka has aptly noted, 'it *was* 1968 that marked the beginning of a process of reconstructing the memory of the Jew in Poland' (italics in the original).[3]

Twenty-one respondents admitted they had only one Jewish parent; out of this number, thirteen people had only a Jewish father. This was very important, if problematic, to almost all of them. They were aware of the Halakhic law according to which one is not Jewish unless born of a Jewish mother (or converted). It is characteristic of the sample of

Polish Jews that a significant number of them (almost 25 per cent of the whole group) cannot be considered Halakhic Jews, and in fact are not considered as such by a portion of those with at least a Jewish mother.[4] It can legitimately be said of Polish Jews in general, not only of those interviewed, that relatively many of them come from mixed marriages, while some of them have only one Jewish grandparent (especially some younger Jews who have only lately discovered their Jewish roots). One of my interviewees, a man in his 40s, said:

> The problem is that my parents ... if we talk about things Jewish ... My father was a Jew, but my mom not. During the occupation my mom several times escaped death by the skin of her teeth. One of the reasons thereof was that she was staying with the Jews and she was kept in the Pawiak prison. So, because she had contacts with prisoners and then when she was in the ghetto, she actually shared the same fate. In point of fact, two times she was lucky to have survived. [PL 22m]

Another person, speaking about her connections with Judaism, declared:

> It is surely not about language, and not about religion. I come from a mixed family; my father was a Jew, my mom was not. I always knew I was a Jew ... My mom was not Jewish, but she was not Catholic, either. She came from a Russian Orthodox household. Both of my parents were nonbelievers, so on the outside the question of religion didn't exist for us. As for holidays, in principle there was matzo bread and an egg for Passover,[5] just as some kind of symbols. [PL 8f]

Talking about what was crucial in defining their Jewish identity, eight people from the sample mentioned language (either Yiddish or Hebrew); seven mentioned Jewish culture in general; six people pointed to Jewish upbringing and/or education; a few spoke of the awareness of their ethnic background; still others claimed simply that Jewish tradition meant a lot to them. It is curious that though several respondents could still communicate in Yiddish – a clear minority in the group – only one of them thought Yiddishkeit, or the culture rooted in the Yiddish language, to be an essential element of his identity [PL 25m].[6] The knowledge of, and attitude to, the Yiddish language is exactly what makes the sample (if not contemporary Polish Jews in general) considerably different from the Jewish community that existed in Poland before the war, or even in the late 1940s and early 1950s. As Irena Hurwic-Nowakowska has observed, a large proportion of the Jews she surveyed between 1947 and 1950 spoke Yiddish and some of them even chose to fill in the questionnaires in Yiddish.[7] Yet those who easily communicated in Yiddish were much more numerous. In fact, Yiddish was considered by a majority as an element defining their ethnic identity. 'The basic elements determining identification with the Jewish people', Hurwic-Nowakowska argues 'seem to be religion (among religious Jews) and the Yiddish language.'[8] This shows that Polish Jewry has undergone a dramatic social change, as will be demonstrated in more detail below.

Many of my interviewees, specifically those born after the war, said they had tried to learn Yiddish or would like to do so in the future. A significant number of respondents revealed they knew just a few Yiddish words, as the language was only used by their parents when they did not want the children to understand the topic of their conversations. A typical story, not only for Polish Jews, but for American Jews, too.

A man born in 1916 described the role of the Yiddish language in his life the following way:

> As far as language, I learned it at home. Not only my parents, but also my brothers and sisters spoke Yiddish. I was raised in this language. Till I was a teenager I only spoke Yiddish – at home and with friends ... I attended *cheder* just for a short time ... but now, after all these years it's hard for me to recall why, after some two–three years, I left *cheder*. I don't know, maybe I didn't like the discipline ... Then, at the age of eight–ten, I used to read a lot in Yiddish, I read Jewish classics. My dad had a poor command of Polish, just to communicate with his clientele, but my mom knew no Polish at all. Until the age of 15, 16, maybe 17, my language was Yiddish, although I already knew Polish, I had this junior high school finals [mała matura]. [PL 12m]

Another person, a woman just under 60, when speaking about language and identity, confessed:

> In fact, my nation I guess are the Poles. For me personally language is really the basic source of unity with a particular social group. I'm not fond of Poland as a homeland, but, as I say, Poland has this one advantage over the rest of the world that it is here that people speak Polish. [Though] my spiritual homeland is France ... First of all I am a Pole, but at the same time a Jew. However, if I heard

someone say 'my nation', I wouldn't think of Israel. [PL 38f]

As striking as it may seem, this woman, whose mother was Jewish and whose father, though not a Jew, died in the Warsaw ghetto, voiced what many other respondents felt – that they are rooted in Polish culture: that for most of them their first language is Polish. Most of the people interviewed stated that they have a double identity. Six people said they consider themselves both Jewish and Polish; another four declared they are Poles of Jewish origin; a few said they are simply Polish Jews. Other answers to the question regarding identity were expressed in less standard ways. One person, for example, said she feels 'more Jewish than Polish', though she is not a Halakhic Jew [PL 27f]. Some other people stressed their attachment to Polishness or more specifically to Polish culture. One person said, 'I love Poland' [PL 44f], while someone else stated that he is both a Jewish and a Polish patriot [PL 20m], and another respondent declared: 'I'm a patriot of *this* homeland.' [PL 35m] This also points to the difference between contemporary Polish Jews and those who lived in this country fifty years ago. Among the latter there were many who considered themselves Zionist and dreamed of emigrating to Palestine as their homeland.[9]

Also, from the point of view of the present research, it was interesting to see what role, if any, religion played in creating Jewish identity of the respondents. What is striking, only a few people stated that religious practice or observance mattered to them as Jews. Some said they had religious parents and remembered holidays being celebrated at their homes. However, this did not necessary imply a continuation of religious practice by my interviewees in their adult life. What is more, a significant part of the sample admitted that religion played only a minor role in their self-identification as Jews. Five people overtly declared they did not believe in God even though they were not asked about it (the question was asked later, but not at the initial part of the interview when the issue of identity was raised). That would suggest they wanted to make sure they would not be identified with Judaism as a system of beliefs. Later, during their interviews, many others also said that, for various reasons, they were unbelievers.[10] In many cases they had at least one parent who was non-believing.

One person revealed that she remembered some kind of Jewish tradition in her home, but that it was a very specific one: it was 'a tradition of reading, a strongly atheistic tradition'. [PL 39f] Another woman, born of Jewish mother and Polish father, having one German grandmother, said that in her parents' household no Jewish tradition whatsoever was present, for I was born in a home where the parents were Communists. My mother came from a fairly poor family, but both a traditional and antireligious one. She was the first to leave home and then enrolled herself and her siblings in a Polish school. She belonged to Jewish leftist organizations before she entered the Communist Party of Poland. At the end of her life she was very much surprised to see so many young people come back to Jewish religion. [PL 41f]

Another person, a man of 50, whose wife is Roman Catholic, said that apart from his parents he had no closer family, and 'at home no tradition was observed. It was not like there was either Jewish or Catholic tradition; we were just totally secular, we had no ties with any religion whatsoever.' When asked whether he remembered any religious symbols being displayed in his home, a *mezuza* or a *menorah*, he answered: 'Nothing, completely nothing. I would say at some point I was even more attached to some elements of the Catholic culture. Why? Because my mom had a cousin who was a Catholic priest.' [PL 4m] The secular character of their families was mentioned several times by my interviewees. Often they mentioned they had been brought up as completely irreligious, that their parents were active in secular Jewish societies, and even that Jews are 'a completely secular nation'. [PL 46f][11]

On the other hand, if being an agnostic or a non-believing person did not contradict one's Jewishness, belonging to the Christian religion was a considerable problem in this regard. Four of the people interviewed claimed they were Roman Catholic by confession. One survived the war in a Catholic orphanage and only then decided to be baptized: 'I accepted it [Christianity] with honesty. I was baptized after, not during the war, under pressure. I did it consciously, I was already thirteen. I took it as something that was mine, I accepted it. I am Catholic to this very day.' [PL 1f] Being aware of the problems her religion causes in terms of identity, she has a clear sense of belongingness to the Jewish nation: 'I feel and ... I think I am Jewish nevertheless, in spite of all confusion. [Yet] I am Jewish not in the eyes of all people; it depends on the definition of the Jew, on who you think a Jew is. In my own opinion I am both Jewish and Polish, and I belong here.' [PL 1f]

Two other Catholic respondents, both men born in the 1920s, were hidden by Catholic families during the war and consequently converted to Christianity. One was helped by a Polish woman who prayed incessantly, and he felt that her prayer was salvific. That convinced him to convert to Catholicism [PL 21m].[12] The other man was hidden by his future wife whose religion was Catholic. That is why he later assumed her religion [PL 47m].

The fourth person was born at the high of the extermination of Polish Jews. As an infant she was saved by a Polish Catholic family. She was baptized and then raised as a Catholic. The interview with this woman was one of the most touching, but also a problematic one. The problem was purely formal. When asked what made her feel that she is Jewish she answered:

> I am not Jewish because I was uprooted from Jewishness when I was six months old. So, I have this knowledge about my origin, but I can't honestly say I'm Jewish, because this is simply not true. I was reared in a non-Jewish environment, in a completely different culture, in different customs, in the Catholic religion. I don't have the instruments that would enable me to feel Jewish. So, I honestly say I'm not a Jew. And that's a pity, I'd like to be [Jewish], only, as I say, there's no way for me to do it. I would like to be [Jewish] as I have a great sentiment for that, I know what happened to my closest relatives, and all this is very important to me. And I'm trying to reach this cultural environment. For example, I sometimes go to synagogue. I just know my parents and grandparents would go there. I'm trying to find there something for myself, but I find nothing ... when I enter a Catholic church ... the bells, the sound of organ, church songs, the smell of incense – this is all mine, it makes me think of my childhood, of safety, of my beloved step mother. I can find something there. That's the truth. [But] my [biological] parents and grandparents were Jews, and traditional Jews. [PL 37f]

Here we do have a problem: should this person be included in the sample? That is the basic question: Does this interviewee fall under the category of Polish Jews? Unable and unwilling to solve the problem myself, I decided to include this interview in my research, for two reasons. One is that the person had received a special letter in which I explained that I was interested in interviewing *Polish Jews living in Warsaw*. Had she told me on the phone, when we were arranging the meeting, that she definitely was not Jewish, I would surely have withdrawn. But she agreed to the interview. The other thing is her deep awareness of her descent and the fact that she is a member of the child survivors group ('Dzieci Holocaustu') which brings together Jewish children who survived the war. On these grounds I had to acknowledge that the person was Jewish, at least in a certain aspect. That is why I have interpreted her words, 'I can't honestly say I'm Jewish' as if they meant, 'Even though I *feel* some connection with Jewishness, I *fear* I have no right to say it.'

The very idea of looking at Jewishness through the prism of religion seemed dubious to a couple of my respondents. One of them, a woman over 50, stated very clearly why, on the one hand, religion should not be regarded as an essential element of being Jewish, and why, on the other hand, converting to any other religion equals rejecting one's Jewishness:

> You can live a peaceful life without any definition of the Jew, [though] the world attempts to squeeze us into a shallow religious definition which is simply inadequate and false. Being Jewish does not mean being religious. The world has changed and for 200 years now this has been a social untruth. The truth, however, is something else, namely that by converting to another religion you cease being Jewish. This holds even for people who are completely secular. Changing your religion is an exclusion. That's a social definition, not mine. This is how it socially functions and it has nothing to do with our own religion. This is also the way I feel about it. Someone who becomes a Catholic ceases to be a Jew. [PL 46f][13]

Completing this overview of the issue of identity of the Polish Jewish sample, I should like to reflect on two quite important aspects of the topic. One is what might be called *external source of identification*, the other is *emotional-declarative identity*.

The element I have labelled 'external source of identification' is simply anti-Semitism. Many – maybe even most – of the interviewees said that anti-Semitic attitudes of the Polish society at large made them realize – and still does – that they cannot escape their Jewish identity. Fourteen people declared that anti-Semitism is one of the elements that influence their sense of identity; some of them pointed exactly to the 1968 purges as the decisive moment for their lives as Jews. That does not mean, however, that the other thirty-five respondents had not experienced some kind of anti-Jewish behaviour on the part of their Polish co-citizens; during the interviews, it was only rarely that the question of anti-Semitism did not arise. What is significant, though, is that for at least these fourteen people, anti-Semitism was an important factor co-shaping their Jewish identity. One of my interviewees admitted:

> I am a Jew also because of the antisemitism on the side of Poland …And I came to the conclusion which is a very sad one, not so much for me as for the people who hear it, that I don't like Poles, [and] that I'm a Jew … The year '68 is a very important date, and the

experiences from that time, to which I then gave much consideration ... after years it led me to unambiguously identify myself [PL 5m].[14]

Some respondents claim that anti-Semitism strengthens Jewish identity or even think (as Sartre did) that 'antisemitism makes the Jew, for if there were no antisemitism in Europe, I'm more than sure that the Jewish population would invisibly blend in to the European society'. [PL 19m] Also, some point to Christianity, and the Church more specifically, as a force spreading animosity against Jews: 'Let us not delude ourselves, even in the Church there was a strong antisemitic attitude ... And it had its foundations all through the ages.' [PL 22m] 'All the antisemitic stories made me distrust religion. It must be true what I heard in the film *Shoah*, namely that the true sources of antisemitism come from that tradition of Christian anti-Judaism.' [PL 29f]

Upon in-depth analysis all the Polish interviews I came to the conclusion that a number of respondents (at least eight of them) identify themselves as Jews through some kind of conscious self-attribution. With some of them it is more emotional – they attribute Jewishness to themselves by way of feelings ('I feel I am Jewish'); with others the process is more declarative or volitional ('I know that I am Jewish, therefore I really am Jewish'). In both cases the attribution to oneself of being Jewish is to some extent vague, unspecific, devoid of concreteness. For most people interviewed, the constitutive elements of their Jewish identity were either their descent from Jewish parents and being brought up as Jews, or observing some basic traditions (even if only in a secular way), or their interest in Jewish history, or in some cases accepting Judaism as their religion, or all of the above. In other words, a large part of the sample could point to some content of their Jewishness; they could name, without much hesitation, particular 'things' that they thought made them Jewish. With the eight people mentioned above, this was not the case. They had problems with identifying themselves as Jews either with regard to their origin, or their rootedness in Jewish culture and knowledge of things Jewish.

In one interview the link between the external identification element and declarative identity seems obvious. To the question whether his Jewish identity was in the first place a matter of birth, or was it, rather, belongingness to the Jewish culture or religion, the respondent answered:

> Undoubtedly the culture. In my case the father was Jewish, which implies the influence of some kind of authority, the significance of the father. First of all, I guess, it is the awareness of being Jewish

and the attitude [of people] around me to the Jews which was a negative one. And that caused contrariness in me: the greater animosity against the Jews there was, the more interested I was and the more I identified [with them]. As far as religious, Orthodox Jews, [according to them] I am not a one hundred percent Jew, 'cause it's the mother that counts. But I didn't bother. [PL 23m]

Even though the man mentions culture, it seems he just uses a notion that is so general that it can signify everything and nothing. He can barely describe the content of this 'culture' and his identity is apparently determined as Jewish out of spite for the Orthodox, on the one hand, and the anti-Semites, on the other. He does, however, mention the Shoah as an important element of his Jewish identity.

Another person described his identity in the following way:

[I am a Jew] by birth. I was born on [my parents'] way to Israel. I spent all of my childhood in Israel. My mother was a goy, but I feel Jewish all the time. I feel a Polish Jew, a Pole of Jewish origin. I am both a Jew and a devout Polish patriot ... To me [a Jew] is someone who feels Jewish, because if he has some Jewish blood and feels Jewish, then he is Jewish. [PL 20m]

Asked whether there is a definition of the Jew which she could agree with, a woman of 40 answered:

One wouldn't know what kind of criteria to take – the halakhic or the Nuremberg ones? For me this is especially difficult for I come from a mixed marriage and for believing Jews I'm not a Jew at all, and for most Poles I am. And for myself? I cannot answer explicitly whether I am more Jewish or more Polish. I have a strong hope I will never have to make it explicit ... I am both here and there and I'd like to leave it just like that and never to be forced to make a final decision. [PL 8f]

A similar problem with determining one's identity was faced by yet another respondent:

This is all quite complicated. Because with me the case is not really unambiguous. There's a problem of ... I don't know how to term it ... a kind of doubleness. I can't identify myself unambiguously [saying:] 'I am a Jew and that's it.' I mean I didn't have the possibility to ... Since my childhood I have never lived in a uniform Jewish community. [PL 11m]

What can be inferred from all interviews quoted above is that these respondents have a deficit of criteria for their own Jewish identity. They find it difficult to specify the content of their Jewishness. As for the Polish part, the problem seems to be non-existent: they live in this country, they are Polish citizens, they speak Polish and know Polish literature and history. But how to give meaning to the Jewish part? They think of themselves as Jews but do not know what it is that makes them Jewish. Therefore they experience a classic situation of cognitive dissonance. In order to reduce the dissonance some start to learn Hebrew or Yiddish, but most of them quit after some time. They read books on Jewish topics, but eventually what they are left with is clinging to their emotional conviction or declaration of being Jewish. On the psychologial level, however, they are probably not satisfied with this argument.

In sum, it can be said that the sample of Polish Jews includes both people who have no difficulties in finding subjective and objective criteria for their Jewish identity, and those who, though they consider themselves Jewish, encounter problems with specifying what their identity is about. For all respondents their first language is Polish, even if it was otherwise in the past. Their attachment to Polishness cannot be denied, for in most cases they actively contribute to Polish culture, and for the most part consider themselves both Jews and Poles, Poles of Jewish origin or Polish Jews. Religiously they are rather liberal, or indifferent. A significant portion of the group are non-believers, though in particular cases they believe in some sort of higher being, but do not strictly observe the Judaic law. Nevertheless, they sometimes go to synagogue, in most cases for Yom Kippur or Passover. For a large part of the respondents, Jewish tradition – containing elements of religious practices – is a vehicle of Jewishness. Only a small proportion of the sample are believing and practising Jews.

PROFILE OF THE SAMPLE OF AMERICAN JEWS

The American Jewish sample included twenty-nine women and twenty-three men. Among them there were three women survivors and one man who survived the war.[15] Seven persons were born outside the United States. Thirty-three respondents were either born in New York City or had lived there since they were at least 14. Thus most of the interviewees spent most of their lives in the city. Thirty-four respondents had a college or university degree, while eleven held PhDs (which means, of course, that people with doctoral titles are over-represented in the sample).[16]

Eleven respondents are members of Orthodox synagogues (including two Modern-Orthodox); two belong to a Lubavitch (Hassidic) congregation; eleven belong to a Conservative congregation; six belong to a Reform temple; two are members of a Reconstructionist and one of a Conservative-Reconstructionist congregation; and six are members of a Secular Humanistic community. It should be noted that the last group, those belonging to City Congregation, which is a Secular Humanistic community,[17] are considerably over-represented. In reality, Secular Humanistic Jews constitute about 1 per cent of American Jewry.[18] Yet members of this congregation were more willing than others to be interviewed, and because of their general openness they were easy to contact.

In the American sample, six interviewees were members of the Workmen's Circle (Arbeter Ring), which is a Bundist–Yiddishist organization; two were members of the Hillel Foundation (operating on university campuses); and one belonged to a Jewish Community Center. Three people belonged to survivors' organizations. Six women were active in various Jewish women's movements. Eleven people were unaffiliated with any religious community and two respondents had no Jewish affiliation whatsoever.[19]

During most of the interviews, the American respondents used clear-cut categories and were more specific about what they understood by Jewishness than the Polish respondents. This may be partly due to the fact that Judaism (culturally, but not always politically) has been developing in America with hardly any obstacles for the last two hundred years. American Jews as a community have developed a variety of religious denominations and have been active in a great many social and political movements. They have founded innumerable organizations and institutions fostering the development of Jewish communal and private life. Last but not least, American Jewry has achieved a social position that guarantees general acceptance and undisturbed involvement in all professions and all walks of life.

Although several Jewish denominations exist in the United States, the group of American Jews is, to a certain extent, easier to describe. First of all, considerably fewer of the American respondents have problems with explicitly identifying themselves as Jews. Out of the fifty-two people interviewed, thirty-nine (75 per cent) asserted that they were born of Jewish parents and considered it an important element of their identity. Also, seventeen people said they had parents or grandparents who were born in Eastern Europe, mostly in Poland or Russia, but also in the

Ukraine, Lithuania or Romania. For a majority of them this fact was not to be disregarded. One had the impression that through their East European ancestors they could find their roots; they knew they were not people 'from nowhere' but came from a particular place on earth. Indeed, this feeling of rootedness was very important to some of them, even an object of pride.

To a significant number of interviewees (fourteen), their education and the way they had been raised by their parents played a crucial role in shaping their Jewish self-awareness. Many of the American respondents said they had been sent to Jewish schools, learned Jewish languages and saw Jewish tradition being practised in their homes, although as children they were not always happy with that.

Recounting the story of her childhood, a 60-year-old woman said: 'On holidays, you know Passover, we had a dinner, and we had a cultural seder, not a religious seder. Hanukah – the same thing. [And] I went to Jewish schools – not Hebrew school but Jewish cultural school.' [AM 15f] Another woman, aged 80, confessed she 'was sent to a secular Yiddish after-day school, to learn the language, to know who I was – without the benefit of the clergy'. [AM 17f] She and her husband, who came from a similar milieu, decided to send their children to a Yiddish school too, so that they would be raised the same way as their parents had been. Yet perhaps the most impressive and moving was the experience described by a professor at Brooklyn College:

> I was brought up as someone who was Jewish 'cause I lived in a Jewish neighborhood ... I can read Hebrew but I can't understand it ... When I was 13 I was bar mitzvahed ... I think that kind of Jewish upbringing is incredibly valuable because ... when someone intermarries they're not bringing anything to the table. On the other hand, my son, he's gonna marry someone who's not Jewish but his kids are gonna be raised Jewish in a meaningful way because he has a certain sense of himself being Jewish and what it means. [AM 1m]

It is symptomatic that most Jews from the American sample seemed never to have had to face the question of whether they are rather Jewish or American. First and foremost, being American means having non-American roots, and most people in the United States are aware of their ethnic origin. Thus, American Jews can easily define themselves as Americans and Jews and no one (including themselves) expects them to declare which came first. In other words, being Jewish in America is as 'normal' as being black, Irish or Latino. People may have different ethnic allegiances, but they all make up American society. Presumably that is why none of the interviewees had any problems with consciously accepting his/her American *and* Jewish identities.[20]

To illustrate the typical attitude of the American respondents toward their Jewish identity, I shall give brief quotations from two interviews, both with women over 70, one born in the United States, the other in pre-war Poland:

> I am thoroughly and fiercely Jewish. I was born to a Jewish family. My father was an Orthodox rabbi who didn't practice. My mother's father was an Orthodox rabbi from Vilna. They came here in 1904.[21] I really consider myself very Jewish – culturally, religiously, even though I'm not 'very Orthodox', but I come from that kind of background and I went to a religious school. [To me Jewishness] it's a kind of an identity: because of my family, because of the culture, because of the history, because most of the people I've associated with in my life have been Jewish though I've worked with non-Jews, but this is a thoroughly Jewish neighborhood. I guess it's a cultural thing. I'm also American, but I'm also very Jewish. [AM 45f]
>
> My sense of identity is, as a Jew ... Jewish in terms of birth, history, culture, and people. Not necessarily in a religious sense. But the religious context of Judaism is part of the Jewish culture, that is part of my fabric. So, even though I was raised in a non-religious environment, in a secular environment, [because of] the fact that my father had been a rabbi who became a socialist, there was a great deal of the religious input even into the secular aspect of my life ... and adult life – in terms of the moral imperative, history – not seen as a ... divine scene as much as a historic scene. [My family] never kept kosher, never kept kosher. The holidays were all done as cultural, historical events. [AM 47f]

What is telling is how often the respondents included in the American sample referred to culture and cultural values of Judaism as principal determinants of their identity. Twenty-six respondents, that is 50 per cent of the whole group, mentioned Jewish culture in defining their Jewishness. Therefore, as was argued in the first chapter, culture constitutes the most important factor shaping the identity of American Jews. One of the conclusions of the *Study of Jewish Culture in the Bay Area* (San Francisco) is that in describing American Jewry, 'the significance of Jewish art and culture has largely been ignored ... [However,] every religious attribute is filled with culture, every cultural act filled with religiosity. Synagogues themselves are great centers of Jewish culture.'[22] The identity-building potential of Jewish culture cannot be over-estimated. Apparently, it is this potential that helps many Jews maintain their sense of being Jewish and belonging to the Jewish community. It provides them with a specific content: 'some-thing' that can attract their attention and encourage them to get involved in Jewish life.

But why is that so? Why does culture occupy the first place in the American Jewish world? Has it always been so? Certainly not. For centuries, Jewishness meant Judaism, and of course not only in North America. Being Jewish equalled belonging to the ethnic religion of all Jews, which implied sharing the same (to a large extent) rituals and theological beliefs. The emergence of *haskalah,* or Jewish Enlightenment, resulted in the process of secularization which also reached the shores of the American continent. Today, American Jewry is a highly secularized society:[23] it shows a strong tendency to turn from faith-religion to culture-religion. Thus, culture has become the secular religion of American Jews. It is an element giving inner coherence to the identity of individuals and gathering them together into a community, and as such it creates a new social structure. This culture-focused life of present-day American Jews is a characteristic feature in the landscape of contemporary America. That is why my respondents so often and with such emphasis talked about Jewish culture. A 50-year-old woman described her identity as follows:

> To me it's the culture and my heritage more than the religious aspect. I was brought up in a very cultural home. My parents were very involved in the Jewish world. My father was a lecturer and a Jewish teacher for many years, and, growing up, my first language was Yiddish. So, I was brought up in a very Jewish environment. My parents were immigrants; [they were] not religious, [they] did not go to synagogue but they were very ... Jewish-orientated. They were not keeping kosher, they did not observe the Sabbath. [PL 15f]

At the same time what one can observe in numerous interviews is that culture replaces faith-religion. And many of the interviewees wanted to make it clear that, if they were unbelievers, Judaism was important to them, but *not as a religion* in its classic sense:

> I grew up in a town that had a strong Jewish presence, but ... [of course] we were a minority. I had a strong sense of Jewish identity when I was growing up – that was more cultural than religious. My mother, for example, [was] not a believer. My father was very

skeptical, I don't know if he actually said he didn't believe a bit. The religious part was not very strong in my family, the cultural identity was very much ... They didn't feel that there was a big contradiction between not being believers and still having a synagogue affiliation. My brothers were bar mitzvahed, for example. For many years I was aware culturally of being Jewish, and it was something that I enjoyed ... Nonetheless, my husband is not Jewish. I really had no conflict about that, because he also is a nonbeliever. [AM 23f]

I'm very attached to Judaism culturally as opposed to religiously, as opposed to a belief in God. We speak ... my son is fluent in Yiddish, and that was very important to me. When he was born I told my mother to speak with him only in Yiddish, and so he fluently understands Yiddish. That was very important to me. All the customs, all the tradition, the language is very important – all of those things ... [As a family] we were more Orthodox than not, we weren't a hundred percent, but more Orthodox than not. [Ours was] a kosher home. I went to an Orthodox synagogue growing up which I eventually rebelled against, but I think that's normal. But I've come back – now that I have a child I've come back to that tremendous connection of that cultural aspect of Judaism. [AM 27f]

I feel very Jewish, I have a very strong Jewish identity. And it's not just a matter that I feel that I just happened to have been born Jewish ... My feelings of Jewishness I'm sure come from my background because I was raised with a very strong Jewish upbringing. My family is Orthodox, except for me. I'm not Orthodox, but I'm very traditional in a lot of ways, in certain things.[24] I had a strong Jewish education; I started going to Hebrew school when I was five, even before I started the first grade. When I finished six grades my parents put me to a yeshiva day school, Orthodox yeshiva. And then I went into high school, also girls' Orthodox yeshiva high school ...And I went to these Jewish religious Zionist summer camps. All my friends were Jewish. So, it's very much part of my particular identity even though I myself have gone away from the ... Orthodox beliefs. Personally I'm not a religious person. I mean I'm actually ... actually an atheist. And yet I keep my apartment kosher. Some things are just in my guts ... I'm very strict about it even though I'm not kosher outside of my apartment. I do belong to a synagogue, but I don't go very often. I go because I want to have the affiliation ... and to have a place for major holidays. [AM 49f]

These are just the most typical and unambiguous enunciations of the respondents regarding the question of Jewish culture, but in no way are they the only ones. As was mentioned above, at least 50 per cent of the interviewees clearly stated that they cherished Jewish culture more than any other aspect of Judaism. But there were, of course, many others to whom culture also matters and who just did not express it explicitly. In many cases, what the respondents talked about were the cultural and/or secular values that they associated with Jewishness, although they did not call it 'Jewish culture'.

Also, many others claimed they were not religious Jews. Nineteen persons said they did not share the belief in God; nine declared they lacked any religious involvement whatsoever (these are two separate phenomena that should not be confused). Here the situation is similar to the Polish sample: many of these people declared that they are unbelievers even before they were asked about faith. They mentioned the issue while answering the first question – the one concerning identity. Hence, it might be inferred that it was important to them to state that they are Jews, but Jews who do not believe in God. It is also striking that, of these nineteen people, none seemed to reveal his/her unbelief out of hate or contempt for the believers. They were not trying to disavow or to discredit faith in God in general, though some may have been critical of certain concepts of Judaism or of particular denominations (mostly of Orthodoxy or Hassidism). A man of 55, for example, said: 'The ultra-Orthodox and the *Hassidim* have blocked themselves off completely from the rest of the world, except in terms of trade. You don't have to worry about them. But they're fanatics, so I discount them.' [AM 3m] Another man, aged 75, speaking about the Hassidim, asserted: 'I believe to this day that it's a fanatical movement of [the] Middle Ages.' [AM 41m]

To be sure, among the interviewees there were a couple of followers of the Hassidic branch of Judaism, too. There were also others who, though not affiliated with Hassidism, spoke approvingly about the movement, such as the person who started to learn more about 'the Orthodox people from Brooklyn, the *Hassidim*. I began to respect them more, not that I believe what they believe in, but respect because before ... I didn't understand them. They were almost an embarrassment. I respect them because they believe in what they believe, and they're strong in that.' [AM 7f]

There is also a significant group of people who do observe the Judaic law and attempt to follow (to a certain degree) the precepts of their religion. Fourteen respondents declared they observe religious practices in their life; many of them also claimed that this is one of the elements determining their Jewish identity. This would most often involve observing the Sabbath, the laws of kashrut (kosher food and kitchen), going to synagogue, or regular prayer. This is how a 56-year-old man, whose parents had a kosher home and observed all Jewish holidays, sees his Jewish identity vis-à-vis religion:

> As my core belief, it probably started with the fact that I was born into a Jewish, and a religious family, and ultimately my education led me to believe that what I practice is true ... I attended a yeshiva throughout my life and went to synagogue regularly. My home is a kosher religious home. My children all attend Jewish schools, we also attend synagogue regularly. [AM 44m]

The religious engagement of the interviewees certainly has several levels of gradation. Not all of them observe the same laws, and not with the same dedication. In other words, the intensity and passion with which their religiosity is lived and expressed differs in a variety of ways. It is noteworthy that sometimes in their own eyes they are not very religious, even though they continue what is generally considered a traditional Jewish way of life. A good example of such an attitude would be the case of a woman over 80 years of age, who confessed:

> I'm both culturally a Jew and also religiously. I'm not very religious, but I do belong to a synagogue and I attend services quite regularly, especially as I'm now retired. I was educated not in a religious way, but we had in this country what we call *folkshule* and this was concentrated on Yiddish. All of my siblings were born in Europe, I was born in Canada. [I came to the USA when I was] about 10 years old— I came to Detroit, [and then moved] to New York in 1939 ... My mother definitely kept kosher. I also keep kosher, [though] I don't change dishes ... but I don't eat pork or shellfish. And I don't mix meat and milk. I observe many holidays. I go to synagogue on Rosh Hashanah and Yom Kippur. I'm planning a big seder for the Passover. [AM 42f]

Yet another particular case deserves to be given close attention. Among the American Jewish respondents there was one who was Catholic by religion – which again opens the question of whether one can be both a Jew and a member of a confession other than Judaism. Since I have already discussed this issue at some length, further analysis here is unnecessary. The person in question is a man who was born in Poland and survived the war partly in hiding and partly as a Catholic worker in Germany. This is how he views his Jewish and Catholic identity:

> I struggled all my life with the question of identity: Who am I, who is my God? I was born in a traditional Jewish home. I had attended a Jewish school in Lodz with all the subjects being given in Polish except Hebrew lessons ... my father and my mother were Polish patriots – they believed in Poland. To one another they spoke in Yiddish, to the children – only in Polish. I didn't know Yiddish, I hadn't learned Yiddish. If I learned some Yiddish expressions it was in New York, years later. My father imbued in me love for Polish literature, and poetry, and history. My Jewish identity was traditional, Zionistic. Before the war, until I was 11, I had virtually no single Polish friend, they were all Jewish. We got stuck in the Warsaw ghetto for over two years. But my Jewish identity, if anything, was strengthened by persecution, by the frozen, starving skeletons. As far as Jewish tradition and religiosity, we went to the synagogue maybe two, three times a year. At home, only the two, three main holidays were commemorated, Passover ... My mother prayed Friday night and we had Friday night supper with fish. [My parents did not keep kosher], but it was a secret. Ham was served in our home. So, it was a traditional, progressive Jewish home ... For many, many years, and still partially until today, I am torn because I came to believe in Christ. This was my last resort – clinging to someone who represented love and understanding. As far as religion, I am officially Catholic. Today I have a few very dear friends who are Poles, and a few who are Polish Jews. We have these theological conversations [with Mr N.N.] very often when I'm there [in Poland]. I'll tell you something I haven't told anybody before [even the Spielberg Foundation]: I pray every night 'Our Father' and 'Hail Mary' simply because I don't know any other prayers. I'm not a great believer; my beliefs have weakened through the years. I don't go to the synagogue, I've been to the synagogue maybe twice in 20 years, friends took me there, out of sentiment ... My loyalty is to America. Americans liberated me from the Germans, enabled me to come, be educated. I am a very patriotic American. I also have deep sentiments for Poles and Poland. [Though,] I could never live in that place anymore ... Being so split asunder, it's a huge cross to bear in life. I have tremendous ties with Polish culture ... I have troubles believing in the divinity of Christ even though I pray to

> him – I pray to him because he was a holy man. I have trouble believing every word of the Gospel just as I have trouble believing every word of the Bible. [AM 41m]

Though faith itself is a source of doubts for this man, it seems he has no problems with identifying both as a Jew and a Catholic. We do not know exactly what it means that his Catholicism is 'official', but it would be difficult to infer from his words that the religion he is affiliated with makes him less of a Jew. What is clear is that Jewishness is his life story which he does not want to deny, or to diminish its significance. Moreover, these two identities do not interfere with his first loyalty to America, which, in turn, is typical for most of the sample.

In sum, we can say that the average person included in the American sample had parents who were either believing/practising Jews or who were secular but observed some basic Jewish traditions. The person interviewed, on the other hand, tends to be more culturally attracted to Jewishness than to have a strong attachment to Judaism as faith. Having Jewish ancestors is certainly an important element (if not the major one) in deciding to get involved in Jewish life. Here is how such a typical identity might be depicted:

> The things that define me as a Jew, in no particular order, is that my family is Jewish, they raised me Jewish. [We had an] involvement with a religious Jewish community – a synagogue. And I went to the Jewish rituals; we had Sabbath every Friday night; I was bar mitzvahed; went to Hebrew school [from the age of 6 or 7 to 15] ... We were Reform Jews. That meant that we didn't keep a kosher home, the home wasn't kosher during Passover, we didn't keep the Sabbath ... in any way whatsoever, except for that we lit candles, said the prayer over the candles, had halah and wine, went to synagogue for the major holidays and celebrated [them] in the home. But mostly it was a social situation – being with other Jews ... I define myself as a Jew ... through a historical sense of activism, what Jews have done in the world, social change. Very much who I am is that lineage which in many ways has nothing to do with it as a religion, but as a culture. And also culturally I'm very, very identified [as a Jew] through the humor and the art, and the cultural productions, and the respect for thinking and learning – things that are associated with religion, but can be separate as well and experienced in a secular way – that's very much what I do. I am not affiliated with any particular

synagogue now, but I do go about once every three weeks in the city ... just go to a different one ... I'm also identified as a Jew through my political engagement and specific affiliations [?] mostly as an activist in the last ten years through working with other Jews and using our Jewish identity as the basis for the actions that we take and the messages that we put up. [AM 51m][25]

2. ASSIMILATION, THE HOLOCAUST AND IDENTITY

Assimilation has threatened Jewish existence ever since the Assyrian and the Babylonian bondage. In order to protect the Jews from dissolving into other societies, especially during diaspora times, Jewish leaders created numerous religio-cultural institutions and laws that were supposed to impede the nation's losing its identity. Yet Jews the world over were never perfectly immune (at least not all of them) to the temptations of other cultures. This was especially true with regard to the Sephardic Jews, who had experienced an enormous influence of the Arabic nations of the Levant and of the Moors' Spain. Ashkenazic Jewry, on the other hand, was exposed to assimilation forces as late as the eighteenth century as a result of the *haskalah* movement, the father of which was Moses Mendelssohn.

In the United States, since it became one political entity, assimilation has been one of the crucial aspects of social and political life. In fact, the constitutional idea of *E Pluribus Unum* – one (nation) out of a multitude (of cultures and ethnic groups) – was an official decreeing of a state-supported assimilation.[26] The first Jewish newcomers to settle on American shores were the Sephardic Portuguese Jews who arrived in New Amsterdam, in 1654. They were soon followed by the Ashkenazic *Dorfjuden* – village Jews from German-speaking Europe.[27] These first Jews were too small a group to think of assimilation, which would immediately have destroyed them. Only when the Europeanized Ashkenazic *maskilim* (enlightened Jews) from Germany arrived in the 1820s, 1830s and 1840s[28] was an already-assimilated Jewry introduced into American life.

Assimilation, however, became an issue for Jews in America when East European Jewish masses started to immigrate to the United States in the 1880s – a process which lasted until the mid-1920s, when American law set stringent immigrant quotas. It was characteristic of the big Jewish communities across the American continent that they comprised innumerable small groups of East European Jews organized on the basis of their place of origin. According to a 1938 survey, in New York City alone there were over 1,800 such small associations – *landsman-schaften*, as they were called in Yiddish.[29]

These Jews, however, were perceived by many German Jews as 'uncouth, destitute, and therefore threatening to their own position in American society ... Rather than withdrawing from the Eastern European Jewish immigrant, however, the German Jews undertook to "Americanize" them as rapidly as possible.'[30] They established relief centres for Jewish immigrants (the first such organization – The Hebrew Emigrant Aid Society of the United States – was founded as early as 1870) and ran special 'educational and training courses and schools for both children and adults'.[31] These mostly Russian and Polish Jews were approximately the same kind of people as their German brethren had been over half a century before them: they were poor refugees. And, like their German co-religionists, they quickly adapted themselves to the demands of American culture; they were also active in creating a new form of Judaism – it is believed that the East European Jews were responsible for the emergence of Conservative Judaism. Yet, if the Germans brought the Reform with them from their native county, Conservative Judaism was organized as a new and a genuinely American Jewish denomination.[32]

A characteristic feature of American Jews was that they were assimilating mainly in large urban areas such as New York, Boston, Chicago and Detroit. First of all, assimilation was easier and less painful in such metropolises. Secondly, each arriving group of immigrants was more willing to settle in places where there already was vibrant Jewish life and where they would not be completely lost and alien. Thus the Jewish quarters in New York's Lower East Side and then in Brooklyn functioned like magnets attracting newcomers. Those whose parents had decided to live in large cities 'were becoming an integral part of the new urban landscape'. Yet what they had to face, despite the progressing process of their Americanization, was 'the disturbing dissonance of anti-Semitism, which they perceived as threatening their security and their aspirations'.[33]

How did the new, urban Jews find out that there was still animosity toward them on the part of American society at large? When the economically mobile Jews moved to the second-settlement areas, they were soon joined by their less assimilated brethren. Eventually, the former found themselves trapped in a Jewish ghetto they had wanted to escape. Furthermore, they started to realize that they had not been really accepted as part of the middle class by their non-Jewish neighbours.

The conclusion was clear, if upsetting: namely, that cultural assimilation was not coterminous with structural assimilation. In other words, economical well-being and Americanized mores did not guarantee a social status equal to that of the WASPs.[34] America of the 1920s and 1930s was a land where anti-Semitism was gaining popularity among the masses and support within the elite.

Another wave of Jewish immigrants from Europe came in the late 1940s and 1950s, a tragic consequence of the Nazi Holocaust and of continuing anti-Semitism in countries such as Poland, Hungary and Romania. They came to an America that was advocating assimilation and to a great extent *was* assimilated.[35] Moreover, they joined a Jewish community that was perhaps the most Americanized minority group. If assimilation was attractive as a potential warrant of social acceptance and an expression of (as it might have seemed) decreasing anti-Semitism, what was at stake was the very issue of Jewish continuity – for indulgence in total assimilation would have surely destroyed the specificity of Jewish identity. Therefore, the question was 'whether, in the aftermath of the Holocaust, Jewish existence continued to have any purpose. A minority of American Jews concluded that the price for identifying with the Jewish people had simply become too high ... What rational case could be made, they asked, for affirming a Jewish identity after Auschwitz?'[36]

In general terms, assimilation was made into an ideology thanks to the well-sounding slogan coined by Isaac Zangwill in his play *The Melting Pot*. The title expression of Zangwill's work became a blueprint for American assimilation. The pouring masses of immigrants were supposed to blend into the American society – as if in a melting pot – and form an alloy of one, homogenous polity. Zangwill's idea of a thorough assimilation was expressed through the words of David Quixano, a Jewish pogrom survivor from Russia, whose vision was that

> America is God's Crucible, the great Melting Pot where all the races of Europe are melting and reforming! Here you stand, good folk, think I, when I see them at Ellis Island, you stand in your fifty groups with your fifty languages and histories, and your fifty blood hatreds and rivalries, but you won't be long like that brothers, for these are the fires of God you've come to – these are the fires of God. A fig for your feuds and vendettas! German and Frenchman, Irishman and Englishman, Jews and Russians – into the Crucible with you all! God is making the American ... The real American has not yet arrived. He is only in the Crucible, I tell you – he will be the fusion of all the races, the coming superman.[37]

The idea of the melting pot was heavily criticized by many an American scholar in the 1960s, in the era of a nascent ethnic America. In their well-known book titled *Beyond the Melting Pot*, Nathan Glazer and Daniel Patrick Moynihan submitted Zangwill's idea to a critique. Basing their argument on the cases of New York's blacks, Puerto Ricans, Irish, Italians and Jews, they demonstrated that even if the melting pot concept might have had some allure for the early-twentieth-century immigrants, it became completely false and unattractive for the third and fourth generations.[38]

Seen against the background of the emerging 'black power', of feminist movements, of the great awakening of Native Americans, and of the more and more numerous Asiatic and Latino immigrants, the idea of assimilation came to be thought of as a completely compromised concept.[39] Instead, multiculturalism or ethnic federalism was proposed as an alternative – and even the right – vision for America.[40] As cultural pluralism was gaining momentum in the 1960s, it 'spurred a Jewish ethnic awareness among American Jews'.[41] This ethnic Jewish awareness, as I have pointed out many times, was not, however, completely devoid of any religious elements. What is more, as Glazer and Moynihan claim, after the war there was a religious revival in American Jewry, but that revival has had relatively little to do with religious faith in God: rather, it is about a need for adherence to a larger group of the kindred. Thus, 'among those without formal religious ties there is a heightened sense of the defensive importance of organized Jewish community'.[42]

In Poland, on the other hand, assimilation was an issue seen almost exclusively as pertaining to the Jewish population. During the times of the First Republic, many different religious and/or ethnic groups lived in Poland without pressure from anyone to assimilate to the Polish culture, for there was hardly anything like an ethnically homogenous Polish culture. The questions of diversity and uniformity were raised in the nineteenth century, when Poland, like most European nations, was developing its national consciousness. Poland, of course, was then non-existent as an independent country, which only strengthened the Poles' hopes and strivings to restore political and territorial sovereignty. At the same time, the *haskalah* was starting to influence Polish Jews. Then the question arose: Can the Jews assimilate to Polish society at large – are they willing to, are they invited to? According to Aleksander Hertz's view, Polish Jews constituted a separate caste within Polish society, at least since the sixteenth century.[43] As Hertz has aptly observed, Jewish assimilation to Polish culture began in earnest after the January Uprising of 1863. It is after that event that 'the mass assimilation of Jews to Polishness was viewed as the sole solution to the Jewish question in Poland; on the other hand, a distance was kept from those new Poles of the Jewish faith.'[44]

In general, in the latter half of the nineteenth century, Jews inhabiting the territories of the former Kingdom of Poland and the Great Duchy of Lithuania (then partitioned between Russia, Prussia and Austria) formed five different sociocultural groups: Ashkenazic Jews; Ashkenazic Jews defining themselves as Polish Jews; Poles of the Mosaic confession; German Jews; and Russified Jews from the 'Pale of Settlement',[45] called *litvaks*.[46] These five groups differed not only nominally – that is, not only in how they saw themselves or were perceived by others; they were different in their lifestyles, in their philosophies, in their economic and political status: in short – they were different from the point of view of assimilation. After 1918 all these Jews became Polish citizens and were put under the same laws – all of them, the most assimilated German Jews and Poles of the Jewish faith, as well as the *litvaks* (who were also assimilated in some respects, but certainly to the Russian rather than the Polish culture), and Ashkenazic Jews (the *Hassidim* and the *misnagdim*) and the Zionistically inclined as well as the secular socialists.

It should also be noted that at the beginning of the twentieth century, both some Jewish milieus and Polish xenophobes were increasingly more inclined to think of assimilation as a failed idea. The chauvinistically oriented Poles would see assimilation as a way of infiltrating 'pure' Polish culture by the allegedly 'vicious' and 'base' traits of the Jews. The anti-assimilationist Jews (the Orthodox, the Yiddishists and the Zionists), on the other hand, tended to view the process as a treason against Jewish culture and/or religion[47] and believed it to be counterproductive. Therefore, I have to agree with Celia Heller who argues that the general opinion that dominated Polish Jewry in the interwar period was that most Jews did not see assimilation (any longer) as a viable solution to their plight.[48]

After the Second World War, as Hurwic-Nowakowska has noted, it was not unlikely for Polish Jews to think of assimilation as a delusive and ineffective process.[49] First of all, the Jewish community changed tremendously after the war. They were not the same people that they had been before the war: they had seen their loved ones perish in the Holocaust and were aware that only a minority of the pre-war Polish Jews had survived. This awareness had a dramatic influence on their way of thinking. In mere numbers, the population of Polish Jews shrank by some 90 per cent: from over three million before the war to less than 200,000 in the years following the catastrophe.[50]

The war, it seems, has also had an impact on how the category of 'the Jew' was perceived. Before the war Jews were identified in most cases on the basis of their confession. Thus there were Jews practising Judaism, and Poles whose religion was Judaism, too. There were also secular people, but, for a majority of them, either their parents or grandparents had been practising, religious Jews. Also, in Nazi-occupied Poland, anyone who had been a member of a Jewish religious community, or a descendant of members of a synagogue, was considered by the law as a Jew.[51] After the war, however, when most of the religious – the most pious – Jews had perished, this was no longer true. As Hurwic-Nowakowska has shown, and as the present study also demonstrates, in the post-war situation, being Jewish has by no means meant belonging to a religious group. With a significant part of post-war Polish Jewry being secular Jews, some even supporting the communist regime, the religious criteria were no longer relevant. We can conclude that those who had survived were by and large secular, assimilated Jews, and this fact implied a considerable change in the identity of the Jew.

At the turn of the nineteenth and twentieth centuries, a specific Jewish group was already starting to appear, namely the non-religious – or, rather, 'no-religion' – Jews: neither followers of Judaism nor of any of the Christian faiths, but still unambiguously Jewish. To make things even more complicated, among Polish Jews a new socio-ethnic identity emerged – those for whom Poland was a homeland (at least a surrogate homeland), but who nevertheless regarded themselves as Jewish, not necessarily by religion but by ethnicity.[52] These ethnic Jews, often patriots of their Polish motherland, not always associated with Judaism, remained a 'separate spiritual faction'[53] which has had an exceptional share in Polish culture. They came to be a significant influence on the development of the new Polish republic – on its political, economic and cultural life, a period which lasted, unfortunately, for only one generation.[54]

It can legitimately be said that the post-war Jewish identity has shifted toward a cultural determination, and, even if religion is still considered important, its importance consists in its functional usefulness; thus it has become but one element among many of Jewish culture.[55] Today, as in the period described by Hurwic-Nowakowska, there are no 'hard' and unquestionable sociological criteria for 'the Jew'[56] (save for the traditional Halakhic ones). That is why we have to rely on the subjective criteria of the people interviewed – whether they regard themselves as Jewish or of Jewish origin. This is partly due to the fact that after the war, Polish Jews were assimilating with surprising rapidity. In contradistinction to American Jewry, they were not only assuming the identity of the host country – they were losing their Jewishness. Insofar as American Jews were simply American Jews (of course, there were also those who practically cut off their Jewish identity), Polish Jews were gradually becoming Poles of Jewish origin, or just Poles. Their Jewishness was becoming non-existent. As Irwin-Zarecka has noted:

> they were convinced that complete integration was now both possible and desirable, and strengthened in that conviction by the democratic public opinion ... In subtle or direct terms, a Jew would be told to change his name and to avoid any public display of his Jewishness; many of those who were not told did so out of concern for the cause ... [They were becoming] 'Poles of Jewish origin', with emphasis placed on the first term and a polite silence covering the rest. Again, individual variations notwithstanding, their Polishness was not to be questioned; their Jewishness gradually to disappear altogether.[57]

I shall now attempt to answer the question: How did the Polish and American Jews interviewed perceive the phenomenon of assimilation? During each conversation, I asked my respondents whether, to them, assimilation constituted a threat to Jewishness, and whether they considered themselves assimilated Jews. Questions concerning their attitude toward assimilation were to be helpful in seeing how the Holocaust is used as an identity-building factor. In other words, answers to these questions were supposed to serve as a supplement to those concerning the role played by the Shoah in the interviewees' identities. In certain cases it was really interesting to compare the respondents' opinions on religion and how they viewed the Holocaust in relation to their Jewish identity. The latter issue will be discussed at length in the second part of this chapter.

In the Polish sample, the largest group constituted people who thought that assimilation is a very ambiguous phenomenon, a kind of 'double-edged sword.' Out of forty-nine Polish interviewees, twenty-seven took the position of 'in-between' – they saw the obvious negative sides of assimilation, yet at the same time claimed that it has some 'pros' as well. Besides that, they were aware that they themselves were in large measure assimilated, a state which they considered to be quite 'normal'. Six people maintained that assimilation was generally a positive thing, while seven respondents were of the opposite opinion. The rest (nine people) were not really interested in the issue of assimilation at all, and could not answer what their stance was.

It was not infrequent that assimilation was commented upon in relation to the Holocaust. Thus a 75-year-old man, a survivor, judging assimilation as exerting a negative influence on the Jews, stated:

> Assimilation has always failed and its crowning achievement was the last war, the Holocaust. Assimilatory tendencies could be observed in big Jewish communities, among the people of science and art. They thought that by occupying the social position that they did they could completely accept the host culture and strike root in the host society and through that erase their past. But life has shown that no assimilation is ever successful. All in all, it strikes the individual in a ricochet. [PL 6m]

A woman aged 64, employed by a Jewish institution, even likened assimilation to the Nazi murder of the Jews:

> Q: *Would you agree with the opinion that assimilation threatens Jewish identity?* Of course. On a par with the Holocaust. [Though] it is painless and beautiful. I mean, I'd not fight it. You have the right to make your own choices, it's your life. But assimilation certainly endangers small nations. But as you can see this nation has persevered, and for a long time. So, maybe it won't be that bad ... Q: *Who do you think is an assimilated Jew?* It's someone who has forgotten his language, or doesn't know it at all. Who knows nothing about his culture, who doesn't care ... Assimilation also means that you don't know the culture ... You have no contacts [with Jews]. You know you have some Jewish ancestors but it's meaningless. You marry a non-Jew and you get drawn in the outward direction. So, to your children and grandchildren being Jewish is a completely alien notion. [PL 13f]

Some other respondents, even if they are persuaded that assimilation does no good, are also aware of the fact that it has affected their lives, that assimilation has changed their lifestyles. One of them said: 'In some sense [assimilation] is a threat. I myself am a completely assimilated Jew. So, looking at myself, it does constitute a threat.' [PL 38f] Other interviewees, on the other hand, held that assimilation is not to be feared, even if it implies intermarriage:

> Assimilation is insignificant. It depends on what kind of assimilation it is. If you know the language of your host country, its customs and

traditions, if you dress like the local people, then it's not a threat. I love Poland. My wife was a Pole, and she was a very good wife; we respected each other and lived together for forty-one years. [PL 7m]

Another person, accepting the fact that she is an assimilated Jew, points to the difference between the assimilation of her father's generation and that of her own:

I'd say [being assimilated] means participating in the [public] life of the country one lives in as far as culture and all other things, while having one's own awareness. I mean you have this awareness only for yourself or you cultivate it and take part in various meetings just because you're Jewish. But this should be seen on an individual basis. I think I am an assimilated Jew, sure, but I'm also a Pole of Jewish origin. I can't find any unambiguous definition of myself. It was of extraordinary importance to me to find out that an assimilated Jew of today is something totally different from what it was before the war. My father always used to tell me he was assimilated, and I understood I was assimilated, too. But there were a couple of things that didn't fit into it. For if he told me he hadn't known any single Pole before the war, I felt there was something wrong with it. My father hadn't known the 'Aryan' side. When he would get on a tram on the 'Aryan' side he'd wonder why people were making the sign of the cross when they were passing by a church. And though, he was very much assimilated. Now that meant something completely different than today. My father attended a Jewish school with Polish as the language of instruction. He knew Polish literature, he read a lot, had a rich vocabulary and a pure pronunciation. How that can be compared to today's assimilation? It cannot. [PL 10f]

Another person, a woman in her seventies, a physician and a university lecturer, said:

I don't agree that assimilation is a threat because I was raised in the spirit of assimilation. Assimilation is a very complicated issue, it's very difficult to explain it. It is that you can be both a Pole and a Jew at the same time ... I know German Jews could be both German and Jewish. Those whom I knew were more Jewish than German. Being assimilated is about not being different. On the other hand, even if you did things impossible, you'd still keep 'a piece' of your Jewish identity. *Q: Do you consider yourself an assimilated Jew?* Yes. Otherwise I wouldn't be here. [PL 42f]

A woman over 50, a computer technician, pointed out that in general terms assimilation is a natural thing in specific circumstances, and it is a condition *sine qua non* of functioning in a non-Jewish society. Moreover, she argued that in our times, who one is is a question of choice and one can determine one's identity in a number of different ways. In her opinion we could speak of a destructive assimilation only in cases where an individual utterly denies his/her Jewish roots:

> It depends on how you understand assimilation. In some way I'm an assimilated Jew. I'm nonreligious, but that's another thing. But at the same time I haven't lost my Jewish identity. I live in this country, in this particular place, I am a citizen of this country, and in a certain way I'm interested in two kinds of things: Polish and Jewish ... This is the twentieth century, we can't live in kind of ghettos. I don't know how I'd feel in a Jewish *shtetl*. Although, I've never gotten so much assimilated as to think of Christmas Eve as my own holiday since we never had it at home. So, when I prepared Christmas Eve for my children, it was, so to speak, artificial. [PL 14f]

In the sample of American Jews only two people said they were uninterested in the issue of assimilation ('It's not something I think about.' [AM 8f]), and one person was unable to say whether she approved of assimilation or not, though she had given it much consideration. On the whole, most American respondents were opposed to the assimilation of Jews into host cultures. Yet only a few of those who found assimilation a danger to Jewish identity said that the process can clearly be observed in people or families where some basic Jewish customs are practised only rarely, or at random, if they are practised at all, and where only some main holidays are celebrated.

Most of those who claimed that they saw a threat for the Jewish people in assimilation pointed to intermarriage as a fundamental problem. About two out of every three respondents said that they considered intermarriage as the most serious jeopardy looming over the future of American (or, more generally, diaspora) Jews. Exogamy is seemingly perceived as a definitely negative phenomenon, because, as one person phrased it, 'Judaism is a family religion, it's a home religion.' [AM 35m] Here are a few typical opinions:

> I'm always worried that the number of Jews will be diminished. Based on that, I do not believe in intermarriage. I have a daughter who's intermarried. It was, and still is, an extremely painful experience. I will never recover from it. Would I intermarry?

Probably, if I fell in love with somebody. However, I would continue being a Jew, I would continue emphasizing Judaism, and I would definitely not intermarry if I am at the point of my life where I'm raising children, 'cause I'd like to pass Judaism to the children. I come from a family that was asked to convert in Spain or leave. They left. And I feel very proud that they did that, that they stood for who they were and what they believed in. And I feel very much to blame, maybe, for that fact that my own child, after so many centuries of continuity, broke that line. [AM 22f]

I hate to see Jews die out. *Q: Do you think assimilation constitutes a kind of threat to Jewishness?* Oh yes. Definitely. *Q: And intermarriage?* That's the worst. Intermarriage is the worst part of it as far as losing our identity. Assimilation is a little different. I guess I'm assimilated, but I'm Jewish. [AM 30f]

I'm against intermarriage and I'm against assimilation. I don't want the Jewish people to disappear as a group. *Q: Do you consider yourself an assimilated Jew?* No. My Jewish identity is very strong. I don't really socialize very much with non-Jews. I would be very upset if either of my children married a non-Jew. I have members of my family who married non-Jews and I'm sorry about that. [AM 42f][58]

Since the issue of intermarriage is not only widely discussed by common people but is a problem that the Jewish law deals with very seriously, it will not be out of place to cite what a professional cantor said on the topic:

In principle, it almost goes without saying that I'm opposed to mixed marriage. I am unhappy with my colleagues who officiate them, and who officiate at marriages with clergy of other faiths. I feel this is a very big step towards assimilation. I can't say enough about disapproval. The extenuation part is that there are circumstances, and ... it's gonna happen. And I do not condemn everyone that engages in mixed marriage. But as a general rule, I could not officiate a mixed marriage without conversion. [AM 19m]

There were a couple of respondents in the American sample who were even more fiercely opposed to assimilation and intermarriage than others. Below is a fragment of the enunciation of a woman belonging to a Hassidic community:

[Assimilation] constitutes a great threat to the Jewish people. I live

> in New York City where there are millions [sic] of Jewish people who don't intermarry, Orthodox, Hassidic. [To them] it is definitely a threat, especially today. The rate [of intermarriage] is so high that they say that assimilation is killing off more Jews than the Holocaust did. Because if you don't have a Jewish mother ... I'm strictly opposed to intermarriage between blacks and whites. I think people should stay with the people from whence they come. [AM 50f]

What is striking is that the woman compares mixed marriage to the Holocaust. Although it is not commonplace to view intermarriage in these terms, she was not the only person to see a parallel between the Shoah and Jews marrying out of the stock; there were other people who had a similar opinion:

> I think assimilation is the most dangerous thing going on, comparable only to the Holocaust. And mixed marriages, if it doesn't result in a conversion and creation of a Jewish family, it's just an extension of the Holocaust. And it's obviously an extension of the assimilation as well. So, assimilation is something to be highly discouraged for Jews. [AM 11m]
>
> I think it [assimilation] is a modern holocaust. People use that term, it's not my own. The tremendous amount of assimilation, or conversion to other faiths, is a loss to us as much as ... anybody who would have died in a camp. To me assimilation is a loss, it's a terrible thing. [AM 12m]

On the other hand, there was one person who said overtly that he found comparing intermarriage to the Holocaust offensive. He was a man of 43, a member of a Conservative synagogue and also active in the Workmen's Circle. He had a story of his own – one concerning mixed marriage. He had once had a serious relationship with a woman whose father was Jewish and whose mother was black. He said that for him to marry her, she would have had to convert, at which suggestion the woman was outraged. Significantly, while recounting the story, the respondent admitted he might be considered a racist because of his position on why he could not marry the woman. At the same time he was aware that this kind of behaviour was emotional in character rather than intellectual; he could not help it. To be precise, his general attitude toward intermarriage was twofold, emotional and intellectual at the same time:

> I have an emotional response and an intellectual response. I had a

reaction to a certain part of the American Jewish community [that] tends to be more Orthodox part of the community and officially fights intermarriage. They say that intermarriage is the new Holocaust. I find that disgusting ... actually blasphemous in a certain way. I like living here in Brooklyn because my neighbors are Mexican, and black, and white, Irish, and Italian, and Jewish – it's all mixed together. *Q: Do you consider yourself an assimilated Jew?* No. I couldn't imagine marrying someone who's not Jewish. And I think that has a lot to do with my identity as a child of a refugee. I feel like I owe something to my people to keep Judaism alive in whatever form makes sense. It doesn't make sense intellectually, it's an emotional feeling. [AM 48m]

Characteristically, in the passages cited above, we can see some similarity to Emil Fackenheim's idea of the 614th commandment which forbids Jews to cease being Jewish lest Hitler should gain a posthumous victory. We can assume that among American Jews Fackenheim's concept was tacitly accepted and perceived as an expression of opposition to voluntary assimilation. Two of my American respondents agreed that that there is some likeness between their views and that of Fackenheim. One said that the Holocaust compels him 'to try to be a better Jew for all those who did not survive. And my grandparents, and my great-grandparents, and many of my cousins who were killed, most of them were Gerer Hasidim[59] who were very Orthodox.' Yet he claimed that the Shoah 'is not the primary [neither] the only [factor shaping his identity,] it's really a minor component of it'. He also maintained that assimilation, understood in terms of sheer numbers, is not the greatest threat, because 'for Judaism to survive it never depended on how many Jews there were. It's never depended on numbers.' [AM 11m] The other person, a 30-year-old man (the youngest of the American informants), said that the Shoah made him reflect on 'the sense that how important it is to continue living a Jewish life'. Asked whether his way of thinking was close to the commandment added by Fackenheim, he answered: 'Yes. I mean, it's that idea. It's not a conscious thing but I can relate to what he said.' [AM 13m]

Interestingly enough, two of my Polish interviewees mentioned Fackenheim even though they were not asked whether they were familiar with his ideas (I simply did not expect Polish respondents to know much about current-day American Jewish theology). One of them said that even though he 'discovered Fackenheim's 614th commandment fairly late in life' [PL 48m], he realized that he had been practising this commandment without knowing it. The other respondent said that he simply accepted Fackenheim's formula. He was convinced that 'Fackenheim's 614th commandment really shows how much the continuation of the Jews after the Shoah depends on me. Each of us here in Poland is a survivor. Maybe in America it's different ... although not. So, in this sense, it's even a greater obligation.' [PL 49m]

We should also note that those interviewees who likened assimilation, and especially intermarriage, to the Holocaust made, in fact, an act of ethical judgment. They saw assimilation as morally reprehensible behaviour, as committing a crime. If those who perpetrated the Shoah did what was morally evil and were to be held accountable for that, by the same token those who are assimilators and who intermarry are to be held accountable for the dwindling numbers of American Jews, which in these respondents' opinion made that behaviour similar – not, of course, in terms of cruelty, but in terms of statistics – to the killing off of the Jews by the Nazis. One more person alluded to the morally questionable aspect of assimilation in the following way:

> Assimilation is very bad for the Jewish people. Definitely. A Jew is supposed to marry another Jew. And it's a very simple reasoning because when a Jew marries a non-Jew, his religious values deteriorate and you don't follow, you don't do anything. Anybody can say they were born a Jew but do you practice? And it's the practicing that makes a person a Jew. And the less you practice the further you go from being ... the best Jew you can be [to] the worst Jew you can be. Now, assimilation puts people to *the worst Jew you can be*, if not un-Jewish at all ... So assimilation is a *deterioration* of the Jewish people. [Italics added.] [AM 6m]

Yet for quite a number of respondents, assimilation is not so unambiguously destructive for the Jewish community. They pointed to both negative and positive aspects of the phenomenon. The first thing they mentioned was a feeling of 'normalcy': being seen and regarding oneself as a common citizen, as someone not to be ashamed of his/her identity. As someone put it, however, 'assimilation is a threat to Jewish identity, I think it's just a normal process and I think assimilation, at least in the United States, it used to be the way it goes'. [AM 3m] Another respondent even said that 'it's nice to assimilate, it's nice to be part of everybody else and to get along with everyone and to share the normal stuff'. She also was wondering: 'Maybe there couldn't be a Holocaust if everyone was intermarried?' [AM 5f] Also, one of the most important gains of the assimilation of American Jews, many argued, is that thanks to American meritocracy, they were able to climb the social ladder with considerably fewer obstacles than had been the case with their ancestors in Europe:

> I think assimilation has been a double-edge sword for American Jews. It was the thing that enabled the majority of the American Jewish population to succeed relatively rapidly in the twentieth century – and I'm a beneficiary of it. But I'm also a beneficiary of a much longer tradition of emphasis on education, and learning, and thinking. So, it's hard to separate those two. And I personally – and I think this is true of a lot of secular Jews – find expressions of very strong Jewish identity, religious identity, the whole idea of the chosen people as very offensive.[60] And yet, there's a way in which I'm critical of American Jewish assimilation if it requires one to hide the fact that one is Jewish. [AM 26f]
>
> It's not that I don't approve of intermarriage, I think that has to be put in proportion. There's a positive aspect to it and I think on a certain level it's even necessary to have some social integration. You can't have social integration with zero percent intermarriage. There's an absolute positive element to cultural mixing and combining of heritages and cultures. [AM 46m]

It is very interesting to analyse the family background of the last respondent cited above. He is a university professor who teaches in the field of Jewish studies. He grew up in a small town in the West, in what he said was a completely assimilated family. This is how he described his home:

> Being Jewish had very little meaning for me as a pre-teen youngster. I didn't have Jewish friends. We always celebrated the Jewish holidays, we went to a classic Reform Jewish synagogue. And my parents were like the 60s liberals. *Q: Did they keep kosher?* No. We [had] a totally non-kosher home. I don't think that I even knew what Sabbath meant. I'm not even sure what Sabbath dinner meant until I went to college. [AM 46m]

Another person, a Modern-Orthodox rabbi, remarked that assimilation was indeed a serious problem for American Jewry, but said that it was not intermarriage in itself that constituted the real problem. To him, intermarriage only indicates a deeper crisis of the identity of American Jews. And this crisis, paradoxically, is a result of the openness of American culture:

> I think assimilation is a very serious threat. The community seems

to be on the brink of a significant decline in numbers and energy because of loss of population to assimilation. [However,] intermarriage is not the worst thing. Intermarriage is a symptom, not a cause – that's the way I would put it. It's a symptom ... And many Jews are living a poor quality Jewish life. In the free world and the Western world there's a tremendous multiplicity, openness, breakdown of barriers, breakdown of stereotypes, and discrimina- tory behavior. So, the paradoxical result is that for Jews, particularly the Jews who are most integrated, is that it becomes a drift out of the community, rather than a drift into it – that's why it's such a threat. [AM 29m]

Two other interviewees claimed that though they generally do see a threat for Jewish identity in progressive assimilation, under some conditions they cherish the values of American open society, even if one of its consequences is that in a number of mixed marriages, the offspring will have no sense of Jewishness. The positive side to it is the very possibility of being part of American society, on the one hand, and enhancing the group's genetic pool, on the other:

Well, the numbers are not going to increase geometrically if there's assimilation because the children of the intermarried parents prob- ably many of them will blend into the majority society. *Q: Do you think it might be better for the Jewish people, for it's survival in demographic terms, to live in a shtetl or some kind of an isolated area?* No. Absolutely not. I like an open society. And if we lose some people – that's their hard luck. [AM 45f]

Q: Do you think intermarriage is a threat to Jewishness? Absolutely. Absolutely. When you have fifty percent of Jews marry out and their children aren't raised Jewish, you're losing, and our birth rate is ridiculous. The other thing is in terms of enriching the genetic pool. I have no problem with intermarriage where there is Jewish continuity. [AM 47f]

In one interview the respondent was very clear about his views regarding intermarriage – namely, that Jews should only marry Jews – and yet at the same time he was able to transgress the frame of religious restrictions and be receptive toward those who have inter- married. This was a rare case when a respondent (and an Orthodox one) opposing intermarriage in general was in favour of accepting within the Jewish community those who, in the judgment of Halakhic law, should be ostracized: 'What I feel is that the people that have intermarried should be ... included in the community to ... a certain extent but I think that we should also encourage Jews to marry other Jews so that there would be continuation of the Jewish people.' [AM 13m]

Of course, there were also interviewees who generally saw assimilation and/or intermarriage in a positive light, without, of course, advocating a total blending into American society and without willing a complete loss of Jewish identity. In their enunciations one could notice some kind of acceptance – maybe not so much of assimilation as a social project to be realized at all costs, but rather an acceptance of the people who are assimilated, who have intermarried, and who are at times marginalized. Also, for some of the respondents, assimilation meant assuming the positive, constructive values of Western civilization:

> I think the threat is when you have people who were raised Jewish with no morals, with no real values. I don't see a threat from assimilation. In some ways I see just as much of a threat from certain kinds of Jewish Orthodoxy that will take Jews away from their understanding that Judaism has certain universal themes that are central to it. And if it doesn't have those universal themes then it's frankly no different than any other tribalism that someone might go into. [AM 1m]
>
> Very hard for me to answer that question because in my own family both my daughters intermarried. So, it's a hard question for me, it's something I had to accept. And I don't have a problem with it because my grandchildren so far are being brought up with very strong Jewish identity but neither of my sons-in-law converted. But they [the children] are learning about both religions and so far it's working. Even with my daughters' in-laws, people that we've always spoken about the Holocaust and spoken about other things. And I find it very nice that we're all getting together, respecting each other's religions. I go to them for their holidays, they come to me for my holidays, and honestly, it's working. So my family ... I have to accept it. And I don't see it as a threat; I see it more as accepting each other, respecting each other. [AM 15f]
>
> We officiated intermarriages [in City Congregation]; we would never suggest that such a marriage not take place. Our movement's view is that a Jew is basically anyone who identifies with those struggles in the history of the Jewish people. Personally I do not believe that the Jewish people are gonna be wiped out by intermarriage. *Q: Do you consider yourself an assimilated Jew?*

> No, I don't. And the reason for that is that I have a very strong identification of myself as Jewish ... When I think of assimilation I think of people who no longer have a distinct identity from other people around them. [AM 38f]

It seems to be of utmost interest and importance to analyse how both Polish and American Jews have interiorized *das Ereignis Auschwitz*. At this stage of the study we shall see whether – and, if so, how – the Holocaust has impacted their Jewish self-consciousness. We shall submit to comparative analysis those parts of the interviews in which the informants were answering the question: 'Has the Holocaust affected your Jewish identity? Do you think that your being Jewish is in some way determined by the Shoah?' All respondents answering the question can be intuitively divided into three groups: those whose identity has been in some important ways influenced by the Holocaust; those who are unaffected; and finally those who do not rule out any such influence, yet claim that it was only one (and not necessarily the most significant) among many elements shaping their identity as Jews. Nevertheless, we have to note with emphasis that virtually all the interviewees said that the Holocaust did affect them in one way or another. However, although most of the respondents in both samples stated that they had been impacted by the European catastrophe qua Jews, some said that the event was significant to them only qua people. Of course, it is not always easy to differentiate between the two things, and in many cases the two planes overlapped. The most typical – and at the same time the most striking – point is how the Shoah has affected my informants' family life, which is a problem they viewed as a Jewish issue, but also as a general psychological one.

Let us start with the Polish sample where twenty-six people said that the Shoah did affect their Jewish identity, which is slightly more than one half of the group. One might have expected a greater percentage of respondents to answer the question affirming that they did experience such an impact on their lives – after all, they are either survivors or children of survivors. Yet if we take into account the fact that quite a number of the people from the second generation were raised with hardly any knowledge of their Jewishness, and that their parents would sometimes refuse to talk about their war experiences to the children, then it seems quite understandable that almost half of the interviewees said the Shoah had an insignificant impact on them or even they were unable to answer the question.

One of the most interesting cases to analyse is a 42-year-old man whose mother is Polish. Answering the first question in the conversation (the general question regarding Jewish identity, but without any explicit or implicit mention of the Holocaust), he said:

> I feel a Jew because the Shoah was something that would have involved my life if I had lived at that time ... [I remember when] my schoolmates tried to pull my pants down, now I can guess they wanted to check up whether I was circumcised. But I'm not, of course. Who would have done it to their child after the war? Besides that, my mother was Polish and there was no *mohel*[61] in Poland ... To me a Jew is a fighter. In World War II my father took part in the Warsaw Uprising [in 1944] and he was a Communist. He also saved over ten people from his family from certain death – he smuggled them out of the ghetto. It all would have affected me, this Jewish bravery. It was not you, Poles, it was us, Jews, it was me. For me the Shoah today is a question of my relation to Poles, to my Jewishness, to my Polishness – not to being a Pole but to my Polishness. The Shoah is the background of my reflections. This is what separates me from Poles. On the other hand, I long for the time when Jew and Pole meant the same to me. [PL 5m]

A 40-year-old woman, who had cooperated with a Jewish organization in collecting testimonies of survivors, confessed:

> When I saw the topic of your dissertation I started to think about what kind of impact the Shoah has upon me. The knowledge of the Shoah has surely influenced me. I guess it has affected my identity in terms that I can't separate myself from the people who had gone through these things if I'm connected with them by blood ... I conducted over 400 interviews and the stories I heard cannot be farther from normal human experiences and that hasn't left me unaffected. [On the other hand,] my Polish friends have more or less normal families, like grandparents, and I never had a grandpa or grandma. These are the kind of wounds that can't leave you unchanged. I don't know whether it was just the Shoah or also the Kielce pogrom and antisemitism in general. All these things overlap one another. [PL 8f]

Another informant, a 51-year-old woman, said how the knowledge of the Shoah has not only impacted but strengthened her Jewish identity, how it helped her retrieve that identity from the depths of the unknown:

> Q: *Do you think that your awareness of the Shoah might have*

affected your Jewish identity? Oh, definitely. When I wanted to find an answer why that happened I started to read books. Thanks to that I could learn what had happened to my father's parents. I don't remember any literature on the topic [being taught] in school. And then, I really experienced it not as literature but as life, life that could have been my own and my parents' who could have not existed. I remember I got obsessed with it, for three years I was reading but this kind of literature. At night I would have nightmares and I'd wake up. There was no one to talk to about it, so I didn't feel well. I was afraid of talking about it – that was after I graduated high school. And then they founded the association 'Children of the Holocaust – Second Generation'. It gathers people born after the war, just like me, people whose Jewish identity had been kept in secret by their parents, people who don't have big families. And it turned out that during these meetings of the association there are four therapists, as if everyone really had some kind of problems. Also those who, after all, hadn't had an immediate experience of that trauma, who don't have that trauma, who didn't live through the Holocaust. [Despite that] each [of us] has his/her individual experiences and it turns out that our generation suffers from complexes, terror and fear occasioned by the Shoah. [PL 10f]

In a few cases the respondents stated clearly and unambiguously that the Holocaust is the one single event that determined their identity as Jews. Asked whether the Shoah has had any impact on her Jewish identity, one person said: 'Well, yes. Actually this is a fundamental component of that identity. Kind of a feeling of obligation – I feel that in me all the time.' [PL 39f][62] Another person, also a child of survivors, said: 'That's the main element, of course.' [PL 40f] Another respondent, another child of survivors, declared:

I would risk the statement that if not for the Shoah I wouldn't have been a Jew – if not for the Holocaust – because my family, as far as I know, had been completely assimilated. They were the kind of Jews who'd never go to synagogue, or if they did it was once a year. So, if not for the Shoah I would probably have been a totally different person. And what happened made me think that I didn't really have much of a choice. [PL 15m]

Speaking in a similar vein, other people underscored the importance of the Shoah for themselves and their children. Many said that the

Holocaust 'intensifies Jewish identity' and that they 'continue to live with the problem' [PL 28f]. One respondent, when asked if the Holocaust had any impact on her Jewish identity, confessed:

> Yes, an enormous impact. That's a crucial point. I was born in a family, in a home which was filled with Polishness. I can say I feel as much a Jew as I feel a Pole. And I suspect that if not for the Shoah, if not for the fact that my father's family – my father was born in Warsaw in a family that had lived in Warsaw for many generations – all of his loved ones, beginning with his parents, died here. Since I was raised mainly in Polish culture, if it hadn't been for the dramatic past of my grandparents, I probably wouldn't have realized my connection to Jewishness, it wouldn't have been so important for me. I am married to a Polish woman and want to transmit my Jewish experiences to my children so that they keep the memory of this nation – and here the Shoah has a fundamental significance. [PL 32m]

Some survivors said that the Holocaust had influenced their identities even in a 'fundamental way'. [PL 44f] One of the two oldest respondents, survivor of a small ghetto near Warsaw, said:

> Not for a single day, not for a moment do I stop thinking about it. You can't imagine such experiences ... They took away my mother, my whole family – over thirty people. I'm an old man but I can't forget ... Till my last day, till I close my eyes. Although I'm more attached to Poland, to Polish culture, to our nation, but always, even in my dreams, this thought never leaves me. I know that innocent people were dying only because they were of Jewish descent. [PL 7m]

A woman who survived Auschwitz said that those who did not live through the things she had experienced cannot imagine the immensity of the war horrors. Although she claimed that her Jewish identity was little affected, if at all, by the Shoah, it is apparent that she had shared the typical fate of Jews during the war:

> I'll make it brief: you, as a young person, are unable to imagine [what I went through]; on my own eyes my father was murdered, almost on my eyes. If it hadn't been for my Polish friends, you wouldn't be talking with me now. For I walked after my father when they took him. These are things you can't imagine. I can't forget the Shoah, I can't forget what I went through and what my

family did. *Q: Do you think that you feel Jewish also because the Shoah affected the Jewish people?* No. I don't have that bond to Jewry – because there are no Jews in Poland. [PL 34f]

For several respondents the Holocaust is an event they do think about, yet it does not constitute the core of their Jewishness. One person said that there was a time when she did perceive the Shoah as a crucial point of reference for her Jewish identity, yet it changed later on: 'The Holocaust for a long time was an important element [of my identity]. Then it ceased being that important, for you can't feel a Jew only because of that horrendous crime and because so many people were murdered. Almost my whole family was murdered. So it can't constitute this one, sole element. But at first it was.' [PL 2f]

One interviewee, a woman aged 51, also argued that the Shoah should not be the only or the most salient factor shaping one's Jewish identity. In fact, she was the only person to allude to the American public discussion on the Holocaust. Her opinion was that that is not necessarily the best way to build one's identity:

> *Q: Does the Holocaust influence your awareness of being Jewish?* Yes, it's also because of the Holocaust, but not above all because of that, and not only because of that. It's neither a necessary, nor a sufficient condition. It is an important condition, an important element of that identity. So, of course it's an important thing but not a component of a definition of the Jew. [PL 46f]

Asked whether it occurs to her to talk about the Holocaust with other people, she answered:

> I don't avoid it and I don't provoke it, either. The subject is just there. It is an essential topic also in a negative context because I think that many of us, many Jews, build their identity on the Shoah. Of course, I'm not talking about the survivors, for they have the right for anything; I'm talking about those who feel a void and [are searching] for something to fill their identity with; and they [ask:] How to perpetuate Jewishness in the contemporary world? The easiest answer is to invoke the Holocaust. This is what's happening, this is how the Holocaust has been invoked in the United States for the last thirty years. In Poland, too, when you want to touch the question of your identity you start talking of the Holocaust. I often think about it terms of a total disagreement with it. The whole issue of Holocaust reparations is an

element of a larger intellectual strategy with which I have nothing
to do and I don't wanna have anything to do. [PL 46f]

Among the six informants (12 per cent) who claimed that the Shoah
had had hardly any impact on them, most said that many of their family
members had not survived the war, which was common to all Polish
respondents. Yet this fact seemingly did not have a direct impact on the
group in question. A characteristic opinion was that they saw the
European catastrophe more as an historical fact and that they did not
feel any 'special attachment to their nation as a result of the Shoah'.
[PL 20m] One of them, a 57-year-old woman, when asked whether she
felt some special bond to the Jewish people because of the Holocaust,
said: 'I guess not. I was raised in a Jewish atmosphere. The only link I
have with the Holocaust is that my grandparents and my family died in
the Holocaust. And I've been afraid that if there were a war such things
could happen. I learned about the Shoah in school. In fact, my parents
didn't tell me anything about it.' [PL 43f]

In the American sample the overall proportions were somewhat
different, especially as far as those who claimed that their Jewish identity
had been unaffected by the Holocaust. Twenty-four people (46 per cent)
said that the Holocaust did have an influence on their feeling Jewish;
eleven respondents (21 per cent) said that their Jewishness had little to
do with the Shoah. Others were undecided or seemed to contend
that their Jewish identity was both independent of the Holocaust and
somehow impacted by it.

Let us start this analysis with a quote from a female survivor who
argued that the Holocaust had in significant ways shaped her identity:

> For me the Holocaust has made me what I am. I am absolutely
> certain that had I not lived through that period of time I would
> have been in some way a different person. I know that my
> view of everything is colored by the experience I had during the
> Holocaust. Absolutely. It is a primary reason why I am what I am.
> [AM 31f]

Here, as was the case with one Polish survivor, the answer is very brief,
somewhat less emotional, but not less firm. It might seem interesting
that the children of survivors were more willing to dwell on the
consequences of the Shoah for their Jewish self-consciousness. Below
are a couple of examples of how the children saw the impact of their
parents' sufferings on their own lives:

Both my parents are Holocaust survivors, and I relate to the Holocaust, I relate to it in terms of ... what it means in terms of history, and what it means in terms of repeating of history, and the Jew's place in the world – why he's so persecuted by the Gentile population. So, the Holocaust is very meaningful to me, and it has affected my parents' lives ... the lack of an extended family relates directly to the Holocaust. I know that when I speak to anyone, they can go to a family gathering where they have hundreds and hundreds of people who are relatives. We can go to a small restaurant and only take one table up. So, we are different because of that reason. [AM 11m]

Q: Do you think the Holocaust may have impacted your Jewish identity? Well, I guess the answer is 'yes', but indirectly. Judaism itself doesn't really have any relationship with the Holocaust. However our lives do have a relationship with the Holocaust because the Lubavitch movement, the leaders, were affected by what happened to them in Europe and my parents were affected by what happened to them in Europe ... And as a son of Holocaust survivors, when I say my prayers, especially at certain times of the year, when we think about those who died, you know, you question God too, like: How did he let that happen? My father, every time you get him talking about it, he can talk for hours and hours and hours about what happened in the Holocaust and the inhumanity of people. Would I be a different Jew if the Holocaust hadn't happened? Well, I think that would have to do with my upbringing. My parents brought me up with a certain fear, I guess, that came from being a Holocaust survivor. Anyone who survived the Holocaust, and I've met plenty of people, whether they openly admit it or unadmittedly, there is a lot of psychological changes that have happened unless ... there were certain people that were lucky and were able to stay in a relatively, if I can use the word, safe environment during the war. [AM 6m]

One interviewee underscored the fact that the Nazi Holocaust had probably significantly impacted her family's attitude toward assimilation. Not only most of her parents' friends were Jewish survivors, but she was sent to a Jewish school – in order for her Jewishness not to dissolve into the popular American culture:

The Holocaust played a vital part in my Jewish identity because my parents are Holocaust survivors. And I grew up also in my early

childhood ... all my playmates, many of my playmates were children of Holocaust survivors because they are the people my parents
associated with socially. And, maybe because of the Holocaust my
parents did not rush to become assimilated Americans but sent me
to [a Jewish] school so that I can learn Jewish history and
culture – not during the day but after regular school. [AM 20f]

Another quotation will illustrate a typical story of an American Jew
who does not have any survivors in his family and who has learned
about the *Churban Europa* mainly from school textbooks and from the
American popular culture. Born in the Pacific West, this 36-year-old
man started his career as a university professor in the area of Jewish
studies. To the question: 'Does the Holocaust play any role whatsoever
in your Jewish identity?' he answered:

Absolutely. *Q: Is it still valid, relevant to your defining as a Jew?*
Absolutely. There's no doubt. No matter how secular or even separated from Jews a Jew is, there is something about that knowledge
that at one time and place in history a government presided over the
attempt to exterminate the Jewish people wherever they were. It
affects a Jew, any Jew in the world, it's impossible to be neutral on
that. I remember actually my mom having us sit and watch a film
called 'The Holocaust', it was in 1978. It was a Hollywood
production. I would have been like 11. And she had the whole
family watch that for like four–five nights. So, my parents made me
watch that. That had a certain impact. My grandparents talked about
it a lot. My grandfather ... had two major themes: Pearl Harbor and
the Holocaust. He couldn't get over what he called the cowardice of
the Japanese. And then the Nazis and the Germans—the two things
he'd bring up time and time again. I was hearing that stuff. *Q: Did
your parents talk about it?* Not really, I have to say. We lived in a
beach town in the West Coast of the United States in a non-Jewish
community. And we weren't religious. I learned about the Holocaust
in a regular history course. [AM 46m]

The next story was told by a rabbi, raised in Brooklyn and educated
in traditional yeshivas as well as in American public schools, and now
a well-known Jewish leader:

Emotionally, [the Holocaust] is an event with tremendous emotional power. I think here I am a typical Jew, at least typical of my
generation. There's some argument whether young people have

the same feeling – I believe the answer is 'yes' despite claims to the contrary. But certainly in my generation, again, it was such a powerful emotion: the feeling of exposure, and risk, and pain, and suffering. It paradoxically led people to identify more – (a) with fellow Jews and (b) with Jewish existence and Jewish faith. And that's pretty my life, too ... My parents lost a good part of their family, and this was communicated; I don't remember the conversations, but it was communicated. *Q: So you remember your parents talk about the destruction of European Jews at the time when it was happening ...?* Not so much talk about. What I remember is my mother cried, and conversations they didn't have in my presence, 'cause apparently they didn't want to upset their children. I also remember right after the war a cousin and an aunt visiting my parents, like a year after the war – I would have been 13. I learned many years later that they had survived an *Einsatzgruppen* shooting; and that's what they had reported to my parents, including the death of family members. At the time that they met I was not told the fact, but I remember the intensity of the pain and of the crying and so on ... When I graduated high school I took an English literature examination. This was 1949, I was 16 years old. You had to write an essay and you had a list of topics – and one of the topics simply said 'Wanted'. That was the topic. On the spot I knew what I was gonna write and I wrote it. And it was basically describing how the Jews of Europe are driven from their homes and are being persecuted, they try to go to different places, and everywhere they go they find there's a big sign saying 'Unwanted'. And the punch line was in the last paragraph; and I said: 'So they're captured, because they can't escape, they're put on a train, they arrive at Auschwitz, the gas chambers, and there's a big sign saying: 'Wanted'. [AM 29m]

There were, indeed, informants who were critical of some aspects of 'Holocaust-identity', so to speak, though the Holocaust was a significant event to them as Jews. The respondent cited below claimed that the Shoah affected her Jewishness in terms of a resolute opposition to racism and other kinds of discrimination. She said that as a Jew, and because of the Holocaust, she is more committed to anti-racism, to non-violent civil resistance, and to fighting oppression. The point she is critical about concerns various uses, and misuses, of the memory of the Holocaust:

I think any group that has gone through a historical trauma is entitled to have a sense of ... a bit more security by belonging to this group. So, we're all survivors in that kind of large sense. But I think it gets very inappropriate when people who have not experienced that kind of suffering use that legacy to ... legitimate any kind of political stance, for example things that I'm critical about – actions of the state of Israel when they say: 'We're a nation founded by survivors of this unique horrible historical experience, and therefore we can just pursue any policy.' I disagree with that. And I think it gets even slipperier in the US because the vast majority of American Jews are very far historically from that experience, although not like metaconsciously in actuality. And I think that Israel and the Holocaust are used sometimes to justify very conservative political positions that I don't agree with. So, it makes me angry when the history is misused. [AM 26f]

As for those who found it difficult to state clearly whether the Shoah did influence their sense of Jewish identity or not, it may be argued that on different planes the event had different connotations for them. Historically it is relevant to them, as is any other fact of Jewish history, whereas in terms of ethnic consciousness it does not bring about much of a change. They would not be 'less Jewish if there hadn't been a Shoah', as one interviewee phrased it, but at the same time 'it is something that has significance' [AM 49f] in terms of historical context. It is exactly this context that another respondent alluded to in his enunciation:

I make reference to the Shoah in the same way I make references to the Chmelnitzky massacres. I make reference to the Shoah in the same way I would make reference to every catastrophe, and that's what 'shoah' means ... I don't believe that one can view the history of Judaism without mentioning the Shoah. That does not mean that it is the ... be-all and end-all of Judaism. [However,] to the Holocaust survivors, for instance, their entire world may be around the Shoah. And I will not judge them harshly for that. The remarkable thing about the Shoah survivors is that for the most part they continued ... *el-al*, onward, upward. [AM 25m]

Another interviewee saw two sides in recalling the Shoah: one is a natural inclination of people whose kinsmen suffered a terrible tragedy, the other is making of the Holocaust some kind of ersatz identity:

I certainly think that the Holocaust or things like that are a big part of Jewish identity even for someone like me who's born after the Holocaust. I think a lot of people use the Holocaust in a sense to bolster their identity, especially if they're not very observant or have nothing else to really hang it on. I suppose to some degree I think part of Jewish identity is unfortunately ... not constant persecution, but frequent enough – one that's not necessarily that far from it. In that sense I think the Holocaust has some part of my identity. But I don't think of myself as constantly referring to it. We've all met people who ... you can't talk with them for five minutes without it coming along. I don't think it's like one of the first two three defining characteristics of my identity. It depends on the context. [AM 43m]

Those who contend that they do not treat the Shoah as an essential element of their Jewish identity do not say they ignore or disregard the event totally. They affirm that they build their identity on 'positive things' rather than on memory 'of persecution', and that generally it is the positive things that are 'the basis of Jewish identity'. [AM 13m] One of the informants, a 51-year-old man working for an important American Jewish institution, explained:

The Holocaust doesn't really speak to me. I shouldn't say that – it does speak to me in the sense that it's the dominant event of our times, except possibly for the birth of the state of Israel. So it certainly does speak to me but *it doesn't speak to my Jewish identity*. What the Holocaust speaks to me is a terrible chapter in the Jewish experience, the most terrible chapter. I'm also upset by those who see the Holocaust as a lens on which to look upon what being a Jews is. It's a very poor lens on the Jewish experience. I also lastly cannot see constructing an identity based upon terrible things happening to Jews. If terrible things happen to Jews I would say: 'So why be Jewish?' It only makes sense if what being a Jew means is worth preserving. Under both circumstances it doesn't matter whether there is a Holocaust or whether there is complete acceptance of Jews. In other words, *it's irrelevant to Jewish identity* ... obviously I have no sympathy for the enemies of the Jews but I'm also not going to allow them to define who I am as a Jew. So I don't think the Holocaust should be relevant. It doesn't mean it's not relevant; it's quite relevant to many numbers of Jews. I think there is a trend in Jewish life increasingly to construct one's identity upon the Holocaust and that trend is one that Jewish leaders need to combat. [Italics added.] [AM 2m]

Here again we have an allusion to Emil Fackenheim. The man cited above rejects such a vision of Jewish identity where the Holocaust is a crucial element building that identity. If Fackenheim said: being Jewish today means saying *no* to Hitler, this respondent replied: no Hitler or any other Jew-hater will be granted the right to determine on what Jewish identity should be based.

In some respect, a similar answer was given by a woman in her mid-70s, who also put much emphasis on the fact that Jews as a nation have a lot of achievements to be proud of. She also argued that the sufferings of the Shoah – the result of extreme inhumanity – do not have the potential to define her identity, although they should not be left to oblivion:

> [My Jewish identity] has nothing to do with the Holocaust. My being proud of what I am is because of all the things that they have accomplished, the Jews have accomplished, since the beginning, like five thousand years ago, and also what the Israelis accomplished. Being proud of what I am has nothing to do with the Holocaust. But the Holocaust is done. As I get older I realize the horrors of it, it affects me more as a human being – how people could be so horrible to each other and so inhuman. That affects me more than anything else, I mean any civilization, any peoples, just the horror and inhumanity against humans. [AM 7f]

Another interviewee, a journalist in a Jewish newspaper and, more importantly, a survivor, said:

> There was Jewish identity before the Holocaust, so the Holocaust was not the catalyst for my Jewish identity. It's just another chapter in the history of being Jewish. It is not a *raison d'être*. For some people being Jewish means either Israel or the Holocaust. For me being Jewish is being Jewish because of the history, of who I am. I'm a descendant of Jews. I can trace my family back to Spain. [AM 47f]

In the final analysis we can draw the conclusion that the respondents' attitude toward assimilation has, in some respects, much to do with their relationship to the Shoah. One general remark is that in both samples about one half of the respondents claimed that the Holocaust did play a certain role in defining their Jewish identity. This may seem somewhat strange, since Polish Jewry is a community that lives in the very place where the mass murder of Jews was perpetrated; thus one could have expected Polish Jews to have a more direct attachment to the memory of the Shoah. One the other hand, we have to take into

consideration the fact that a significant number of Polish Jews interviewed in Warsaw did not straightforwardly oppose assimilation. The
reason thereof may be twofold: first and foremost, many contemporary
Polish Jews, though children of survivors, had been raised in a non-
Jewish way. Their parents fairly often did not practise Jewish rituals or
customs at home; they sometimes even did not want their children to
be aware of their Jewish roots. Secondly, in numerous cases, survivor-
parents were not willing to reveal their tragic war experiences to their
children. Therefore, for many of the Polish interviewees, their Holocaust consciousness only appeared when they were adolescents or even
later in life. Many of them were aware that they had fewer relatives than
their schoolmates, but did not relate that fact to the destruction of Jewry.

In the American sample, with rare exceptions, most respondents were
aware of their Jewish identity and learned about the Holocaust earlier
than their Polish kinsmen. Of course, it was characteristic for both
samples that in the homes of most of the informants who are children of
survivors their parents did not talk about the Shoah. Yet the American
interviewees had always known they were American Jews, while many of
the Polish respondents had thought, for some time, they were just Poles.
Also, more people in the American sample opposed assimilation than
was the case with the Polish group. The Polish respondents – or many of
them, at least – were aware that Polish Jewry is very much assimilated;
they were so much immersed in the Polish culture, involved in Poland's
public life and aware of its discontents that in consequence their Jewish
identity was, not infrequently, merely symbolic. It is curious, however,
that while many Polish informants said that they were to a certain extent
assimilated, only a few of them admitted unambiguously that they were
completely assimilated – though indeed many were. Even among those
who had no attachment to Jewish religion, nor any knowledge of the
Jewish languages, and even if they did not observe important Jewish
customs – even these respondents often claimed that they were only
partly assimilated because they had a strong feeling of being Jewish.

In the American sample, on the other hand, most of the interviewees
were aware of, and did not deny, the fact that they were Jews assimilated to American culture. It is worthwhile mentioning, however, that
psychologically it was easier for the American respondents to admit
that they were assimilated than for the Polish respondents. First and
foremost, despite some traces of animosity toward the Jews, America
is almost free of anti-Semitism.[63] Thus there are hardly any reasons for
the American Jew to overtly discredit assimilation or to fear being fully

immersed in American life. The situation of Polish Jews is quite dissimilar. Though their rights to Polish citizenship are not questioned, anti-Semitism in Poland is far from non-existent. Although it is not as violent and brutal as it was the 1920s and 1930s, it is more disturbing and vivid than in the United States. Therefore, for some Polish Jews, it might be somewhat more difficult to say that they are assimilated to the Polish culture, because part of Polish culture, including public life, contains the seeds of anti-Semitism. On the other hand, as some Polish interviewees have noted, even if a Jew were 100 per cent assimilated, s/he would always have a 'chance' to meet with anti-Semitic prejudices. One may say: 'If they always consider me a Jew what's the point in insisting that I'm assimilated?'

It seems expedient at this point to dedicate a passage to the issue of assimilation versus acculturation. As we have seen, most respondents replied to the question regarding assimilation by stating what they think of this phenomenon and whether they consider themselves assimilated Jews. A few of my informants, however, made a distinction – and rightly so – between assimilation, traditionally understood, and acculturation. One of them said: 'I think being assimilated to me is something different than being acculturated.' [AM 5f] Another person argued that 'there is partial assimilation, or acculturation, or whatever it might be called'. [PL 49m] I am convinced that these respondents are right in their presumption that assimilation is not exactly the same as acculturation, especially in the context of the Jewish diaspora. I should like to make it clear that I do not refer here to the sweeping definitions of assimilation that some sociologists have put forward: namely, that assimilation is a process of mutual transmission of cultural and economical values leading to absorption of an alien element by one or more groups.[64] I assume the typical notion of assimilation implicitly accepted by all scholars working in the area of Jewish studies: when we speak of assimilation of the Jews we mean gradually losing the characteristic religio-ethnic elements of their culture, together with accepting new social patterns from the host culture. Thus understood, assimilation may be superficial and partial or else it can be thorough and total. Also, we should not neglect the fact that assimilation is considered, by and large, as a negative phenomenon for the minority group.

Acculturation, as I understand it, is devoid of a pejorative connotation and refers to a process whereby an individual or a group adapts itself to a dominant culture. Here I deviate to a certain extent from Celia Heller's definition, which reads that acculturation is about 'individuals moving away from the traditional Jewish culture and toward the culture of the larger society'.[65] If we were to accept that concept of acculturation it would barely differ from that of assimilation. The problem with this definition is that it is too general; it comprises both the idea of assimilation and acculturation *sensu stricto*. What I would propose is a concept that does justice to the notions of assimilation and acculturation as two distinguishable phenomena and, on the other hand, conforms with my interviewees' convictions. I view both assimilation and acculturation as two distinct processes, not contrary to one another but differing in degree and scope. While acculturation is an almost inevitable, even quasi-automatic or unconscious process, assimilation is forced or voluntary, conscious and purposeful. Both phenomena occur in a situation of culture contact; thus we need two social entities – two groups, or an individual and a group.[66] When a minority, or one of its members, encounters the majority group which performs the role of host group, acculturation must occur as if out of necessity because, in the long run, total isolation or ghettoization is not only unproductive and unfunctional but also unfeasible.

Acculturation includes assuming from the host culture such elements as: civil institutions, certain modes of comportment, dressing, dietary customs and language. The problem with language is that normally it is one of the most important elements determining a culture, and totally giving up one's language would signify accepting assimilatory patterns. With the Jewish diaspora, however, it is much more complex an issue. For what is the mother tongue of the Jews? Any language any Jew speaks. Of course, only three generations ago, for a majority of East European Jews the very expression 'mother tongue' (*mameh loshn*) was coterminous with the Yiddish language. This, however, was only a local language which would not be understandable to Jews from Morocco or Ireland. Obviously there is also Hebrew, which is the language of the Bible and the Talmud and contemporary Israel. But for innumerable Jews the world over, their mother tongue was and is a language other than these two; it could have been Ladino, German, French, Spanish, Russian, Polish or some version of Hebrew-Arabic. Therefore, in the context of the Jewish diaspora, after so many centuries of using tens of different languages, abandoning any one of them in favour of another one cannot be considered an element of assimilation. That is why I view the acceptance of either Polish or English as one of the mechanisms of acculturation and not assimilation.[67]

I should also refer to an extremely interesting and practical distinction that Heller makes between cultural assimilation and identificational assimilation.[68] First of all, she maintains that in interwar Poland, Jewish acculturation meant Polonization. And this seems to be true – assuming some elements from the Polish society was not tantamount to a complete loss of one's Jewish identity; therefore it was not total assimilation. At the most it could be called cultural assimilation but certainly not identificational assimilation, for most of those who took on some features of Polishness, especially the language, did not want to cut off their Jewishness. Therefore acculturation is a *selective process*: pick-and-choose, whatever you find of value you may treat as an element of your own culture. The *selectivity* of this process is what marks a sharp difference between acculturation and assimilation. Through this selective adoption of particular aspects of the Polish culture, Polish Jews were Polonizing themselves. But they did not abandon their Jewish identity altogether. Those who did cease regarding themselves as Jews and wanted to be just Poles underwent identificational assimilation. Hence, if we agree that the sum of all processes leading toward progressive integration of an individual or a group into a given host society is called assimilation, then the initial stages of this assimilation can be labelled cultural assimilation or acculturation. This could be illustrated in the following way:

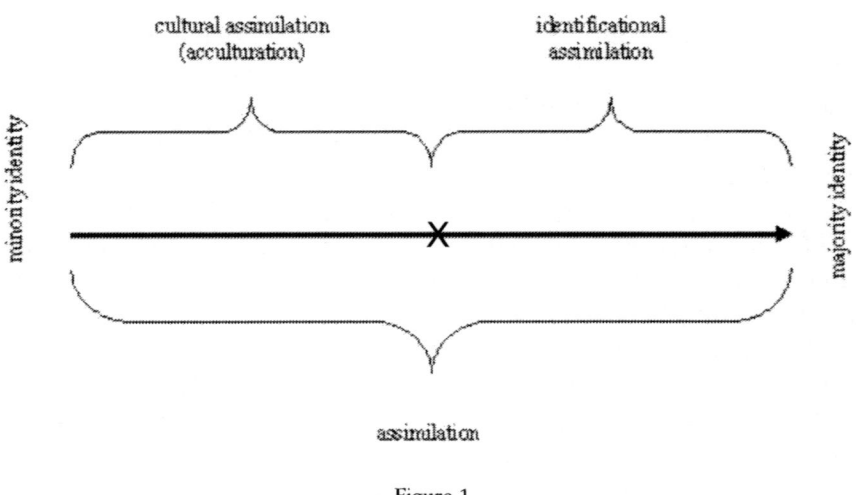

Figure 1

There is yet another difference (apart from scope and degree) between assimilation *sensu lato* and acculturation. It is no less important that while acculturation consists mainly in acquiring new values and enriching one's original identity with specific elements of the dominant culture – without at the same time losing essential features of one's inherited cultural framework – assimilation involves abandoning the world of one's ancestors and erasing various traces of the minority identity. In short, it is 'relinquishing one's cultural identity and moving into the larger society';[69] as such, assimilation can be perceived as a destructive phenomenon. Thus the difference lies in the direction of cultural movement: acculturation means adding new elements (inward movement), whereas assimilation implies removing old elements (out-ward movement). The breaking point between these two movements is marked with the letter 'x' in Figure 1. In other words, during the process of acculturation, an individual or a group acquires an additional identity, while what happens during assimilation is, first of all, pro-gressive losing of the old identity. In fact, even etymologically, the word acculturation gives us a hint that it has to do with some gain and not with a loss: *to a-cculturate means to a-ppropriate and ac-quire (Latin quaerere, to search for, to obtain) additional cultural values, to make them one's own (proper) and thereby obtain a new social status.*

Hence, we may conclude that the respondents from both samples are to be found somewhere around the 'x' point. Some of them have certainly crossed the border of identificational assimilation and identify themselves as Jews only to some extent. This holds true especially for a number of the Polish interviewees. In the American group, on the other hand, no one claimed s/he was more American than Jewish or that his/her Jewish identity held a secondary position. That is perhaps why more American Jews were strongly opposed to assimilation than Polish Jews. That is also why relatively many American respondents were concerned about the loss of Jews in numbers.

Also, we have to bear in mind what one of the Polish informants said: namely, that assimilation is a phenomenon that really took place in the late nineteenth century and until the Second World War. Nowadays in Poland it is difficult to talk about assimilation, not to mention acculturation, for Polish Jews are in a significant measure assimilated, except that they still assert they *are* Jews. In the American group, one would say, most of the respondents are well-acculturated, most of them may be even located exactly at the 'x' point, but their Jewish identity is more vivid, unambiguous and tangible.

Two more important remarks should be made regarding the intervie-wees' relationship to the Holocaust. One is that there is no correlation whatsoever between their attitude toward assimilation (and the degree of assimilation or acculturation they achieved) and the impact of the Shoah on their Jewish identity. Those who are very much assimilated, as well as those who are only to some extent acculturated, argued that the Holocaust means a lot to them as Jews. Yet we may note that those who were religiously observant or very traditional were somewhat less prone to ascribe to the Shoah a leading role in shaping their identity. On the other hand, among those for whom the European catastrophe is only a minor factor determining their Jewishness we have observant believers and secular assimilators alike.

Another remark which I think is not unimportant, pertains to the fact that the survivors find the Shoah an element that has deeply affected their personalities. The same was true in most cases with regard to the children of survivors, especially in the United States. Yet with both survivors and their children it is not always easy to discern whether the impact of the Holocaust was upon their Jewishness or their whole personality. One thing is clear: *a permanent and persistent feeling of a lack of close family, of relatives.*

Most children of survivors in the American sample and virtually all Polish children of survivors confessed that they felt an inexorable sadness and sorrow because of their small families – families whose many members had been murdered by the Nazis. One of the interviewees put in straightforward terms: 'We are a nuclear family.' That was true in many cases: survivors with hardly any relatives, no parents, often no siblings, maybe an uncle or an aunt. And a similar situation with their children: no grandparents, aunts or uncles. In fact, to many an informant, the word 'aunt' was empty; they knew theoretically what the notion 'my mother's sister' might mean but existentially such terms were empty to them. And this was experienced by many, especially by the Polish interviewees, as an aspect of post-Holocaust Jewishness: to be Jewish means to be devoid of an extended family.

So, even if they did not always put it in clear terms, even if not all of them said 'That's how the Shoah affected my Jewishness', objectively it may be argued that being deprived of one's relatives is a characteristic trait of Jewish post-Holocaust identity in Poland, and in America – as far as the survivors and their children are concerned.

Finally, I should like to make some comments regarding the outcome of my research and the study conducted by Joanna Wiszniewicz.[70] Wiszniewicz argued that 'the Holocaust memory turned out to be, as might have been predicted, one of the most important motives' mentioned by her Polish Jewish respondents. She also stated that parental transmission of the experience of the Shoah was probably the 'basis of the ... identity'[71] of her informants. Marcin Starnawski, who interviewed several Polish Jews of the 1968 emigration, concurred with her conclusion.[72] It seems to me that one has to be very careful when making such sweeping statements.

First of all, in qualitative research we have to be aware of the limitations of our conclusions, for we never base our observations on representative samples. Moreover, as Wiszniewicz admits, those of her respondents who belonged to the 1968 generation (she interviewed them in the United States) were 'affected by the shock of the antisemitic campaign [of 1968] and by the dramatic circumstances of their departure, they accomplished a thorough redefinition of their identity ridding it of numerous Polish identities. Then they based their newly built identity on the knowledge of the Holocaust.'[73] Though she said that she did not analyse in depth the differences between those who emigrated to America after 1968 and those who did not leave Poland, Wiszniewicz has noted that for those of her interviewees who had stayed in Poland, 'it was not the Holocaust but Jewish tradition that became the crucial element of their mature Jewish identity'. This remark, however, was not mentioned in Starnawski's article. Yet it seems very important, for it sheds more light on the results of Wiszniewicz's research. Even though she initially asserted that, 'as might have been predicted', the critical element in the interviews she had conducted and the basis of her respondents' Jewish identity was the memory of the Holocaust, she later explained that this, in fact, pertained only to the '68 emigration. And this particular information should not be overlooked. As could also be seen in my research, it is hardly possible to draw a general conclusion as to the Jews' identificational strategies vis-à-vis the Shoah. Only one half of my interviewees declared that the Holocaust was one of the key factors shaping their Jewish identity. As for the rest of the informants, they were less decided, and less eager to express their views in clear-cut categories, and it is therefore important to describe those views in a carefully nuanced way. Despite a tendency amongst scholars to present their observations in black and white, we should, rather, attempt to illustrate our findings with a whole gamut of colours, in many shades.

NOTES

1. The question was: 'What does it mean for you to be Jewish? Is it just a matter of birth? Or is there something else that you think is important for your identity – language, culture, religion?'

2. An interesting article, dealing with the issue of the Jewish identity of Polish Jews who emigrated from Poland after 1968, was published a few years ago. See Marcin Starnawski, 'Historically Conscious Cosmopolitans: Jewish Identity and the '68 Generation of Polish Jews in Exile', *East European Jewish Affairs*, 32 (Winter 2002).

3. I. Irwin-Zarecka, *Neutralizing Memory: The Jew in Contemporary Poland* (New Brunswick, NJ: Transaction Publishers, 1989), p.63. Henryk Grynberg has said that March 1968 was a time of brutal, scandalous purges. And even though apologies were offered by the Polish authorities in the 1990s, no wrongdoers have been punished so far. He also recalled that Adam Michnik once called March 1968 'a pogrom without bloodshed' (suchy pogrom), to which Grynberg ironically responded that there was no bloodshed also in the sense that all perpetrators have been left unpunished ('Marzec uszedł sprawcom na sucho'). Grynberg, *Monolog polsko-żydowski*, p.34.

4. Two people from the sample said matrilineal Jewish descent was a condition of being a Jew. However, a person born of a Jewish mother declared: 'I surely don't like the halakhic definition, namely that a Jew is he whose mother was Jewish, because that's too narrow a definition. In our situation ... that [kind of a definition] is absurd ... [It] is unacceptable to me.' [PL 24m]

5. She used the word 'Easter', which in Poland can be employed both in Christian and Jewish contexts.

6. When preparing the interview scenario, I talked with a Jewish person who happened to be a sociologist by training. When we were discussing the question of languages, the person said I should avoid asking my interlocutors whether they knew Yiddish, as the issue had allegedly no relevance to contemporary Polish Jews.

7. Out of 817 questionnaires sent to Hurwic-Nowakowska (the return rate was about 6 per cent), fifty-one were filled in in Yiddish, which means that these people found it easier to write in Yiddish than in Polish. I. Hurwic-Nowakowska, *A Social Analysis of Postwar Polish Jewry* (Jerusalem: Zalman Shazar Center for Jewish History, 1986), p.16.

8. Ibid., p.51.

9. See Hurwic-Nowakowska, *Social Analysis of Postwar Polish Jewry*, pp.17f, 52. In the late 1940s, many Polish Jews did leave Poland for Israel or considered such a possibility, mostly because of the strong and violent anti-Semitism they encountered after coming back to their home towns. See Irwin-Zarecka, *Neutralizing Memory*, pp.48ff.

10. A significant percentage of people claiming to be atheists were also observed by Hurwic-Nowakowska in her 1947–50 research. Out of 817 respondents, 461 (close to 60 per cent) said they were non-believing. See Hurwic-Nowakowska, *Social Analysis of Postwar Polish Jewry*, Table 10.

11. Six respondents also stated that they had one or both parents who were communists; in one case the interviewee's brother was tried as a communist even before the war and was later removed from the party for Trotskyism. One person interviewed was himself a member of the pre-war Communist Party [PL 12m].

12. This man, born to Jewish parents, though having a very limited knowledge of Judaism, said: 'My family was completely assimilated, more attached to Polishness, I would even say attached to the fight for independent Poland ... So, I didn't feel I was Jewish ... I always went to purely Polish schools and I don't know this language [Yiddish] at all, which seems strange to my [Jewish] kinsmen; they even don't believe I am a Jew ... They still keep saying I pretend and have hooked myself to the Jews for no apparent reason.' [PL 21m]

13. Not fully understanding why one could be a Jewish atheist but not a Christian Jew, I asked one respondent, when discussing the topic of Jewishness and conversion, whether she could explain it to me. This is the answer I was given: 'Mind you, obscurantism and intolerance are phenomena of world-wide range. Can one be a Jew being a Christian? After all that's what Christ was. According to the categories [accepted by] the believing, Orthodox Jews, if their son or daughter assumed the Catholic faith, they were regarded as if they had been dead. Ignorance has no limits.' [PL 42f]

14. The same person also said: 'I wouldn't like people to like me just because I'm a Jew. I am in

perfect agreement with those who claim that philosemitism and antisemitism are one and the same thing.' [PL 5m]

15. The man could speak really perfect Polish, with no foreign accent whatsoever. Yet our conversation, like all those conducted in New York, was in English. Also, one of the women could speak Polish quite fluently.

16. The American Jewish population has a markedly high level of education in general; nonetheless, the number of PhD holders in this sample is greater than the national average among American Jewry. Though official statistics do not show the estimates of how many American Jews hold doctoral titles, we can assume that it is no more than 10 per cent of the population. Data provided by the 1990 National Jewish Population Survey (NJPS) indicates that some 33 per cent of core Jews (group including Jews by religion and Jews by birth – currently non-religious) have postgraduate degrees, while almost 22 per cent are college graduates. This data, however, does not show how many of the postgraduates have a master's degree and how many have PhDs. It seems reasonable to assume that if 33 per cent of the group in question have at least a master's, then not more than 10 per cent of the whole population have doctoral degrees. See *CJF 1990 National Jewish Population Survey [NJPS]* (accessed 9 March 2002). <http://web.gc.cuny.edu/dept/cjstu/08th.jpg>, Table 3A. According to the 2000–01 *NJPS*, 53 per cent of American Jews aged 18–24 are in college or graduate school, while the same is true for 30 per cent of those aged 25–29. See *UJC 2000-01 Jewish Population Survey, January 2004* (accessed 1 February 2010), http://www.jewishfederations.org/local_includes/downloads/5067.pdf.

17. The Society for Humanistic Judaism was founded in 1969 by Sherwin Wine and is a member organization of the International Federation of Secular Humanistic Jews. According to Wine and other prominent Secular Humanistic Jews, this movement is based on the conviction that Jews are first and foremost an ethnic and cultural community, where religion is one of its ever-changing elements and does not necessarily have to include theistic beliefs. 'The intensity of "feeling Jewish" is not a function of cultural exposure or theological belief. It is related to the individual's awareness of his situation in society and in history.' S. Wine, *Humanistic Judaism* (Buffalo, NY: Prometheus Books, 1978), p.89. The Secular Humanistic Jews Federation's 'Statement of Principles' clarifies that

> Jewish history is a human story, Judaism, as the civilization of the Jews, is human creation. Jewish identity is an ethnic reality. The civilization of the Jewish people embraces all manifestations of Jewish life, including Jewish languages, ethical traditions, historic memories, cultural heritage, and especially the emergence of the state of Israel in modern times. Judaism also embraces many belief systems and lifestyles. As the creation of the Jewish people in all ages, it is always changing.
> (24 October 1986, Detroit, Michigan).

See R. Kogel and Z. Katz (eds), *Judaism in a Secular Age: An Anthology of Secular Humanistic Jewish Thought* (New York: Ktav Publishing House/International Institute for Secular Humanistic Judaism, 1995), pp.365–6, 370–1.

18. 'According to the NJPS, the national distribution of American Jews by denomination in 1990 was as follows: Orthodox: 6 per cent; Conservative: 35 per cent; Reform: 38 per cent; Reconstructionist: 1 per cent; "just Jewish": 10 per cent; other answers: 10 percent. See S. Goldstein, 'Profile of American Jewry: Insights from the 1990 National Jewish Population Survey', *American Jewish Year Book* (1992), table 19 (accessed 1 February 2010). According to the *UJC 2000-01 Jewish Population Survey*, the figures changed to the following: Orthodox: 10 per cent; Conservative: 27 per cent; Reform: 35 per cent; Reconstructionist: 2 per cent; "just Jewish": 26 per cent.' See J. Ament, 'American Jewish Religious Denominations,' in *United Jewish Communities Report Series on the National Jewish Population Survey 2000-01* (February 2005), table 2 (accessed 1 February, 2010).' http://www.jewishfederations.org/ local_ includes/downloads/7579.pdf.

19. As Marshall Sklare argues, there are actually no reliable statistics on synagogue affiliation in the United States. He says that in small communities approximately 80 per cent of the Jewish population are affiliated to a religious congregation. This is somewhat different, however, with regard to metropolitan areas. In Boston the figure is 53 per cent, in Detroit 49 per cent, while for New York, which is a very specific city, as Sklare claims, 'no study is available [but] observation suggests that the affiliation rate is measurably lower than it is in any other large

city'. M. Sklare, *Observing America's Jews* (Hanover and London, MA: Brandeis University Press/University Press of New England, 1993), p.45. See also J. Wertheimer, *A People Divided: Judaism in Contemporary America* (New York: Basic Books, 1993), p.47.

20. In fact, a few people remarked that they had these two (distinct) identities; others just took it for granted. One respondent said: 'I consider myself to have two ethnic ... or, if you will, cultural identities which at this point of my life – I'm 60 years old – are pretty much defining myself. One is American, and the other one is Jewish.' [AM 23f]

21. Her father came to America in the 1920s.

22. 'The Emergence of Jewish Cultural Identity', *Jewish Culture News*, Spring 2003 (accessed 2 July 2003) [pdf document]. <www.jewishculture.org.jcn>.

23. As I argued in the first chapter, and as Marshall Sklare has noted, East European Jews had experienced the process of secularization even before they came to the American shores, only to become more divorced from traditionally understood religion in the United States. See Sklare, *Observing America's Jews*, p.37.

24. All three fragments cited above depict a situation where the respondent had been raised in an Orthodox family and then quit strict religious observance and affiliation with Orthodoxy, which seems to be characteristic of a large proportion of American Jews. According to Sklare, however, while most adult Jews would not describe themselves as Orthodox, they would say not that their *parents* were Orthodox, but that their *grandparents* were. Also, tellingly, Sklare reports that among first generation Jews, 53 per cent use separate plates for meat and milk dishes. The practice is observed by only 25 per cent of the second generation and 16 per cent of the third. In any case, since the period we have in mind is the early 1930s until the late 1950s – exactly the time when deep social changes within American Jewry were under way – we can assume that both views are complementary to one another rather than contradictory. See Sklare, *Observing America's Jews*, p.38. It is also noteworthy that there is little correlation between the fact of having religiously active parents and the interviewees' current religious options. Many of those whose parents followed the Judaic law do not keep the same law themselves. Among them are a number of atheists; there are also those who chose for themselves one of the more liberal branches of Judaism, and only a small proportion of the sample are those who, like their parents, do observe most precepts of Judaism.

25. Of course, what is untypical in this interview is that the person is not affiliated with any particular religious congregation. Yet, as he put it, he goes to a different synagogue every once in a while, which indicates that the social aspect of being Jewish is also expressed through participating in collective religious Jewish life.

26. See P.D. Salins, *Assimilation, American Style* (New York: A New Republic Books/Basic Books, 1997), p.11.

27. See H.M. Sachar, *A History of the Jews in America* (New York: Vintage Books, 1993), pp.13–17.

28. See ibid., pp.38–43.

29. See C.I. Waxman, *America's Jews in Transition* (Philadelphia, PA: Temple University Press, 1983), p.47.

30. Ibid., p.42.

31. Ibid., p.42, 55. As Lucy Dawidowicz contends, 'by 1920 New York's City College and Hunter College, both free schools, were estimated to have Jewish enrollments amounting to 80 to 90 percent of the whole student body'. L. Dawidowicz, *On Equal Terms: Jews in America 1881–1981* (New York: Rinehart & Winston, 1982), p.92.

32. See A.J. Feldman, *The American Jew: A Study of Backgrounds* (New York: Bloch Publishing, 1937), pp.46f.

33. H. Feingold, *A Time for Searching: Entering the Mainstream 1920–1945* (Baltimore, MD: Johns Hopkins University Press, 1992), p.1.

34. See Waxman, *America's Jews in Transition*, pp.64–6. A similar phenomenon could be observed in the nineteenth and early twentieth centuries in Europe. Jews, even those assimilated to a significant extent and identifying themselves with the Gentile societies they lived in, were perceived as an alien and dangerous group. In many of the European nations they were denied the right to be part of the tissue of these nations. This, as Paweł Śpiewak has noted, was a process of alienation of the Jews from the European societies, an alienation they did not want but that was forced upon them. See P. Śpiewak, 'Szoah, drugi upadek', *Więź*, 333–4 (July–August 1986), pp.7–10.

35. All Jewish immigrants who came from Europe between 1945 and 1954 constituted a 150,000-strong group. Less than 10 per cent of them were East European Jews who 'settled in the Williamsburg section of New York. These are the Hasidic Jews, most Orthodox of all the Orthodox.' J. Yaffe, *The American Jews: Portrait of a Split Personality* (New York: Random House, 1968), p.8.
36. E.S. Shapiro, *A Time for Healing: American Jewry Since World War II* (Baltimore, MD: Johns Hopkins University Press, 1992), p.1.
37. I. Zangwill, *The Melting Pot* (New York: Macmillan, 1909), pp.37f.
38. See N. Glazer and D.P. Moynihan, *Beyond the Melting Pot: The Negroes, Puerto Ricans, Jews, Italians, and Irish of New York City*, 2nd edition (Cambridge, MA: MIT Press, 1970), p.xcvii.
39. In fact, by the late 1930s some scholars were already claiming that the idea of pan-American assimilation was not a success. There was one exception to this, however, for, as Feldman argued in 1937, even though 'the "melting pot" theory ... in general American life failed, within American Jewry [it] has worked and still works successfully'. Feldman, *American Jew*, p.49.
40. See Salins, *Assimilation, American Style*, p.11.
41. S.L. Goodman (ed.), *The Faith of Secular Jews* (New York: Ktav Publishing House, 1976), p.30.
42. Glazer and Moynihan, *Beyond the Melting Pot*, p.293.
43. See A. Hertz, *The Jews in Polish Culture*, translated by R. Lourie (Evanston, IL: Northwestern University Press, 1988), pp.116, 119–23.
44. Ibid., p.116.
45. 'The Pale of Settlement' (or 'The Jewish Pale') – a special area established by Czar Catharine II in 1871, comprising part of Bielorussia, Lithuania and Ukraine, where Jews were allowed to settle. In 1904 the territory was extended from the Baltic Sea to the Black Sea.
46. See D. Grinberg, 'Warianty i ewolucja tożsamości narodowej Żydów na ziemiach polskich', in R. Żebrowski (ed.), *Studia z dziejów Żydów w Polsce*, vol.1 (Warsaw: Żydowski Instytut Historyczny, 1995), p.145.
47. 'In the ghetto, during the occupation, Jews often treated converted Jews as national traitors.' Hurwic-Nowakowska, *Social Analysis of Postwar Polish Jewry*, p.28.
48. See C.S. Heller, *On the Edge of Destruction* (New York: Schocken Books, 1980), p.211.
49. In her study on Jewish identity (1947–50), she found that many of her respondents had a pessimistic view of assimilation, as was clearly seen in the responses she quoted: 'I consider Jewish assimilation unhealthy, not useful and leading nowhere (example: German Jews).' 'I do not believe in the long-term existence of cultural–national distinctiveness of Jews in Poland. Should the present trend continue, Polish Jews will be in danger of complete disappearance within thirty years.' 'For Jews, assimilation is not the way. I hold *shmendryks* [assimilationists] in contempt.' 'My attitude is that of revulsion and contempt. Our contemporary so-called Aryans or Marranos are nothing but a bunch of cowards, idiots and people without dignity.' This was said despite the fact that significantly more assimilated Jews managed to survive the catastrophe than the most pious and traditional ones. Hurwic-Nowakowska, *Social Analysis of Postwar Polish Jewry*, pp.110–11, 114–15.
50. Hurwic-Nowakowska has found out that in 1947, as the records of the Central Jewish Committee show, there were over 88,000 registered Jews in Poland. The number, however, included only those who 'between March 16 and April 6 [contacted one of] the Jewish Committees [which] conducted registration for the distribution of *matzo* for Passover'. However, according to the Central Jewish Committee's survey from the period from January to June 1946, there were over 240,000 Jews in Poland. Whence the great difference? Hurwic-Nowakowska convincingly argues that the first half of the year 1946 was still a time of intensive mobility of the Polish society and especially of the Jews. Thus, in the first survey, many Jews were registered more than once, because they registered each time they changed their places of residence. On the other hand, after the infamous Kielce pogrom of July 1946, thousands of Jews left Poland. Yet after the pogrom many Jews might have wanted to hide their identity for fear of any future possible anti-Jewish riots. That is why the 1947 survey indicates such a low number. All in all, though the real number of Jews residing in Poland at the beginning of 1947 is unknown to us, it may be assumed it was somewhere between 100,000 and 150,000. Also, we have to be aware of the fact that there were more Jewish returnees coming back to Poland in the late 1940s and the early 1950s – they were coming back as Polish repatriates from the Soviet Union. Ibid., p.20; see also pp.15–19, 30.

51. See ibid., p.26.
52. See Grinberg, 'Warianty i ewolucja tożsamości narodowej Żydów na ziemiach polskich', pp.145–7.
53. Ibid., p.146.
54. It should be noted, however, that the more those assimilated Jews were involved in Polish culture and Polish life, the less Jewish they were becoming, which implied that they ceased to be regarded as Jews by the Jewish community at large. As Celia Heller has observed, even if these assimilated Jews held prominent offices in the public administration, they

> were rarely elected [to these] offices by Jews. When they held such office, it was usually because they had been appointed by Polish central or local government authorities. In 1927 elections to the kehillot [local Jewish communities], the assimilationists suffered an unexpected defeat: they were eliminated from the boards and councils of most, even in the cities where they formerly dominated.'

Heller, *On the Edge of Destruction*, p.186.
55. It seems that Hurwic-Nowakowska had already observed that tendency in the late 1940s. In her study she quotes several respondents who claimed that their Jewish identity was purely secular. 'A thirty-nine year-old worker from Warsaw [said:] "I respect and believe in the Jewish tradition and I celebrate holy days as safeguards of tradition. I believe not in God but in good men." ' Hurwic-Nowakowska, *Social Analysis of Postwar Polish Jewry*, p.73.
56. See ibid., pp.28f.
57. Irwin-Zarecka, *Neutralizing Memory*, p.50. Speaking about Jewish identity in post-war Poland, especially focusing on the survivors, some authors paid closer attention to the phenomenon of name changing. For many European Jews the only possible way to survive Nazi persecution was by assuming a new, non-Jewish-sounding name, and living with a new identity. In my interviews I did not ask my respondents about their names – whether they themselves or their parents had changed family names. I did not deem it particularly relevant to my research, and I thought it might create an embarrassing situation for both myself and the interviewee. However, reflecting on this question ex post, I can infer that if the issue of changing names had been a crucial one for my informants, they would have mentioned it. The fact that not one of my respondents alluded to it may imply that changing Jewish names to so-called 'Aryan' names was not important to them in the context of our conversations. The problem has been analysed in depth by Hurwic-Nowakowska, *Social Analysis of Postwar Polish Jewry*; B. Engelking, *Holocaust and Memory: The Experience of the Holocaust and Its Consequences: An Investigation Based on Personal Narratives* (London: Leicester University Press, 2001); and specifically by M. Melchior, *Zagłada i Tożsamość* (Warsaw: IFiS PAN, 2004).
58. The fear of intermarriage is not a new phenomenon for American Jews. What is more striking is that there was reservation on the part of German Jews living in the United States toward the marriages of their children with Jewish immigrants from Eastern Europe. As James Yaffe argues, 'The dreaded "intermarriage", which filled so many Germans with horror, inevitably took place on a large scale. Today there are very few German families which aren't tainted with a heavy dose of Russian blood.' Yaffe, *American Jews*, p.15.
59. Hassids from Góra Kalwaria (Ger or Gur, as it was pronounced in Warsaw Yiddish), a town situated about twenty kilometres south of present-day Warsaw.
60. It is characteristic that only a minority of respondents in both samples entirely rejected the concept of chosenness. Even though the idea is obviously a theological one, many of the secular people interviewed claimed that Jews are in one way or another a chosen people. Those who were declared non-believers explained their stance, saying that they understood chosenness as specialness, which to them has been proven throughout the ages of Jewish history. What they meant by specialness was most often the Jewish tradition of education and the immensity of intellectual achievements of Jews and people of Jewish origin (the respondents sometimes mentioned Freud, Einstein, Jewish Nobel Prize winners). Those with at least some basic faith in God claimed that it is the Jews' mission to carry the light of ethics to the nations (which is exactly how the early-twentieth-century Reform viewed the idea of Jewish chosenness). Some ironically said: If we are chosen – we are chosen for suffering. Still others argued that it was the Jews themselves who had chosen God's Torah, rather than that God chose them for some special task. A few of the interviewees said they did not share the belief that Jews are the chosen people, or that in their opinion this idea is harmful and should be abandoned altogether.

61. A specially skilled male member of a Jewish community appointed to perform ritual circumcision in accordance with the Jewish law, in present times often a physician.
62. That respondent learned about her Jewish identity when she was 5. One of her kindergarten friends, a Jewish girl, told her about her lineage and said 'that the Shoah happened in Poland, that Poles helped the Germans', while her mother 'didn't talk about it for she wanted to hide her ancestry; she thought it wasn't a good lineage in Poland' [PL 39f].
63. There is one exception, however, namely part of the black population which once marched arm in arm with American Jews fighting for civil rights for all Americans. Yet, beginning in the 1970s and 1980s, the partnership started to fall apart. Nowadays, if Jews experience anti-Jewish prejudices or even brutality, these come mostly from some black people, as often happened in Brooklyn. It is also the case that anti-Semitism is sometimes used for base political reasons in some milieus of the American Polonia, specifically in the Chicago area.
64. See J. Szacki, *Historia myśli socjologicznej* (Warsaw: PWN, 2003), p.613.
65. Heller, *On the Edge of Destruction*, p.12.
66. Z. Bokszański et al. (eds), *Encyklopedia Socjologii* (Warsaw: Oficyna Naukowa, 1998), s.v. 'Akulturacja', by E. Nowicka.
67. In fact, when Heller speaks about 'Warsaw Polish-language dailies owned by Jews and aimed at Jewish readers before and after independence', even she does not claim that any Polish-language Jewish newspaper was obviously assimilationist. She contends that 'the pre-independence, *Nowa Gazeta*, was ... an "assimilationist" newspaper', and so much so that it overlooked Jewish interests. 'Contrariwise, the *Nasz Przegląd* [Our Review], founded in 1923 (it was to become one of the best newspapers in Poland), was consciously on guard to satisfy and protect Jewish interests.' Needless to say, *Nasz Przegląd* was a Polish-language paper. Heller, *On the Edge of Destruction*, p.214.
68. See ibid.
69. J.W. Berry, 'Acculturation and Psychological Adaptation: An Overview', in A.-M. Bouvy et al. (eds), *Journeys into Cross-Cultural Psychology: Selected Papers from the Eleventh International Conference of the International Association for Cross-Cultural Psychology held in Liège, Belgium*, (Amsterdam: Swets & Zeitlinger, 1994), pp.131f.
70. J. Wiszniewicz, 'Pierwsze powojenne pokolenie polskich Żydów: Rodzicielski przekaz pamięci Holocaustu a tożsamość żydowska', *Biuletyn Żydowskiego Instytutu Historycznego*, 191 (September 1999).
71. Ibid., p.41.
72. See Starnawski, 'Historically Conscious Cosmopolitans', p.10.
73. Wiszniewicz, 'Pierwsze powojenne pokolenie polskich Żydów', p.44.

CHAPTER FIVE

Concepts of Torah and God: Did the Nazi Destruction Destroy Jewish Faith?

1. HUMAN TRADITION OR DIVINE REVELATION?

'All the so-called "holy books" are but poetry for me' – a man in his 50s, a scientist, said during an interview in Warsaw in reply to the question: 'What is your attitude to the Torah? Does it have any impact on your Jewish identity?' [PL 18m] Then he added that even the ethical system and the values that have their origin in the Bible appear to him in the first place as literature. Taking the Bible as a piece of literature or a civilizational document seems to be a quite frequently occurring phenomenon within the Polish group. Another person said it is for him 'a historical work of literature'. His relation to the Bible is also in a way emotional: it is of value to him 'mainly because many million people have read it for centuries'. [PL 4m] However, on the religious level he does not identify himself with 'these books', as he puts it; moreover, in the general context of his life they 'do not play any role'. What is important to this man is the physical or material continuity of the Torah as an object or a written text, which in fact agrees with the respect he has for the generations of people who read it.

That predominantly humanistic attitude to the Bible might be thought of as fairly typical of a number of non-believing people. A Polish woman born a couple of years before the Second World War said:

> The Bible is a beautiful old book from which everything originates – that whole culture that calls itself Christian and usurped ... took a lot from these books. So, it's the fundament of our culture and of the psychic construction of the Western world; [it is] the most important script of our civilization ... It does not tell about religion but about historic events ... It is important also to nonreligious

people because of its great value for the civilization – from any point of view. [PL 13f]

The interviewee is glad that the Bible is a Jewish book, written by Jews and for Jews. Here the aspect of temporal and generational continuity appears: she appreciates the inspirational function of the Bible as a source of intellectual and moral qualities over 'the last thirty-three centuries'. Therefore, she admits, 'I'm proud of it'. That high esteem in which she holds the Torah is not based on any sort of religious emotion, quite the contrary – what the woman affirms, and what should be emphasized, is that the Bible is not a religious work. On the other hand, religion does not seem to her a destructive phenomenon, either. She even says: 'Unfortunately, I am not a religious person. I am saying "unfortunately", as I think religion is something beautiful. This is not easy, apparently. One cannot lie to oneself.' Not only does she approve of religion in general, but she is also of the opinion that 'it is not unlikely that there is something beyond man and nature, [though I think] God is an unrevealed being. He does not intervene in human lives.' [PL 13f]

To some people the Torah or the Bible[1] has a considerable meaning as an ethical reference point, as a collection of moral maxims. A Polish person claiming that 'the Jewish religion makes part of the secular Jewish culture and does not demand from man to believe in the supernatural' confessed that the Torah was very important for his Jewish identity and concluded: 'This is a total of [written] experiences of my nation; it builds up my ethnic and ethical self, my place in the world.' [PL 19m] This man was the only person interviewed in Warsaw to state overtly and precisely that his own ethical system was an emanation or, to put it less poetically, an outcome of the biblical text. Some others' enunciations were more practical about this point, suggesting that the Torah it is a 'signpost' or that it teaches how to become a better person: 'I consider the Torah to be the [divine] revelation. To me it is a life signpost, a point of reference. It conditions my identity and I think that the better one understands it and practices in life the better human being one becomes. So, for me the two things are convergent with one another.' [PL 45m] On the other hand, a few Polish Jews expressed quite contrary opinions regarding the ethical value of the Torah: an academician, about 50 years of age, admitted that it is 'an important script telling about the essence of spiritual life of Jews'. [PL 3m] He stated, however, that to him 'it is not a spiritual rock or a fundament of values' and that 'my behavior is not motivated by the Decalogue, rather is it inspired by pure humanistic morals'. He knows the Bible very poorly but is convinced that 'it is possible to think of one's Jewishness beyond any Bible-based criteria'. A woman over 70, a retired physician, asked with a slight irritation in her voice: 'Why do I have to read the whole Torah just to find one moral principle? I don't have to read it to know one mustn't steal or kill.' [PL 17f] The Bible means nothing to her; it is not a divine revelation. She says she is 'completely irreligious' and repudiates all religions, including Judaism, although she appreciates spiritual life. Her last word on the topic is a comparison. The woman compares Catholicism, Russian Orthodoxy and Judaism to the theatre. Yet she is of the opinion that 'people need it'.

Another person saw the issue of ethical value of the Bible as a more nuanced, even problematic, one. He said:

> If this book shapes [such moral postures as] humanism, solidarity, honesty, decency, then I'm in favor of it ... If we assume that the Torah gives you 'wings', if it brings forth encouragement and delicacy, then that's a positive thing. But if you're trying to draw some other conclusions which throw a negative influence, then ... I believe that what is good in these books should be supported, but when they speak of destroying the adversary, about slaughtering enemies and whole towns, and if those who analyze the books and teach [them], and if they're unable to change it, they should at least soften it, mitigate it. [PL 25m]

This view is quite characteristic of a majority of the Polish sample. Even if many respondents did not put their opinions in a straightforward manner, what they have in mind is clear: it is human reason rather than the so-called holy scriptures that constitutes the base of ethics. Human ethical reason (Weber's *Wertrationalität*) judges the ethics of the Torah, and not vice versa. From the sociological point of view this is a fact of great importance; it means that historically, through the ages, a significant proportion of Jews – as the sample analysed shows – have evolved from Torah-inspired ethics to reason-inspired ethics. In other words, a part of modern Jewry has come from Moses to Kant. This will be clearly seen in the analysis of the American group, too.

Quite a number of Polish interviewees claimed to have some relation to the Bible, mainly because they perceive it as *the* Jewish tradition or *the* nexus with that tradition, although that relation is often superficial or marked with a kind of magical character. Only a few people who were asked about the meaning of the Torah in their lives did manage to go beyond such popular expressions as: 'It is to me what it was to my ascendants. It must have been something great and sacred to them. I respect it and consider really sacred.' [PL 26f] It is curious that to some people who regard themselves agnostics or atheists, the Bible represents a communal and cultural value, though it has no theological meaning for them:

> In no sense am I a religious person. I am a nonbeliever, which implies that to me the Torah is part of [my] national and social tradition. But to me it does not have this aspect of sacredness. I don't consider it to be [divinely] revealed ... Does the Torah directly influence my life? Rather not, It's not something that guides me in my life; what does guide me is my own [moral] code. This code, however, converges with the Torah in many points. In our culture ethics generally comes out from the Torah, from the Bible. [PL 24m]

Yet in some cases there appears a tension between the cultural and the theological, which in turn may provoke problems, as can be seen in the following fragment:

> I know the Bible is something one cannot question or negate. You know, for generations, millions of Jews ... so why should I have a different approach to it, in terms of acceptance? On the other hand ... if you were raised an atheist ... how can I now turn 180 degrees and act contrary to my inner feelings? But when I had these conversations with the rabbi, it raised my self-esteem. And today it is my conviction that this culture and this tradition, everything that Jewishness carries with itself, should be cultivated and known; so just because I am part of this nation I must simply know it ... Also, I was upset that my parents actually didn't really try to pass it on to me. I felt like I was uprooted and put in a vacuum and didn't know where I belonged to ... I don't know how to say it. I don't resist in the sense of negating it. But on the other hand, I just can't get fully into it. [PL 22m]

However, asked about the Torah, a man under 50 answered that he loved 'to read it, to comment on it, to discover new things in it'. [PL 48m] Despite his approval of the traditional interpretation suggesting that the Torah had been dictated to Moses by God, he finds historical critique of the biblical text 'extraordinarily fascinating'. Another person who identified himself as a religious Jew declared: 'To me the

Torah is a record of revelation, which is a source and a trace of the higher order. It is a record of things human and of the history of Israel. It's a medium of responsibility in relation to the higher instance' [PL 49m].

A few of the people interviewed frankly admitted they could easily do without the Bible. A relatively large number of them confessed they did not know that book, they had not been taught the Torah. A woman over 50 who said: '[my] parents were a hundred percent Jews, [and my] children are a hundred percent Jews', added: 'I don't think the Bible can have any influence on my Jewish identity. I'm not religious because I was brought up that way. I know there are people who need religion; I don't. I don't need it yet, maybe some day ... One never knows. Different things happen. Altogether I find it difficult to talk about religious topics.' [PL 14f] She also talked about her son, and how she had been shocked when he had turned towards religion: 'on Sabbath he wouldn't go out to buy a newspaper. But after some time it passed off.' [PL 14f] The same woman straightforwardly said she had probably never been in a synagogue and confessed her disbelief in God.

Many other Polish interviewees admitted they personally do not believe that the Torah possesses some sacred character (by and large because they are unbelievers); to some of them it is even unimportant as an identity-building factor. But at the same time, they claimed that the book is important for the Jewish nation as a whole:

> I was raised [in a] nonreligious [atmosphere]. I look at the Torah from the historical perspective. The Torah has been binding up the Jews and in this respect I have a great attachment to it because it is thanks to this book that the nation has been preserved as a nation. [Yet] I don't have the feeling that this book was given by God. I just don't feel it. [PL 32m]
>
> I treat the Torah as a legend, as history. In point of fact, mine is a nonreligious attitude to it. [Is it important for my Jewish identity?] Definitely not. [Though] I think as a sociologist that religion has been that binding element that enabled this nation to survive. [PL 40f]
>
> For me [the Torah] has a rather historical meaning. I am more of an atheist. [But] I couldn't imagine the Jewish nation's coming into existence without the Torah. This people has survived thanks to reading this book and using what is written there as a guide. Otherwise it wouldn't have survived. So, the Torah does have a great significance. [PL 43f]

The American group is similar to the Polish one in that quite a number of the American interviewees claimed that they they were not really interested in the Bible, or, at least, they knew very little about it. These were basically (but not without exceptions) people who had been brought up in secular homes where reading or studying the Torah was not really practised. On the other hand, hardly anyone from the group was troubled by my questions concerning the Bible. In contradistinction to the Polish respondents, even if they were poorly versed in biblical stories and teachings, by and large they were not embarrassed by these questions. I could easily ask them about such topics as the inspired or the divine character of the Torah, and in most cases they would answer without any feelings of uneasiness. For instance, a 70-year-old woman said: 'Well, Torah, I never read it, I never studied it. It's something that certainly shouldn't be destroyed in any way.' When asked, 'Do you accept the view that the Bible is the word of God given to Moses and then passed on through the generations?', she answered:

> I don't feel it that way. If people wanna believe that way, let them believe that way. I don't feel that I personally need it. I don't need to go to the synagogue. I don't have to do it – I feel it inside. I know what I am. I can't say what I believe in because at this point I don't know what I believe ... [AM 7f]

Yet, even among the respondents who were raised in non-religious households, many were given some basic schooling in the Bible. They may have been exposed to biblical teachings in their secular (quite often Bundist-style) schools or in the Jewish Centers they and their families attended. For example, a man in his fifties confessed: 'I was raised a very secular kind of person. I went through the motions of some religious training and I did the same thing with my son. But I attended more socially in vein, it wasn't religion; Torah doesn't speak to me in any way.' [AM 3m] Of course, there were others whose knowledge of the Torah was in fact non-existent. Though they knew some particular stories, they had never read the book and 'don't revere it in any way'. [AM 38f] Some claim they are not very much interested in learning more about it even now: 'I would like to ... take the time to reread it ... to read it, actually, for the first time, because I learned the stories but I didn't read them. I find historical analysis or discussions of the Bible as history very, very interesting. But I'm not willing to do it, so I guess it's not at the top of my list.' [AM 23f] Still others, though they often maintain that the Torah means a lot to them, are sceptical or even ironical about the alleged divine origin of the biblical text: 'I'm interested in it as literature, as history. [*Q: But is it revealed, inspired?*] No. You know, you run around the desert – you hear voices. [*laughter*] So, maybe ... the voice of God, I don't know.' [AM 34f]

A majority of the American interviewees claimed that for them the Torah is mainly a piece of literature, poetry, and a historical work. To many this is also an important record containing ethical teachings that can be practised by Jews, and even by non-Jews. However, there were voices saying that 'it's a very important book historically but not morally'. [AM 20f] All in all, one could argue that the view that was most typical and thus shared by a sizeable proportion of the American sample was that the Torah is inspiring in terms of literature and in terms of tradition – understood either as history or as ethical values, or both. For instance, a man over 50 said:

> I've read it a couple of times. The whole Exodus has its miraculous touches, but as a writer I understand the uses of literature to fire the imagination and to get people excited about something. My father always said: 'You don't have to take the Bible literally', which of course is heresy to some people; he said: 'It's a form of poetry.' I agree. So, I'm comfortable with it as ... a work. I see it as a work of literature, but not necessarily of a divine spirit. I don't see it as a divine spirit at all. [AM 37m]

Quite a similar view was expressed by another person, who underscored the significance of the Torah for the human mind and for Jewish self-awareness: 'I think intellectually it's interesting to me. It's interesting to me as a source text of Judaism. In a historical framework the tradition of study and intellectual development around the Torah interests me.' [AM 10f]

Speaking about the value of the Bible, a man over 40 offered a *sui generis* interpretation of Judaism:

> I view the Torah in two regards. On one hand I have a ... Shintoist reaction to it. Shinto [is] the Japanese religion which reverences myths and legends, even though you don't believe in them at all. You reverence them, because they are part of your tradition. And the second aspect is that after three thousand years of ... evolution, intellectual and religious evolution, a great deal of useful ... knowledge can be garnered. [AM 25m]

It is curious that this far-Eastern, non-theistic outlook on religion was shared by many other respondents from the American sample. Interestingly enough, a number of them claimed that the Bible was important to them in terms of ethics and continuity with the Jewish culture even though they considered themselves atheists. What many respondents from the American sample thought in this respect might well be summarized in the assertion that the Bible is a 'completely human-made document which contains some very important morals'. [AM 43m] Thus they testified to the fact that not only the Torah, but also the whole of Jewish religious tradition, has been transformed – at least to a certain degree and in some milieus – into what I have called secular religion:

> To me [the Torah] is ... important because I feel I'm part of the Jewish people, and this is the book of the Jewish people, so it's part of our heritage, part of our history. In a sense I study it a lot because I belong to a Jewish group that meets once a month – a *havurah*. I just like it because I like to keep the connection with my background. So, we discuss the Torah every month and I find it fascinating. It's a wonderful work of literature. I think there is a lot of ... good ethical teaching ... I told you I'm an atheist... [*laughter*] Obviously how can I believe the Torah is divinely inspired? Of course not. [AM 49f]
>
> Was it dictated by the word of God to the hand of Moses? That's just part of our story – and it's a good story. I don't object to the story, the story is lovely. But could it possibly be true? And I'm simply a nonbeliever. Maybe. But I can't believe ... That doesn't make sense. It's just not the way life is. God doesn't go around dictating. [AM 31f]

The ethical aspect of the Torah teachings was also emphasized by other interviewees[2] (who more often than not questioned the view that the Bible is divine revelation):

> I look upon the Torah as being a very interesting tale ... I think [it's a] composite of a lot of different things that were put together. As an instrument of instruction in terms of a way to live, a code of ethics, I think it's wonderful ... if you could subscribe to everything that it says. It's a very strong foundation for being an ethical person. [AM 3m]
>
> [To me the Bible is] legend, folklore, intellect. Perhaps a certain degree of intuition and wisdom as well. Observation of human experience and what seems to make sense, what seems to work in

the society, kinds of values that help the society. But I don't think it's divine. [AM 23f]

In the American sample there were, of course, those who deemed the Torah to have a considerable influence on their religious and spiritual life, too. They differ from the group previously described in that they see the Bible as a condition *sine qua non* of the existence of Judaism and as a guide for their lives. They reflect on the issue of divine inspiration and revelation and sometimes agree that these attributes can be ascribed to the Bible. Also, a fact not to be overlooked is that they usually consider God to be the author – or co-author – of the book. Some are so explicit on this issue that they say that 'Moses is the prophet, and he was maybe the only prophet to be able to hear the word of God directly'; therefore the Torah is 'God's word and lessons'. [AM 11m] Several people were very specific about this question:

> The Bible is the blueprint of Judaism. You can't have Judaism without the Bible. To me all of Judaism comes from the Bible; it comes from every word. All of the laws, all of the things that have happened in the Bible are the blueprint of how you're supposed to live ... how the Jews are supposed to live their life, well, how anybody is supposed to live their life. The Bible, it has rules for Jewish people and non-Jewish people. Like I say ... there wouldn't be Judaism if it wouldn't be for the Bible ... I do believe that God ... in some ways told Moses what should be written and how it should be written ... I guess you could say: the spiritual and the physical – Moses was the physical and God is the spiritual. [AM 6m]
>
> [The Torah] is the center of my life. As an Orthodox Jew, the Torah is the guide ... We believe that God gave the Torah. I believe the Torah is divine, the word of God. ... Basically, it's the number one guide. And the other guides are secondary. [AM 16m]
>
> It's a way of life. I believe that God gave the Jewish people the Bible and then it was brought down in its original form through the generations. I believe it's all divine, all handed out ... it's the word of God, I believe, and it's a way of life. [AM 44m]
>
> It tells me how to run my life; it's a guideline for a way of life and it was written for me by God. [Q: *Was it passed directly from God to Moses?*] A hundred percent ... I never thought the Torah is a book. The Torah is a direct conversation between me and God, directly I feel that he speaks to me as an individual. [AM 50f]

There was also a group a respondents who, though they did not consider the Torah to be a direct revelation of God, believed that it was religiously important because of its cultural value. Here again we should keep in mind that the religious aspect they meant was a secular and communal one and not theological. Therefore, they saw the significance of the Torah in its social function; they underscored its identity-building character. To some of them, that the Bible was produced by the Jewish people is a fact of consequence: in the biblical stories they find the historical narrative of their nation. Thus they see the Bible as a symbol that implies immersion in the sacred–secular Jewish history. Even though it is not necessarily God who gave them the Torah, the Torah is to be valued and respected as an essential record of Jewish culture and a fundament of their social life – 'it's a good story', a story that keeps the Jewish people together and makes a *one* out of *many*.

One of my American interviewees not only questions the view that the text has a direct divine provenance; she gives a rational explanation of the origin of the Torah. To her, as to many others, the book is a purely human work. Indeed, hers is a sociological and historical way of interpreting religion. What is of crucial importance here, however, is her remark that the text 'may have been inspired by a *belief* in God'. This is what it actually means – that the Torah is a human-made document: it is not inspired by God, but by human belief in God. Or more precisely, it is of no relevance whether there is a God or not. What is crucial here is that people who created the collection of books called the Bible thought that a divine force wanted them to obey certain rules, and made them into a nation. The interviewee is aware of the process of formation and accumulation of various moral and political ideas that led to the emergence of biblical doctrine. It is evident in what she says that it was not some supernatural entity, but human beings who were in fact responsible for creating the system of Judaic faith. The woman claims that this kind of religious system provides the group with a higher sanction regulating their behaviour. Whatever those who established the system intended to decree as good or evil has gained the legitimacy of a supreme power to whom they alluded. This testifies to the fact that people usually tend to seek objective criteria for judging their comportment and hope to find psychical safety in these criteria.

The brief investigation conducted by the respondent is just an exemplification of what many others thought of the issue under consideration but did not deem it necessary to describe in a detailed analysis. Many of them, however, would concur with the conclusion that the Bible is an outcome of human intellectual and moral inspiration, and that it is a revelation of the depths of the human mind. Among the Polish respondents there was one person who also saw the crux of the problem, not in God but in the idea of God. The person, a neurologist in his mid-50s, said that his opinion in this respect is that 'God is the need of God rather than his very existence.' [PL 18m][3]

Amongst the American sample there were some who represented what one might call a 'holistic' approach. They attempted to see all things together: to combine the cultural and theological values of the Torah and affirm its relevance in virtually all aspects of life. They often emphasized the fact that, to them, the Bible stands as a symbol determining their ethnic *and* religious identity. A 33-year-old man declared:

> [The Torah] is a lot of different things. It changes all the time. In its simplest form it's ... the story of understanding of where the Jews came from and what makes the nation and the religion. It has import for the nation, it has import for the religion, it has import for some of the things that you might call 'cultural'. You can't separate them. It [is] the history and the philosophical, theological, and moral basis ... over what this nation is. [AM 35m]

For other respondents, the holistic outlook may at times take on the form of a inherently conflicted view, as was the case with a man who recognized lofty moral teachings in the Bible but also condemned what he said was awful in it:

> Certainly, logically I believe that it's a completely human-made document which contains some very important morals. [Yet] there are some things which are just awful from the point of view of freedom, dignity, economic progress. On the other hand, I was brought up in a very religious home and there was a sense of respect and reverence which I still experience with respect to that, so it's definitely a conflicted view. I'd like to think in important ways that biblical morals influence me, but I don't obey a lot of the very specific rites or very specific ... Jewish culture laws. [AM 43m]

Also, in certain cases the interviewees would express quite unusual opinions regarding the Torah. I will quote just one such interview, one conducted with a 50-year-old woman, an elementary school teacher and the daughter of a Conservative rabbi:

> I teach it [the Torah] – this is what I teach. I prepare children for

their bar and bat mitzvah, and we always start with a portion before I begin to teach their chant. I read the *parashah*,[4] and then I teach the liturgy – the cantilations ... How much I believe in it? I'm not sure. But I find it a very interesting story. We learn so much from so many of the stories, and we've built on the Bible. [Do I believe it was divinely inspired?] No, I don't. I cannot understand, I can't see how it was. [Yet] I build a lot around it. It's not the Bible ... But I believe in *gematria* – it's a play on numbers. And for some reason I believe in it. Maybe it's a lot of traditions, a lot of customs, it's the customs that keep me going. Customs are very, very important. [AM 9f]

What may seem curious in this interview is that the person, raised in a traditional household of a rabbi, and being someone who teaches children the Torah, looks at the Bible from a rather secular perspective. To her the Bible functions as a point of reference and a fundament of the cultural context. What is more, she even finds mystical inspiration in the Bible, for *gematria* is a kind of mystical or magical use of mathematics. This said, however, we should note that for the interviewee, the origin and the nature of the book is not an issue she would examine: it is not so much important *what* the Bible is and who its author is, but it is important *how* it impacts people's lives and identities. In other words, for this person – and for many others too – the onto-logical aspect of the Torah is relatively less interesting than the phenomenological or the functional aspect.

Last but not least, we have several respondents who were more critical than others about the Bible. Without completely discrediting the book, they admitted to having found some negative elements in it. In most cases they pointed to human behaviour as shown in particular biblical stories. According to these respondents, some of those stories are morally unacceptable from the point of view of the contemporary reader. This kind of approach to the Torah is an example of independ-ent, non-theological ethics. Proponents of such ethics judge biblical narrative against their own system of values, which they usually con-sider to be on a higher stage of moral evolution than that included in the Bible. This, however, does not keep them from cherishing the book in other respects, as we can see in the following passage:

Heinrich Heine called the Torah the portable homeland [of the Jews]. On the other hand, when I see very religious Jews clinging on almost slavishly to all the laws that were extrapolated from the

Torah in the Mishna and the Talmud, I get very frustrated. I really wanna move away from that. I'm much more in the spirit of the law rather than the letter of the law. Some of the things in there I probably find offensive. [AM 46m]

Others just say the Bible depicts *all* types of human behaviour. That is why 'in the Bible there's a lot of bad things, too'. [AM 32f] And those 'bad things' as well as good things are in the Bible because it narrates the annals of human beings: 'What I find particularly interesting about it is that here's the holy book that supposedly really portrays the human as very human. There is revenge, there is hatred, there is love, there is murder.' [AM 22f]

In summary, we have seen that both groups, Polish and American Jews, tend to view the Torah as a Jewish book that contains important religious and cultural meanings. We should bear in mind, however, that the term 'religious' is used here in a specific sense – it does not refer to faith and theological doctrine, but to tradition cultivated in Jewish homes: to customs, rituals and ways of interpreting the world. Most respondents from both samples see the Bible as a culture text, a piece of literature, or a record of Jewish history. To these people the Bible has little – if any – meaning as a text shaping the idea of God. Most of the Polish and American interviewees stated that they did not really perceive the Torah as a direct revelation of God's word to Moses. Yet it should be noted that whereas the American respondents had very few problems in talking about these issues, many people from the Polish sample found the very same questions troubling and difficult to answer. Also, though some American respondents said they were not interested in the Torah, and many claimed their knowledge of the book was scant (which subjectively may be true), they were nevertheless considerably better educated in the Bible than the Polish group. Perhaps most of the interviewees in both groups subjectively thought of themselves as knowing little about the Bible, but, objectively, people from the American sample seemed more familiar with the Bible than those from the Polish group.

Whence the difference? There are no easy and unquestionable solutions to this problem. Both Polish and American respondents – but especially those from the Polish group – come, in significant numbers, from secular homes. And even if their parents kept some religious practices and attended the synagogue, they did so more culturally than out of deep theological convictions. This is relevant particularly with regard to the American group. As for the Polish Jews interrogated, many of them were raised not only in secular households, but in families where any sign of Jewishness was a rarity. Instead, what they knew about their parents was that they were loyal Polish citizens, sometimes even actively engaged in the communist regime. Those communist families seemed to have had no need for a Jewish identity, at least until 1968. Others, who were politically and ethnically neutral, wanted to gradually rid themselves of their Jewishness and secure a safe future for their children, which was not unimportant in post-war Poland where anti-Semitism was still a problem. But, of course, the situation of the Polish interviewees born before the war was in many respects different. All of them had had some Jewish education and were raised in homes that were, at least nominally, Jewish. Accordingly, people from this group had practically no problems with defining their identity: they felt either Polish Jews, or Poles of Jewish origin, or both Polish and Jewish, but the Jewish side was never missing, nor was it questioned by them.

So the secular homes of Polish Jews were different from those of secular American Jews. In post-war Poland, secular life equalled lack of Jewish identity for a majority of Jews. Thus, the Polish respondents, in many cases, were bereft of any knowledge of Jewish beliefs, customs and practices. Many others just knew that they were Jewish, but that did not imply any concrete involvement in Jewish life, which, to be precise, was virtually non-existent from the 1950s to the late 1970s.

On the American continent, meanwhile, secular Judaism was by and large 'very Jewish', though not in theological terms. Most of those American interviewees who received secular upbringing were educated in Jewish culture and history, and were even taught basic knowledge of the Torah. Most of those who attended Jewish schools, either before or after the war, were also taught Hebrew. Therefore, their rootedness in Jewish tradition may seem more tangible and self-evident to themselves.

The cultural context of American Jewish life also makes it understandable why a number of respondents from that sample viewed the Torah as a record of sacred–secular Jewish history, whereas this category was practically absent in the Polish group.[5] What I call here the 'sacred–secular' dimension of Jewish history is that it is perceived as sacred by people who claim they do not believe in the God of the Torah. In order to avoid a misunderstanding of my concept of sacred–secular Jewish history, I should make clear in what sense the word 'sacred' is used here. Among the many meanings of the adjective 'sacred' there is one that corresponds with the Hebrew term *kadosh* (root *k-d-sh*). The basic meaning of the word *kadosh* is: something different, something separated from other things. In this sense God is *kadosh* and Israel is *Am ha-kadosh* (the holy people). Also, in the Talmud, there is a tractate titled *Kdoshin* which deals with holy or sacred things in contradistinction to ordinary things. *Per analogiam*, it may be argued that Jewish history is sacred – first of all in a theological sense (accepted by both Jews and Christians), but also in terms of the specialness of that history as seen against the background of the histories of other nations.

Moreover, the specialness of Jewish history in the eyes of Jews may be understood as a natural attachment to one's family, relatives and close friends – the obvious social surrounding. That is why American Jews who regard themselves as secular can think of their history as a special or sacred history. Furthermore, they can see the Torah as a sacred book, but in secular terms, since to many of them it is sacred as a piece of literature and the fundament of their culture. Hence it follows that they deem Jewish history sacred, as their whole culture is sacred to them *qua Jews*. And this, in turn, is a perfect example of ethnic religion. To many of the American interviewees, and also to American Jews in general, Judaism is a way of being Jewish, of keeping one's ethnic identity.

Yet the problem of secular sacredness of Jewish history is not as simple as it might seem. We have in both groups – but more so in the Polish than in the American one – a distinction that the interviewees made between the functional and the ontological aspect of the Bible. As for its social role, many of them said that it has different meanings to them as individuals, on one hand, and to the Jews as a nation on the other. It is really striking that a significant number of American and even more Polish interviewees said they 'did not need' the Torah to feel and to be Jewish, while most of them thought the book to be of utmost importance for the Jewish nation as a whole. When asked whether they could imagine the very existence of the Jewish people without the Bible, almost all my informants answered that this would be unthinkable to them. If not for the Bible, they said, there simply wouldn't be the Jewish people. And if, in fact, there were no Bible, the Jews would have invented 'another Bible'. Thus it can be argued that to a significant proportion of Polish and American Jews, the Torah has little influence on their individual Jewish identity, though they deem it to be crucial for the Jews as a community.

It is also telling that in both samples a majority of respondents said that, to them, the Torah is mainly a piece of good literature. But what exactly does this statement communicate? It probably means that is what we have been taught – the system of education we participated in sees the Bible as one of the fundamental works of literature, a product of the Mid-Eastern and Mediterranean civilization. Thus, American Jews as well as Polish Jews unconsciously presented themselves as children of the societies they live in and as well-educated citizens. We may assume, therefore, that the answer 'the Bible is literature' is not so much a Jewish response but the response of a middle-class citizen for whom the Torah is part of the social tradition of his/her civilization.

Yet another issue that appeared to be essential to most of the respondents in both groups was the question of ethics. Again, in both samples there were those who claimed that the Torah was important to them as an inspiration for being a morally decent person, and that it provided them with a code of ethical principles that can be followed by believers and non-believers alike, but there were also those who disagreed with this standpoint. The latter argued that although the Bible may be valued as literature, it fails to offer the kind of ethics they could accept. While the ethics it imposes on Jews are too restrictive, some of the interviewees claimed that it often depicts utterly immoral behaviour.

One thing that marks a sharp difference between Polish and American Jews in their relation to the Torah is the view that the book is a condition *sine qua non* of the existence of Judaism and *the* guide determining the Jewish way of life. More American respondents than Polish ones stated that, to them, the spiritual and theological meaning of the Torah was the crucial one. In this respect the American sample therefore appears to be more traditionally and typically Jewish, since in traditional Judaism *Torah is a way of life*. Seven respondents from the American sample asserted that the Torah constitutes an important basis for their lives: it is 'the blueprint of Judaism' [AM 6m]; 'the guidebook for practic[ing] Jewish life' [AM 13m]; 'the number one guide' [AM 16m]; 'a way of life' [AM 22f, AM 44m]; 'a guideline for a way of life' [AM 50f]; and it contains 'laws and lessons' that one ought to follow in one's life [AM 11m]. All of these seven people were members of Orthodox or Hassidic congregations, which confirms the fact that these two branches of American Judaism stick to the tradition of viewing the Torah as the centre of Jewish life and opt for a literal interpretation of the Bible. Thus, the more liberal the synagogue one is a member of, the more liberal the views one holds on the Torah. This is also true with regard to the Polish sample, in which only three people said that the Torah is to them the centrepiece of Judaism, and that they see it personally as a life signpost, an essential 'reference point'. [PL 45m] These three people, all men, are also members of the Jewish (Orthodox) Community of Warsaw.[6]

2. HOW IS GOD (IM)POSSIBLE?

How can there be a God if there was a Holocaust? This question and many other religiously-oriented questions triggered by the Shoah haunt people nowadays, both Jews and non-Jews, believers, agnostics, and atheists, too. One of the two major hypothetical assumptions of the present research has been that the occurrence of the destruction of European Jews has brought about a considerable decline in the belief in a personal God within the communities of Polish and American Jews. In the course of the interviews, all the respondents were asked whether their awareness of the Holocaust and knowledge thereof had any impact whatsoever on their view of God or on what they thought of the idea of a Higher Being. Also, similar questions were posed that focused on the issue of religion vis-à-vis the Shoah, and on the problem of the sense of life and values that people find most important to follow. All these questions were meant to provide me with data regarding the interviewees' basic world views and belief systems.

The object of ultimate interest was whether the person had or had not asked him/herself the question: 'If the Holocaust was possible, is it possible that God exists?' The answers were fairly differentiated. The least feasible and the least legitimate thing would be to try to indicate how certain standpoints may be determined by such variables as age, sex or educational level. In fact, there is practically no correlation even between the interviewed Jews' ages and their opinions on the Absolute. It would surely be illegitimate to claim that people who experienced the tragedy of the Holocaust have lost religious faith; nor is it true to say that those born after the war find religion something 'natural' or easy to live with. Among the interviewees there were people who claimed they were deeply involved in Jewish faith and religion; there were others who were indifferent; and finally there were those who reject both religion and the existence of the Absolute.

It is very interesting to see how the people interviewed differ not only in their views and in the intellectual constructions they make, but also in their emotional reactions, and to analyse the words they use when speaking of religious beliefs. In both samples we can distinguish four groups of respondents on the basis of their relationship to the problem of the Holocaust in a theological context:

1) those who were raised in secular homes: they are non-believers and say that the question of God and the Holocaust is not really an issue for them
2) respondents who, though non-believers, find the whole question interesting and sometimes even claim that the occurrence of the Shoah only confirms that they are right in rejecting any theistic outlook
3) believing interviewees for whom the destruction of European Jews did not destroy their faith in God
4) those who admit that the Shoah does constitute a serious challenge to their faith, a challenge that has led them to non-belief.

Let us first analyse the interviews with Polish Jews. A number of them, when asked about their view of God and whether it might have been affected by the Holocaust, answered that there is no correlation between the two things because 'it has to do with religion' [PL 3m], which to them is an alien theme; therefore what others may perceive as a problem to them is not a problem at all. They often claim that their disbelief does not depend on the fact that there was a Holocaust: 'If I were a believer', a 42-year-old man said, 'I'd say that there is a God, but I'm a nonbeliever and I say: there is no God. But that's not because of the Shoah.' [PL 5m] Other people concurred with that:

> Generally I find it difficult to talk about religion ... I am a completely nonreligious person, I've been brought up without religion. My parents were atheists, but atheists by their own choice ... They both stopped believing after the war, and that had something to do with the Shoah ... Although not my father, for my father must have left religion even earlier since he had held strong Communist views before the war ... I myself, I never felt God, that is why I can't answer this question. To me, there is no connection [between the Shoah and the fact that I'm a nonbeliever]. [PL 8f]
>
> For me it's a very difficult question. I wasn't raised in any religion whatsoever, tota zero. However, I sometimes dream of there being a higher force that could help me in specific situations. But having failed to encounter such help I think I agree with the old saying that people did it to people. So you shouldn't confuse it with divinity. Actually I haven't given it much thought but ... the Shoah has not affected my current outlook. [PL 9f]

A woman in her 50s recounted a similar story:

> That fact that I'm a nonbeliever has nothing to do with the Shoah.
> That's just how it is. My father was an atheist even before the war
> ... I didn't have any problems with that, but my father quit reli-
> gion though his parents were believing, religious people. The same
> goes for my mom, although I don't know for sure about her.
> Sometimes she'd light candles and pray in secret. [PL 14f]

Some of the Polish interviewees said they were well aware of the
argument that the Holocaust questions the existence of God, but
affirmed they nevertheless did not need to mention this argument to
justify their disbelief. A 50-year-old woman said she had heard others
ask whether God is possible if the Shoah was possible. Though she
understands the reasoning, this is not what she would personally argue
if she had faith:

> If God existed he couldn't intervene in mundane life, because that
> would be senseless. He would have to intervene every time and
> ceaselessly ... And I reject divine intervention in general, so why
> would it have to be otherwise with the Holocaust? But if I were a
> believer my reflections on the Holocaust would have been deeper.
> So the point is that because I don't believe in God at all, even in
> the case of the Holocaust God is for me a being or a notion that
> has no impact on me – only people do. [PL 28f][7]

Another 50-year-old woman said she knew very well that the idea of
God was a psychic phenomenon and a construct many people have
recourse to, but that she herself did not need it, even facing the Shoah:

> For me, the problem does not pertain to me, because before I had
> the awareness of the Holocaust I had been aware that actually ...
> God may be a construct of sorts that helps people to find them-
> selves in the world. It is not a construct I refer to. I don't rule out
> the possibility that I will refer to it someday. [PL 40f]

Among the Polish interviewees there were also those who were not
believers and claimed that the Holocaust did not have any impact on
their outlook regarding the idea of God, but who said that they envied
the believers, and at times had some kind of longing for the experience
of faith in God. Yet neither their unbelief nor the longing has anything
to do with their awareness of the Shoah:

> I guess I was raised, as far as philosophy, in kind of a materialistic

world view, and I was taught to believe in man in the first place ... That's why I never believed [in God] ... I have some problem with the lack of religion on my side, I feel I could do with it. I think it's easier to live with religion, no matter what kind of religion. However, I don't see here any connection with the Shoah. [PL 8f]

It seems expedient to quote one more interview, illustrating the views of non-believers for whom the Nazi Holocaust does not constitute a breach, a civilizational scandal and a turning point in what might be called personal philosophy of life. It is not just one example among others: it can serve as an explanation of all the interviews from the group analysed. It provides an answer to the question: Why would an atheist refuse to use the Shoah as absolute evidence against the existence of God? Here is what the person argues:

Saying that God doesn't exist because there was a Holocaust is in fact a religious question; it is faith that God exists. I feel that it's like all hazy, and it doesn't pertain to me. And the awareness that I'm Jewish didn't push me to put these questions anew. If I were a believer this would be a fundamental question' [PL 39f].

In the next group to be analysed are people who argue that they do not believe in God regardless of the Holocaust, but who, nevertheless, contend that the Jewish catastrophe confirms the validity of their view and constitutes, as it were, additional proof that there can be no supernatural being. Thus, a man just under 50 asserted: 'This [the Shoah] exactly is a proof of the nonexistence of God. It's impossible for God to exist; that's what such instances as the Holocaust demonstrate. I'm positive that I've never encountered any examples of God's intervention and God's existence – neither in literature, nor in my life, nor anywhere.' [PL 23m]

The shock some of the respondents have experienced is intellectually externalized as a pure contradiction of two elements: God imagined as an all-powerful, all-loving being on one side, and the unimaginable suffering of the Shoah on the other. A woman born ten years before the Second World War, whose family was killed in Treblinka said: 'If there is any supreme power, why did the Shoah happen? If God is almighty how could he have allowed that? How could he have allowed the destruction of his chosen people, as they say? That is another reason why I don't believe in God. Faith in God and the Holocaust are irreconcilable.' [PL 17f]

Another woman, not a Halakhic Jew, born in a secular home, and whose father was a communist, said she has been and still is a non-believing person. She belongs to the group of people interviewed who claimed overtly that the Holocaust has had an impact on what they think of God. Though she was raised without religion, she explained:

> I know how important it is for religious Jews, and in a sense I envy them – I envy them being religious in general, but I can't make the effort, I just know it would be an intellectual effort. I have a deep conviction that things like faith one gets from home – certain habits and emotions that go back to early childhood. And I know that's beyond my reach. [PL 10f]

The woman then said that the question of God and the Shoah must have shaken the minds of many religious Jews just as it shook her world view, even though she never believed in God. She admitted:

> I can't get over it in any way. No answer has satisfied me so far and I've posed the question to many rabbis. These two things [God and the Shoah], you can't square them with one another. I think that even if I had been religious till the time [I learned about the Shoah,] I would have stopped [believing afterwards]. All else I consider pure rhetoric and manipulation. I'm surprised that after the Shoah there are still religious Jews – survivors. I can't understand that ... After what happened I will never believe [in God]. [PL 10f][8]

The third group we will focus on are those respondents who are believing religious people whose faith has not been destroyed by the *Churban Europa*, although it might have been weakened in some cases. Certainly these are not people who would be unmoved by the cruelties of the Shoah, but what they claim is that the Nazi regime succeeded in large measure in destroying their people but not their belief in God. One of the most interesting, even intriguing, cases was the man who said he loved to comment on the Torah. His was indeed a thought-provoking concept. He said that his knowledge of the history of the Holocaust was pretty vast, but emphasized the fact that cruelty is not an invention of the twentieth century. To support his opinion he pointed to the Bible:

> I don't understand the Shoah. I mean, I understand it intellectually. But there is a plane on which it is perfectly untransparent ... I know there are people younger than me who get paralyzed and whose lives get consumed by the awareness of the Shoah. I don't

have that at all. [Though] I'm a compulsive reader of books on the Warsaw ghetto and I search for pieces about my family. For the last twenty years I've been reading everything accessible to me [published] in the languages I know. But you don't get used to it, on the contrary – it's horrible ... But it's not only the Shoah, it's the reality of Canaan, too. We had entered Canaan and we slaughtered the aborigines, one by one. My attitude to this is similar to the Shoah: I truly don't understand it. If ... on the Lord's order we entered the land and slaughtered them all, including children, then there's a serious misunderstanding ... I don't believe in such a God. I don't believe in a God who makes people murder children and who burns them in ovens. But I do believe in the God who's the author of this book. So, I don't understand, I demand explication. And after I die I will clamor, I will yell to have it explained ... I don't have any problem [with the question of whether there can be a God if the Holocaust happened]. So much so that I'm actually astonished by those who, because of this event, are doubtful about God. The Shoah is for me a paralyzing proof of the authenticity of divine revelation. God created us as free ... And apparently human freedom adds something to the world created by God, something that the world needs and something that wouldn't exist if not for us. [However] the Shoah was not the price that *had* to be paid. The Shoah was historically avoidable. Yet God who takes our freedom seriously couldn't have intervened for the sake of some part of humanity. [PL 48m]

It might be inferred from this passage that the man's autonomous intellect does not allow him to accept unconditionally the image of God as it is sketched in classical Jewish texts. Yet his faith – his basic frame of reference – is not destroyed, as he claimed, but at the same time his value system produces puzzling questions. Indeed, his are *questions* of *why* and not *assertions* such as 'This is why God cannot exist.' The difference is clear: the latter case would imply the destruction of his frame of reference, while the former means that the questions would not be posed if not for the frame of reference – both elements are intrinsically linked. Faith and questions seem to coexist.

The same argument – human freedom – was raised by a woman born just before the war in Moscow. Though she held quite a pessimistic view on life in general, she did not want to blame God for the suffering of Jews. Instead she saw the history of man as a partnership between humanity and its creator:

I believe that ... I can accept the view that God wanted to create a partner for himself ... We cannot, however, project human judgments on divine judgments. It's difficult for a living and suffering human being to understand it all, for usually people, I guess religious people, see God as a care-taker, a father or someone like that. Then we can have grievance against him, but anyway it's an inscrutable being. I wouldn't involve God in it. I think it's humans, humans exclusively. They've been given free will and nothing can justify them ... But the Jews didn't perish; Jews will persevere. That was God's intention – and this is what chosenness is all about. [PL 13f]

A similar view was presented by one of the very religious, practising Warsaw Jews. Interestingly enough, he was one of the people who had been raised in Catholic homes. He then found out his Jewish origins and became a devout member of the Orthodox congregation. This is his comment on the concept of God's non-existence in the light of the Shoah:

This is not a question I would pose myself. Of course, I know this attitude. For me the Holocaust is a human work. It is the specific political and social factors and various forces that were in people and interpersonal relationships that led to what happened. God shouldn't be put into it ... One of the fundamental assumptions of Judaism is free will. God does not intervene in the realm of human actions by deciding for people. And man has also the freedom to do unimaginable evil. That's why even the worst scenario is possible for people – and this scenario was realized in the twentieth century. That, however, does not exclude God from history, for it is he who made such actions feasible for people. [PL 45m]

A woman who left the Warsaw Ghetto after its liquidation (she was then less than 10 years old) and was hidden in a Catholic orphanage, recounts:

Many people say: where was God then? I could not ask such a question in those days. Today I say to myself: I am too stupid for it. There's probably nobody who could answer that question. I always say it must have been [the acts of] providence, for I had no chances to survive. Everything was against my survival ... Why did I survive? I don't know. Providence watched over me ... Someone guided me. I couldn't survive one day without people's help, therefore someone must have sent me those people. [PL 1f]

But since she had been raised in a religious Jewish family, it was not difficult for her to 'accept religiosity' and belief in God. Though the religion she accepted is not the same as the religion her parents had practised:

> When I found Christianity in the orphanage, everything was new for me. It was as if I had left hell in 1944 and found myself in Paradise. It was Christmas time and, as a child, I liked it all very much. I did not accept everything at once, but I was soaking everything up. I wanted to be one amongst many. I was baptized after the war, not during the war, under pressure.[9] [PL 1f]

The woman also wonders whether she, as a religious person, should think that the Shoah was inescapable. She concludes: 'Catastrophes like that did happen in human annals. Perhaps it had to happen for the state of Israel to be created.' [PL 1f]

In fact, during the war, among believing Jews the attitude of waiting for God's help and having hope in his mercy was a normal thing. We can learn about this by reading the letters written by Polish Jews under Nazi occupation. They often encouraged each other not to despair, and to trust God, to pray to God for deliverance.[10] Religion played an important psychological role for people who faced death and suffering. As Ludwik Hirszfeld, Catholic by religion, Jew by birth, recounted, when he visited the church at Grzybowski Place, in the Warsaw Ghetto, and attended the mass, he was embraced by 'the coolness and the ambience of the temple. The crowd was immersed in prayer ... We are united by the feeling of a higher community ... Everything was an echo of the Great Harmony.'[11]

An interesting view was expressed by a man who actively belongs to Warsaw's Orthodox synagogue yet argues that God is not a given and should not be taken for granted. He says that the Holocaust may prove to be a real challenge for the believer. To him, however, the destruction of European Jews did not constitute a serious existential problem, as it seems.

> My take off point is not some kind of a childish faith which assumes that if there is a God in whom I believe then all must be well. Rather, my take off point is a sort of agnosticism, a conviction that generally with God you don't know ... So, in this sense awareness of the Shoah doesn't impact [my faith]. Of course I know the literature and the various reflections on the subject, but I personally think that the Shoah is lethal for a naive faith in providence. This

has never been my faith, that's why I don't have problems with it. Generally speaking, it's not easy to believe in God if by Jewish God you mean a God who takes care of the Jews immediately and protects them. The belief that it really is so is quite an essential element of Jewish tradition. If it's understood literally then of course it's hard not to despair ... On the other hand, there's another idea of God that's equally important in Jewish tradition – it's a God who cares for us to carry on in our lives, us all, us people, us Jews. And this conviction is left untouched, it can be even strengthened. [PL 49m]

For me, the most interesting cases, however, were those of respondents who had been believers once but to whom the Holocaust – as total anomie and a theologically inexplicable event – meant that they could no longer believe in the biblical God. Their views may serve as an illustration of some kind of theology of the death of God. The destruction of European Jewry caused in them an enormous mental and emotional shock which brought an end to their faith. Yet what may seem striking is that very few of the people questioned admitted that they had lost their faith because of the Shoah. The first case I would like to analyse here is that of a woman who, at the time of the interview, was not a non-believer. She said she had regained faith after a period of rebellion against, and denial of, God:

I call it the period of rebellion. I had such a period of rebellion, of total separation from God and from any kind of religion. At that time I called myself an atheist ... That was a period of rebellion against God who I said was not, just didn't exist, if he let such things happen, and if innocent people perished. If one human being could kill another human being and go unpunished then God simply doesn't exist ... Today the Shoah is still to me something unexplainable and incomprehensible, but unfortunately it's a fact one has to face. I've come back to religion, but I rebelled so awfully for a long time. And it's not that I've forgiven God for there was nothing to forgive. [PL 2f]

A second case that is a clear example of someone who lost his faith after the Holocaust is a man who survived the war:

I had a long discussion with a [Catholic] priest, quite an enlightened one, and he was surprised that I'm an agnostic. And I am an agnostic, I don't believe. He asked me why, what's the reason? I answered that if innocent children were murdered, their heads were smashed against a wall, and there was no force that would react to that – that convinced me to become an agnostic, and I don't believe. I have nothing against the believers. If they're authentic and honest [in their faith] then I fully respect all philosophies and it doesn't matter to me which religion [they adhere to] ... Because of this historical injustice and those victims I'm a complete agnostic. For me God does not exist. [PL 6m][12]

In the course of virtually all the interviews, the respondents were asked about what they thought were the reasons for the Holocaust. Some of them alluded to the theme even without being asked. A few respondents said they were aware of some extremely religious (that is, ultra-Orthodox) interpretations of the Shoah. One of them said: 'I don't see it like the rabbis do who contend that the Holocaust is punishment for sins, that people didn't observe the Torah and didn't observe certain rules for centuries, and so on. I can't agree with that, because even if ... well, can you say OK to the murder of millions of people?' [PL 22m] Another person was surprised: 'After the Shoah there are those, like these sects, whose explanation is that people sinned so heavily and that it was God's punishment. I don't believe in that.' [PL 25m] Indeed, what these two interviewees alluded to was an explanation which some of the Hassidic leaders had proposed: namely, that in accordance with the holy scriptures, Jews were punished for their transgressions. Another attempt to account for the *Churban Europa* was made by some of the Zionist leaders, who claimed that the Shoah was an unavoidable condition for the establishment of the state of Israel. And this is what one of the Polish respondents said: 'From the point of view of the Zionists it was OK that all Polish Jewry was murdered. Whether there is any sense to it – that's another story. The changes that took place after the war led to the creation of Israel.' [PL 31m]

In general, most Polish respondents maintained that the idea that the Holocaust was God's punishment is unacceptable to them. They think this for either theological or humanistic reasons. Of course, the non-religious simply do not seriously consider the very possibility of divine punishment because of their lack of belief in any deity. More interestingly, however, most of those who are believers, or who at least do not overtly call themselves atheists, also rejected the theory that sees the Shoah as divine retribution for sins. The quotation below will serve as an example of that kind of reasoning. Although it is more articulate and carefully considered than the average response to the question under analysis, it summarizes most of the arguments raised by many other interviewees:

> I don't think one and half million innocent children had to die for sins. It seems that this interpretation goes into extreme, and I don't agree with it, at least not completely ... Of course, I believe in divine providence and God's intervention in history. I believe in that God freed Jews from Egypt in an unusual way. But these are exceptional events and God intervenes in history when he wants. Certain historical processes led to a situation when this happened. What impacted it was also sort of an accumulation of hatred beginning a couple of centuries ago, and a mixture of political and social factors. I do think the Holocaust was not unavoidable ... *Q: Do you agree with such an interpretation that the Holocaust may have been necessary for the state of Israel to be created?* I don't agree. That's an interpretation I protest against. You can't legitimize the existence of the state of Israel, or the need to build it, by pointing to a tragedy that's going on ... [Also,] I don't agree with the stance according to which Israel is a necessity because of the Holocaust. [PL 45m]

There were, however, a few respondents in the Polish sample who asserted that the destruction of European Jews may have been, if not intended, then at least permitted by God. These were, of course, those who did not rule out the possibility of God existing. One person said, not without hesitation, that 'maybe it was all planned by God; apparently it had to be so' [PL 25f], whereas another respondent was more convinced about it: 'the Holocaust was performed by God'. [PL 4m] It may seem interesting that none of my respondents referred to Marcion's (considered one of the early Christian 'heretics') idea of a dual God. It is noteworthy that a well-known Polish survivor and writer, Hanna Krall, did mention in one of her stories the concept of a comforting and good God, on the one hand, and of a perfidious and evil one on the other. These two deities constituted the bright-and-dark axis of her view of the world.[13]

One person, however, was more specific on the issue of God's permitting the Shoah: a man about 75 years of age, a survivor who fought the Germans as a Polish soldier in General Berling's army. He told a story of a Jew who came to Poland in the 1970s or 1980s in order to find the place where his loved ones were killed. When he saw the spot, the man fell on his knees and began to hit the ground with his fists and cry: 'Lord, our God, how could you have allowed that?' After recounting the story, the respondent said:

> Why didn't I have the same feelings as the Jew hitting the ground with his fists? If we have the warning: 'Observe God's command-ments', if it was proclaimed by some prophets' mouths (I can't tell you exactly where and who wrote it and by whose inspiration), then I was warned. The Jewish nation received a first and a sec-ond warning. Therefore I say: Can I have grievance against God? [PL 35m]

While analysing the American Jewish sample I will use the same four-group division, though the third group (those who believe in spite of the Shoah) seems to provoke more problems than was the case with the Polish sample. In contradistinction to Poland, in America there were a considerable number of respondents whom I call the 'Kaplanian–Kantian believers'. I have in mind people who do not believe in the God of the Bible, who reject the idea of a personal, all-good deity to whom one may pray. They do not discredit the very notion of God, but what they mean by this term is a cosmic force that created the con-ditions for the development of the world and is actualized in human-ity as an ethical inspiration. Even if this being-force is alluded to in prayers, it is alluded to more for symbolic and cultural reasons than for theological reasons. Therefore, though these respondents did not call themselves atheists, their faith differs in significant ways from that of devout Orthodox believers. I shall define in clear terms in the analysis that follows whether those who have been categorized as belonging to the third group are 'classical' believers or the 'Kaplanian–Kantian' believers.

It might seem curious that relatively few of the American respon-dents stated that their disbelief or agnosticism had nothing to do with the occurrence of the Shoah. Not more than five people said they would be secular-oriented even if there had been no Holocaust. The quotation given below is an illustration of a typical, brief answer by a person from the first group:

> Since I don't believe in God ... I know that it's some poetry that you read here, Jewish poetry in Yiddish and in Polish, they invoke God, and they're not religious people. God has nothing to do with it in my view. I don't have a view of God, because I don't believe in God. *Q: Has it ever occurred to you that the Holocaust is yet*

another piece of evidence that there is no God? I know a lot of people think that way, but I don't. *Q: So, had the Holocaust not happened you would still be a nonbelieving person?* Right. [AM 34f]

Another interviewee made it clear that his secular outlook had less to do with the Holocaust than with a rationalist world view:

I don't believe in magic, I don't believe in divine will. I don't believe in divine justice. I don't blame God for the Holocaust ... *Q: Does it occur to you to raise the question: 'If the Holocaust was possible is God possible?'* No. Even an atheist doesn't need to make that statement. *Q: But for some atheists that is the final argument contra ...* Yes, for some of them it is. My atheism has absolutely nothing to do with the Shoah. It has to do with ... common sense. [AM 25m]

Still others claimed that their atheism had to do with a rejection of any theistic view on the ground of ethical sensitivity. To them, while ethics is independent of belief in God, there have been lots of atrocities in the world of which the Shoah is but one example – and all these atrocities make the existence of God unthinkable to them. Therefore, from the ethical standpoint, the traditional (biblical) idea of God is for them a concept they cannot accept:

I'm not one that believes that what the Holocaust demonstrates is how could there be a God. You know, 'cause how could God let this happen? ... I think in Judaism there's the ability to separate the notion of a higher being from this notion of following a set of ethical laws that allow you to be a humane person. And that's what you should be thankful for: that you have these sets of behavior that allow you to function in this world. You know, because God – who knows? So in that sense I'm an agnostic. And I think the notion of God is irrelevant. [AM 1m]

Q: Do you think you wouldn't be a secular person had the Holocaust not happened? No, I would have been secular anyway. If anything, the Holocaust for me ... reinforced in my mind that there was no God. That people were all we had to lean on, and that people had to lean on each other. There's been an awful lot of horrors since that: dropping of the atom bomb, the slaughter that is going on in various countries in Africa right now, child soldiers. This is not any different, in some senses, from the Holocaust. Perhaps it's different in the sense that the Holocaust was an attempt to wipe out an entire people which most of this stuff is not, but the horror is as great ... I see it as ... a signpost along a long road; it's a large signpost, but it's not the only one. *Q: Have you ever heard in yourself a voice saying or anyone else saying: 'If the Holocaust was possible God is impossible'?* Sure, I have heard other people say that. *Q: Is it part of your personal reasoning?* No. My reasoning has to do with the fact that in general ... I am with Sherwin Wine.[14] I simply do not believe that there is ... a divine or a spiritual being outside people. I've never had a religious belief, a belief in God. My nonbelief in God came from much earlier. I always thought that the people who said: 'If the Holocaust could happen there is no God' that they were in many respects bitter. I don't feel that way. [AM 38f]

We should note that in the last interview quoted, the respondent said that, if anything, 'the Holocaust reinforced [my conviction] that there was no God'. That makes the person belong to both the first and the second group, in a way. Though she does not refer to the Shoah in the first place, it does have some importance to her in terms of her atheism. On the other hand, there were respondents whom I would put in the second group yet who show some features characteristic for those from the first group. A 60-year-old woman active in New York's 'City Congregation', which is a Secular Humanistic community, said she never had faith and therefore she did not lose it because of the Holocaust – it was just 'one more argument against' the idea of God:

The times that I'm living in I consider post-Enlightenment times ... That's really the background with which I can't square supernatural belief. I'm not a ... metaphysical atheist as much as I am ... may I say, a moral atheist in the sense that whether or not there is ... a Supreme Being, I don't believe it. I think I have to rely on myself, my own courage, my own honesty, my own talents, and those of the people of the world. ... I'm not uncomfortable with the word 'atheist' ... I don't know how to explain all the horrible injustices in the world if there's a loving God and a powerful God. It doesn't comfort me. In fact it gives me more discomfort ... to think that there really is a being or a force that could intervene and doesn't intervene, and sits back and watches ... what we do. I know there are answers for all of this, but none of them convinces me ... *Q: Do you think there might have been any impact of the*

Holocaust upon what you think of religion in general? I think that it's harder for me ... That's increasingly incomprehensible to me about how people really do maintain their belief in God ... after the Holocaust ... after the horror of the Holocaust, that's like the final, may I say, nail in the coffin [*laughter*]. That's not a good metaphor ... maybe it is ... it makes it more difficult for me to understand how people continue to find faith. Living without faith is not ... sadness for me ... I can't say I would have had faith if it hadn't been for the Holocaust. No, I don't; it's just one more barrier; one more reason ... to not have faith, it seems to me. [AM 23f]

What convinced this person to be a 'moral atheist', as she put it, was *also* the awareness of the Shoah. Thus it was not exclusively this event that made her a non-believer, but all injustices of the world. All the sorrows and sufferings of humankind led her to take up the option of total ethical responsibility of the human species for its fate: we people are alone in this world, and it is only on people that we can rely; there is no higher instance or force that could be helpful. The respondent maintains that the Holocaust was a final, if horrible, confirmation of the validity of this view. That kind of reasoning, to be sure, was characteristic of other interviewees from the second group, too. A 53-year-old woman, for example, asserted:

Well, if by religion you mean the belief in an all-powerful, all-knowing supernatural force – yes, the Holocaust certainly confirmed my belief that there couldn't possibly be such a force and have allowed the Holocaust or other atrocities to take place. I would not understand any possible reason for allowing this ... In my opinion the Holocaust is just another proof of the nonexistence of God, whether it's Christianity or Judaism. As far as Christianity, the problem was that they were not involved in the Holocaust, they stood by basically, with the exception of some very brave and good human beings ... And Jewish religion, I think, played ... as far as the way the Jews reacted during the Holocaust, I feel that those who were extremely passive ... some more of them might have been able to have been saved if they weren't waiting for God to help them. But that's true of all people in the world. [AM 20f]

What is interesting in this quotation is that for the person inter-viewed, the *Churban Europa* constitutes proof of the non-existence of any deity. Although other things are not unimportant, the destruction of European Jews made it completely clear, the interviewee contends, that there can be no God or a force of good that would let the Holocaust happen. Another respondent evidently thought in these terms – that the Holocaust morally and socially excludes the possibility of there being a God. Yet it is telling that for this person the Shoah meant destruction of the belief in God, but *not* of Judaism as a secular religion and a civilization. She was extremely critical, however, of the very religious people who build and support theological faith – the Hassidim:

> Even when I was 21 at the time of the Second World War, I couldn't come to terms, and I [still] cannot understand how a survivor can believe in God. My God, we Jews have our murderers and rotten people but we are not so bad, so terrible for our God to have allowed ... I'm not talking about fighting in a war. But why have we sinned? Where have we, as Jews, sinned so much that a God would allow that? This is a phenomenon I can't understand. *Q: So, you question, in a way, the validity of Judaism after the Holocaust?* Not Judaism! A belief in a God. How could a God have allowed!? It's not that they were fighting a war. But to allow six million to go to the oven? We are not such a terrible people. We are human like everyone else. *Q: You asked: 'If there is a God, could he have allowed the extermination of his people?' Do you think the Holocaust provides you with another or the decisive proof against the existence of God?* Yes! Yes! I can never doubt it. It ... reaffirmed and confirmed my feeling. As I have said, living among Orthodox Jews, humans just like me ... Their indifference, their selfishness, their lack of ethics ... We live in the same building, and they wouldn't let their children play with my children. Why? What? Was I going to give their children pork? The kids were playing. Now, come on ... and condemn me because to them I'm worse than a goy? ... And so, my answer was: 'Listen, if there is someone upstairs, at the end, I'll go first.' I don't eat the pork outside and inside keep a kosher home. See, this is day-to-day living. [AM 17f]

The woman was born in 1921 of parents who had immigrated from Russia and 'left their religion behind but remained Jews'. She was raised in a purely secular milieu and sent to a secular Yiddish after-day school. Among her friends, 'not one of the boys that I knew was ever bar mitzvahed'. And she never had the need for religion. 'I can be a good Jew', she thought, 'and a good human being without studying the religion.' [AM 17f] Knowing that in the 1920s and 1930s, secular American Judaism and, specifically, the Bundist and Yiddishist circles, were even anti-religious, it seems hardly surprising that the woman criticizes the idea of God and the behaviour of the Hassidim in the same breath. To her the Shoah is just a final and a fundamental sign which demonstrates how harmful and lethal religious beliefs and practices are.

Let us now move our attention to the third group, which includes respondents who were more or less believing people, who claimed that the Holocaust did not have any serious impact on their religious view – at least, it did not destroy their faith in God. It should be noted at the very outset of this analysis that in the American sample, the third group proved to be the most problematic one. Firstly, as has already been said, there are a significant number of interviewees whom I have classified as the 'Kaplanian–Kantian believers'. Secondly, sometimes it is even difficult to judge whether a particular person belongs to the first, second or third group. There was a person, for instance, who says she has never been religious. She finds it difficult to 'turn to God', the way people usually do, because of all the suffering – the Shoah included – that humanity has endured through the ages. The interviewee says:

> We turn to God for help, for justice, that is because we need it. I'm not sure that so-called God … really is interested, [and that] he really cares. And I'm not sure what God does because if you think of all – forget the Holocaust as such at the moment – but think of all the terrible things that have happened to people. [AM 33f]

This person inquires whether God can be a caring one, whether he is interested in what happens to human beings – and therefore she seems not to exclude the very possibility of the existence of a deity. On the other hand, she identifies herself as a non-religious person and refers to the world's suffering as if it were a classical atheistic argument showing that there can be no God. In other words, she simultaneously reflects on two issues: whether God is good and caring, and whether God does exist. Her position is not untypical, although most respondents were more specific on this topic. On the other hand, a large proportion of the interviewees categorized in the third group are to some extent undecided. Their position is quite often that there must be some God, some-thing-that-rules-the-world that exists despite the

Shoah, while they contend that that this cannot be a personal, biblical God, someone who hears prayers and offers help.[15]

Most of those who belonged to the third group were of the opinion that it was humans who were responsible for the Holocaust and not God. If anything, they may have been angry with God or argued with him, but that did not imply the rejection of his existence. Asked whether it ever occurred to her to think that if the Holocaust was possible, God's existence seems impossible, a 50-year-old woman answered:

> Sure ... It might be harder for some people because they say: 'How could God let that happen?' I know that some people gave up being Jewish and gave up God after their experiences. But I think that it's really the people that did it. It isn't God that did it. God created the world and we have the choice to be good or bad ... And I don't know if I was really in those camps, would I say: 'God has forsaken me?' No. And I could see why someone would think that. I don't think I can answer the question completely. I hope that I would believe even more in God. Really there might be some forces beyond me. I mean I do believe there is a universal creator, a force of nature all beyond people. I don't think that this is an easy question to answer at all. I do question sometimes: 'Why was it allowed to happen in such an extent?' [AM 5f]

One might infer from this passage that the person interviewed seems in a way divorced from the horrors of the Holocaust. For even though she admits to asking troubling questions regarding the issue of 'Why was it allowed?', she also hopes she would believe even more in God had she been incarcerated in a camp. It is curious that there is one event that perhaps touched her more than the destruction of European Jewry: it is the terrorist attack of September 11, 2001. In all sincerity, she said: 'When this stuff happened with the terrorists I was really scared ... That's much more real to me than the Holocaust of Europe. I think it's the new Holocaust, actually.' [AM 5f]

Another subject that seems important and should be commented on is one concerning doubts. In fact, when people admit they pose difficult questions they actually have doubts. Even if the respondents belonging to the third group consider themselves believers, they often confess that they sometimes have doubts, that they question what normally they think is true. Sometimes, however, they argued that even though they have 'questions of "why" ', they have faith as well [AM 16m]. That is exactly the situation two Orthodox men described:

Doubts everyone is going to have. I'd be surprised to meet someone who's never had a doubt. In high school my saintly East European rabbi, who was a Holocaust survivor, said to me: 'You think I don't have doubts?' To hear that I was stunned because he was a man who did everything imaginable. I realized doubts are natural and understandable. My answer to your question though is twofold: as an historical fact the Holocaust cannot cause greater doubt in God's existence than the death of a one-month-old child which happened five thousand years ago, it's happened for ever. So in that sense whether God exists or not cannot be determined by the Holocaust any more than any other tragedy, despite the enormity of it. The Holocaust as a theological problem to me is no greater theological problem than the book of Job. More than that, what I would say is what the Holocaust represents is Dostoyevski's view: when God is dead all is permitted. The absence of God unfortunately means the absence of constraints. And when human morality becomes the absolute morality, when there are no absolutes, when human being is an absolute, then God help us frankly. In other words the notion of that there is a God and that God stands behind the universe is a perpetual Jewish statement or perpetual religious statement of affirmation that things will be OK. If I don't have that God, I have no guarantees whatsoever ... And I'd say if there is a God sometimes I wonder what that God has been doing all these years. But ultimately I would say I do believe in that deity because there must be something beyond me, there must be something beyond the world of humanity, there must be something beyond the building across the street. There has to be some kind of other reality which suggests that there is a spiritual plane which guarantees the basic goodness of human existence. I've never understood the atheist position because the atheist position basically says we can go in any kind of a number of different directions one of which is the destruction of ourselves. [AM 2m]

There are some people in our synagogue that specially make that an issue: 'Where is the sense of life?' 'What's the reason?' 'What are we here for?' I think we kind of search for the sense of life in religion. I would have to think about it a little more ... Well, in a negative way, as being a child of survivors, and if you think about what happened, that could make you very sarcastic towards religion: 'How could that happen?' 'How could we have religion and what is the sense of life if God allowed that to ...?' I mean, that's a real problem. *Q: Do you personally ever experience any doubts thinking of the Holocaust and of the millions who were killed in it and people who went through it?* Yes, I think about that very often and even though I believe in God ... I can't honestly say that I believe in God one hundred percent, you know, high nineties. But as a son of a survivor, there is that doubt, there is that doubt. I've seen so much and heard so many stories. I believe in God, that's why it's in high nineties, it's not a fifty-fifty thing. But I just can't understand how God could allow to kill so many innocent children and people. It wasn't only Jews, it was millions of Russians. It was a world war, there were millions and millions killed. It's a real problem. That's why I say like it's kind of justified for those people who say that maybe there is no God, even though it's a really small chance to me that there is no God. And just people like you now, the scientific approach, you know, how man evolved, to me that's only a few percent possibility: one, two, three percent. But it does lurk in the back of my mind that if there was a God how was it possible for him to allow such a ... I mean there are no words for World War II ... and World War I or the Holocaust ... I definitely believe ... yeah, it's a possibility, even though it's a small possibility but it is a possibility that maybe the scientist are right – there is no God. I don't think that that's the case but because of what happened, I mean, it's a real tough argument. [AM 6m]

The voices of those who do have doubts were many; sometimes they verged on disbelief or agnosticism. Many respondents asserted that they thought they had a belief in God, or they wanted to believe, but eventually admitted that anything is possible. Therefore, even though they hoped to find equilibrium in faith in God, they asked whether God – understood as good and omnipotent – really exists, which is less certain after the Shoah. Below are a couple of examples:

Q: So the question: 'If the Holocaust was possible, is God possible?' has never entered your mind? No. Just that I don't understand God. I question him. There's a number of questions. 'God where were you? Why didn't you stop this? Why?' But he's not giving me the answer. He's not talking to me directly that I can hear. Maybe he is

– I don't know. In Jewish theology, or philosophy, or whatever we want to call it, the question is: 'Does God predetermine everything?' And if he does, then we don't really have free will. Yet Judaism believes in free will. God created nature, created the world with a certain pattern: 'Now, people, you're on your own. This is the way the world is going to be. This is what I've created' ... Therefore we must say: Whatever we do, we do. It's God's will but I don't understand it. If I understood him he wouldn't be God. If I can understand him, he would be limited to the extent of my personal comprehension, like a picture in a frame. [AM 12m]

Q: *Does it ever occur to you to pose that question: If the Holocaust happened can God exist?* Always. Always. That question's always there. And for other ... You know, there's lots of tragedies in the world. I ask: 'Is there a God?' Which is one of the reasons I'm back in Judaism – my mind is searching my own religion for that. Yeah, that question is always on my mind. And the Holocaust just ... makes it very evident – where was he? But that question is always on my mind, personally: 'Is there a God' Where is he?' It's a question [*laughter*] that drives me crazy ... And I would imagine it pertains to the Holocaust too, 'Is there a cause, a reason? Or is it all random?' And I think knowing whether there is a God (some people can believe – I'd like to know) would tell me that it's not random, that there is a reason, and that I just don't know the answer ... that there is some plan. I'd like to believe that. [AM 14f]

Doubts, as it turned out in one interview, are feelings that rabbis also experience. In a conversation with an Orthodox rabbi, the problem of the lack of faith seemed to be one of the crucial questions we dwelled upon. The rabbi told his story of doubt provoked by the Shoah and his gradual return to a more stable faith. Interestingly enough, he did not say he stopped asking troubling questions or that he regained perfect joy and tranquillity:

[My first] immersion, reading and studying ... it was totally shocking and totally overwhelming. I would get up in the morning, having read the whole night before. If you're an Orthodox Jew, you put on your *tales* and *tefilin* and you pray. I even put on my *tales* and *tefilin*, and I found I could not pray. I mean I didn't feel emotionally that I could pray ... [*laughter*] I was feeling either rage at God or I was feeling a lack of belief. I'm not sure which was worse, but anyway, I didn't feel like praying, let's put it that way. It was so painful and vivid that I honestly did not feel that I could genuinely say at this moment that I believe ... When Richard Rubenstein began to write God is dead he really became a pariah in many ways, you know, in religious circles, rabbinic circles. And I defended him very strongly. My argument was: You may disagree with him, and I disagree with him, too, but there's a piece of us that has to admit the integrity and the truth of what he's saying. In a certain sense I thought it was a genuine religious response to say: 'If this happened, then God is dead or God can't exist.' My main disagreement with him is the finality of that view, that it's too easy. That was too easy, because in a way it resolved the tension – it's done – and I felt that the Holocaust you should leave in tension, you should not resolve the tension. So, if there was more tension to be torn between belief and disbelief, I felt that was intrinsically more correct than to resolve the tension. *Q: Does it mean that you still experience that struggle in yourself, a struggle between belief and disbelief? Is it that there are still these two parts of your self?* Actually, then more true than now. I sometimes think it's like grief ... working through grief. There are moments when you believe and there are moments when it's just not real. *Q: Do you still experience that kind of ...?* I'd say much less. Much less. [*laughter*] Then it was all the time. I compare it to a grief response. I began to overcome the first round of grief and to be more affirmative. And it was a combination of this feeling ... a certain feeling of empathy or compassion for God, and a certain feeling about suffering, God is also suffering. Be that as it may, it became a more positive feeling. I felt a sense of shared grief, rather than a sense of either anger or ... 'This can't be a God; I can't believe in such a God – such a God can't exist, it just can't be possible.' So, there was a shift in the balance. But even now, sometimes when I hear what a lot of piety ... it evokes this reaction that's almost like anger: 'How can you talk so piously, so comfortably?' [There is something that] reminds of the question of doubt and lack of faith. [AM 29m]

There were also a considerable number of respondents who can be classified in the third category only if we accept the concept of a believer as comprising not only traditionalists but the non-traditional, 'Kantian–Kaplanian' believers, too. This subgroup included both those who were raised by believing parents as well as those who were reared in secular families; their attitude toward the idea of God was that it is hardly possible that there is a caring God who helps people, but there is (or has to be) some kind of higher, superhuman power. This position I have called Kantian, because it contains a stress on independent, autonomous ethics and on responsibility which rests exclusively on human beings. At the same time, it is also a view that is clearly Kaplanian, for, just like Mordecai Kaplan, the founder of Reconstructionism, it maintains that God is not a person one can pray to; it is a higher power, a cosmic force that actualizes itself through human striving for good. Many a respondent also had a conviction or a feeling that one has to believe in something that transcends man, and that belief in a higher order is functionally positive.

A 60-year-old woman said she had been raised in a secular home but she believed 'in something'. She explained the change in her life in the following way: 'As you get older, you have crises in your life, and you have to have some kind of belief. I can't tell you exactly what it is but I do believe in something. I don't know if it's the Holocaust itself that gave me ... but life crises as you get older. I feel you have to have some kind of belief.' [AM 15f] It is a belief in something unspecified, uncertain, but providing the individual with a meaning of life. It is a reality or an idea that helps answer what Paul Tillich has called questions of ultimate concern. The belief in a higher power also makes it easier not to panic in the face of aging, suffering and dying. Hence, many people, at some stage of their lives, find faith psychologically unavoidable, even though it does not offer viable answers to catastrophes like the Holocaust.

An 84-year-old former nurse said she does not know 'what God is' or 'who God is', she is still searching for an answer. She admitted, however: 'I feel that there is some kind of a supreme power that manages things that happen.' [AM 32f] Yet she could not completely get over the fact of young children dying of cancer, whom she saw when she was working as a nurse; neither could she understand what motivated Nazis such as Dr Mengele to commit unimaginable crimes: 'How could such intelligent, educated people think of such horrors of torture, of what they did? And I ask, if there is a God why does he create people to do such things? I feel if there was truly a loving God, he would create people to do good, to be good, to be humane.' [AM 32f]

Another interviewee stated that 'it's easier to believe in a God who protects his children and doesn't allow them to ... be murdered'. The

God she believes in – or wants to believe in – is perhaps not a caring one: rather, it is a higher power that guides human history. She says she is undecided about whether it is hard to believe in a helping God after the Holocaust:

> I've given it some thought. I think this question of what God is ... is perhaps a little more complex than either Judaism or Christianity have defined it to be. My belief in God? I have a desire to ... believe. And it's not destroyed by history, it's not. However, believing in the Orthodox religion ... I personally love the wisdom. I go to the Torah, I even look at Christian texts, I look at Buddhist – I go to the wisdom. I'm not skeptical, if that's what you're asking, because that happened. You know that poet in the film [we saw the other day], Rosa, she says: 'He shouldn't have burned us, but God is one and there is no other.' And that's about what I believe. There is this higher power. [AM 35f]

The 'Kantian–Kaplanian' kind of belief was shared by many others, too:

> I think that if God created a natural world and a human being with a capacity for violence ... there's this level of violence, and there's this level of violence. And I don't think that God intervenes in history, to the extent that I believe that God exists, which is a kind of an imaginative act. I say that there is a benign ... force that produces in our world what's beautiful and that has creativity in it, and that has feeling of love and so forth. I don't believe that there's an ongoing kind of finger that comes in and saves some people and doesn't save others, and kills millions, averts accidents, or forgets to avert accidents. [AM 10f]
>
> I had the experience of a DP camp. Do you know what goes on in DP camps? I remember Mr Levin, for example. My father continued to pray, all the time. And I thought you have to do that. I mean, if my father does it, then that's what you have to do. Mr Levin said to my father once in front of me, in front of the children: 'Mr Goldberg,[16] why do you pray? Nobody is listening.' And my father was shocked. And Mr Levin said: 'Mr Goldberg, I prayed all the years of my life ... and what did I get for it? I lost my wife, I lost my children, I lost my parents, I lost my siblings. I've got no one! Why should I continue to pray? What for? Who's paying any attention?' And when I heard it, I want you to know, these words were not wasted on me. I've been thinking about it

ever since ... I'll accept the fact that human beings need a spiritual side; apparently, we are betraying that, we need spirituality. But prayers? catechisms? *Q: Did you ever ask the question Mr Levin did before you met him? During the war did it come to you mind to ask where God was?* I never asked that question until I heard Mr Levin ask it. I don't think I thought it was permissible to ask that question. And another man that had made me the non-observant that I have become was a Russian doctor. When we were liberated by the Russians the doctor said: 'We can't help you much, we don't have much but we'll give you whatever we have. However, you must not eat it at once. You must eat little tiny bites, eat often, but very little, tiny bites. And nothing fatty.' And my father wanted to know if the food was kosher. And the doctor said: 'You are worried about kosher after God permitted to happen what happened!? Look at your children! You are worried about kosher?' *Q: Did you ever ask the question: 'If the Holocaust was possible is God possible?'* Yes, I played with that question. But I don't think God is out there, I think God is in here. And if we don't make the world more liveable, then his absence is greater. If we make the world better, then his presence is greater. I see God as something undefinable, a great mystery, if you will. And the presence of that great mystery is determined by our relationship – if it's loving relationships, helpful, caring, then God is manifest. [AM 31f]

There were also those who claimed they believed in God though they differed significantly from the position of the Orthodox or Hassidic groups. In some cases their reproaches toward religion and the idea of deity were aimed not at God as such but at his idea as propagated by those Orthodox milieus. One of the women interviewed, the only Sephardic woman in the sample, said:

The Holocaust obviously makes it [the issue of God and human suffering] even a stronger point. The one thing I can tell you is that what I absolutely abhor is those very Right-wing fundamentalist Jews who feel that this is God's punishment for something Jews did wrong. That is stupid! That is ridiculous! That is insane! That is harmful! That is dangerous! And that is not a Jewish belief. I think that came across very strongly. I mean, if that's the kind of God that exists – thank you very much. [AM 22f]

Of course, there were respondents who maintained that their faith

in God was practically unaffected by the European catastrophe. This is
how they view the question of God's existence vis-à-vis the Holocaust:

> You hear of so many people who perished in the Holocaust singing
> out *Shema Israel* and then they went to the gas chambers. So
> where was God? Here they were screaming out to God, singing
> their last words to God if he could help ... But I think that the
> Holocaust has not had an impact on me in terms of my relation-
> ship with God. I believe that there is this being, and I think my be-
> lief is because of ... I've gone through some difficult times and I've
> always had the strength, and I've always come through. People say
> I have a very positive attitude, and I think it's because I have this
> belief ... I believe that God has a reason for everything. There was
> a reason – I don't know what the reason was – for the Holocaust.
> I don't know. Where was he? But he was there because he's
> always there. God, he's definitely there – in the Holocaust. And
> why he did what he did, I don't know. Why he allowed these mil-
> lions to perish I don't know. Nobody knows. [AM 9f]
>
> I definitely believe God is very possible. It's hard to me to
> explain it, but as I've gotten older and I've studied Hassidism, I
> understand that this is a waiting room, that there is a better place
> that we will eventually go to, and that one day when the Messiah
> will come all this will be revealed and we will understand the
> answers. This is written in the Torah that nothing bad comes from
> God, only good comes from God. [AM 50f]
>
> The idea of little me versus ... God, the concept of God... who
> am I to question the concept of God? Accepting that this hap-
> pened by God is totally unacceptable to me. There was never any
> reason for me to be able to justify this in terms of God. But the
> idea that we survived – call us whatever you want, an ethnic
> group, a religious group – from ancient times being dispersed –
> that we survived is very meaningful to me. I don't know what
> God's purpose is in terms of eternity ... I cannot understand it.
> Am I angry? Extremely angry. I think that humanity needs God,
> the concept, the idea of God. Obviously I think we are pro-
> grammed to have a need for God. When I am in extreme stress, I
> automatically turn to God. I don't understand why God visited
> this on us, I just don't begin to understand. God being the
> omnipotent being ... God could not be detached from this.
> Whether, as some people say, this is free will ... God has created
> us in his image by giving us free will and it's man who committed

this, and this is the price we pay for free will, I still cannot sort of separate God, free will or not, from this catastrophe. [AM 52f]

When talking with the interviewees, the issue of God's punishment turned out to be very problematic, especially for the believers. In traditional, rabbinic–biblical Judaism, God may intervene in history to punish people. For my respondents, however, this really was an idea they could hardly concur with. They argued that the evil one experiences should be blamed on the human beings who have committed it and not on God. But the theological plane on which suffering has something to do with punishment for sins puzzled many of them. They found it extremely difficult to accept the biblical view that God's pedagogy sometimes consists in punishing people:

What the Germans did was evil; it cannot be explained away. And just what happened on September 11th is an act of evil. And the idea how could God allow the Chmelnitzky pogroms of 1648–1650 where hundreds of thousands of people were slaughtered; the Petlura pogroms – entire communities were wiped out. There is no period in history where the Jewish people had not been persecuted, and I'm sure there were people then who would have said: 'How could God allow this to happen?' This is an age-old question and it's not God who did it. God created man and made it possible for man to have free choice … And if people kill it's because they choose not to follow the path of righteousness – why blame God for that? What happened in Auschwitz is simply the most extreme [evil] … We traditionally, in our prayers, at the High Holidays, at the Sabbath, we do say: 'Mipnei hataeinu galinu me-artzeinu': 'We were exiled from our country for our sins.' For anyone today to say, like unfortunately some of the Satmar[17] *Hassidim* who blame the Holocaust, as you say, on the fact that Jews did not observe the Torah … I think it is absolutely an abomination to say that my grandfather who was beaten up by the Nazis at the Kristallnacht … that he died, because he committed sins. This is nonsense. That is something that is beyond our realm. We dare not enter the realm of judging people. That is something that is clearly reserved to God Almighty … But to blame anybody for the *Churban Europa* I think is terrible. I think that the crime that was committed is so horrible that we should not blame anybody, I mean, obviously the perpetrators, who are the ones who committed the crime. [AM 24m]

I think the moral claim of the prophets that God has redeemed you and will hold you accountable for not living up to the covenant, you'll be punished if you don't live up to the covenant, I think it already began to change under the rabbinic experience of exile, in a sense that theology is finished. It's not theologically or morally tenable any more. It is not viable today. Given the fact that God does not protect those who are faithful to the covenant, the notion: 'Therefore I will punish you if you don't live up to the covenant' is I think grotesque. I respect the biblical text, but for someone today to apply that – that the Jews are being punished for their sins – I find this not only grotesque but morally offensive. I think the Orthodox rabbis, they are the most prone to do this. [AM 29m]

I totally disagree with the interpretation that somehow the Jewish people brought it on themselves or that it was God's retribution for the sins of the Jewish people ... As a historian I can see the confluence of certain factors like long history both in the Catholic Church and in certain regions in that part of the world of antisemitism, plus the influence of ... external political factors like economic decline of Germany, and the whole disarray that was generated by the revolutions of the early 20th century, and the human need to have a certain kind of security, and the strength of that need being so powerful that it could lead people to scapegoat a group to the point of mass-murder. [AM 26f]

The last category includes those respondents who rejected faith in God as a result of their reflections on the destruction of European Jews. Interestingly enough, only four of all American respondents can be said to have lost faith because of the Shoah. And even they claimed that there were other things – the existence of violence and evil in general – that made them question the existence of God. However, it should be made clear that it is very difficult – if it's possible at all – to draw a line of division between the fourth group and the 'Kantian–Kaplanian' section of the third group. One of the features which characterize those classified in the fourth group is that they tended to more overtly admit they saw the Holocaust as a proof demonstrating the non-existence of God. Another thing that might differentiate the 'Kantian–Kaplanian' believers from the fourth-group unbelievers is that the former had doubts but claimed they still believed in some kind of (subjectively defined) God, whereas the latter did not share that belief. On the other hand, the division presented in this analysis may be legitimately questioned as arbitrary. We should keep in mind, however, that the whole problem discussed here is a very delicate one, for it deals with people's deepest feelings and convictions. Therefore, it is an issue which is susceptible to many different interpretations, and other methodological approaches to it are also possible.

A 44-year-old woman, a child of a survivor, who reacted very emotionally to almost all questions related to the Holocaust, asserted that her unbelief in God had much to do with the destruction of European Jews. Although she observed some major Jewish holidays, she was not motivated by faith: rather, she did it partly to please her mother, and partly for herself and her child to be immersed in Jewish tradition. It is noteworthy that the woman was married to a non-Jew, a son of Polish émigrés. Though they were both unbelievers, they wanted Jewish symbols and traditions to be present in their home. And this is what the interviewee said when asked about her attitude toward religion:

> *Q: You told me at the beginning of our conversation that your identity is more of a cultural kind as opposed to religious. Has the Holocaust affected your attitude towards religion?* Yeah, it certainly did. My issues are with God, and that's what I mean when I say 'the religious part of it' as opposed to the cultural part. When you go to temple and you pray to God, that's, yes, that was definitely influenced by the Holocaust. I have felt for a long time and I still feel, although it's changed a little bit, you know, if God exists, if he's there, and he's so great, and he's so powerful, how could he allow something like that to happen? How could he allow all these people to have suffered. It's not even ... so much all the time the death – it's the suffering. People die all the time, but to have people suffer ... [*she starts crying*] and ... to lose their families the way they did ... *Q: What you feel about it – is it just doubts or rather a kind of evidence against the existence of God?* Yeah, I guess that is how I have felt it – evidence against the existence of God. Because if there is a God, then how could this God who, everybody says, loves people so much, how could this God allow it to happen? [AM 27f]

The next example is a case of a follower of Secular Humanistic Judaism, which is definitely a non-theistic religious movement. The man said he had not been satisfied with any of the mainstream Jewish denominations in America. Even Reconstructionism, though that is what his father suggested to him, seemed to him 'still theistic':

I think the notion of God, for me, is certainly affected by the Holocaust – the notion of a personal God was affected ... it's incomprehensible to me that anybody can ... I don't understand how people believe in God in the face of this experience. How could a loving God ...? *Q: Do you happen to hear in yourself the question: If the Holocaust was possible, is God possible?* Yeah. A personal God – who answers prayers – is that possible? ... I didn't formally embrace Secular Humanistic Judaism until I met the people of the City Congregation. And I was unaware of a formalized organization of this type. I was literally always involved with an organized Jewish community. I felt that it was important, I had an identification with Judaism; I wanted a connection to a community, but I was always, consistently disappointed and ... disaffected by my involvement in the formalized congregations. Unquestionably Orthodoxy and Conservative were not comfortable for me. In Reform ... Well, I came away from anything angry, because it was just too much of an intellectual compromise. *Q: Did the Holocaust play any role in your turning towards atheism?* Sure, sure. *Q: You were raised in ... You told me your family belonged to a Reform temple.* Yeah. I mean the thing that's characteristic of so many Jews: They belong, but they don't believe. [AM 28m]

The other interviewee, though not a survivor *sensu stricto*, 'grew up in a small town in southern Germany during the Hitler years'. Two of her aunts had been in Theresienstadt; one of whom died there. Also, her father had been incarcerated in Dachau before the family managed to flee Germany in 1939, when she was a 15-year-old girl. Thus we can assume the person was influenced in a significant way by what she had seen in Nazi Germany and what her close ones had gone through. This is her story:

On the night of November 9, 1938 when the windows in our house were shattered and my father was picked to be taken ... he ended in Dachau. My mother had insisted that as we went to sleep at night we would always say the *Shema*. I think the implication to me was that if you didn't you might not wake up in the morning. That night I announced loudly to my mother: 'I am not saying the *Shema* tonight because I just don't believe it makes any difference.' I never after then felt compelled to ... I find I like to participate in services in the Hebrew which I can read but not translate particularly because when I read it in the English I freeze because I'm really basically a nonbeliever. But I like the tradition, the singing, the ritual, and I'm glad it's continuing. I don't think it's hypocritical, I think I know what I'm doing. I don't think my attitude towards religion has changed particularly because of the Holocaust. I think I would have probably arrived at the same position ... *Q: Does the fact that you define yourself as a nonbeliever depend on the Holocaust in any way?* I'm not at all sure. It may have started that way, but I strongly suspect I probably would have arrived at where I am because I have a very skeptical nature. I don't think I need to have a belief system ... in an interactive deity to make me function. *Q: Does the question 'If the Holocaust was possible is God possible?' seem familiar to you?* Oh, of course. That's what I was saying when I was 14 years old. How can God tolerate evil on a massive scale? I think some other true believers have it easier because they believe in after-life and divine punishment. [AM 39f]

In sum, what could be observed in the American sample is that one half of the respondents seemingly believe in some kind of God, be it a personal, biblical Father-God or an undefined superhuman force. Among these twenty-six respondents there were two survivors and four children of survivors. The faith of two of these survivors and two of the children of survivors can be described as the Kaplanian belief in a superhuman, a-personal deity.

Of the six survivors from the sample, one person belonged to the first group (unbelievers unaffected by the Shoah) and three people have to be placed somewhere between the third and the fourth group. Of the sixteen people who have survivors in their close family (including seven children of survivors), ten are believers – four of them have at least one parent who is a survivor. Among these sixteen people there was one who claimed she could not believe in God because of the Shoah. This woman, aged 44, has a mother who survived the war in Poland. In the course of the interview it turned out that she had been under the strong influence of her mother in terms of thinking through the prism of the Shoah. She said that her mother had always talked about her war experiences, and the respondent was severely traumatized by her parent's stories. She was very emotional during the interview and several times it had to be stopped when she started to cry. Subjectively speaking, this was one of the most moving interviews conducted in New York. What is not to be overlooked, however, is that her mother kept on being religious after the Shoah and did not become an atheist.

What is apparently striking is the relatively significant number of interviewees who have some kind of belief in God, either in a traditional sense or otherwise. Yet among these twenty-six people there is none who, having been an atheist, would have gained faith in God as a result of the European catastrophe – neither a survivor, nor anyone born after the war.

What conclusions can be drawn in the final comparative analysis of the Polish and the American sample? In both groups, those who do maintain a belief in God hold a majority: sixteen respondents in the Polish group (32 per cent) and twenty-six in the American (50 per cent). Also, in the Polish sample, and to a lesser extent in the American sample, many *survivors* have placed themselves in the believers' subgroup. The same was true with respect to *American children of survivors*. With the Polish respondents, the situation was that those who were not survivors themselves were virtually all children of survivors. Thus, in the Polish group, apart from the eight survivors classified in the believers' subgroup, there were also eight non-survivors in the same cluster. It is interesting to compare the number of believers with the number of those who were either agnostics or atheists in both samples. The breakdown of non-believers in the first two subgroups is as follows: twelve Polish Jews (including four survivors) said they were atheists, regardless of the Shoah, while eight of them (including two survivors) claimed that the Holocaust only confirmed and strengthened their unbelief; in the American sample, eight interviewees belonged to the first group (one survivor) and six were categorized as members of the second group (one child of survivor). Therefore, summing up subgroups 1, 2 and 4, we can see that in general terms, respondents from the Polish sample tended to be more atheistically oriented than was the case with the American group. Twenty-three Polish Jews (including seven survivors, with an additional one situated on the borderline between groups 3 and 4), constituting some 46 per cent of the whole sample, and nineteen American Jews (including one survivor and two children of survivors), constituting almost 36 per cent of the entire sample, chose not to believe in the God of the Jewish scriptures.

In the two samples analysed, the category of non-believers refers also to the respondents who claimed they had lost faith because of the Shoah (group 4). It is extremely interesting that only a small proportion of both samples claimed to have lost their faith because of the carnage of the Holocaust. This was the case of three interviewees in the Polish group and five interviewees in the American group. In the former group, in the fourth category there was one survivor; another one, however, was undecided whether he actually had lost faith in a deity; he said that 'during the catastrophe there was no God', but was unsure if this statement expressed his general world view [PL 47m]. In the latter group, no American survivor was classified in the fourth subgroup, yet there was one child of a survivor, and another one was undecided; there were also three survivors who could be put between groups 3 and 4 (there were five such people in total. If the respondents who were genuinely affected by the Shoah and verged on non-belief were to be taken into consideration, we can say that the faith of four Polish interviewees has been seriously challenged by the destruction of European Jews, and the same could be said of ten American respondents.

We can make another interesting observation when comparing both groups, namely that there were significantly more Polish respondents than American interviewees who said they had no opinion on the issue of God vis-à-vis the Holocaust, or who just did not know what to think about it and were not willing to make the effort to express a personal view, or who said they were completely uninterested in the whole topic and thus could not offer their view. In the Polish group there were nine such respondents (18 per cent), whereas only four American interviewees (over 7 per cent) took a similar position – or rather a lack of position.

We have, therefore, three major points upon which to comment: (1) A relatively large number of American interviewees have been categorized as believers, whereas in the Polish sample the subgroup of believers is significantly outnumbered by the subgroups of unbelievers (one out of two survivors from both samples belongs to the third subgroup); (2) Unexpectedly few respondents have fallen into the category of the fourth subgroup; (3) Many more Polish interviewees than American ones were uninterested in the problem of how to reconcile the idea of God with the Shoah.

1. Though American Jews constitute one of the most secularized minority groups in the United States, 50 per cent of the interviewees admitted to having some kind of belief in God. It is worthwhile noting that their statements concerning faith in a deity were not uttered by accident in a situation they could not have expected. On the contrary, they expressed their views on the idea of God in very specific circumstances: it happened during a planned interview and they were responding to questions pertaining to the destruction of European Jews. The significance of the context in which the answers were given cannot be overestimated: the interviewees were faced with the Holocaust, and

yet so many of them claimed that they retained some kind of religious belief *in spite* of the great catastrophe. Moreover, it is very striking that out of six survivors in the American sample, two turned out to be believing people. The young age of the survivors at the time when the Holocaust was perpetrated cannot provide a complete explanation of this fact. For even young children were severely traumatized by what they had experienced. Thus, one might have expected a significant number of them to reject or question, at some point in their lives, the idea of deity. It is even more striking in the Polish sample, where out of seventeen survivors only one person lost his faith because of the Shoah, while eight survivors claimed not to be agnostics or unbelievers.

A possible answer to this problem – and perhaps the best one – can be found in Victor Frankl's concept of the 'search for meaning'.[18] According to Frankl, man's most important, if difficult, task is to find meaning. But is does not necessarily have to be a meaning of life, it can be a meaning of suffering. And that is what the survivors must have faced: the problem of whether there is any sense in their pain and distress. Frankl contends: 'Once the meaning of suffering had been revealed to us, we refused to minimize or alleviate the camp's tortures by ignoring them or harboring false illusions and entertaining artificial optimism.'[19] It is telling in this context that virtually all respondents in both samples said they did see some meaning in their lives and that life was worth living. It was only rarely that an interviewee would assert that the Shoah demonstrates the contingency of our existence. One such person was a Polish survivor who said that she had tried to commit suicide several times, which she thought would have been a solution to the feeling of existential vacuum [PL 13f]. This is exactly the kind of situation Frankl calls a 'lack of the awareness of a meaning worth living for'.[20] We can thus imagine that some of the survivors could have 'worked through' their Holocaust trauma (not in terms of overcoming it completely, but in the sense of facing it) by turning towards a belief in God – which did not necessarily imply involvement in any religious practices. The woman cited above regarded herself as a non-religious person, though she believed that God had created the world and had given human beings free will.

This squares very well with Frankl's idea of the search for meaning, which term signifies in practice a state when an individual attempts to find a source of meaning outside of him/herself. That is why his *logotherapy* (Greek *logos* stands for 'meaning') is more future-oriented and seeks for relationships with *others* in order to help the patient master his/her trauma, in contradistinction to classical Freudian psychoanalysis which is retro- and introspectively-oriented.[21] In boundary situations, such as the Holocaust, there are few 'things' which can serve as anchor points and potential sources of meaning. Hence in many/some cases, people find relief, or even regain psychic sanity, when they acknowledge that there is a higher order, or a higher being, which embraces all events and gives meaning to all sufferings even if the meaning is not immediately accessible to the traumatized person. This situation might be called an existential trust – that there is Somebody who knows the real meaning of each particular pain and death. Frankl calls it a 'supra-meaning'. According to his theory (and clinical practice), this kind of mental–emotional process is therapeutic in character and functions as a 'life-saving procedure'.[22]

Of course, the same kind of process could be carried out by a child of survivor or any other believing person reflecting on the Shoah. And this is what many respondents from both samples have done: they turned to God, the Higher Being, or the Cosmic Ground of Being, hoping that he/it knows what the actual meaning of the Holocaust was. It is symptomatic, however, that in our times many people who seek help from on high choose to believe not in a personal deity, but in a supernal, divine force, which holds true especially with regard to the American sample. That conclusion concurs with what Robert Reeve Brenner has observed in his survey on the faith of Holocaust survivors living in Israel. He claims that many of the survivors who had lost faith after the war tended, over time, to move 'toward the profession of belief in an impersonal God'.[23]

Yet even the believers – in a traditional God or otherwise – do have doubts; they do ask: 'Why?' Brenner saw it in his research, and Frankl was aware of the unavoidable question, too. The latter, in his book, recounted the story of his own daughter, who once asked him why people 'speak of the *good* Lord'. Frankl's reply was that 'the *good* Lord sent you full recovery' from measles, to which she retorted: 'But, please, Daddy, do not forget: in the first place he had sent me the measles.'[24] Earlier in his book, however, Frankl offered what seemed to him a solution to this problem: namely, he said that 'it is a dangerous misconception of mental hygiene to assume that what man needs in the first place is equilibrium or, as it is called in biology, "homeostasis", i.e. a tension-less state'. The Austrian scientist contends that it is rather the contrary: 'What man actually needs is not a tension-less state but rather the striving and struggling for some goal worthy of him.'[25] The paradox of the human being, Frankl believes, is that he is the inventor of the gas chambers of Auschwitz and Treblinka, but it is also he who entered those chambers 'with the Lord's Prayer or the *Shema Yisrael* on his lips'.[26]

And these final reflections are perhaps the most problematic in the context of this study. For if the decision to survive for the sake of one's family, or to refuse to despair of one's fate for the sake of the tasks one wants to perform for a larger community, can serve as real – even corpo-real – sources of meaning for one's future life, the same cannot be said of reciting a prayer when coming to the place of one's death. Even if the very pious Hassidim found some consolation in saying their prayers in the last moments of their lives, can this act provide any meaning to those who have survived? To think of one's loved ones, that they said their prayers but have not survived – does that reveal an ultimate meaning of suffering? If anything it can serve as a spiritual tranquilizer, a last resort in a situation of extreme stress when life will no longer be continued. But, for the living, the supra-meaning as described by Frankl will lend itself to questions such as: 'Why did he send the measles?' As we have seen, in some rare cases the answers provided could be very puzzling: it was God's punishment. The same was observed in Brenner's study of survivors: several respondents answered that 'it's not difficult to come up with very suitable and acceptable reasons for God having brought about the Holocaust ... The Talmud, too, can be consulted for explanations of God's punishment of the people Israel.'[27]

Nevertheless, the 'hard' facts are such that for one half of the American interviewees and for a proportion of Polish respondents, the search for meaning might have motivated them not to completely abandon faith in God. They eventually chose some nebulous, indeterminate belief, rather than clear-cut non-belief. They chose uncertainties, inconsistencies, contradictions and tensions rather than certainty and consistency. So, in terms of functionality of faith in a supra-meaning, Frankl proved to be right. And this is also what one of the American respondents put briefly – namely, that in his opinion it was more correct not to reduce the tension than to solve the problem completely by turning to disbelief [AM 29m]. In other words, despite the tension, or maybe even because of its activating force, 'believing in God became a new form of psychotherapy', as Sherwin Wine has aptly remarked.[28]

Another issue we have to try to elucidate is the number of those who were atheists/agnostics regardless of the Holocaust (including those for whom it was just the final 'nail in the coffin'). In the Polish sample we had twelve interviewees in the first group and eight in the second, making twenty altogether. Among the American respondents, eight belonged to the first group and six to the second group, which is fourteen altogether. Again, knowing how secularized American Judaism became in the twentieth century, one might have expected rather the opposite – more non-believers raised in secular homes in America. It is even more striking if we take into account the fact that in the American sample there is an over-representation of Secular Humanistic Jews. If not for them, the number of secularly-oriented people and those who gave up faith in God for reasons other than the Shoah would have been even smaller. Then, why do we have so many non-believers in the first two groups in the Polish sample and relatively fewer of them among the American respondents? Two answers seem acceptable, one to the question 'Why so many' and the other to the question 'Why so few?' respectively.

As has been demonstrated in this chapter, a large proportion of the Polish interviewees were reared in secular homes where hardly any Jewish traditions were observed, not to mention any belief in God. Also, more than 20 per cent of the Polish respondents learned about their Jewishness only at some point in their childhood or adolescence. In short, until a certain point in time many of them lived without any Jewish or religious consciousness. What is not unimportant, either, is the fact that six of the Polish interviewees had at least one parent who was a communist, while many others' parents worked in government institutions. Hence, for these people, the lack of belief in God, or even declared atheism, was something natural. They did not have to invoke the Holocaust; they just knew there was no God, because their parents said so.

With regard to the American group, one might have legitimately thought that there would be considerably more respondents who were raised in unbelieving families. After all, from the 1920s until the late 1940s, American Judaism had gone a long way from traditional religion-centred culture to secular religion. Also, it might be assumed that in the late 1940s and early 1950s, when thousands of East European survivors were coming to American shores, their testimonies would have led even more of their American brethren to unbelief. Did that really happen? On the one hand, as Brenner has demonstrated, many survivors tended to become atheists during or shortly after the war, and after twenty or thirty years, some of them came to the conclusion that there might have been some impersonal, divine power over man. On the other hand, many other survivors coming to the United States established new centres of Orthodox Judaism and helped the existing ones to flourish. Samuel Heilman argues that many of the Haredim, or pious Hassidic Jews, who landed on the American soil were resolute to continue their faith-world in the new places. After the great trauma, they thought it was their obligation to save whatever could be saved from the world of their fathers:

> After the Holocaust there was no going back. Now even the most traditionally oriented of Jews were forced to reincarnate the past. A new religious framework was created by the survivors. The circumstances of their new incarnation was, however, significantly different from their previous one. Not only were they in new and very different sorts of places, they were carrying on their struggle to maintain their tradition and their opposition to modern western culture in the capitals of this very culture, becoming most concentrated in New York City, the quintessential modern megalopolis ... Being survivors was an important element of the *haredi* world. With only a fraction of their leadership surviving the war ... post-Holocaust, New World *haredim* had a special sense of mission. They felt that they could and should resurrect the world they remembered.[29]

Thus, from the early 1950s on, the Orthodox community was gaining strength and influence. Many young men, brought up in secular homes and fascinated by the quickly developing and exotic world of the Hassidim, all of a sudden wanted to study in their yeshivas. Moreover, at about the same time, a new movement was started within American Jewry: *baalei teshuvah*, that is the repentants or the returnees to 'real' Judaism. The *baalei teshuvah* would include mainly those who felt they would be at home with Orthodoxy and those who wanted to affiliate with Conservative Judaism. Then, in the 1960s, the 'new ethnicism' started and many minority groups saw a chance for themselves to become more visible on the American scene at large. The 'hyphenated' identity appeared: Jewish-American, Irish-American, Afro-American. But being part of an ethnic minority was not so easy as it might have seemed at first – one had to have some concrete content of one's identify, to have some characteristics that distinguished him/her from the general American society and from other minorities. With Jews, the problem was that there was little else to point to than Jewish religion. Of course *Yiddishkeit* was still alive in America, but for the hundreds of thousands of native-born Jews, the Yiddish culture was more distant than Jewish religion (understood theologically or culturally). Hence, it may be inferred that from the 1960s onwards, many of those who were coming back to Jewishness were, in fact, coming back to religion, even if the religion they practised consisted of a set of traditions and belief in a superhuman force many still called God.

2. Why so few interviewees in both samples (three in Poland, or almost 6 per cent, and five in America, or less than 10 per cent) asserted that they had lost faith in God as a result of the *Churban Europa*? Brenner's research revealed that of survivors residing in Israel, 16 per cent of his respondents lost their faith because of the Holocaust.[30] Of course, in the two samples analysed here, survivors constitute only a part, but nevertheless the numbers seem relatively low. Bearing in mind Victor Frankl's theory, we might answer that for many (or even most) people, finding supra-meaning is a condition *sine qua non* for their mental sanity and sometimes for sheer survival. Therefore, there are few people who can carry on in life without the God-hypothesis. Right after the war the percentage of unbelievers who rejected faith in God because of the Shoah might have been greater, but now many of them have died.

There were five people in the American sample (three survivors) and one (a survivor) in the Polish sample who should be placed somewhere between the third and the fourth group. This can point to the fact that apart from those whose unbelief was unambiguous, there were also respondents who had been really seriously shaken by the European catastrophe, and they actually rejected God but were afraid of saying so, and afraid for themselves. They could not be classified in the third group because if they did believe anything, it would be hard to describe the content of their beliefs; nevertheless, they could not make the effort to declare themselves atheists or agnostics. They just led this endless struggle.

Also, for the new generations the Holocaust is becoming ever more distant and existentially irrelevant. They may read a lot about it, they may even teach it, but nevertheless it does not affect their lives. What does affect their lives, as *many* American respondents asserted, are events such as the terrorist attacks of September 11, or the massacres in former Yugoslavia and Rwanda, or singular examples of evil which they encounter in everyday life.

Another answer to this question may be that so few people lost their faith because there was no faith to lose. As a matter of fact, Judaism has virtually never developed a doctrine of God. God was not somebody to speculate about; he was a father and lawgiver whose commandments the Jew should observe. This view of God, however, was unconditionally accepted by the masses, while the educated people, especially since the Haskalah, saw God as the origin, the basis for our existence, the cosmic creator. 'Ultimately God was turned into a vague retired superstar who was so distant and mysterious that nothing positive could be said about him. Any atheist could almost be comfortable with the God of Maimonides. But then why bother with God at all?'[31] This may be one of the reasons why so few interviewees lost their faith in God: 'most people believed – but there was nothing to believe in',[32] and thus nothing to lose. If their faith had little to do with a 'real' biblical God there was no use losing it. There would be no difference anyway.

Why did so few respondents lose their faith ...? Why should it be otherwise? Why does the question impose itself with such overwhelming power? It seems that there is a tendency to think of survivors as people who question the existence of God. Brenner has aptly remarked that 'the most publicized survivors are surely those who lost their faith in God'.[33] But it would probably be more accurate to say that many survivors wrestle with or rebel against God than deny God. This would be best exemplified by Elie Wiesel. In his *Night*, Wiesel declares that God is dead – he is hanging on a gallows, in the body of a young boy. Yet Wiesel is not an atheist; his is a literary quarrel with God, whose existence he does not negate. We may also think of Imre Kertész, Calel Perechodnik; ... Perechodnik, for instance, writes that before the war he was a believing person. But what are his very first words in his 'life confession'? 'Prayer – I am incapable of prayer, belief – I do not believe.'[34] How did he become a non-believer? It was his father's faith that led him to question God: 'I could not listen to an adult, normal person, and a Jew, contend that the murder of the Jewish people was a result of sins against God committed by Jews, and that this whole catastrophe was in accordance with God's will and had been foretold by Jewish prophets.'[35] Thus, reading Wiesel, Kertész, Perechodnik and others, we unconsciously begin to believe that all survivors do or at least should deny God. And if the survivors do, other Jews should also abandon faith. But facts do not conform to our speculations.[36]

3. The third point to dwell on is: Why so many Polish interviewees, as contrasted with only a few American ones, were simply uninterested in the issue of how the destruction of European Jews may have impacted religious faith. If there can be any answer to this question, it is that many Polish Jews, especially those who decided to stay in Poland (and were not forced to leave the country) after March 1968, were

those whose identity was not vividly Jewish and who did not practise Jewish faith. In the 1970s and 1980s there was no formal Jewish religious organization in Poland. What did exist was the Socio-Cultural Society of Polish Jews (Towarzystwo Społeczno-Kulturalne Żydów), an organization officially approved by the communist regime. In many Jewish homes (if they were indeed Jewish) faith was taboo and God was never mentioned; thus, the problem of how to reconcile his alleged existence with the occurrence of the Shoah never arose. In contradistinction to the secular religion of American Jews, the secular lives of Polish Jews were by and large immune to any mention of God, even a Jewish God. Whereas in America, throughout the 1960s, 1970s and 1980s, God was fiercely discussed, denied, fought and defended, in Poland God was limited to the Christian population, and Polish Jews – the few of them that were still there – were becoming less and less Jewish and did not deem it worthwhile to have debates about the existence of God. Perhaps that is why there is no contemporary Jewish theology in Poland.

There is still one more comment I would like to make on the issue of disbelief and belief in a non-personal God-Cosmic Force. We have seen that a significant number of interviewees in both samples have shown some kind of inability to believe in the God of their fathers, to continue the faith in the biblical God. One would think that a natural reaction would be to assume Richard Rubenstein's position: The Shoah has demonstrated that there can be no God – unless s/he is conceptualized as a monster whose thirst for human blood is quenchless: the only God there is, is Holy Nothingness: cold, unmerciful Universe. Yet this was not the choice many respondents would have made. Instead, a good number of those who ruled out any possibility of traditional faith in God claimed that they believed (or *wanted* to believe) in a deity, a cosmic force which governs this world, a kind of impersonal providence. Through such statements they showed themselves to be very close to Mordecai Kaplan's idea of Judaism as a civilization wherein there is room for religion but faith in a personal God is excluded. It seems that the views on ethics and Torah held by many of the Polish and American respondents are also in conformity with the Kaplanian system. They believe that ethical laws were not given by God but were invented by human beings; that Torah is not a revelation of God but a valuable cultural Jewish legacy. Last but not least, they are attached to the Jewish people and not to the Jewish religion, which is a perfect realization of Kaplan's idea of 'peoplehood'. The words with which

James Yaffe has characterized Kaplan's Reconstructionism fits many of the interviewees very well: 'What this philosophy does is to remove Torah, and therefore God himself, from the center of Judaism, and put the people in his place.'[37] It seems, therefore, it is psychologically more 'digestible' to accept a world view where God is an empty idea but nevertheless the notion of God is not completely uprooted, than to 'convert' to a theology without God, where the silence of the cold Universe announces God's death.

NOTES

1. One person was not even sure what the word 'Torah' meant; someone else thought the two names referred to different books.
2. In fact, as James Yaffe maintains, ethical values are considered by many American Jews as a core element of Judaism, even the only one that makes the survival of the Jewish religion in America worthwhile. See J. Yaffe, *The American Jews: Portrait of a Split Personality* (New York: Random House, 1968), p.301.
3. It is very meaningful from the point of view of this research that what convinced the man to see God in terms of a psychological need rather than an actual existence was the Holocaust. This problem is analysed in Chapter 5, section 2: 'How is God (Im)Possible?'
4. A portion of the Pentateuch which is read on Sabbath – every week a different fragment.
5. Among the Polish interviewees, however, there was one person who said that the Torah 'was made sacred by tradition and its sacral character [*sakralny charakter*] is an outcome of its long-lastingness and the important place it has occupied in Jewish life'. [PL16f]
6. Until the late 1990s, the Orthodox community was the only organized religious congregation of Jews in Warsaw. In 1999 a liberal Jewish association/congregation – Beit Warszawa – was established and formally registered three years later. The three men, however, were members of the community not because of the lack of any other religious Jewish group, but because of their conviction that this is the way they want to live their Jewish lives.
7. Yet the same woman said that she accepts the reasoning of those who lost their faith after the war *because* she is a non-believer herself: 'I can understand them because I am an atheist. These are my reflections, and it's not only the case that I was brought up in a particular way. I can simply fathom it on the basis of my own considerations.' [PL 28f] It may be argued, therefore, that this person rejected the possibility of the existence of God without necessarily referring to the Holocaust, yet she is of the opinion that the event has an enormous potential to bring others to unbelief.
8. To Grynberg, after the Shoah, practising Judaism as a religion is a luxury he can't afford. See H. Grynberg, *Monolog polsko-żydowski* (Wołowiec: Wydawnictwo Czarne, 2003), p.64.
9. She was then at about the age of *bat miztva*: that is, the Jewish ritual during which a 12-year-old girl confirms her adherence to the Jewish religion (Hebrew *bat miztva* means 'daughter of commandment'). Quite a similar story was told by Michał Głowiński in his testimony published in W. Śliwowska (ed.), *The Last Eyewitnesses: Children of The Holocaust Speak* (Evanston, L: Northwestern University Press, 1998), pp.57–60.
10. The authors of those letters comforted one another: 'Pray for us, do your best, and Lord God will help [us] all.' 'God will have mercy on us.' 'Thank God I have not collapsed, for everything comes from the Kind Creator.' 'Let God, blessed be his name, say to the Angel of death: Enough! Would to God that we are spared. God save us! Pray for mercy for us.' R. Sakowska

(ed.), *Archiwum Ringelbluma: Listy o Zagładzie* (Warsaw: Żydowski Instytut Historyczny/PWN, 1997), pp.25, 56, 87.

11. L. Hirszfeld, *Historia jednego życia* (Warsaw: Czytelnik, 2000), p.363.
12. Loss of faith in reaction to the cruel events that people saw with their own eyes was not infrequent during the war, as we can find out by reading the letters of victimized Polish Jews. We should note, however, that what many lost was not only faith in God, but faith in man, too: 'I don't believe in anything anymore. [I don't believe] in any Providences [*sic*] if they allowed such pure and innocent human beings go to the slaughter like sheep ... I am most disturbed by the awareness of impotence. Man is a beast which has to wash himself, be clad, and gobble. I can find no comfort.' Sakowska, *Archiwum Ringelbluma*, p.79.
13. See H. Krall, *Sublokatorka* (Warsaw: Iskry, 1989), p.17.
14. Sherwin Wine is the founder of Secular Humanistic Judaism in America.
15. In a sense they could constitute a separate group of the 'undecided'. However, the fact that they do not call themselves atheists or agnostics, and that their belief in some supra-human force has not been not destroyed by the Shoah, makes it reasonable to put them in the third group. Among the undecided there were also people who maintained that they did not openly negate God, but found it problematic to unconditionally accept the idea of a deity. For example, one such survivor said:

> I am not a synagogue person. I will accept the intellectual component of Judaism, but the transcendent ... I'll give you a definition, somebody said it: 'I'm a secular Jew who fears God.' It's there, but it's not there. I am totally immune to any kind of indoctrination, conversion. I'm a Lithuanian Jew, which is the rational Jew – I'm a *litvak*. I'm born in Warsaw, but I'm a *litvak* and a rationalist ... We joined a Reform synagogue. I said: 'Look, Judaism is a buffet – pick and choose.' You don't have to leave it ... But in terms of the divine, it's ... a big question. [AM 47f]

16. Both names, Levin and Goldberg, are not the actual names given by the interviewee. The names have been changed in order for the respondent not to be identified.
17. One of the Hassidic sects of Hungarian origin.
18. See V.E. Frankl, *Man's Search for Meaning: An Introduction to Logotherapy*, translated by Ilse Lasch (a newly revised and enlarged edition of *From Death-Camp to Existentialism*, Boston: Beacon Press, 1963).
19. Ibid., p.78.
20. Ibid., p.107.
21. See ibid., p.98.
22. Ibid., p.79.
23. Brenner, R.R., *The Faith and Doubt of Holocaust Survivors* (New York: Free Press, 1980), p.92.
24. Frankl, *Man's Search for Meaning*, p.121.
25. Ibid., p.107.
26. Ibid., p.137.
27. Brenner, *Faith and Doubt of Holocaust Survivors*, p.219.
28. S.T. Wine, *Judaism Beyond God* (New York: Ktav Publishing House, 1995), p.31.
29. S. Heilman, *Defenders of the Faith: Inside Ultra-Orthodox Jewry* (New York: Schocken Books, 1992), p.31.
30. See Brenner, *Faith and Doubt of Holocaust Survivors*, p.109.
31. Wine, *Judaism Beyond God*, p.30.
32. Ibid., p.31.
33. Brenner, *Faith and Doubt of Holocaust Survivors*, p.109.
34. C. Perechodnik, *Czy ja jestem mordercą?* (Warsaw: Karta / Żydowski Instytut Historyczny, 1995), p.5.
35. Ibid., p.194.
36. It is worthwhile noting that it was really widely believed after Auschwitz that many people lost not only their faith in God but also in society. They questioned the objective validity of the

social values and ideals ('advocated by the Establishment', as Saul Goodman argues) and turned toward ethics based on individual conscience. The Six-Day War of 1967 was another factor undermining the general trust in socially approved concepts and in the benefit of assimilation. It was that event that 'helped awaken an ethnic consciousness of American Jews'. S.L. Goodman (ed.), *The Faith of Secular Jews* (New York: Ktav Publishing House, 1976), p.31.

37. Yaffe, *The American Jews*, p.87.

CHAPTER SIX

Postscript: Memory Reconsidered

1. HISTORY OUTMODED: MEMORY AS A NEW FORM OF HISTORY

Although people have been interested in their past almost since times immemorial, history as a science is a relatively young field of research. Of course, thanks to Tukidides, Herodot or Joseph Flavius, we know many things that would otherwise have been buried in the inaccessible depths of the past. The problem with these ancient historians, however, is that they often failed to distinguish between facts and myths or even hearsay. Their task was to record what happened before or during their lifetimes, but they did not bother to double-check the sources on which they based their theories. That is to say, they lacked what we now call 'the critique of sources'. I do not mean to charge them with overlooking the methods we use today, for that would be an anachronism; I only argue that what is meant by 'history' today was not necessarily what the ancient 'historians' wrote about.[1]

It is a widely accepted opinion that modern history was invented, as it were, in the nineteenth century.[2] As was the case with most sciences, specifically medicine and other natural sciences, history had to be submitted to the judgement of critical thinking, which excluded mythologies, superstitions and folk beliefs. It is no accident that history was born in the century of the 'positive method'. In other words, if not for positivism, history would not have appeared as a modern science in the academic arena. One of the essential elements of the newly accepted method was a specific relation of the historian to the sources he relied on. That critical approach put much stress on the objective side of the events to be described, instead of the subjective and individual aspect. What that implied, in fact, was not only looking with scepticism at the documents one referred to, but also determining which of them could be relied on and which had to be excluded from analysis because of some sort of flaw that was found in them (most often their extremely biased character).

History was not only invented in the nineteenth century, but also became very popular at that time. In spite of numerous attempts to the contrary, the old Europe was falling apart and many new states were created (such as Belgium, Germany and Italy). Also, many ethnic groups, no matter whether or not they had separate states, were found to form or strengthen their identities by referring to their particular histories as fundaments. The birth of nationalism was in large measure due to the emergence of history as a science and as a powerful tool enabling various ethnic and cultural groups to accentuate their distinctiveness. That happened to the Belgians, Poles, Hungarians and, in a certain way, to the East European Jews, especially to the Bundist and the Zionist milieus.

Traditional nineteenth-century and early-twentieth-century history aimed to be an objective science, not influenced by non-rational factors such as theological doctrines or popular mythologies. (This attitude reached its peak in Rudolf Bultmann's concept of the *demythologization* of the Gospels.) This kind of history tended to look for universal schemes of the evolution of the world through time. Hegel's idea of unchangeable laws of history, subsequently taken over by Marx and his followers, was a perfect incarnation and expression of that 'positive' belief that, just as the Earth revolves in accordance with the cosmic laws of physics, so human history is a realization of some irremovable laws (which in Marx developed into historical materialism). The focus on the general and not on the particular, on the societal and not on the individual, was a characteristic trait of that concept of history.

In today's postmodern parlance, 'normal' history would be labelled as a 'totalizing discourse' – one that, in the search for objectivity and certainty, suppresses the single person with his/her individual experiences, ambiguities and uncertainties. History looks for facts and pretends that what it finds are events that actually did take place in a particular context that is to be believed as the real one – or so the typical postmodern critique goes. This claimed social independence of history, as Milchman and Rosenberg argue, is the most problematic of its features:

> we are not prepared to accept a vision of history which sees the past 'the way it really was', which, because it is 'objective', makes it possible for the 'facts' to speak for themselves. The conception of objectivity which underlies such a vision would mean that history, in contrast to memory, is not socially mediated, and structured by its cultural determinants. We do not intend to eliminate the notion of objectivity altogether, but we do reject a conception of objectivity with a capital 'O', a conception which is suprahistorical and transcendental.[3]

Such an anti-objectivist view of history can be thought of as an epitome of postmodernism per se. Unwillingness to grant real objectivity to historical findings is becoming fashionable for many contemporary scholars – historians, sociologists and philosophers. Thus it might be said that history as a science is, in fact, losing its hitherto accepted significance and is even becoming despised for its alleged totalizing character. It is being accused of introducing ideologies masquerading as objective knowledge. Historical objectivity has been considered for some time now as a powerful myth, but a myth nevertheless. It seems only natural, therefore, that a majority of scholars have adopted the concept of 'oral history'. In point of fact, oral history is not literally oral, but in its narrative, epic form it resembles the act of recounting or storytelling. Oral history, as distinguished from traditional history, is closer to the truth and yet not interested in reaching the final Truth (as a matter of fact, advocates of postmodernism reject the idea of Truth). This also holds true with regard to the Holocaust. It has been one of the most 'thoroughly documented and studied' periods of human history, but also one that brought forth countless oral testimonies, as Geoffrey Hartman has observed.[4] However, it is not exclusively postmodernists who oppose the idea of objectivity in history; it is perhaps an ever more pervasive conviction that the historian does not and cannot recreate past events. The faith that history can bring actual events to our consciousness 'has ceased to be tenable, since we know that the act of recreating the past involves decisive subjective moments, and that a gulf separates facts from meaning'.[5] Thus, although history of the Shoah is perhaps the most extensively researched period of human annals, memory of the Shoah is seemingly more important and more vividly present in scholarship as well as in the American wider public sphere, both on the conscious and unconscious planes.

As has been already noted, the nineteenth century was one that focused on history as an identity-building element. Yet that longing for and concentrating on the past is not limited to Romanticism. On the contrary, the second half of the twentieth century saw an even greater and ever-growing interest in things past. As Charles Maier has aptly put it, 'Western societies have been living through an era of *self-archeologization*.' (Italics added.)[6] The continuing fixation on the past has had its perfect expression in the new kind of museum – state-of-the-art multimedia museums. Whereas traditional museums would exhibit actual artefacts and documents (and therefore offered the visitor the real historical objects), the new ones would *represent* the past through reconstructing ancient tools, households and performing (re-living) scenes or situations that happened in the old days. While traditional institutions proposed static history, the new ones gave an opportunity to refresh or even introduce new elements in the visitors' memory – to educate them. Thus, the new kind of history is not about presenting events and facts, but about *re*presenting them; it is not about counting things but rather about *re*counting stories. The new history is a story which is supposed to vibrate with memory and to animate memory. It is a narration of experiences rather than a report on facts. It has less to do with critical thinking, probing different viewpoints, than with easily accepted opinions and popular, imaginative, uncomplicated convictions. Therefore, it is difficult not to agree with what Arno Mayer said about memory, namely that it

> privileges piety and consensus over freethinking and criticism. It tends to foreclose discussion rather than to free and encourage it. Memory is not intrinsically or even primarily a fount of 'dangerous' thoughts and subversive intentions, even if, under certain circumstances, it certainly can and does contribute to fueling liberalizing dissent and rebellion. The memory of Auschwitz has become overly static, inflexible, and undialectical, with the accent almost exclusively on the unfathomable barbarity of the Nazis and the monstrous degradation and suffering of the victims … This foreshortened view marks a withdrawal from history rather than a commitment to it.[7]

Typical examples of modern memory-centred institutions are museums such as the Yad Vashem Holocaust Museum in Jerusalem and the United States Holocaust Memorial Museum in Washington, DC. The latter, designed and built as a place that takes the visitor (who, to be precise, is a not a visitor but a witness) back to the 1930s and 1940s, marks a new stage in museum construction. It is a four-storey educational centre: a sacred space where the witness-visitor is surrounded by documentary–visual art presentations: footage of the actual sites of extermination, slide shows, Nazi Party gathering recordings (*Parteitäge*), blown-up pictures of young SA-troopers, dozens of maps and diagrams, and, finally, pictures of piled-up dead bodies looked on by American liberators. The witness-visitor can enter a real cattle railway car, one in which thousands of people must have been transported to extermination centres located across Nazi-occupied Poland, where most of them found their deaths. One can try to imagine what it felt like in a ghetto when standing by a replica of the only preserved fragment of the Warsaw ghetto walls. Moreover, there is a special section of the museum designed for the youngest visitors. A child accompanied by his/her parents enters a typical middle-class apartment in a German city. This is where some little Daniel lived with his mom and dad. There is his desk, his toys, the kitchen where he had his meals. Then the child observes how Daniel's life gradually changed: he was not allowed to play soccer with his 'Aryan' schoolmates; his parents had to face serious financial problems. Then the whole family was forced to leave their apartment and was taken to a terrible place surrounded by barbed-wire fences ...

Thus, historical reality is transformed into a canvas into which a narrative is woven. The narrative museum uses history in order to produce a memory experience so that the witness-visitor, while 'walking through' the experiences of the victims, acquires a new memory. The victims' memory then becomes his/her own in the process of 'memorial visiting'. To this end, everyone who enters the Washington Holocaust Museum is handed an identity card with a photograph and a short biography of an actual Holocaust victim (either a survivor or not). In this way the visiting takes on a more personal character. The witness-visitor identifies (or so the authors of the idea assumed) with the person represented on the card. What naturally follows is a feeling of sadness and empathy. The visitor, after having witnessed what his/her imagined friend had gone through, internalizes the awareness of being a victim, identifies with all the oppressed and is likely to protest against violence. But the question arises: Does this emotional identification have any practical impact on the visitor's behaviour? If one acquires a perception of him/herself as a victim, will that necessarily stimulate him/her to refrain from using violence in one's real life? When the identification is with the victim and his/her vulnerability, the perpetrators are always 'them' – some others. Hence, it seems that the educational aspect of the museum can be watered down to a sentimental affection instead of motivating the visitor to think in terms of: 'Given extremely unfavourable conditions, I too could become an oppressor or even a murderer.' That kind of consciousness could probably alert one to the danger of committing violence oneself, rather than seeing others as potential aggressors. This, however, is simply an illustration of the times we live in – times when memory is used, and sometimes abused, as an instrument. It is also characteristic that in these memory-focused times, one of the central places is occupied by the myth of the victim. Memory, viewed not as memorization (*mémorisation*) but as commemoration, as Paul Ricouer claims, has become a hallmark of our era which is *une époque commémorative*.[8] In this commemorational epoch, victim status plays a crucial role, for it is around the victims that all commemoration takes place.

Even if history is being replaced (at least to some degree) by memory, the link between the past and identity is not weakened. Yet now it is not only history that constitutes the focus of personal and group identity: memory enters the scene and starts to play an ever more important role in identity politics. The past is, for our generation, like a narcotic: we become addicted to it[9] and it desensitizes us to almost everything that is not the past.[10] Even if we build our identities more on memory than on history, it is still the past that we incessantly refer to. 'Memory is certainly a prerequisite of identity, which rests on an awareness of continuity through time. The hunger for memory has been a remarkable cultural feature of the last decade.'[11] The memory-that-replaced-history is in large measure based on testimonies and memoirs, especially as far as the Nazi Holocaust is concerned.[12] Since the process develops in the public sphere – not only in museums, but also in the academe, in the arts, in literature and film – we are facing a phenomenon that might be called a mobilization of cumulative collective memory.

As could be observed in the previous two chapters, the issue of memory as a prerequisite of identity is very much present in the interviews with my respondents. Most of the Polish informants had direct experience of the war or were children of those who survived. As has been noted, not all of them inherited the knowledge of the Holocaust from their parents, but living in Poland they acquired the identity of victims as Poles. Afterwards, when they found out the Jewish side of their identity, their self-perception as victims became even stronger. Of course, those who had been aware of their parents' identity and war stories were even more imbued with the awareness of being a victim. In America, on the other hand, memory of the Holocaust as a factor shaping my interviewees' self-consciousness was transmitted to them either through the family or, more often, through school, from the media, or from films and books.

2. HOW IS COLLECTIVE MEMORY POSSIBLE?

The notion of collective memory was invented and made known by the French sociologist Maurice Halbwachs. It has been used by most students of history and social sciences; it has provoked numerous commentaries and polemics, and motivated other scholars to present their views on memory and the social aspect of life. If we are to discuss the very concept of collective memory and see how it can be understood today, possessing the knowledge and experiences of the latter half of the twentieth century (which were inaccessible to Halbwachs), we must analyse the concept in its original version, as formulated by Halbwachs. According to his view:

> it is in society that people normally acquire their memories. It is also in society that they recall, organize, and localize their memories ... when I remember, it is other who spur me on; their memory comes to the aid of mine and mine relies on theirs ... There is no point in seeking where they [memories] are preserved in my brain or in some nook in my mind to which I alone have access: for they are recalled to me externally ... It is in this sense that there exists a collective memory and social frameworks of memory; it is to the degree that our individual thought places itself in these frameworks and participates in this memory that it is capable of the act of recollection.[13]

What Halbwachs proposes is a view based on the psychology of the individual and on the theory of society. This particular area – the point where the individual encounters the group – is exactly the essence of the concept of collective memory. And herein lies the difficulty, too. For it is hard, even impossible, to judge which influences which, which is dependent on which. Nevertheless, the object of our interest remains clear: the interrelation between one's memories and the convictions and beliefs of the society one lives in. Even though we are unable to demonstrate who is the primal actor (the 'first mover' or initiator) in this process of mutual exchange,[14] we can examine the very mechanisms of the process. The basic data we possess are that the individual has his/her own content of memory, on the one hand, and that society as a group subject has its beliefs and grounded views concerning the past, on the other hand. Now, how do these two memories, or 'consciousnesses', exist? Are they totally isolated from one another? Are they one and the same thing?

As Halbwachs has emphasized, the interrelation between the individual and the group was much more simple and clear in primitive tribes than it is today in modern (or postmodern, post-industrial) societies. In those primitive tribes the burden of preserving and transmitting memory rested on the elder members who were the guardians of shared memory. The distinctions between the tribe as a whole, the clan, the family and the individual were not so vivid, neither were they very important. That is why all members of a primitive group *shared* a common memory rather than let their individual memories be shaped by group memory.[15] Their memory was an incarnation of the memory and tradition of the generations that had preceded them: it had a continuous present character. Hence, the present was shaped after the memory of the past, while in our times the situation seems to be the opposite: it is rather the past that 'remains under the influence of the present social milieu'.[16] This *presentist* view of memory is characteristic of Halbwachs's parlance. Analysing the way group memory functions in contemporary societies, he underscores the present as an essential element that determines the actual shape of the collective framework of memory. Although Halbwachs himself does not use the term, it might be argued that the present aspect of memory is tantamount to the actual *interest* of the group that perpetuates the memory of its past. That means that the past itself is not the most important, it is just a pretext for creating a certain collective consciousness that will supposedly help the group achieve its purposes. Thus, Lewis Coser is right to conclude that 'collective memory is essentially a reconstruction of the past in the light of the present',[17] if it is not simply formed *in order to meet the needs* of the present.

How does this presentist aspect of collective memory function in practice? Before examining this problem, we have to point to an important distinction that both Halbwachs and Yerushalami introduce in their theories. They contend that there is a difference between memory (*mneme*) and recollection (*anamnesis*).[18] 'Memory', Yerushalami says, 'will be that which is essentially unbroken, continuous. Anamnesis will serve to describe the recollection of that which has been forgotten.'[19] Another difference between the two phenomena is that the former refers to the general and universal, whereas the latter refers to the individual and the singular. Collective memory contains images and concepts that are common to a group of individuals. A single person uses his/her memory through recollecting past events, in which process s/he is helped by society.[20] Recollection almost always takes place in a social context: it is triggered by contemporary events and people, through the spread of information; through gossip; through public activities such as going to work, reading papers and books, watching news and films; or in more private circumstances such as meeting with relatives and acquaintances; writing and receiving letters; making phone calls, and so on. That is why Halbwachs can say that 'the mind reconstructs its memories under the pressure of society'.[21]

To a certain degree, collective memory is never complete, though it tends to be more static than history. That is because collective memory undergoes changes, as it were, invisibly and gradually, and not with successive leaps, turns and sudden movements as may happen with history. Group memory is a 'dual movement of reception and transmission'.[22] One is constantly under the influence of society and, while reflecting on one's own past, adds to the beliefs of the group. That is, the present of society is a powerful determinant of the individual's memories and at the same time it must be touched by the particular pasts of all its members. In this way, singular experiences of individuals (when submitted to reflection) reshape collective memory and create a 'new present' that will appear in the future.

It might seem striking that Halbwachs maintains that the past of a person

> is not preserved but is reconstructed on the basis of the present ... the collective frameworks of memory are not constructed after the fact by the combination of individual recollections; neither are they empty forms where recollections coming from elsewhere would insert themselves. Collective frameworks are, to the contrary, precisely the instruments used by the collective memory to reconstruct an image of the past which is in accord, in each epoch, with the predominant thought of the society.[23]

In this passage we have two important points. One is that the past is not preserved but can be reconstructed; the other is that the frameworks of collective memory are not made up of an aggregate of individual recollections. We have to consider these two points separately.

First, what does Halbwachs actually mean when he says that the memories of the past are rather reconstructed than preserved? Through his own research on dreams, he is convinced that memories do not subsist 'in an unconscious state';[24] they are not recorded in any part of the human brain. This, however, seems really problematic, for if there is no trace of past events, how can they be *re*-constructed? *Ex nihilo*? If, as Halbwachs maintains, collective memory is not a substance existing 'in' society, then the reconstruction of memories cannot have its origin in the public sphere. Yet there is another concept that Halbwachs uses which might prove useful here: it is the idea of image. The past is remembered as images: therefore memory is a collection of images that are stored in some place. Where is the place? It is present in the mind of the individual – existing there either consciously or unconsciously. Thus, we experience problems with recalling the past, not because it is not pre-served in our brains, but because of the specificity of 'storage' memory exercises. The events we do not remember or cannot recall are simply 'too well' stored in our memory and we are unable to retrieve them.

And this is where the collective frameworks of memory come into play: we may be reminded by our relatives of something we have for-gotten, or, on the other hand, society (school, newspapers, secular and religious public ceremonies) can, by accident, help us in recalling things we thought we no longer remembered. Thus the role of social institu-tions in *collective remembering* seems of utmost importance. These institutions act as catalysers of recalling. Therefore, we remember not only in person but also through others. But what these others recall may not necessarily be exactly what we have forgotten, nor an accurate recollection of the event that actually happened. That is why collective memory (in this case, collective remembering) is often discordant with the facticity: it is an image of what we now think might or should have happened in the past. As such, collective memory bears in itself the seed of the present; it is a compromise between the present and the past.[25] If the above is true, then the dichotomy of *mneme* and *anamnesis* (in collective terms) should be more carefully considered, if not questioned. For even though commonsensical reflection would support the distinction between memory and remembering (the one static; the other dynamic), phenomenologically the two notions do not seem so distant from one another. How can memory exist if not through millions of individual acts of recollection (or an intrapersonal discourse)?[26] There is no one single 'collective social mind' in which memory could be stored. What can be stored is subjective knowledge of particular events and people that every individual possesses. When we recall these things/people we simply retrieve bits of information stored in our brains. But if not for our acts of recollection, would we be aware of our memory at all? Could there be memory without remembering? Counterfactually speaking, we would be unable to coin the very notion of 'memory', were we incapable of recalling events that happened in the past. Thus, collective memory is an interactive phenomenon – it comes into existence whenever individuals interact with their society in looking back toward the past and trying to 'pull' it into the present.[27]

Halbwachs also argues that collective memory is not a combination of individual recollections. Nevertheless, he believes that individual memory is an aspect of group memory, as we have seen. The problem may be explained not only by the importance he attaches to the distinction between memory and recollection. It is likely that what he means is that while each human being possesses his/her own capacity for remembering things, collective memory is not 'democratically' shaped by all members of a group and their recollections. Collective memory cannot exist outside of the public sphere; and the public realm, to be sure, has its kings and servants. In other words, there are words and memories that are more influential and more societally fitting than others. Hence, the collective frameworks of memory are constructed not by common people, but by the leaders of a group – be they political or religious leaders.

Can we then legitimately claim that 'contemporary *public memory* [is] different from traditional *collective memory*',[28] as Geoffrey Hartman does? It seems as if Hartman is playing with words, and assumes that the word 'public' has taken on a different meaning than it used to have in the past. But the adjective 'public' has always been used in reference to affairs that are not kept in private but are accessible and/or known to a larger group of citizens. What, then, is so specific about public memory? According to Hartman, 'it is this nervous effervescence [of the media] that marks modern experience and the rise of public memory in distinction from collective memory ... public memory ... strikes us as a bad simulacrum, one that, unlike the older type of communal or collective memory, has no stability or durée, only a jittery, perpetually changing yet permanently inscribed status.'[29]

One cannot avoid the impression that the difference Hartman has in mind is mostly technical: it is that public memory is created and popularized by the media and, as such, it is unstable. Yet in times of no mass media, collective memory was also constructed and spread in the public sphere by public persons: shamans, clan leaders, the caste of priests, prophets, sages, scholars and universities, and, last but not least, state officials. This was always part and parcel of the public life of all societies. No kind of group memory could, *ex definitione*, function outside of the public domain. Even though the constructors of collective memory often constituted a separate, privileged subgroup (as is, to some extent, still the case nowadays), collective memory – that is their product – circulated within the general public. Otherwise it could not perform its unifying, sense-building and identity-building role, as it always has.[30]

3. HYPERTROPHY OF MEMORY: MEMORIALIZATION AS
A POLITICAL ISSUE

We have seen how memory has become more important than history and how it has attracted the attention of present-day societies. My main interest in this chapter is how collective memory functions within American Jewry. It is my conviction, based on personal observation as well as on the observations of other authors, that the memory of the Holocaust is an exceptionally powerful factor shaping American Jewish identity. The memory (or memories) of the Shoah is being invoked in innumerable public ceremonies. In fact, these ceremonies can be called 'memory-actualization' or 'memory-realization', or even 'memory-reification'. This means that memory of the European catastrophe is becoming (or has become) an object of veneration, and at the same time it is a 'plastic substance' that is being modelled by some of American Jewish groups and leaders.

Using one's memory for the purpose of identity-building and keeping it alive can hardly be reproached with any rational argument. For the point is not that memory of the past had better not be dealt with by a given group; the problem is *what kind* of memory is used and popularized.[31] It may be disputable, but it seems as if Holocaust memory were immune to history or even counter-historical. That does not deny, of course, the fact that history of the Holocaust has developed to an immense size, and the *Churban Europa* is now one of the best researched and documented periods in human annals. Yet memory lives its own life; its itinerary runs in parallel to that of history. It is interesting to learn what Yerushalami has to say on this topic:

> I have no doubt whatever that its [the Holocaust's] image is being shaped, not at the historians anvil, but in the novelist's crucible. Much has changed since the sixteenth century; one thing, curiously, remains. Now, as then, it would appear that even where Jews do not reject history out of hand, they are not prepared to confront it directly, but seem to await a new, metahistorical myth, for which the novel provides at least a temporary modern surrogate.[32]

It is worthwhile stressing that it is not just the common people who have moved the focus of their interest from history to memory; it is also the historians (or maybe it was the historians in the first place) who have made history more memory-like. The very act of remembering and retrieving memory is now phenomenologically the main object of study for many professional historians.[33] Indeed, as Charles Maier has pointed out, 'memory has become not just a glass through which the past is viewed perhaps darkly, but, so to speak, a viscous experience'.[34] That would explain, at least to a certain extent, why many contemporary ethnic, cultural and religious communities dwell so much on memory. They become attracted to how their past is remembered and narrated; they are attracted by the spectacle of memory, and the viscosity thereof makes them unwilling and maybe even incapable of trying to find balance between history and memory – the balance that could bridge factual truth and faithfulness to one's own existence, as Ricoeur has postulated it.[35]

Thus the collective memory of American Jews is also an experience of attraction and viscosity. The central point of reference for many of them is the Holocaust. And the memory-actualization of the Holocaust – transforming the event into the content of memory and making memory Holocaust-centred – has now become indispensable to a part of American Jewry. The fact of being a survivor, or a survivor's child, or belongingness to a nation of Nazi victims, is viewed by many a Jew as a common denominator of the whole group. Although history is unable to deny that conviction (in spite of the attempts of Holocaust deniers), this belief is nevertheless not grounded in history but in collective memory. It is within these frameworks of memory that many American Jews construct their identities. And attending public ceremonies commemorating the Shoah proves both practical and unavoidable. This is just how collective memory of this group functions: much of its content deals with the catastrophe. And here again we can be astonished by Charles Maier's deliberately provocative view:

> Let me risk bad taste by beginning with the most egregious branch of what might be called the memory industry, that is Holocaust commemoration. Major museums to commemorate and supposedly teach the lessons of the Holocaust are going up in Washington, Los Angeles and New York. Whereas in many respects these will be museums of history, I have suggested that they are part of a memory industry. I believe this is a fair characterization since it is the aftermath of memory and only secondarily the pursuit of history that motivates historical activity; historical research utilizes memory ... In its impulse to be retrieved and not to be explained, collective memory must claim some liturgical impulse [for] memory involves sacralization ...[36]

We might ask why memory sacralizes certain events while it

condemns others for oblivion. That, however, is not so difficult to guess. Memory is simply 'drastically selective;'[37] it focuses on those points of the past that bear with them the greatest identificational potential. Now that even history itself is becoming less and less distinguishable from memory (with many historians preferring 'storytelling' to gathering and interpreting data[38]) it is all too clear and understandable why memory, with its viscous and selective character, is perceived as an ideal vehicle of identity.

Also, we have to be aware of the fact that memory, as Berel Lang has observed, is an institution in itself.[39] Whether it is a personal or a social phenomenon, memory always functions as an institution; its task is to assure the individual's/the society's connection with the past. Therefore, it can be argued that the very term 'memory' refers both to a mechanism (or process) and to the product of the mechanism. The institution of memory produces and perpetuates memories.[40] Our very ability to remember is memory, and what it stores is memory, too. The institutionalization of memory, however, should not necessarily be understood in pejorative terms. It is a cultural fact typical of our times: as it is so easy to publish and popularize, so to speak, one's memory (or memories), the process of its institutionalization is inevitable:

> Culture now would turn individual memory into the systematic forms of expression: the axioms of historical explanation, the compilations of statistical data, the devices of fiction and poetry, the aspirations of theological summary. And then it would move further to turn these single lines .... into institutions with a larger and corporate reach: laws and trials, museums, libraries, centers of research, courses of study, conferences, monuments of bronze and stone. The individual memory, the individual imagination, the individual conscience ... organized themselves.[41]

What is of highest importance in the passage cited above is that individual memory, when it undergoes the process of structurization, becomes collective memory. In fact, 'collective memory cannot take form and persevere without organization and orchestration'.[42] If, therefore, the emergence of collective memory as an institution is a neutral, or value-free, phenomenon, can one say memory becomes sometimes politicized? And can there be a hypertrophy of memory?

Generally speaking, any human activity can prove politically useable, and thus it can be used (and abused) for political purposes. This is what Charles Maier has called 'search for a useable past'.[43] And memory is no exception here – it can be, and at times is, misused for political purposes. As David Roskies claims, 'abuse[d] Holocaust memory forms part of a much larger mobilization of group memory for the sake of group survival',[44] which can be observed in the American Jewish community. To be sure, the meaning of the word 'survival', as used here, refers not only to the biological level of a nation's existence. It also points to dangers threatening its cultural and/or religious identity. But that struggle for cultural survival can sometimes turn into the will to dominate the scene of public memory, to produce powerful collective memory which will confirm and guarantee an exceptional character of a particular group. That is perhaps why several authors maintain that the memory of the Shoah has been deformed and distorted just because of the issue's being raised in political affairs.[45]

But what exactly are those distortions and abuses of the Holocaust? What are the actual political profits that some American Jews hoped to gain? We can find brief answers to these questions in Berel Lang and Arno Mayer. Speaking of the deformations of the Holocaust, Lang says:

> as with any reformulation or abstraction moved by events opaque in their density or menace, the way was open in this institutionalization for a variety of falsifications: in the self-justification pursued constantly by theories and ideologies, by individual and cultural sentimentality which sought by a turn to the past to elude the severities of the present ... although it is necessary to recognize that the deformations of the Holocaust have not been as extreme as they might have been, still the evidence is plain of violation and exploitation: in the political rhetoric which directs charges of genocide or Nazism against acts that, terrible as they are, are clearly not *that* ... [and also] in the many varieties of Holocaust 'business' from which writers and speakers on the Nazi genocide have been unable or unwilling to dissociate themselves ...[46]

Mayer, writing about the history and memory of the Judeocide, argues:

> historical narratives and interpretations ... have been – and continue to be – shaped and instrumentalized to exalt rulers, to generate founding legends, to promote national identities, to brace belief systems, and to rationalize abuses of power ... Indeed, the purpose of heralding a collective memory is less to preserve an immutable receding past than to readjust and enliven it for use in arguments over policies for today and tomorrow: to deny or minimize the instrumental aspects of collective or social memory

is to misconceive it ... In 1976, at Yad Vashem's Wall of Remembrance, Mordechai Gur, then Israel's chief of staff ... declared the Holocaust to be 'the root and legitimation of our enterprise', and insisted that the army 'draws its power and strength ... from the holy martyrs of the Holocaust and from the heroes of the [Warsaw ghetto] revolt'.[47]

As the Nazi Holocaust and its memory were becoming more politicized, there arose the issue of competing for being acknowledged as a victim. Victimhood came to be seen 'as a valuable possession'. Not only Jews (especially those in the American diaspora), but 'other peoples also want[ed] the status of victimhood'.[48] According to Charles Maier, this change in the perception of victimhood was brought about by the phenomenon he calls 'hunger for memory'. Victimhood ceased to be thought of as pitiable; instead, it came to be prized.[49] Retaining its basic identificational function, memory started to focus not only on heroes but also on victims. This, however, is not surprising as far as Jewish memory is concerned, yet it is a new phenomenon on the American public scene. The presentist character of memory helped transform it into an important sphere of social life and even a commodity. Halbwachs's frameworks of memory thus became less a reconstruction of the past and more a construction of new values and identities vaguely linked with the past. Collective memory started to be seen and to function as 'a semi-opaque and self-referential activity'. This process affected not only memory but history too: 'causal analysis [was] replaced by representation'.[50] Therefore, what we are dealing with here is a significant transformation of memory (from multidimensional to unidimensional, politically useable) and a decomposition of traditional history.

As strange as it may seem, to some authors the problem with Jewish memory is that it is now focused almost exclusively on Jewish suffering. Arno Mayer has noted that 'the exaggerated self-centeredness, if not entrenchment, of the Jewish memory of the Judeocide ... entails the egregious forgetting of the larger whole and of all other victims'.[51] Controversial reproaches were also formulated by Charles Maier, who believes that renewed memory of the Holocaust may sometimes imply 'aggressive exploitation of the dead [and] a more exclusive property right in suffering'.[52]

We are finally driven to ask vexing questions: Can there really be a surplus of memory? Can memory be counterproductive? Can there be an overproduction and banalization of Holocaust commemoration? We should always be cautious in giving straightforward answers to such questions, for we are dealing with the memory of the dead and of the living, with unimaginable human suffering. It seems, nevertheless, that those who have criticized the overabundance of Holocaust imagery in public life are in large measure right. The object of their criticism, and of mine, is not memory (or history) per se. Rather, it is the uses of the past that now tend to be more and more concerned with social and political benefits. It is the legitimizing function of Shoah commemoration that is a problem, *not the Shoah itself, nor the commemoration itself.* Certain aspects of collective memory of the Holocaust may seem questionable when that memory is instrumentally used in order to justify some dubious or controversial political stances.[53] Also, what might be puzzling in terms of social relations is the (sometimes) exclusionary character of Holocaust memory. On the one hand, every individual and every group has the right to build their identity on anything they consider important and meaningful. Yet, on the other hand, centring a group's life and consciousness on death and victimhood can cause social friction and animosity instead of preparing a stable ground for the perpetuation of the group's cultural identity. Just as anti-Semitism is not a 'mysterious guarantee of the survival of the Jewish people',[54] so is the focus on the Shoah not a warrant of their cultural and social unity and development.

NOTES

1. Although we employ the word 'history' with regard to many ancient records and religious narratives, we have to bear in mind that they were not produced by historians, in the modern meaning of the term. This also refers to most biblical concepts of history (and to the Bible as 'history' as well), for, as Yosef Hayim Yerushalami has noted, they were 'forged not by historians, but by priests and prophets'. On the other hand, Yerushalami maintains that biblical stories form, in fact, 'actual historical narrative' and should be considered 'the most distinguished corpus of historical writing in the ancient Near East'. Y.H. Yerushalami, *Zakhor: Jewish History and Jewish Memory* (Seattle, WA, and London: University of Washington Press, 1996). p.12.
2. According to Yerushalami, this is in large measure due to the process of secularization of thinking about the past. In other words, modern history, especially Jewish history, differs from the previous concept of history in that it has become secularized. See Yerushalami, *Zakhor*, p.91. The developing process of secularization of history (or historicization of Judaism) has led to a tension – or more than that, an opposition – between Jewish history and Jewish memory. See H. Bloom, Foreword, in Yerushalami, *Zakhor*, p.xix.
3. A. Milchman and A. Rosenberg, *Eksperymenty w myśleniu o Holokauście: Auschwitz, Nowoczesność i Filozofia* (Warsaw: Wydawnictwo Naukowe Scholar, 2003), p.140.
4. G.H. Hartman, *The Longest Shadow: In the Aftermath of the Holocaust* (Bloomington and Indianapolis, IN: Indiana University Press, 1996), p.3.
5. G.M. Kren, 'The Holocaust as History', in A. Rosenberg and G.E. Myers (eds), *Echoes from the Holocaust: Philosophical Reflections on a Dark Time* (Philadelphia, PA: Temple University Press, 1988), p.3.
6. C.S. Maier, *The Unmasterable Past: History, Holocaust, and German National Identity* (Cambridge, MA: Harvard University Press, 1997), p.123.

7. A.J. Mayer, 'Memory and History: On the Poverty of Remembering and Forgetting the Judeo-cide', *Radical History Review*, 56 (Spring 1993), pp.7f.

8. Ricoeur alludes here to Tzvetan Todorov and Pierre Nora. See P. Ricoeur, *La Mémoire, l'histoire, l'oubli* (Paris: Seuil, 2000), pp.97, 104f.

9. See C.S. Maier, 'A Surfeit of Memory? Reflections of History, Melancholy and Denial', *History and Memory*, 5 (Fall–Winter 1993), p.140.

10. In any case, we should keep in mind that neither history nor memory guarantees direct access to the past. Every time we try to reach events from the past, we act as 'after-mediators' and cannot avoid all kinds of biases. See Mayer, 'Memory and History', p.8.

11. Maier, *Unmasterable Past*, p.149; see also p.139. Arno Mayer's contention is that memory is even 'in fashion these days'. Mayer, 'Memory and History', p.7.

12. The ambiguous, dialectical relation between history and memory can be judged differently by scholars representing different philosophical schools. To Mayer, as we have seen, the problem is that history is being put aside by the omnipresence of memory. To Hartman, on the other hand, the situation seems to be the reverse: 'As events "pass into history", and they seem to do so more quickly than ever, are they forgotten by all except specialists? "Passing into history" would then be a euphemism for oblivion, though not obliteration.' Hartman, *Longest Shadow: In the Aftermath of the Holocaust*, p.60. It might be argued that the very fear of the past passing from memory to history is an expression of the dominance of memory. In other words, the memory-centered narrative (which is an example of deconstructive thinking) strives not to let events be 'swallowed' by the allegedly corrupted, depersonalized historical discourse that seeks objectivity. In fact, for Hartman, if there is any truth of the past, it lies within the domain of memory rather than history, especially with regard to the Holocaust. For history, so he claims, tends to look for similarities and contextualizes particular occurrences, whereas memory dwells on the unrepeatable and the singular; 'rampant analogies between the Holocaust and other catastrophes or disputed actions ... weaken memory and the truth.' Ibid., p.10.

13. M. Halbwachs, *On Collective Memory*, edited and translated by L.A. Coser (Chicago, IL: University of Chicago Press, 1992), p.38.

14. This phenomenon can easily be observed in how the Holocaust is being remembered and taught, and how knowledge about it is being popularized. For one thing, what we call the collective memory of the Shoah is shaped by the survivors, eyewitnesses and the first historians of the Holocaust such as Reitlinger and Hilberg. For another, after tens of years the survivors are influenced by other survivors and also by the historians' narratives; then we have the second generation survivors and scholars whose perception of the Holocaust has been impacted by those who went though it. Moreover, there are also those survivors who have begun to speak about their war experiences only recently – after having read lots of survivor testimonies and historical works, after having seen tens of documentaries and feature films. Thus, what we now call 'Holocaust memory' is a kind of social space that is an amalgamate of singular, individual testimonies – either published or unpublished but spread among relatives and friends – and scholarly works by historians, sociologists, psychologists, philosophers and theologians; we have Holocaust courses in school and university curricula, Holocaust museums, memorials, Hollywood productions, and even Holocaust comics. All these now form the social frameworks of Holocaust memory.

15. See Halbwachs, *On Collective Memory*, p.48.

16. Ibid., p.49.

17. Lewis A. Coser, Introduction, in Halbwachs, *On Collective Memory*, p.34.

18. See Yerushalami, *Zakhor*, p.107; Halbwachs, *On Collective Memory*, passim.

19. Yerushalami, *Zakhor*, p.107. Paul Ricoeur, too, argues that there is an important difference between memory and recollection. In his view, *anamnesis* is more active and it demands a volitional involvement, *anamnesis* implies research. *Mneme*, on the other hand, is rather static and passive. Ricoeur describes it as *pathos*, a Greek word which signifies, in the first place, not suffering but sensing, feeling. See Ricoeur, *La Mémoire, l'histoire, l'oubli*, p.67.

20. See Halbwachs, *On Collective Memory*, p.43.

21. Ibid., p.51. It is worthwhile noting that Halbwachs distinguishes between personal memory of an individual concerning his/her own life, and historical memory that refers to events one has not experienced in person. On the face of it, this view seems sensible, but upon further consideration it should be deemed incongruent with Halbwachs's general concept of the collective frameworks of memory. For if anything that we recall takes place within these

frameworks, why would our autobiographical recollections be excluded from the scheme? On the contrary, it seems that even our most personal, intimate memories must *of necessity* refer to the social world, for the way we perceive ourselves is always rooted in our position in a group (family, workplace, ethnic community, state). Moreover, the way we see ourselves (be it in the present or in some point in the past) is often a projection of how others see us. In other words, the image we have of ourselves is not infrequently a manifestation of group awareness and/or group beliefs. In present times, just as in the past, family plays the role of a bridge between the individual and the society at large. It is in the family that we acquire our first personal experiences and make contact with a larger group. Initially, it is exclusively through family that collective memory becomes interwoven into our own memories. Then, in school and other public institutions, collective memory exercises an ever greater influence on the memory of the individual. For more on the issue of collective memory and family, see Halbwachs, *On Collective Memory*, pp.54–83.

22. Yerushalami, *Zakhor*, p.110.
23. Halbwachs, *On Collective Memory*, p.40.
24. Ibid., p.39.
25. This happens when human reason is trying to bring more coherence to memory. As Halbwachs has convincingly pointed out:

> when reflection begins to operate, when instead of letting the past recur, we reconstruct it through an act of reasoning, what happens is that we distort the past, because we wish to introduce greater coherence. It is then reason or intelligence that chooses among the store of recollections, eliminates some of them, and arranges the others according to an order conforming with our ideas of the moment. From this come many alterations.

Ibid., p.183.
26. Halbwachs, too, believes that in spite of there existing collective memory, one always has one's own memory which participates in group memory:

> everyone has a capacity for memory [*mémoire*] that is unlike that of anyone else, given the variety of temperaments and life circumstances. But individual memory is nevertheless a part or an aspect of group memory, since each impression and each fact, even if it apparently concerns a particular person exclusively, leaves a lasting memory only to the extent that one has thought it over – to the extent that it is connected with the thoughts that come to us from the social milieu. One cannot in fact think about the events of one's past without discoursing upon them.

(Ibid., p.53.)
27. This interactive aspect of collective memory is what Halbwachs calls *discoursing* upon the past. The discourse, even if it is silent and intimate, is not a pure monologue, but a dialogue between the individual self and the voice of society as it is internalized in the individual.
28. Hartman, *Longest Shadow*, p.106.
29. Ibid., pp.106f.
30. Hartman has found followers of his theory in Milchman and Rosenberg, who claim:

> 'Hartman's politicized collective memory', no less than his public memory arises with the demise of collective memory and the traditional communities in which they were constructed. What links these different ways in which people(s) remember is that each one is a social or cultural memory. Moreover, if memory is socially or culturally constructed, culture is itself inextricably bound to memory.

Milchman and Rosenberg, *Eksperymenty w myśleniu o Holokauście*, p.134. It seems, however, that there is little evidence to support a sharp distinction between the collective and the social. Therefore it is probably reasonable to stick to Halbwachs's classical term (remember Ockham's razor).
31. Paraphrasing Yerushalami's view that 'the choice for Jews as for non-Jews is not whether or not to have a past, but rather – what kind of past shall one have' (Yerushalami, *Zakhor*, p.99), we could say: 'the choice is not whether or not to have a memory, but what kind of memory to support'.
32. Ibid., p 98.
33. See Maier, 'Surfeit of Memory?', p.137.

34. Ibid., p.138.
35. See Ricoeur, *La Mémoire, l'histoire, l'oubli*, p.648.
36. Maier, 'Surfeit of Memory?' pp.143f. In this context, Paul Ricoeur spoke of 'la sacralisation et ... la monumentalisation' of Holocaust memory, which can eventually become 'la mémoire blessée, voire malade', wounded or sick memory. Ricoeur, *La Mémoire, l'histoire, l'oubli*, pp.336f.
37. Yerushalami, *Zakhor*, p 95.
38. Berel Lang argues that 'the writing of history is restricted either to a bare assembly of chronicles or to narrative "storytelling" in which the line between fiction and nonfiction is blurred. That there has been an emphasis recently on just these conceptions of historiography is undoubtedly due to the inadequacy of past efforts at causal explanation—but it is clear that these recent alternatives to the latter, whatever else they accomplish, rule out neither the possibility nor (more importantly) the need for explanation.' B. Lang, *Act and Idea in the Nazi Genocide* (Syracuse, NY: Syracuse University Press, 2003), p.167.
39. See ibid., p.xxv.
40. According to Arno Mayer, 'the principle and production of memory ... may be said to date from the Great War of 1914–1918. This colossal conflict was the first major phase of the Thirty Years War of the twentieth century ... While Verdun became emblematic of the slaughter of World War I, Auschwitz became emblematic of the slaughter of World War II.' Mayer, 'Memory and History', p.9. It can be said that the production of mass death finds its consequence (more precisely: one of its many consequences) in the emergence of mass (that is, collective) memory. This seems to be true in reference to the triad 'Verdun–Auschwitz–Hiroshima'. Each of the three place names has become a symbol of a particular kind of death: fields of death in Verdun (pre-modern death); factory of death at Auschwitz (modern, industrialized death); plasm of death in Hiroshima (postmodern, hi-tech death). And all three of them have generated an enormous, institutionalized, public memory.
41. Lang, *Act and Idea*, p.229.
42. Mayer, 'Memory and History', p.12.
43. Maier, *Unmasterable Past*, p.2.
44. D.G. Roskies, 'Group Memory' [review of Peter Novick's *The Holocaust in American Life*], *Commentary*, 108 (September 1999), p.65. Maier contends that one of the 'subtext[s] of Holocaust commemoration [was that] it has served to impose a certain unity of the Jewish community in the United States'. Maier, 'Surfeit of Memory?', p.146.
45. See especially Alter, 'Deformations of the Holocaust', pp.48–54; G. Schoenfeld, 'Auschwitz and the Professors', *Commentary*, 105 (June 1998), pp.42f.
46. Lang, *Act and Idea*, p.230.
47. Mayer, 'Memory and History', p.13.
48. Maier, *Unmasterable Past*, p.161.
49. See ibid., p.164.
50. Maier, 'Surfeit of Memory?', p.141.
51. Mayer, 'Memory and History', p.17. Edward Linenthal has observed: 'what came to be known as "the Holocaust" was often indistinguishable, in the immediate postwar years, from the millions of noncombatant casualties due to terror bombing of civilian populations, epidemic illnesses, or starvation.' An important change in consciousness occurred in the 1960s, the decade of the Eichmann trial and the Six-Day War: 'during the mid-to-late 1960s, American Jews became less reticent about being Jews in public, as ethnic particularism became an accepted form of cultural expression'. At that time many people, Abraham Joshua Heschel among them, would ask: 'Will there be another Auschwitz, another Dachau, another Treblinka?' Linenthal, *Preserving Memory*, pp.5, 9.
52. Maier, *Unmasterable Past*, p.164.
53. See H. Arendt, *The Origins of Totalitarianism* (San Diego and New York: Hartcourt, 1985), p.9.
54. Ibid., p.8.

Conclusion

In the introduction to this book I presented my hypothetical assumption that *the Holocaust, as the destruction of the Jewish people on an unheard-of-scale, has had a tremendous impact on all contemporary Jews. First and foremost, it must have shaken their belief in the God of the Bible, leading many of them to atheism. It seems very probable that the survivors – those who experienced the horrors of the Shoah with their own bodies and minds – will be, because of the torment they went through, in a large percentage non-believers. Also, the Shoah must have affected what it means to be a Jew today.* That was my ideal type. Does it have to be modified, after confronting it with reality? Was it helpful in exploring the social attitudes and concepts of contemporary Polish and American Jews in relation to the Shoah?

It seems extremely difficult, or even risky, regarding the delicate nature of the issue, to put forward any firm and unquestionable statements. A first general conclusion is that the working hypothesis cannot be accepted in its original form. As could be seen both in the published texts analysed and in the interviews, opinions on the subjects I was exploring were significantly differentiated. Among Jewish authors who have written about the Shoah, only a few claimed to have lost faith in God as a result of their experience and/or awareness of the Jewish catastrophe. The same turned out to be true with regard to the people interviewed: only a minor proportion of respondents from both samples admitted that the Holocaust made them reject the idea of the biblical God.

My deep conviction, after having read Richard Rubenstein's works, was that many Jews would share his view: namely, that after Auschwitz, faith in a personal God is impossible. This seemed quite likely, since the tragedy touched the Jewish people; thus the Jewish people – I thought – would in significant numbers lean toward atheistic positions. I thought that this would be quite logical: history has denied God's presence in its midst, and therefore it has denied the existence of this God whom the Torah describes as a God who intervenes in history, and whom the Jews traditionally regarded as a father who cares for their lives. As we saw in Berkovits and Fackenheim, this did not happen on the theological plane. What is more, until Rubenstein's famous *After Auschwitz*, there was virtually no debate in the United States on the subject of God's existence in light of the Shoah. Among the very Orthodox and Hassidic thinkers, the idea of the biblical God was fiercely defended. They used traditional theological paradigms that interpreted suffering – and actually anything that happens – as God's acting. They applied their biblical–rabbinic vision of history to the period of the Holocaust as if it were just one of the chapters of Jewish history. This was only confirmed by the fact that they automatically employed the term *Churban Europa* to define the destruction of much of Europe's Jewry. Thus, the Orthodox milieus have continued to see history as 'God's playground', an area that belongs to the sacred sphere of religion. In short, they refused to secularize history, as was the case with almost all other Jewish denominations. Their view of history remained rooted in mediaeval theology, which used philosophical terminology and categories to explain the facts of ordinary life as meaningful in the realm of religion.

Yet there were, too, some Orthodox thinkers who were to some degree non-traditional, although it would be difficult to call them radical. Eliezer Berkovits, for example, said that to him, faith after the Holocaust was as incomprehensible as unbelief. He agreed that the Holocaust was a scandal, and at the same time he did not completely reject that vision of history that needs the divine power to make history sensible. Also, he referred to the classic rabbinic concept of *hester panim*, the hidden face of God, in order to justify the immensity of Jewish suffering during the war. This opinion was not shared by another Orthodox thinker, David Weiss Halivni, who objected to the use of *hester panim* as the paradigm of divine invisible presence in history. Halivini rightly argued that the biblical category of *hester panim* implied the idea of divine punishment for sins. Here he was in complete disagreement not only with Berkovits but with all of the Hassidic rabbis such as Shapira and Wasserman and their followers, who had interpreted the Holocaust in terms of God's retribution and of sacrifice.

In the Orthodox world, the most inspiring and thought-provoking reflections on the Shoah were those presented by Irving Greenberg, a neo-Orthodox rabbi. In truth, his concepts and his personal experiences were close to those shared by a significant number of my American interviewees. He claimed that after the Holocaust, belief in God can best be perceived as 'moment faiths'. He also underscored the tension between belief and unbelief, which in his opinion is a genuine struggle experienced by a believing person who faces the Shoah in all seriousness. Greenberg also pointed to a very important change that has been brought about by the European catastrophe. According to him, after the Shoah, man has become the senior partner in the covenant with God; that is why it is on human beings that all responsibility now rests. This is the new burden that modern man has to bear: the burden of adulthood and maturity, as the existentialists used to call it. This, however, is just one step away from the secular humanists' faith of many of my Polish and American interviewees – and not very far, either, from Rubenstein's view of the cold universe where God is Holy Nothingness. Although they differ very much from one another in their reasoning (Greenberg comes to his conclusion as a result of his reflections on the covenant, while Rubenstein's concept appears to be the consequence of a complete rejection of the idea of covenant and chosenness), the practical implications of their ideas are quite similar to each other: we can only rely on ourselves; whatever we do we are not helped by any supernal power, and therefore history is devoid of its traditionally approved sacral–theological character.

Contrary to what I had expected, very few of my respondents, both in Warsaw and in New York, appeared to have been influenced by the Holocaust in their attitude toward the idea of God. They did not share the convictions of Rubenstein. Rather, they were closer to that of Greenberg, or even Kaplan, who was simply uninterested in any theological implications of the Shoah. Therefore, my initial working hypothesis that *many* Jewish people would lose faith in God upon reflecting on the Holocaust has found no confirmation in reality. It turned out that in both samples there were *few* people who did lose faith because of the Shoah. If there were unbelievers, their atheism or agnosticism was an outcome of the way they had been brought up. This, in fact, is what many of my respondents have said: in most cases their belief and values systems were shaped by their parents and, to a lesser extent, by the schooling system. It can be argued, therefore, that our views are not so much shaped by what we experience but by what we are taught. More often than not, we perceive historical events the way our parents do, and appropriate them so that they fit in with our general world view, our frame of reference. On the other hand, it is quite rare for people to change their frames of reference on the basis of their own (and still less of someone else's) experiences. Victor Frankl has shed light on this problem, saying that we have a need to find meaning in our lives, and the idea of God has proved to be very useful in this regard. Also, the need for safety, as Maslow's theory insists, is one of the basic needs we experience as human beings; this need can be relatively easily satisfied by a belief in God, even if it involves numerous incongruities and inconsistencies. Perhaps this is why a significant proportion of the interviewees clung to some kind of belief in a power beyond themselves. This, to be sure, only rarely appeared as a traditionally understood faith in the God of the Bible. More often it was faith in a Kaplanian–Kantian God, especially in the American sample. The need to find meaning in history was apparently so strong that some of the respondents said that, in their opinion, there must have been some reason for the Holocaust in God's plans. A few even asserted that the Holocaust could have been – or in fact was – performed by God, which is exactly what many of the Hassidic rebbes maintained.

With regard to the identity of my respondents, the impact of secularization could be observed in both samples interviewed. Interestingly, this impact was much more visible than the expected influence of the Shoah. As the American thinker Harvey Cox affirms, 'pluralism and tolerance are children of secularization'.[1] And this was also the case with my respondents: as secularized people they represented a whole gamut of different visions of Jewishness. What they made up was not a religion-centred group, but rather a community of memory and of secular values,[2] which in fact assures to each of its member the right to hold his/her own personal views on religion. Cox again aptly remarks: 'For some, religion provides a hobby, for others a mark of national or ethnic identification, for still others an esthetic delight. For fewer and fewer does it provide an inclusive and commanding system of personal and cosmic values and explanations.'[3]

Thus, for most of my American respondents, the axis of their Jewish identity was Jewish culture, or culturally-understood Judaism. This phenomenon had its roots in the interwar period when American Jewry was becoming ever more secularized, often expressing their Jewishness through involvement in Bundist or Yiddishist organizations. Also, because of the social movements of the 1960s, the rise of ethnic America and the appearing cult of victimhood, American Jews started to be more visible as an ethnic minority. The Holocaust then emerged as a vehicle of Jewish identity. In addition to the Holocaust, Israel was becoming more and more important to American Jews as its safety was threatened by its Arab neighbours. That is how the 'myth of Holocaust and redemption' emerged, as Jacob Neusner has put it. Many other authors have also remarked that in the late 1960s and the 1970s, the Shoah was becoming the hallmark of Jewish identity, but it also started to play an exceptional role in American popular culture at large. The Jews' seeing themselves as victims of Nazism, or of anti-Semitism *tout court*, resulted in elevating American Jewry to the pedestal of victim culture. The Holocaust then became a code word for Jewish experience, and every Jew was entitled to feel a victim of the Holocaust, if only victim by proxy.

The awareness of the danger of anti-Semitism, despite its declining influence in America, and the progressive assimilation, as well as the rising rate of intermarriage, made the fear of the disappearance of the Jews in the United States ever greater and left a vivid mark on American Jewish identity. In Poland, the situation in the 1960s was to some extent similar. Anti-Semitism was actually on the rise, which made most Polish Jews realize that they were not only Poles but Jews as well – or, at least, others perceived them as such. Characteristically, for most of my Polish respondents, anti-Semitism was an important factor in acknowledging their Jewish identity. That is why a considerable number of them had an externally-shaped identity. Many others are Jews by a strong volitional act; their identity can be called emotional–declarative, for when talking about the content of their Jewishness they point to little more than the mere fact of being Jewish.

The American interviewees much less frequently based their identity on purely declarative grounds. What almost all of them pointed to as a crucial element of their Jewish identity was Jewish culture. It might be argued that American Jews, or at least the group interviewed, are for the most part cultural Jews. If they belong to religious communities they do so mostly for reasons of social affiliation. And it is curious that they don't find membership of a synagogue problematic, even if they are non-believers, for the synagogue, and the synagogue centre, is one of the focal points of American Jewry. Thus the slogan 'belonging without believing' is much more than a slogan; it is a depiction of social reality. The expression 'without believing' may signify that they are just atheists, but it can also mean that many members of Jewish congregations do not share the traditional faith in the biblical God. Many believe in Kaplanian Judaism – ethnic, cultural and secular religion of the Jewish people – even though very few of them are affiliated to Reconstructionist congregations. This, at least, is the situation I observed in the sample interviewed in New York.

Interestingly enough, some of the American Jews interviewed favoured what could be called the 'sacred–secular' dimension of Jewish history. In other words, to them, Jewish history is sacred (special), but in a secular – that is, non-theological – way. It was the genius of the Jewish people that made their history special, and not some higher instance. Generally speaking, American Jewry has 'invented' a well-organized *secular religion* – secular insofar as the term 'religious' is understood as pertaining to the societal and symbolic plane of the phenomenon. Thus, Judaism as a secular religion makes use of the Bible (seen as a culture text), of rituals and customs (*rites de passage*), and provides a psychological background for Jews as an ethnic community unified by common experience. Whether Polish Jews interviewed in Warsaw could be called adherents of Judaism as a secular religion is not so sure. Though they are, for the most part, secular people, they do not seem to be interested in secular Judaism any more than in traditional (that is, Orthodox) Judaism. They often cherish the secular values of Judaism, such as justice and learning; they find themselves attached to the history of the Jews; sometimes they even appreciate the identity-building aspect of the Torah; but they relatively rarely get involved in Jewish community life, even outside the synagogue. If they do belong to a Jewish organization it often consists of being enrolled in a list. Therefore, the category of 'belonging without believing' could be applied to the sample of Polish Jews only with difficulty.

If respondents from both groups saw assimilation as a negative phenomenon, although this was more clearly observable in the American sample, they wanted the Jewish people to continue its physical and cultural existence. Whether they were highly assimilated or religious Orthodox, they did not favour a total 'dissolution' of Jews in the majority society. Knowingly or not, most of my respondents followed the 614th commandment postulated by Emil Fackenheim: *to remain Jewish lest Hitler should gain the final victory*. This is perhaps why Fackenheim is the most frequently cited contemporary Jewish theologian: his concept of continuing Judaism to make Hitler's *Endlösung* impossible answers a common need of the Jews to confirm to themselves that their will to live is stronger than the Nazi obsession to annihilate them. Even if Fackenheim's was a religious commandment, it has won wide acceptance among Jews as a post-Holocaust version of the old commandment that Jews must remain Jews. Now seen more in ethnic and cultural than in religious terms, this commandment seems to play a unifying role among Jews.

I have demonstrated in this book that the impact of the Shoah upon

Polish Jews (at least those interviewed) was not as great as is usually assumed. While one half of the Polish informants admitted that their Jewish identity was in important ways affected by the catastrophe, the other half was rather ambiguous on this topic. For the most part, people from this other half did not assert that the Holocaust was irrelevant to them, yet they could not agree with the statement that awareness of the Shoah constituted a crucial element of the their Jewish identity. It is interesting that in the group of American Jews, over 20 per cent of them claimed that the Holocaust had very little to do with their Jewish identity. Another 30 per cent found it difficult to say whether the Shoah does or does not play an important role in their self-identification. The conclusion which derives from these observations is that we should be very careful in formulating and constructing generalizing theories; we ought to be especially cautious with statements such as: 'The Jews build their identity on the Holocaust.' While this may hold true with regard to part of Polish and American Jewry, 50 per cent of that population seek and find the basis of their identification without necessarily referring to the *Churban Europa*.

It seems, therefore, that the following methodological rule should be considered very attentively: although the sociologist is obliged to comply with strict standards of research, to assure its reliability and validity, it is desirable that s/he keeps a certain distance from the outcomes of his/her research and takes a measure of self-criticism.

Self-criticism and distance is also needed when we analyse the problem of history versus memory, memorialization, the politics of memory and misuses of memory, building and using victim status, rivalry for victimhood. Although politicization of Holocaust memory is a fact difficult to question, we should keep in mind that it pertains for the most part only to some milieus, or particular organizations. For want of other substance of their Jewishness, many Jews have found the Shoah as *the* element on which to base their identity. Yet many others express their Jewish identity through Jewish culture, religion – theistic or secular – and education. In short, the Holocaust can be used, and abused, by those who have a deficit of criteria of their own Jewishness. But to say that all Jews lack meaningful criteria of their identity would be an utterly illegitimate claim.

In a final remark, I would like to underscore that this work sought to sketch an overview of the historical and social changes that Polish and American Jewry have undergone since the end of the war. I have tried to show that we face problematic questions the very moment we

start exploring the reactions of American Jewry in the 1950s. It is difficult to affirm with all certainty whether, right after the war, there was
an animated Holocaust debate. On one hand, among East European immigrants themselves the topic was an important one, though they would
rarely speak about their war experiences in public. Also, as David Myers
has demonstrated, tens of articles on the Shoah were published in Jewish American periodicals. So, to say that the Holocaust was
silenced or totally irrelevant until the Eichmann trial is to ignore the
facts. Yet on the other, if seen from the perspective of the 1980s and
1990s, the presence of Holocaust discussion in the 1950s seems scant
and marginal. At the same time, in Poland, Polish Jews were recovering
from an unimaginable shock and were trying to rebuild Jewish life. In
speaking about war atrocities one did not refer to the 'Jewish Holocaust'
or 'Jewish genocide'. War memories were omnipresent in Polish society, and, on the surface, there seemed to be little difference between
Jewish and Polish suffering, all the more so because state policy was
to level the history and the memory of the war. Jews were well aware,
however, that the Nazi exterminatory policy toward them was of a
special kind, but, immediately after the war, they had almost no time
to reflect on their war experiences, as they had to face a new danger,
that of the unfathomable Polish anti-Semitism. Murders of individual
Jews, pogroms, beating and brutalizing the Jews in railway stations
and on trains – all that made them struggle for a better Poland. Many
of them thought a socialist Poland would bring them peace – not necessarily to them as Jews, but as citizens. Therefore there was no use
in raising the issue of the specialness of Jewish fate during the war.
The illusion of a Poland free of anti-Semitism ended with the 1968
purges. Yet the Jewish Historical Institute (and the organizations that
preceded it) kept collecting testimonies from the survivors as early as
1944 and 1945. Jewish memory was being 'stored' in the archives,
for even in inter-generational transmission it was often absent. That
is why Holocaust research started in earnest in Poland only in the late
1980s and 1990s.

Shortly before finishing my work on this book I was asked why one
of my basic assumptions was that the Shoah has probably caused a significant proportion of the Jews to abandon faith in God. The answer
to this question is twofold. On the one hand, reading some of the books
and articles about the Holocaust, I had the impression that atheism as
a response to this horrendous catastrophe is quite frequent in contemporary Jews – not only in the survivors, but in the next generation, too.

But this was not only my impression. For, as Marcus and Rosenberg have written, 'The relinquishing of faith in a just God by survivors in some ways is the most expected reaction after the Holocaust.'[4] On the other hand, I had my personal reflections. It is not by coincidence that on the first page of this book I have placed a passage ending with the words: '*One of the Germans grabbed the infant and cracked its skull against the wall of the hospital room.*' To students of the Holocaust this may be a picture they often find in their everyday work. Yet I refuse to see it as just one element in the drama of history. For me, this extreme cruelty, multiplied a million times, has to have some consequences. And the burning children, women, and men ... I can't pretend I don't hear their screams. It is not that I am insensitive to the suffering of a single human being. However, it is relatively easy to explain away the suffering or untimely death of one person among a million. But to account for the gehenna of millions of innocent people? The human mind ceases to function in a normal way and belief systems are heavily challenged when faced with such horror. Because of those flames of human flesh and children's blood splashed over the walls and sidewalk, I find it impossible to believe in a God who is a strength and refuge to the inflicted and who wipes away tears from all faces, as the prophet Isaiah had argued.

NOTES

1. H. Cox, *The Secular City* (London: Penguin Books, 1966), p.17.
2. Judaism as a religion is not extraterrestrial-centred. Weber put it in a similar vein: 'We have already made some observations concerning the total sociological structure and attitude of Judaism. Its religious promises, in the customary meaning of the world, apply to this world, and any notions of contemplative or ascetic world-flight are as rare in Judaism as in Chinese religion and in Protestantism.' M. Weber, *The Sociology of Religion*, translated by E. Fischoff (London: Methuen, 1956), p.246.
3. Cox, *Secular City*, p.17.
4. P. Marcus and A. Rosenberg, 'The Religious Life of Holocaust Survivors and Its Significance for Psychotherapy', in P. Marcus and A. Rosenberg (eds), *Healing Their Wounds: Psychotherapy with Holocaust Survivors and Their Families* (New York, Westport, CT, and London: Praeger, 1989), p.239.

Bibliography

Adelson, J., 'W Polsce zwanej ludową' [In a Poland Called 'People's'], in Tomaszewski (ed.), *Najnowsze dzieje Żydów w Polsce* (1993).

'A Distance From the Holocaust: A Symposium', Editors' Introduction, *Tikkun*, 4 (May–June 1989).

Aleksiun, A., *Dokąd dalej? Ruch syjonistyczny w Polsce (1944–1950)* [Where To Next? The Zionist Movement in Poland (1944–1950)] (Warsaw: Trio, 2002).

Alexander, E., 'Stealing the Holocaust', *Midstream*, 26 (November 1980).

Alter, R., 'Deformations of the Holocaust', *Commentary*, 71 (February 1981).

Alter, R., 'Vistas of Annihilation', *Commentary*, 79 (January 1985).

Altizer, Th. J.J. and Hamilton, W., *Radical Theology and the Death of God* (Indianapolis, IN: Bobbs-Merrill Co., 1966).

[Anonymous], 'Dlaczego nie wstępuję do gminy?' [Why I'm Not Going to Join the Community?], *Midrasz*, 2, 2 (June 1997).

[Anonymous], 'Od rozproszenia do poszukiwań: Kilka osobistych pytań na temat żydowskiej tożsamości' [From Dispersion to Searching: Some Personal Questions on Jewish Identity], *Midrasz*, 5, 5 (September 1997).

Arendt, H., *The Origins of Totalitarianism* (San Diego and New York: Hartcourt, 1985).

Arendt, H., *Eichmann in Jerusalem: A Report on the Banality of Evil*, revised and enlarged edition (New York: Penguin Books, 1994).

Bańkowska, A., Jarzębowska, A. and Siek, M. 'Morderstwa Żydów w latach 1944–1946 na terenie Polski na podstawie kwerendy w zbiorze 301 (Relacja z Zagłady w Archiwum Żydowskiego Instytutu Historycznego)' [Jews Murdered on Polish Territories in 1944–1946: A Study Based on a Search Query in Collection 301 (Holocaust Accounts in the Archives of the Jewish Historical Institute)], *Jewish History Quarterly*, 3 (September 2009).

Bauer, Y., *The Holocaust in Historical Perspective* (Seattle, WA: University of Washington Press, 1978).

Bauer, Y., 'Whose Holocaust?' *Midstream*, 26 (November 1980).

Bauer, Y., 'Is the Holocaust Explicable', in Y. Bauer et al. (eds), *Remembering for the Future: Working Papers and Addenda* (Oxford: Pergamon Press, 1989).

Bauer, Y., 'A Critique of Phillip Lopate: Don't Resist', in 'A Distance from the Holocaust: A Symposium', *Tikkun*, 4 (May–June 1989).

Bauman, Z., 'Hereditary Victimhood: The Holocaust's Life as a Ghost', *Tikkun*, 13 (July–August 1998).

Bauman, Z., *Modernity and the Holocaust* (Ithaca, NY: Cornell University Press, 2000).

Berenbaum, M., 'The Nativization of the Holocaust', *Judaism*, 35 (Fall 1986).

Berenbaum, M., *After Tragedy and Triumph: Essays in Modern Jewish Thought and the American Experience* (Cambridge: Cambridge University Press, 1990).

Berenbaum, M., (ed.), *The World Must Know: The History of the Holocaust as Told in the United States Holocaust Memorial Museum* (Boston, MA: Little, Brown, 1993).

Berendt, G. and Grabski, A., *Między emigracją a trwaniem: Syjoniści i komuniści żydowscy w Polsce po Holocauście* [Emigrate or Stay: Zionists and Jewish Communists in Poland after the Holocaust] (Warsaw: Żydowski Instytut Historyczny, 2003).

Berger, D., 'What Do American Jews Believe? A Symposium', *Commentary*, 102 (August 1996).

Berger, P.L., 'The Desecularization of the World: A Global Overview', in P.L. Berger (ed.), *The Desecularization of the World: Resurgent Religion and World Politics* (Washington, DC: Ethics and Public Policy Center, 1999).

Berkovits, E., 'The State of Jewish Belief: A Symposium', *Commentary*, 42 (August 1966).

Berkovits, E., *Faith After the Holocaust* (New York: Ktav Publishing House, 1973).

Berkovits, E., *Crisis and Faith* (New York: Sanhedrin Press, 1976).

Berry, J.W., 'Acculturation and Psychological Adaptation: An Overview', in A.-M. Bouvy et al. (eds), *Journeys into Cross-Cultural Psychology: Selected Papers from the Eleventh International Conference of the International Association for Cross-Cultural Psychology held in Liège, Belgium* (Amsterdam: Swets & Zeitlinger, 1994).

Bielecki, C., 'Szok Marcowy' [The March Shock], *Polis*, 27 (April 1998).

Bokszański, Z. et al. (eds), *Encyklopedia Socjologii* (Warsaw: Oficyna Naukowa, 1998).

Brenner, R.R., *The Faith and Doubt of Holocaust Survivors* (New York: Free Press, 1980).

Bronsztejn, S., 'Badania ankietowe ludności żydowskiej Dolnego Śląska' [A Questionnaire Survey of the the Jewish Population of Lower Silesia], *Biuletyn Żydowskiego Instytutu Historycznego*, 47–8 (October–December 1963).

Burg. A., 'Postsyjonista? Z Abrahamem Burgiem rozmawia Elżbieta Kossewska' [A Post-Zionist? Elżbieta Kossewska in Conversation with Abraham Burg], *Więź*, 601–2 (November–December 2008).

Cała, A. and Datner-Śpiewak, H., *Dzieje Żydów w Polsce 1944–1968: Teksty źródłowe* [The History of Jews In Poland 1944–1968: Source Texts] (Warsaw:Żydowski Instytut Historyczny, 1997).

Cargas, H.J. (ed.), *Telling the Tale: A Tribute to Elie Wiesel on the Occasion of his 65th Birthday* (St Louis, MO: Time Being Books, 1993).

Cargas, H.J. (ed.), *Problems Unique to the Holocaust* (Lexington, KY: University Press of Kentucky, 1999).

Cohen, A., *The Natural and the Supernatural Jew* (New York: Pantheon Books, 1963).

Cohen, A., *The Tremendum: A Theological Interpretation of the Holocaust* (New York: Crossroad, 1981).

Cox, H., *The Secular City* (London: Penguin Books, 1966).

Dashefsky, A. and Shapiro, H.M., *Ethnic Identification among American Jews: Socialization and Social Structure* (Lexington, MA: Lexington Books, 1974).

Datner, H., 'Przez tę pamięć' [Because of That Memory], in a symposium, 'Siedem głosów' [Seven Voices], *Midrasz*, 5, 5 (September 1997).

Datner, H. and Melchior, M., 'Żydzi we współczesnej Polsce – nieobecność i powroty' [Jews in Contemporary Poland – Their Absence and Returns], in Z. Kurcz (ed.), *Mniejszości narodowe w Polsce* [Ethnic Minorities in Poland] (Wrocław: Wydawnictwo Uniwersytetu Wrocławskiego, 1997).

Dawidowicz, L., *On Equal Terms: Jews in America 1881–1981* (New York: Rinehart & Winston, 1982).

DellaPergola, S., 'World Jewish Population 2001', *American Jewish Yearbook 101*, accessed 4 March 2002, <http://sites.huji.ac.il/jcj/dmg_worldjpop_01.htm>.

Denzin, N.K., 'Reinterpretacja metody biograficznej w socjologii: znaczenie a metoda w analizie biograficznej' [Reinterpreting the Biographical Method in Sociology: Meaning Versus Method in Biographical Analysis], in *Metoda biograficzna w socjologii* [The Biographical Method in Sociology], ed. J. Włodarek and M. Ziółkowski (Warsaw and Poznań: PWN, 1990).

Dorff, E.N., 'What Do American Jews Believe? A Symposium', *Commentary*, 102 (August 1996).

Dreyfus, Jean-Marc, 'Comment l'Amérique s'est identifiée à la Shoah', *Le Débat*, 130 (May–August 2004).

Driesen, G.B., 'Revisiting the Chosen People', *The Reconstructionist*, 60 (Fall 1995).

Eckardt, A.L. and Eckardt, A.R., *Long Night's Journey into Day: A Revised Retrospective on the Holocaust* (Detroit, MI: Wayne State University Press, 1988).

Editorial, *Times Literary Supplement*, 26 August 1939, p.503.

'Editorial: God and History', *Tikkun*, 2 (February 1987).

Eisen, A.M., *The Chosen People in America: A Study in Jewish Religious Ideology* (Bloomington, IN: Indiana University Press, 1983).

Eisen, A.M., 'Kaplan and Chosenness: A Historical View', *The Reconstructionist*, 50 (September 1984).

Eisendrath, M.N., 'The State of Jewish Belief: A Symposium', *Commentary*, 42 (August 1966).

Eisenstein, I., 'The State of Jewish Belief: A Symposium', *Commentary*, 42 (August 1966).

Eliaeson, S., *Max Weber's Methodologies: Interpretation and Critique* (Cambridge, UK: Polity, 2002).

Engelking, B., *Holocaust and Memory: The Experience of the Holocaust and Its Consequences: An Investigation Based on Personal Narratives* (London: Leicester University Press, 2001).

Fackenheim, E.L., 'The State of Jewish Belief: A Symposium', *Commentary*, 42 (August 1966).

Fackenheim, E.L., *Quest for Past and Future* (Boston, MA: Beacon Press, 1968).

Fackenheim, E.L., *God's Presence in History: Jewish Affirmations and Philosophical Reflections* (New York: New York University Press, 1970).

Fackenheim, E.L., *The Jewish Return into History: Reflections on the Age of Auschwitz and a New Jerusalem* (New York: Schocken Books, 1978).

Fackenheim, E.L., *To Mend the World: Foundations of Post-Holocaust Jewish Thought* (Bloomington, IN: Indiana University Press, 1994).

Fein, L., *Where Are We? The Inner Life of American Jews* (New York: Harper & Row, 1988).

Feingold, H., *A Time for Searching: Entering the Mainstream 1920–1945* (Baltimore, MD: Johns Hopkins University Press, 1992).

Feitman, Y., 'The Master Race and the Chosen People: A Look at the Nazi Ideology in a Torah Light', in Wolpin (ed.), *Path Through the Ashes* (1986).

Feldman, A.J., *The American Jew: A Study of Backgrounds* (New York: Bloch Publishing, 1937).

Festinger, L., *A Theory of Cognitive Dissonance* (Stanford, CA: Stanford University Press, 1962).

Feuer, L.S., 'The Reasoning of Holocaust Theology', *Judaism*, 35 (Spring 1986).

Finkelstein, N.G., *The Holocaust Industry: Reflections on the Exploitation of Jewish Suffering* (London and New York: Verso, 2001).

Fisher, J., 'God After the Holocaust: An Attempted Reconciliation', *Judaism*, 32 (Summer 1983).

Flanzbaum, Hilene, *The Americanization of the Holocaust* (Baltimore, MD: Johns Hopkins University Press, 1999).

Frankl, V., *Man's Search for Meaning: An Introduction to Logotherapy* (a newly revised and enlarged edition of *From Death-Camp to Existentialism*), translated by Ilse Lasch, 2nd edition (Boston, MA: Beacon Press, 1963).

Freedman, S.G., *Jew vs Jew: The Struggle for the Soul of American Jewry* (New York: Simon & Schuster, 2000).

Frejlak-Koźmińska, E., 'Poland as the Motherland of the Jews: Jewish Strategies of Making Postwar Poland a Home', *Kultura i Społeczeństwo*, 43, 1 (January–March 1999).

Frelick, W.H., 'Mordecai Kaplan's Idea of God', *The Reconstructionist*, 46 (November 1980).

Friedland, E.L., 'O God of Vengeance, Appear!' *Judaism*, 37 (Winter 1988).

Gebert, K., 'Marsz Żywych' [March of the Living], *Midrasz*, 2, 2 (June 1997).

Gebert, K., 'Otworzyć synagogę?' [Should the Synagogue be Opened?], *Midrasz*, 2, 2 (June 1997).

Gebert, K., 'Tożsamości Żydów w Polsce: "Nowa", "Dawna" i "Wysnuta z wyobraźni" ' [Jewish Identities in Poland: "New", "Old" and "Drawn out from Imagination"], *Polis*, 21 (March 1997).

Gifter, M., 'A Path Though the Ashes: Some Thoughts on Teaching the Holocaust', in Wolpin (ed.), *Path Through the Ashes* (1986).

Glazer, N., *American Judaism* (Chicago, IL: University of Chicago Press, 1957).

Glazer, N., *American Judaism*, 2nd revised edition, with a new introduction (Chicago, IL, and London: University of Chicago Press, 1989).

Glazer, N. and Moynihan, D.P., *Beyond the Melting Pot: The Negroes, Puerto Ricans, Jews, Italians, and Irish of New York City*, 2nd edition (Cambridge, MA: MIT Press, 1970).

Goldberg, D.T. and Krausz, M. (eds.), *Jewish Identity* (Philadelphia, PA: Temple University Press, 1993).

Goldenberg, R., 'Is There an "Essence of Judaism" After All?' *Judaism*, 38 (Winter 1989).

Goodman, S.L. (ed.), *The Faith of Secular Jews* (New York: Ktav Publishing House, 1976).

Gordis, D.M., 'What Do American Jews Believe? A Symposium', *Commentary*, 102 (August 1996).

Gordis, R., 'Does Secular Judaism Have a Future?' *Judaism*, 30 (Spring 1981).

Grabski, A. and G. Berendt, *Między emigracją a trwaniem: Syjoniści i komuniści żydowscy w Polsce po Holocauście* [Emigrate or Stay: Zionists and Jewish Communists in Poland after the Holocaust] (Warsaw: Żydowski Instytut Historyczny, 2003).

Greenberg, I., 'Cloud of Smoke, Pillar of Fire: Judaism, Christianity, and Modernity after the Holocaust', in E. Fleischner (ed.), *Auschwitz: Beginning of a New Era? Reflections on the Holocaust* (New York: Ktav Publishing House, 1977).

Greenberg, I., *Living in the Image of God: Jewish Teachings to Perfect the World: Conversations with Rabbi Irving Greenberg as Conducted by Shalom Freedman* (Northvale, NJ: Jason Aronson, 1998).

Grinberg, D., 'Warianty i ewolucja tożsamości narodowej Żydów na ziemiach polskich' [The Evolution and the Different Kinds of National Identity of Jews Living on Polish Territories], in Żebrowski (ed.), *Studia z dziejów Żydów w Polsce*, vol. 1 (1995).

Grynberg, H., *Monolog polsko-żydowski* [A Polish-Jewish Monologue] (Wołowiec: Wydawnictwo Czarne, 2003).

Gutman, I., 'Remarks on the Literature of the Holocaust', *In the Dispersion*, 5–6 (Spring 1966).

Gutman, I. (ed.), *Encyclopedia of the Holocaust* (Tel Aviv, New York and London: Sifriat Poalim Publishing House, 1990), s.v. 'Holocaust'.

Halbwachs, M., *On Collective Memory*, edited and translated by Lewis A. Coser (Chicago, IL: University of Chicago Press, 1992).

Hartman, D., *Maimonides: Torah and Philosophic Quest* (Philadelphia, PA: Jewish Publication Society, 1986).

Hartman, G.H., *The Longest Shadow: In the Aftermath of the Holocaust* (Bloomington and Indianapolis, IN: Indiana University Press, 1996).

Heilman, S.C., *Jewish Unity and Diversity: A Survey of American Rabbis and Rabbinical Students* (American Jewish Committee, 1991).

Heilman, S.C., *Defenders of the Faith: Inside Ultra-Orthodox Jewry* (New York: Schocken Books, 1992).

Heilman, S.C., *Portrait of American Jews: The Last Half of the 20th Century* (Seattle, WA: University of Washington Press, 1995).

Heller, C.S., *On the Edge of Destruction* (New York: Schocken Books, 1980).

Helmreich, W.B., 'The Impact of Holocaust Survivors on American Society: A Socio-Cultural Portrait', *Judaism*, 39 (Winter 1990).

Helmreich, W.B., *Against All Odds: Holocaust Survivors and the Successful Lives They Made in America* (New York: Simon & Schuster, 1992).

Hertz, A., *The Jews in Polish Culture*, translated by Richard Lourie (Evanston, IL: Northwestern University Press, 1988).

Hertzberg, A., *Jewish Polemics* (New York: Columbia University Press, 1992).

Hirsh, R.A., 'Jewish Identity and Patrilineal: Some Second Thoughts', *The Reconstructionist*, 49 (March 1984).

Hirsh, R.A., 'The Nuances of Chosenness: A Reconstructionist Approach', *The Reconstructionist*, 50 (September 1984).

Hirszfeld, L., *Historia jednego życia* [The Story of One Life] (Warsaw: Czytelnik, 2000).

Hurwic-Nowakowska, I., *A Social Analysis of Postwar Polish Jewry* (Jerusalem: Zalman Shazar Center for Jewish History, 1986).

Husik, I., *A History of Mediaeval Jewish Philosophy* (New York: Atheneum, 1973).

Husock, H., 'Red, White, and Jew: Holocaust Museum on the Mall', *Tikkun*, 5 (July–August 1990).

Irwin-Zarecka, I., *Neutralizing Memory: The Jew in Contemporary Poland* (New Brunswick, NJ: Transaction Publishers, 1989).

Israel, S., 'Ethnicity, Geography and Jewish Community', *The Reconstructionist*, 60 (Spring 1995).

Jacobs, S.L., '(If) There Is No "Commander"? ... There Are No "Commandments!" ' *Judaism*, 37 (Summer 1988).

Jacobs, S.L. (ed.), *Contemporary Jewish Religious Responses to the Shoah* (Lanham, MD, New York and London: University Press of America, 1993).

Jager, E., 'Take Back the Holocaust', *Midstream*, 44 (July–August 1998).

'Jewishness and the Younger Intellectuals: A Symposium', *Commentary*, 31 (April 1961).

Kahn, L., 'Another Decade: The American Jew In the Sixties', *Judaism*, 10 (Spring 1961).

Kaplan, M.M., 'The State of Jewish Belief: A Symposium', *Commentary*, 42 (August 1966).

Kaplan, M.M., 'The God Idea in Judaism', in M.M. Kaplan (ed.), *The Jewish Reconstructionist Papers* (New York: Jewish Book House, 1936).

Kaplan, M.M., *Judaism as a Civilization: Toward a Reconstruction of American-Jewish Life*, 1981, reprinted with an introduction by A. Eisen (Philadelphia, PA: Jewish Publication Society, 1994 [1934]).

Karp, A.J., *Haven and Home: A History of the Jews in America* (New York: Schocken Books, 1984).

Kersten, K., *Polacy – Żydzi – komunizm. Anatomia półprawd* [Poles – Jews – Communism: Anatomy of Half-Truths] (Warsaw: Nezależna Oficyna Wydawnicza, 1992).

Klinghoffer, D., 'What Do American Jews Believe? A Symposium', *Commentary*, 102 (August 1996).

Knobel, P., 'What Do American Jews Believe? A Symposium', *Commentary*, 102 (August 1996).

Kogel, R. and Katz, Z. (eds), *Judaism in a Secular Age: An Anthology of Secular Humanistic Jewish Thought* (New York: Ktav Publishing House/International Institute for Secular Humanistic Judaism, 1995).

Krajewski, S.,'Solidarity and Martial Law: The Jewish Dimension', *Studium Papers*, 13, 2 (April 1989).

Krajewski, S., 'Przymierze obowiązuje' [The Covenant Is Binding], in a symposium, 'Siedem głosów' [Seven Voices], *Midrasz*, 5, 5 (September 1997).

Krajewski, S., 'Schematy. Z dr. Stanisławem Krajewskim rozmawia Agnieszka Niezgoda' [Schemes: Agnieszka Niezgoda in Conversation with Dr Stanisław Krajewski], *Polis*, 27 (April 1998).

Krajewski, S., *Poland and the Jews: Reflections of a Polish Polish Jew* (Kraków: Austeria 2005).

Krall, H., *Sublokatorka* [The Tenant] (Warsaw: Iskry, 1989).

Kren, G.M., 'The Holocaust as History', in Rosenberg and Myers (eds), *Echoes from the Holocaust* (1988).

Lamm, N., 'The Face of God: Thoughts on the Holocaust', in Rosenberg and Heuman (eds), *Theological and Halakhic Reflections on the Holocaust* (1992).

Lang, B., 'The Concept of Genocide', *Philosophical Forum*, 16 (Fall–Winter 1984–85).

Lang, B., 'Translating the Holocaust: For Whom Does One Write?' *Judaism*, 48 (Summer 1999).

Lang, B., *Act and Idea in the Nazi Genocide* (Syracuse, NY: Syracuse University Press, 2003).

Lapin, D., 'What Do American Jews Believe? A Symposium', *Commentary*, 102 (August 1996).

Last Stone, S., 'What Do American Jews Believe? A Symposium', *Commentary*, 102 (August 1996).

Lazerewitz, B. et al., *Jewish Choices: American Jewish Denomination-alism* (Albany, NY: State University of New York Press, 1998).

Lederhendler, E., *New York Jews and the Decline of Urban Ethnicity, 1950–1970* (Syracuse, NY: Syracuse University Press, 2001).

Lemkin, Raphael, *Axis Rule in Occupied Europe: Laws of Occupation – Analysis of Government – Proposals for Redress* (Washington, DC: Carnegie Endowment for International Peace, 1944).

Lichtenstein, A., 'The State of Jewish Belief: A Symposium', *Commentary*, 42 (August 1966).

Liebman, C.S., *Aspects of the Religious Behaviour of American Jews* (New York: Ktav Publishing House, 1974).

Linenthal, E.T., *Preserving Memory: The Struggle to Create America's Holocaust Museum* (New York: Columbia University Press, 2001).

Lipset, S.M. and Raab, E., *Jews and the New American Scene* (Cambridge, MA: Harvard University Press, 1995).

Lipstadt, D.E., 'Invoking the Holocaust', *Judaism*, 30 (Summer 1981).

Lopate, P., 'Resistance to the Holocaust', in 'Distance from the Holocaust: A Symposium', *Tikkun*, 4 (May–June 1989).

Maccoby, H., 'Theologian of the Holocaust', *Commentary*, 74 (December 1982).

Magurshak, D., 'The "Incomprehensibility" of the Holocaust: Tightening Up Some Loose Usage', *Judaism*, 29 (Spring 1980).

Maier, C.S., 'A Surfeit of Memory? Reflections of History, Melancholy and Denial', *History and Memory*, 5 (Fall–Winter 1993).

Maier, C.S., *The Unmasterable Past: History, Holocaust, and German National Identity* (Cambridge, MA: Harvard University Press, 1997).

Mamlak, G., 'The Holocaust: Commodity?', *Midstream*, 29 (April 1983).

Marcus, P. and Rosenberg, A., 'The Religious Life of Holocaust Survivors and Its Significance for Psychotherapy', in Marcus and Rosenberg (eds), *Healing Their Wounds* (1989).

Marcus, P. and Rosenberg, A. (eds), *Healing Their Wounds: Psychotherapy with Holocaust Survivors and Their Families* (New York, Westport, CT, and London: Praeger, 1989).

Mark, B., 'Dziennik (Grudzień 1965 – Luty 1966)' [Diary (December 1965 – February 1966)], *Jewish History Quarterly*, 226, 2 (June 2008).

Mayer, A.J., 'Memory and History: On the Poverty of Remembering and Forgetting the Judeocide', *Radical History Review*, 56 (Spring 1993).

Maza, B., 'Why?', in Jacobs (ed.), *Contemporary Jewish Religious Responses to the Shoah* (1993).

Medved, M., 'What Do American Jews Believe? A Symposium', *Commentary*, 102 (August 1996).

Melchior, M., *Zagłada i Tożsamość: Polscy Żydzi ocaleni 'na aryjskich papierach': Analiza doświadczenia biograficznego* [The Holocaust and Identity: Polish Jews Who Survived Using 'Aryan Papers': Analysis of a Biographical Experience] (Warsaw: IFiS PAN, 2004).

Melchior, M., 'What Does the Holocaust Tell Sociologists: Identity as a Stigma', in S. Rejak (ed.), *Thinking after the Holocaust: Voices from Poland* (Warsaw and Cracow: Muza, 2008).

Meyer, M.A., 'Anti-Semitism and Jewish Identity', *Commentary*, 88 (November 1989).

Milchman, A. and Rosenberg, A., 'Remembering and Forgetting: The Social Construction of a Community of Memory of the Holocaust', in A. Rosenberg, J.R. Watson and D. Linke (eds), *Contemporary Portrayals of Auschwitz: Philosophical Challenges* (Amherst, NY: Humanity Books, 2000).

Milchman, A. and Rosenberg, A., 'The Need for Philosophy to Confront the Holocaust as a Transformational Event', *Dialogue and Universalism*, 13, 3–4 (2003).

Milchman, A. and Rosenberg, A., *Eksperymenty w myśleniu o Holokauście: Auschwitz, Nowoczesność i Filozofia* [Experiments in

Thinking the Holocaust: Auschwitz, Modernity, and Philosophy]
(Warsaw: Wydawnictwo Naukowe Scholar, 2003).

Miles, M.B. and Huberman, A.M., *Analiza danych jakościowych*
[Qualitative Data Analysis] (Białystok: Transhumana, 2000).

Mintz, A., *Popular Culture and the Shaping of Holocaust Memory in
America* (Seattle, WA: University of Washington Press, 2001).

Morgan, M.L., *Beyond Auschwitz: Post-Holocaust Jewish Thought in
America* (New York: Oxford University Press, 2001).

'My Jewish Affirmation: A Symposium', *Judaism*, 10 (Fall 1961).

Myers, D.G., *Annotated Bibliography of Holocaust Writing in American-
Jewish Magazines, 1945–1952* (1999) (accessed 24 November 2003),
<http://www-english.tamu.edu/pers/fac/myers/annotated_bib.html>.

Neusner, J., *American Judaism: Adventure in Modernity* (Englewood
Cliffs, NJ: Prentice Hall, 1972).

Neusner, J., 'Beyond Catastrophe, Before Redemption', *The Reconstructionist*, 46 (April 1980).

Neusner, J., *Stranger at Home: 'The Holocaust', Zionism, and American
Judaism* (Chicago, IL, and London: University of Chicago Press,
1985).

Neusner, J., *The Religious World of Contemporary Judaism: Observations
and Convictions* (Atlanta, GA: Scholars Press, 1989).

Norden, E., 'Yes and No to the Holocaust Museums', *Commentary*, 96
(August 1993).

North, S., 'Poland Rediscovers its Jews: An Interview with Malgorzata
Niezabitowska', *The Reconstructionist*, 53 (July–August 1988).

Novak, D., 'What Do American Jews Believe? A Symposium',
Commentary, 102 (August 1996).

Novick, P., *The Holocaust and Collective Memory: The American
Experience* (London: Bloomsbury, 2000).

Oppenheim, M., 'Irving Greenberg and the Jewish Dialectic of Hope',
Judaism, 49 (Spring 2000).

Orbach, W., 'The Four Faces of God: Toward a Theology of Powerlessness', *Judaism*, 32 (Spring 1983).

Oshry, E., *Responsa from the Holocaust* (New York: Judaica Press,
2001).

Papazian, P. 'A "Unique Uniqueness"?' *Midstream*, 30 (April 1984).

Paszko, K., *Polacy i Żydzi w dialogu w latach 1979–1997* [Poles and
Jews in Dialogue 1979–1997] (Warsaw: PWN, 2006).

Pawlak, G., 'Historia opowiedziana' [A Story Told], an interview with
Grażyna S. Pawlak, *Polis*, 21 (March 1997).

Paziński, P., 'Kafka ważniejszy od Tory?' [Kafka More Important Than the Torah?], *Midrasz*, 31, 11 (November 1999).

Perechodnik, C., *Czy ja jestem mordercą?* [Am I a Murderer?] (Warsaw: Karta / Żydowski Instytut Historyczny, 1995).

Pfefferkorn, E. and Hirsch, D.H., 'Elie Wiesel's Wrestle With God', *Midstream*, 43 (November 1997).

Plaskow, J., 'The Problem of Evil: A Conversation', *The Reconstructionist*, 57 (Spring 1992).

Połoniecka, A., 'Przynależę do narodu' [I Belong to a Nation], in a symposium, 'Siedem głosów' [Seven Voices], *Midrasz*, 5, 5 (September 1997).

Putnam, H., 'Judaism and Jewish Identity', in D.T. Goldberg and M. Krausz (eds.), *Jewish Identity* (Philadelphia, PA: Temple University Press, 1993).

Reines, A.J., 'Ontology, Demography, and the Silent Holocaust', *Judaism*, 38 (Fall 1989).

'Rethinking the Holocaust: A Symposium' [editors' introductory note], *Tikkun*, 2 (January 1987).

Ricouer, P., *La Mémoire, l'histoire, l'oubli* (Paris: Seuil, 2000).

Roiphe, A., 'The Politics of Anger', *Tikkun*, 1 (January 1986).

Rosenbaum, A.S. (ed.), *Is the Holocaust Unique? Perspectives on Comparative Genocide* (Boulder, CO: Westview Press, 1996).

Rosenberg, A., 'Was the Holocaust Unique? A Peculiar Question', in I. Walliman and M.N. Dobkowski (eds), *Genocide and the Modern Age: Etiology and Case Studies of Mass Death* (Westport, CT: Greenwood Press, 1987).

Rosenberg, A. and Myers, G.E. (eds), *Echoes from the Holocaust: Philosophical Reflections on a Dark Time* (Philadelphia, PA: Temple University Press: 1988).

Rosenberg, B.H. and Heuman, F. (eds), *Theological and Halakhic Reflections on the Holocaust* (Hoboken, NJ: Ktav Publishing House, 1992).

Rosenfeld, A.H., 'The Americanization of the Holocaust', *Commentary*, 99 (June 1995).

Rosenfeld, A.H., 'Letters', *Commentary*, 100 (September 1995).

Roskies, D.G., 'Group Memory' [review of P. Novick, *The Holocaust in American Life*], *Commentary*, 108 (September 1999).

Rubenstein, R.L., 'The Symbols of Judaism and Religious Existentialism', *The Reconstructionist*, 25 (1 May 1959).

Rubenstein, R.L., 'The Vocation of the Modern Rabbi', *The Reconstructionist*, 25 (27 November 1959).

Rubenstein, R.L., *The Cunning of History: Mass Death and the American Future* (New York: Harper & Row, 1975).

Rubenstein, R.L., *After Auschwitz: Radical Theology and Contemporary Judaism*, 1st edition (Indianapolis, IN: Bobbs-Merrill, 1966).

Rubenstein, R.L., *Power Struggle: An Autobiographical Confession* (Lanham, MD: University Press of America, 1986).

Rubenstein, R.L., *After Auschwitz: History, Theology, And Contemporary Judaism*, 2nd edition (Baltimore, MD: Johns Hopkins University Press, 1992).

Rubenstein, R.L., 'Religion and the Uniqueness of the Holocaust', in Rosenbaum (ed.), *Is the Holocaust Unique?*(1996).

Rutkowski, A., 'An Exhibition on the Occasion of the 10th Anniversary of the Warsaw Ghetto Uprising', *Biuletyn Żydowskiego Instytutu Historycznego*, 6–7 (April–September 1953).

Sachar, H.M., *A History of the Jews in America* (New York: Vintage Books, 1993).

Sacks, J., 'Judaism and Politics in the Modern World', in P.L. Berger (ed.), *The Desecularization of the World: Resurgent Religion and World Politics* (Washington, DC: Ethics and Public Policy Center, 1999).

Sakowska, R. (ed.), *Archiwum Ringelbluma: Listy o Zagładzie* [Ringelblum's Archive: Letters from the Holocaust] (Warsaw: Żydowski Instytut Historyczny – Wydawnictwo Naukowe PWN, 1997).

Salins, P.D., *Assimilation, American Style* (New York: Basic Books, 1997).

Scheindlin, R.P., 'Museum of Death, Museum of Life', *Tikkun*, 8 (November–December 1993).

Scheinman, A. ,'Bikrovei Ekodeish: The Six Million Kedoshim', in Wolpin (ed.), *Path Through the Ashes* (1986).

Scherman, N., 'An Understanding of the Holocaust in the Light of Moshe Prager's "Sparks of Glory" ', in Wolpin (ed.), *Path Through the Ashes* (1986).

Schoenfeld, G., 'Auschwitz and the Professors', *Commentary*, 105 (June 1998).

Schorsch, I., 'The Holocaust and Jewish Survival', *Midstream*, 27 (January 1981).

Schulweis, H.M., 'The State of Jewish Belief: A Symposium', *Commentary*, 42 (August 1966).

Seeskin, K.R., 'The Reality of Radical Evil', *Judaism*, 29 (Fall 1980).

Seltzer, R.M., 'Judaism According to Emil Fackenheim', *Commentary*, 86 (September 1988).

Shapira, Rabbi K.K., *Sacred Fire: Torah from the Years of Fury 1939–1942*, edited by Deborah Miller and translated by J. Hershy Worch (Northvale, NJ: Jason Aronson, 2000).

Shapiro, E.S., 'Jewishness and the New York Intellectuals', *Judaism*, 38 (Summer 1989).

Shapiro, E.S., *A Time for Healing: American Jewry Since World War II* (Baltimore, MD: Johns Hopkins University Press, 1992).

Shapiro, R., 'A Naturalist Affirmation of Chosenness', *The Reconstructionist*, 50 (September 1984).

Shapiro, R.M., 'Holocaust: Usankcjonowanie terminu historycznego [Holocaust: Sanction of a Historical Term], *Biuletyn Żydowskiego Instytutu Historycznego* 169–71 (January–September 1994).

Silberman, C.E., *A Certain People: American Jews and Their Lives Today* (New York: Summit Books, 1985).

Silver, D.J., 'Choose Life', *Judaism*, 35 (Fall 1986).

Singer, D., 'From Judaism to Jewishness', *Commentary*, 90 (July 1990).

Singer, Isaac B., *Wrogowie* [Enemies], trans. Ludmiła Melchior-Yahil (Warsaw: Amber, 1998).

Sklare, M., *Observing America's Jews* (Hanover and London, MA: Brandeis University Press/University Press of New England, 1993).

Soifer, P.E., 'Remembrance and the Victims' Covenant', *The Reconstructionist*, 46 (April 1980).

Soloveitchik, J.B., *Halakhic Man*, translated by Lawrence Kaplan (Philadelphia, PA: Jewish Publication Society, 1983).

Soloveitchik, J.B., 'Kol Dodi Dofek: It Is the Voice of My Beloved That Knocketh', in Rosenberg and Heuman (eds), *Theological and Halakhic Reflections on the Holocaust* (1992).

Sorasky, A., *Reb Elchonon: The Life and Ideals of Rabbi Elchonon Bunim Wasserman of Baranovitch*, edited by N. Scherman and M. Zlotowitz, translated [from Hebrew] by E. Simcha Wasserman and L. Oschry (New York: Mesorah Publications, 1982).

Stannard, D.E., 'Uniqueness as Denial: The Politics of Genocide Scholarship', in Rosenbaum (ed.), *Is the Holocaust Unique?* (1996).

Starnawski, Marcin, 'Historically Conscious Cosmopolitans: Jewish Identity and the '68 Generation of Polish Jews in Exile', *East European Jewish Affairs*, 32 (Winter 2002).

Szaynok, B., *Ludność żydowska na Dolnym Śląsku 1945–1950* [The Jewish Polulation of Lower Silesia 1945–1950] (Wrocław: Wydawnictwo Uniwersytetu Wrocławskiego, 2000).

Szyc, E., 'Gdzie Byłeś?' [Where Were You?], in a symposium, 'Siedem głosów' [Seven Voices], *Midrasz*, 5, 5 (September 1997).

Śliwowska, W. (ed.), *The Last Eyewitnesses: Children of The Holocaust Speak* (Evanston, IL: Northwestern University Press, 1998).

Śpiewak, P., 'Szoah, drugi upadek' [The Shoah: A Second Fall], *Więź*, 333–4 (July–August 1986).

Śpiewak, P., 'Szok Marcowy' [The March Shock], *Polis*, 27 (April 1998).

Stannard, D.E., 'Uniqueness as Denial: The Politics of Genocide Scholarship', in A.S. Rosenbaum (ed.), *Is the Holocaust Unique? Perspectives on Comparative Genocide* (Boulder, CO: Westview Press, 1996).

Szacki, J., *Historia myśli socjologicznej* [A History of Sociological Thought] (Warsaw: PWN, 2003).

Tal, U., 'On the Study of the Holocaust and Genocide', *Yad Vashem Studies*, 13 (1979).

Tec, N., *When Light Pierced the Darkness: Christian Rescue of Jews in Nazi-Occupied Poland* (New York and Oxford: Oxford University Press, 1986).

Tendler, M.D., 'The State of Jewish Belief: A Symposium', *Commentary*, 42 (August 1966).

Tomaszewski, J., *Rzeczpospolita wielu narodów* [The Commonwealth of many Nations] (Warsaw: Czytelnik, 1985).

Tomaszewski, J., 'Niepodległa Rzeczpospolita' [The Independent Commonwealth], in Tomaszewski (ed.), *Najnowsze dzieje Żydów w Polsce w zarysie* (1993).

Tomaszewski, J. (ed.), *Najnowsze dzieje żydów w Polsce w zarysie (do roku 1950)* [Outline of the Recent History of the Jews in Poland (until 1950)] (Warsaw: PWN, 1993).

Tych, F., *Długi cień Zagłady* [Long Shadow of the Shoah] (Warsaw: ŻIH, 1999).

Warszawski, D., 'Mieszkając na ziemi popiołów' [Living on the Soil of Ashes], *Polis*, 27 (April 1998).

Waxman, C.I., *America's Jews in Transition* (Philadelphia, PA: Temple University Press, 1983).

Weber, M., *On the Methodology of the Social Sciences*, translated and edited by E.A. Shils and H.A. Finch (Glencoe, IL: Free Press, 1949).

Weber, M., *The Sociology of Religion*, translated by E. Fischoff (London: Methuen, 1956).

Weinbaum, L., *Polish Jews: A Postscript to the 'Final Chapter'?* (Jerusalem: Institute of the World Jewish Congress, 1998).

Weinberg, Y., 'The Destruction of European Jewry: A Churban of Singular Dimensions', in Wolpin (ed.), *Path Through the Ashes* (1986).

Weiner, H., 'The State of Jewish Belief: A Symposium', *Commentary*, 42 (August 1966).

Weiss Halivni, D., 'What Do American Jews Believe? A Symposium', *Commentary*, 102 (August 1996).

Weiss Halivni, D., 'Prayer in the Shoah', *Judaism*, 50 (Summer 2001).

Wertheimer, J., *A People Divided: Judaism in Contemporary America* (New York: Basic Books, 1993).

Wertheimer, J., 'What Do American Jews Believe? A Symposium', *Commentary*, 102 (August 1996).

Wertheimer, J., 'Judaism Without Limits', *Commentary*, 104 (July 1997).

Wiesel, E., *Night*, in E. Wiesel, *The Night Trilogy* (New York: Hill & Wang, 1987).

Wiesel, E., 'Some Questions That Remain Open', in A. Cohen et al. (eds), *Comprehending the Holocaust: Historical and Literary Research* (Frankfurt/Main: Verlag Peter Lang, 1988).

Wine, S.T., *Humanistic Judaism* (Buffalo, NY: Prometheus Books, 1978).

Wine, S.T., *Judaism Beyond God* (New York: Ktav Publishing House, 1995).

Winer, G., 'The Religious Dimension of Yiddish Secularism', *Judaism*, 41 (Winter 1992).

Wiszniewicz, J., 'Pierwsze powojenne pokolenie polskich Żydów: Rodzicielski przekaz pamięci Holocaustu a tożsamość żydowska' [The First Post-War Generation of Polish Jews: The Legacy of the Holocaust Handed down by Parents with Regard to Jewish Identity], *Biuletyn Żydowskiego Instytutu Historycznego*, 191 (September 1999).

Wiszniewicz, J., *Życie przecięte: Opowieści pokolenia Marca* [Life Cut Through: Stories of the March Generation] (Wołowiec: Wydawnictwo Czarne, 2008).

Wojdowski, B., 'Judaizm jako los' [Judaism as a Fate], *Puls*, 62 (May–June 1993).

Wolf, A.J., 'The State of Jewish Belief: A Symposium', *Commentary*, 42 (August 1966).

Wolf, A.J., 'The Centrality of the Holocaust Is a Mistake', in Berenbaum, *After Tragedy and Triumph* (1990).

Wolf, A.J., 'The Shoah in America', *Judaism*, 48 (Fall 1999).

Wolpin, N. (ed.), *A Path Through the Ashes: Penetrating Analyses and Inspiring Stories of the Holocaust from a Torah Perspective* (New York: Mesorah Publications, 1986).

Woocher, J.S., *Sacred Survival: The Civil Religion of American Jews* (Bloomington, IN: Indiana University Press, 1986).

Yaffe, J., *The American Jews: Portrait of a Split Personality* (New York: Random House, 1968).

Yerushalami, Y.H., *Zakhor: Jewish History and Jewish Memory* (Seattle, WA, and London: University of Washington Press, 1996).

Zangwill, I., *The Melting Pot* (New York: Macmillan, 1909).

Żebrowski, R. (ed.), *Studia z dziejów Żydów w Polsce*, vol.1 [Studies on the History of Polish Jews] (Warsaw: Żydowski Instytut Historyczny, 1995).

Index

Page numbers ending in 'n' stand for notes. Numbers are sorted as if spelled out, e.g. 'six' for '6'.

A